Oil and Class Struggle

Edited by Petter Nore and
Terisa Turner

Oil and Class Struggle

Edited by Petter Nore and Terisa Turner

Zed Press, 57 Caledonian Road, London N1 9DN 821362

Oil and Class Struggle was first published by
Zed Press, 57 Caledonian Road, London N1
9DN in April 1980.

ISBN Hb   0 905762 38 X
     Pb   0 905762 27 4

Designed by Mayblin/Shaw
Diagrams by Janet Brown
Typeset by Donald Typesetting
Proofread by Penelope Fryxell
Cover photograph from Associated Press
Printed by Redwood Burn Ltd.,
Trowbridge and Esher

Contributors to this Volume

The editors of this book are **Petter Nore**, Norwegian oil economist and editor with Francis Green of *Economics: An Anti-Text* and *Issues in Political Economy: A Critique,* and **Terisa Turner**, Canadian energy consultant, lecturer at Rutgers University, U.S.A., and author of *The Political Economy of Nigerian Oil* and *State Capitalism and Public Oil.* The other authors are: **Dr. Renfrew Christie**, formerly St. Anthony's College, Oxford; **Dr. Patrick Clawson**, New School for Social Research, New York; **Ruth First**, Durham University lecturer and author of several books including *Libya: the Elusive Revolution* and *Barrel of a Gun;* **Wolfgang Hein**, University of West Berlin; **Mohssen Massarrat**, Iranian civil engineer and economics lecturer at Osnabruck University; **Edward Shaffer**, formerly a petroleum economist with Walter J. Levy and now professor at the University of Alberta; **Joe Stork**, author of *Middle East Oil and the Energy Crisis* and member of MERIP (Middle East Research and Information Project) in Washington D.C.; **Michael Tanzer**, energy consultant, head of the Economic Development Bureau and author of *The Energy Crisis* and *The Political Economy of International Oil and the Under-developed Countries;* Union negotiators from **Trinidad's Oilfields Workers Trade Union**; and an anonymous Iranian oil worker.

Permissions

Zed Press wishes hereby to thank the following for granting permission for it to reproduce articles that originally appeared in their journals: (i) Monthly Review for M. Tanzer's 'The State and the Oil Industry in Today's World' (*Monthly Review*, March 1978); (ii) Sage Publications for T. Turner's 'The Transfer of Oil Technology and the Nigerian State' (*Development and Change*, 7, 1976), subsequently revised for this volume; and (iii) Intercontinental Press for 'How We Organized Strike That Paralyzed Shah's Regime — Account by an Oil Worker' (*Intercontinental Press*, Vol. 17, No.3, 29 January 1979).

Contents

Tables, Figures and Maps

1. Introduction
Petter Nore and Terisa Turner

Class Struggle and Oil: The Five Dimensions

Oil production gives rise to acute contradictions between social classes. In the
past Marxist writers have concentrated their analysis of the oil industry mainly
on the antagonism which exists between the national and international bourgeoisies, represented respectively by nation states and oil companies. This
tension between governments and companies is the first of what we regard as
five types of class struggle around oil. However, the aim of this book is to show
that while analysis of this dimension is important, it is not sufficient for a full
understanding of the present-day oil industry.

It is also necessary to consider oil as a commodity produced and marketed
within capitalist relations. Energy is the commodity on which the world's largest
multinational corporations are built. It is the resource that is synonymous with
national, military and economic power. Oil and other energy sources have the
strategic capacity to unlock 'frozen labour' by fuelling machines. The more
machines, the higher is the workers' productivity, and the greater the profits
for capital. This makes the energy industry the lynch-pin of modern capitalism.

The second and most direct form of class struggle around oil is the confrontation between capital and oilworkers within the industry. Historically, the
small number of skilled workers in oil have exerted great influence through
strikes and take-overs during major social upheavals such as the Russian Revolution in 1917, the Mexican and Iranian oil nationalizations of 1938 and 1951,
and again in Iran during the popular struggle against the Shah's regime in
1978-79. Furthermore, the multinational character of oil capital has united
oilworkers worldwide, with the result that they are among the best placed to
act in international solidarity against capital. No other workforce operates
such advanced technology for communications and mobility; few industries
are so dependent on a constant flow from production to consumption, and
therefore so vulnerable to strike action. We must therefore focus our investigation on class struggle between oilworkers and the corporations at the
national *and* international levels.

A third form of class struggle around oil takes place among factions and
classes for control of state power within oil-producing countries. The focus in
this book is on Third World, and especially OPEC, states as arenas for class

struggle. But interesting parallels are evident in the Canadian context. Oil production gives rise to large state revenues. The very existence of these large sums gives impetus to class and factional struggle to control the state and preside over the spending of these oil revenues. The antagonism that results is often between a landed oligarchy and a 'modern' bourgeoisie, or between commercial capitalists and a nascent industrial bourgeoisie — each class or faction having specific relations with sections of the international bourgeoisie. Antagonisms within an oil-producing state become especially acute when capitalist relations are generalized within the country. Such conflict notwithstanding, the ruling elements have demonstrated the ability to co-operate, and often to confront, the majority of workers and peasants.

Fourth, and most fundamental, is class struggle between the exploited and ruling classes in oil-producing countries, and on an international scale. Confrontation at this level especially manifests itself in the wake of generalizations of capitalist relations within producer countries often associated with efforts to industrialize through spending oil revenues. It is the most important form of class struggle, since it concerns antagonistic relations which are unresolvable short of reorganizing the social formation and its international links. This national feature of oil-producing countries has its counterpart in the international confrontation between corporate exploiters allied to their own state apparatuses on the one hand, and exploited producers and consumers on the other. Capitalist competition cuts across the global unity of the two classes. Capitalist relations foment competition within each class to generate a hierarchy of power, based most fundamentally on differences in the levels of organization of the productive forces. But this hierarchy is also expressed through national identity, race, and sex differences, through which capital has organized the global workforce for exploitation, and which are used by capital to divide the workforce ideologically and thus maintain this exploitation.

Nevertheless, the international bourgeoisie and global workforce are both becoming more united, each within itself, by the process of accumulating surplus value or struggling against this process. Nowhere is the integration of national bourgeoisies into an international ruling class occurring faster than in oil, as the case of the ever stronger co-operation between the U.S. and Saudi Arabian states makes clear. In turn, oilworkers and consumers are impelled, by this integration, towards common strategies and struggle. In short, the internationalism of class struggle in oil is the cutting edge of much broader solidarity.

The fifth and final form of class antagonism is conflict among factions of the international bourgeoisie, each based in a major industrial power. Growing factionalism coincides with the integration of the international bourgeoisie, just as the emergence of corporate monopolies and oligopolies coincides historically with intense competition among capitalists. Competition among multinational corporations for energy resources and export markets is today balkanizing OPEC and the Third World into spheres of imperialist interest. This produces both greater dangers of war associated with inter-imperialist rivalries, but also greater possibilities for successful workers' struggles.

Two theoretical perspectives are crucial to an extended understanding of class struggle in the oil industry. First, theoretical understanding of the peculiarities of oil production is needed. Marxist analysis must tackle the question of rent, and the question of the relationship between oil — the least labour-intensive form of energy — and other types of energy.

Second, analysis of the nature of the state in oil-producing countries is needed. These states receive large revenues from the rent of the international capitalist system. They therefore are the key to the accumulation process in oil-rich countries. But in whose interests does the state use the oil revenues? And why? Unless we answer these questions, we cannot fully understand a country's oil policies, nor its relationship to multinational oil corporations.

Scope of This Book: Overview of the Contributions

This book analyses the various forms of class struggle at a general and theoretical level, and through case studies. In doing so, it seeks to develop the two perspectives mentioned above. Christie makes a theoretical analysis of the capitalist system's demand for energy. He concludes that this demand is intimately related to the nature of the accumulation process, and in particular to capital's need to maintain profits and replace truculent labour with machines. Mechanization in the South African mines provides a case study of this process.

Masserat's translated work is the first systematic attempt in the English language to relate an analysis of the oil industry to Marx's discussion of rent. While highly controversial, it is a valuable starting point for Marxist discussion of oil and energy. The chapter concentrates on how the rise of rent-earning OPEC states can actually be a barrier to accumulation both in oil, and worldwide. His theoretical starting point is the OPEC states, seen as representatives of an international land-owning class. Using this framework, Masserat examines trends in the world oil industry since the 1960s.

Nore also examines these general trends, but concentrates on oil nationalizations and their effects. While sharing much of Masserat's theoretical framework, Nore sees the state more as a capitalist than as a representative of landed interests. This conception follows from the growth of state oil corporations. The state capitalist view also follows from the state's active intervention in the industrialization process in some countries.

Hein stresses the importance of understanding the nature of the oil-producing state, especially as a distributor of oil rents to the rest of society. Ruth first discusses the characteristics of oil-producing 'rentier states' within a framework of a general understanding of the post-colonial state. Clawson assesses the development of capitalist relations, and hence the state, as determined in the final analysis by the dynamic of capital accumulation on a world scale. Turner likewise emphasizes an oil producer's integration into the world capitalist system as a determinant of national class character and factionalism in the state.

In addition to presenting new theoretical tools to deal with the oil industry and to understand the state in oil-producing countries, the chapters present case studies of five OPEC members, two non-OPEC Third World societies, and two industrialized countries (South Africa and Canada). All the chapters analyse the effects that oil production is having on class composition. The following overview groups the case studies according to the five forms of class struggle associated with oil production.

Tanzer concentrates on the conflict between producer states and the leading oil companies (the so-called 'majors') in the case of Puerto Rico and shows that the majors are in fact dispensable. Potential oil producers do *not* have to accept oil-concession contracts that give all profit, control and production to the majors. Tanzer describes the experience of Vietnam, India and Mexico to demonstrate that there are alternative oil exploration strategies to those dependent on the multinationals.

Turner goes beyond the conception of the state as a 'black box' (whose internal workings are unfathomable) to explain why capital accumulation is not taking place in Nigera. She analyses the factional conflict between commercial compradors and industrializing technocrats in the Nigerian state, and links these factions of the bourgeoisie to their international progenitors. Oil technology is not being transferred to Nigeria, she argues, because the dominant comprador faction benefits from maintaining the foreign oil companies' control. Clawson likewise shows how the development of Iranian capitalism and its relationship to oil can be understood in terms of a conflict between different factions of the Iranian ruling class. In particular, this is a conflict between the 'traditional' or semi-feudal elements and a 'modernizing' bourgeoisie as industrialization gets under way. Shaffer in turn describes how, in the Canadian case, oil production has led to conflict between a nascent bourgeoisie in Alberta and the traditionally powerful bourgeoisie of Eastern Canada.

Class struggle, initiated by oilworkers, is treated in four important chapters, two of them written by oilworkers themselves. In Turner's chapter on Iran, written in Spring 1979, she analyses the role (and implications) of the Iranian oilworkers in bringing down the hitherto apparently impregnable dictatorship of the Shah. And, in the case of Venezuela, Hein shows how the workers' shifting alliances with the state bureaucracy and sections of the national bourgeoisie have shaped Venezuelan policies. Lastly, in the case of Trinago (Trinidad and Tobago), the conflict is an immediate struggle between oilworkers and the giant oil company, Texaco. But Trinidadian workers are aware that the multinational character of corporate employers makes *international* class struggle necessary.

The Trinago Oilfield Workers Trade Union (OWTU) links the struggle against Texaco with the campaign by radicals in the U.S.A. for American companies to pull out of racist South Africa and with the struggle of Southern African revolutionaries generally. 'Global Texaco' unifies U.S. Americans, Trinidadians and black South Africans against multinational capital. The OWTU document states: 'A defeat for Texaco here in Trinago is a victory for the liberation armies in Southern Africa.' Similar thinking is evident in the United Nations' consideration in late 1978 of an oil embargo against South Africa to enforce independence for Namibia and Zimbabwe.

In First's discussion of Libya and Stork's treatment of Iraq, it is clear that the key determinant of oil policies is the relationship between a bureaucratic state capitalist ruling class and the international capitalist system. The virtual absence of any national bourgeoisie makes analysis of factional struggle almost redundant in explaining contemporary oil policies. We are therefore back to Tanzer's starting point with companies and governments, albeit from a different angle. Simultaneously, the Libyan and Iraqi governments' policies are examined in relation to the working class. The nature of the accumulation process in the wake of the influx of oil revenues is, in the last analysis, determined by working class resistance to the intensification of the extraction of relative surplus value.

How does oil production affect the long-run prospects for international class struggle? Christie's chapter argues that, as energy prices rise and conservation technology is not developed fast enough, capitalists will be less able to answer worker militancy with mechanization. Thus multinational capitalists will be forced, increasingly, to seek competitive advantages by use of state intervention and force. The rush for resources in the Third World and growing imperialist involvement throughout Africa and elsewhere are indications of this drive to compete through means other than energy-intensive mechanization. Consequently, Christie argues, the energy price rise in the next decade or so offers workers a crucial opportunity for political advance. But at the same time it increases the dangers of war that are associated with growing inter-imperialist rivalry.

The Special Importance of Saudi Arabia

The position of Saudi Arabia is vital for an understanding of issues related to oil, class struggle and future developments in the world system. First, the country exports more oil than any other. And second, the formation of an international bourgeoisie is nowhere more dramatic than in the integration of the Saudi and U.S. states via the 'big four' American oil multinationals: Exxon, Texaco, Socal and Gulf. The Saudi/U.S. faction of the world bourgeoisie is in the immensely powerful position of controlling both large proportions of Western Europe and Japan's oil supplies, and these countries' access (via exports) to the lucrative Saudi domestic market.

Saudi Arabia is by far the most important OPEC country and world oil producer because of its huge reserves and large current oil production. It is the 'swing producer' — the country capable of supplying (if it so wishes — which it may not always, as its cutback in oil output in 1979 as a result of the U.S. inspired Israeli-Egyptian peace treaty so kindly illustrated) the difference between world demand and supplies from other oil producers, both OPEC and non-OPEC. The vital question is: will Saudi Arabia agree to produce sufficient oil for Western demand, pending a transition to other forms of energy? A subsidiary issue is who will get this oil, which is controlled by the U.S., but needed by European and Japanese capital?

In 1977 world consumption of oil was 49.5 million barrels a day (m.b.d.), excluding the centrally planned (socialist) economies. OPEC produced 30 m.b.d. or 61 per cent of total world consumption. Saudi Arabia alone accounted for over a quarter of OPEC production and almost a fifth of world consumption in 1977. The country's huge reserves of some 147 billion barrels (compared to 68 billion in Kuwait, 65 billion in Iran or 33 billion in the U.S.) mean that Saudi Arabia stands as the world's pre-eminent energy storehouse.

But Saudi Arabia cannot spend all its oil money. This desert country, where only 10 per cent of the land is arable and the population numbers only eight million, does not need all the revenues it earns from such vast oil exports. These totalled some $27 billion in 1975, or about $3,800 per capita. This inability to absorb income could lead to production cuts. However, the U.S. has undertaken to ensure that Saudi Arabia continues to provide such large quantities of oil and spends the income. What is the special relationship between the two countries which allows the U.S. to assume such a responsibility?

After the Second World War, the U.S. replaced the British as the dominant Western power in Saudi Arabia through 'Aramco' (the American Arabian Oil company — composed of Exxon, Texaco, Socal and Gulf). A December 1977 U.S. government report stated that:[1]

> . . . the United States, by virtue of its commercial oil interests' long-standing monopoly over the disposition of Saudi crude, now reinforced by the 1974 conclusion of a 'special relationship' embracing economic and military agreements, is very widely regarded among its allies and by Arabs and Iranians as having secured preferential and near-exclusive access to Saudi oil. Given the extraordinary importance of Saudi oil production to the world generally, the U.S. relationship is considered key to supply security.

The U.S. government is committed to maximizing this giant producer's financial absorptive capacity, which includes 'domestic economic plans and goals, foreign investment opportunities, foreign policy goals as reflected in Saudi foreign aid and military purchases.'[2] According to the U.S. government report:[3]

> It may not be possible to determine an optimal level of Saudi oil production (this issue is one of the most contentious within Saudi Arabia), but money usually can be spent and a more realistic picture might emerge if all likely opportunities for utilization of revenue are included.

There is space here for examining only one of the four opportunities defined by the U.S. for spending Saudi oil money: 'domestic economic plans and goals'. The second five-year development plan (1976-80) envisages total expenditures exceeding $140 billion. In the late 1970s some 50 per cent of the population is dependent on agricultural and nomadic herding activities, while 40 per cent of the labour force is engaged in services, including retail trade, construction and government service. Only 4 per cent work in the oil industry. Remaining workers are in small-scale industries in three main areas: textiles, food processing and furniture, which all produce for local consumption. Inflation is running perhaps as high as 40 per cent. The plan's objectives are: (1) to diversify the economy and reduce its overwhelming dependence on oil income for government revenues (95 per cent), foreign exchange earnings (virtually 100 per cent), and as a share of gross domestic product (87 per cent); (2) to develop a broad industrial base as a means of diversification; (3) to develop human resources; and (4) to contribute to the increased standard of living of the population as a whole. These goals are to be accomplished while maintaining the religious and moral values of Islam and assuring the defence and internal security of the kingdom.

The main thrust of the development plan is to develop huge energy and capital-intensive industrialization projects: the gas gathering system which Aramco is supervising, five refineries (producing for export), two additional fertilizer plants, seven chemical plants, as well as steel and aluminum production. These projects and the vast infrastructural developments they require are centralized on two giant industrial estates planned for the Red Sea and Gulf coasts. A labour force much larger than Saudi Arabia can generate is required to execute these projects. This is a major danger to Saudi monarchical rule, especially since Palestinians are a key migrant workforce in the Middle East, and transmit throughout the Arab countries advanced ideological and organizational forms.

But the Saudi planning structure, which dates from 1965, cannot process spending authorizations fast enough and most projects are delayed several years. The infrastructure is inadequate, inflation is runaway, foreign labour is a threat and the oil boom is disrupting Saudi society and ruling class values. For Saudi Arabia, as with other OPEC countries, it is clear that abundant capital does not necessarily lead to economic development. Among the obstacles to Saudi development which the U.S. report itemized are: the small size of the population; the consequent small size of the domestic market, exacerbated by the fact that many people remain outside the monetized economy; poor relations with other states in the region (which preclude exports as a means of enlarging the market); the small size of the indigenous labour force, which is further circumscribed by lack of training, illiteracy, prohibitions against female participation in the labour force and other social values; *Wahhabi* conservatism; misgivings regarding the social and political consequences of reliance on foreign labour; the unwillingness to see economic developments erode the traditional moral basis of the society; inadequate infrastructure; inadequate technological know-how; the unwillingness of private investors to commit themselves to long-term projects, because they prefer quick returns, and low risk endeavours; and climatic and physical limitations.[4]

Despite increases in costs because of project delays and the inflated prices that have to be paid for modern technology, Saudi Arabia is still unable to spend the oil income generated by oil exports, at the given level of Western demand, on development projects. With a 1978 surplus of $50-60 billion and prospects for continued surpluses, the question of investment opportunities for these funds becomes, in the U.S. view, '. . . critical to continued access to Saudi oil... and should be encouraged as a means of giving the Saudis a larger stake in the health and well-being of the industrialized economies.'[5] With larger demands for Saudi foreign aid (of which Egypt is at the time of writing the main beneficiary), and Western encouragement of military purchases, spending may be kept at a high enough level to make possible and acceptable the continued high levels of oil production.

The second question is: who gets the oil? U.S. companies control, but Japan and Western Europe consume, most of it. Although Aramco transferred 100 per cent ownership to the Saudi Arabian state oil company, Petromin, in 1977, the continued role of Aramco is significant: the four U.S. majors still supply technological and managerial services to the company and in exchange have access to 7 m.b.d. of Saudi production out of a total of almost 9 m.b.d. in 1978. The U.S. oil multinationals can distribute the 7 m.b.d., which is over four times the volume of U.S. oil imports from Saudi Arabia in 1978, to international consumers without Saudi restrictions on its final destination.

It is widely agreed that, by the late 1980s, the industrial world – including, eventually, the U.S.S.R. – will be competing on an unprecedented scale for the remaining available Middle East oil supplies. Given the extraordinary importance of Saudi oil production to the world, the U.S. 'special relationship' is considered by American policy makers to be crucial to American security. Moreover, while the U.S. has a link to Saudi Arabia (but no longer Iran from 1979) which other advanced capitalist countries do not have, the U.S. still imports only one-fifth of its oil from Saudi Arabia, with the bulk of Saudi exports going to Europe and Japan. The 'oil security role' arrogated by the United States is precisely that government's power to direct, when necessary, that the 7 m.b.d. of U.S. controlled Saudi crude be allocated to the U.S. (where demand is escalating and where, by 1978, no conservation measures had been legislated to restrict imports, despite international pressure and President Carter's undertakings), rather than to Western Europe and Japan whose industries are becoming less competitive internationally due, importantly, to high energy costs. According to the U.S. govermnent:[6]

One can argue that while the oil benefit is nowhere near so great to the United States as it is to European and Japanese importers for which it is vital, the U.S. relationship with Iran and Saudi Arabia serves the collective security interests of its allies in helping assure a continuous and adequate flow of oil – if not yet at a price which is within their capacity to pay . . . [But] will the U.S. Government come to affect the destination of these 7 million barrels per day, exercising its influence through the American oil companies? Or will the companies be able to continue to supply, unhampered by considerations other than the meeting of their contractual commitments?

The future development of the world system depends on how broad questions related to Saudi Arabia are resolved but, more crucially, also on the understanding of what oil means for struggle within and between classes and action based on this understanding.

Petter Nore and Terisa Turner
October 1978, New York.

References

1. U.S. Senate, Committee on Energy and Natural Resources, *Access to Oil — the United States Relationships with Saudi Arabia and Iran*, Washington D.C., U.S. Government Printing Office, Publication No. 95-70, December 1977, p. xi.
2. Ibid., p. 42.
3. Ibid.
4. Ibid., pp. 44-5.
5. Ibid.
6. Ibid., p. xi.

2. Why Does Capital Need Energy?

Renfrew Christie

Introduction

The Rockefeller Foundation records the weight of expert opinion to be
substantially in agreement that the world today is moving into a chronic
tightness or even absolute shortage of oil supply. Because of this looming oil
scarcity, we are entering a lengthy and potentially cataclysmic period of
transition from cheap oil to far more expensive alternative sources of
energy. Some time in the late nineteen-eighties, rapidly rising oil prices
together with an actual physical shortage of oil will produce a prolonged crisis
of great magnitude, according to the Rockefeller Foundation.[1] Another
authoritative view along the same lines has been put forward by the normally
cautious Director-General of the Energy Division of the Commission of the
European Economic Community, who sums up the predicted energy crisis
of 1988 in one word: 'disaster'.[2] In contrast to these pessimistic predictions,
the World Bank claims that there will *not* be any shortage of oil during the
next two decades, because non-OPEC underdeveloped countries will make
discoveries of major new oil fields.[3] The World Bank continues, however, to
refuse to finance actual drilling for oil in these countries.[4] Nevertheless, when
conservative people with vast quantities of information at their disposal use
words like 'prolonged crisis' and 'disaster' in a serious way about the future,
it is necessary to analyse the situation with great care. This chapter makes
an initial suggestive contribution to such an analysis by posing four related
questions. Is there an energy crisis? Why does capital in general need energy?
Why do energy capitalists in particular need energy? And how would any
energy crisis affect relations between capital and labour?

Is There an Energy Crisis?

There is no way of knowing in advance whether the Rockefeller Foundation
or the World Bank is correct about the energy crisis of 1988. After many
years in the energy industry, Edith Penrose rightly reminds us that nobody
knows much about oil production capacity except in the short term. The
relation between exploration and production is so tenuous, and lead times are
so long, that expectations can be wildly wrong. She also points out that governments and companies can and do manipulate predictions to serve their
special interests.[5] These often may be quite short-term interests, but the long-
term predictions may be dramatically swayed. It is precisely because of the

high degree of uncertainty about long-term energy supplies that states and capitalists can make these manipulations. No one can prove them wrong before the event, and of course predictions, like any observations, can alter the event. Oil companies presumably have more information at their disposal than the public because they are able to keep some things secret. It may be in their interests to have the public believe that there is (or is not) a future energy crisis. A careful analyst must therefore approach all energy predictions with great caution. Both overt and covert special pleadings must be discounted. For this reason it is perhaps better to start not from questionable statistics, but from a logical examination of the tendencies prevalent in the capitalist mode of production. By starting from first principles, such as the tendency for the organic composition of capital to increase, more may be achieved than by a futile attempt to make sense of the published physical counts of buried hydro-carbons.

There is patently no energy crisis in nature. Neither the earth nor the sun will become too cold for humanity in this millenium or the next. Nature is not running out of energy. Its molecules and atoms are, and will remain, adequately stuck together. Nature has energy aplenty. What matters is how and why human beings unlock that energy. People have the ability to unlock nature's energy in enormous quantities, as the surviving inhabitants of Dresden, Hamburg and Hiroshima can testify. If there is an energy crisis, therefore, it must be seen less at the level of the *forces of production* and more at the level of the *relations of production.* In other words, if there is an energy crisis it is a crisis less of humankind's relations with nature, and more of relations between human beings. It is in the social use of energy under capitalism that the crisis may arise, not in nature. If there is a crisis it will be a capitalist crisis, not a natural crisis: the next ice age is some distance removed from us. Therefore it is capitalism that first must be understood, rather than the physical number of buried hydro-carbons, which is a secondary question, albeit still a very important one.

One inadequate way of answering the question of whether there is a capitalist crisis arising in the energy supply part of the Western political economy has been to do so in terms of 'equality' and 'inequality'. Correct in so far as it goes, this analysis states that there certainly is a crisis because of the unequal distribution of ownership and consumption of energy resources. The greed of a very small fraction of humanity, largely but by no means exclusively living in North America, has led to a situation where a tiny number of people consumes so much energy that an energy crisis is at hand. Most of humanity already has an energy crisis, and this may affect even the capitalist class in the next decade.

By dealing with all human beings, the 'inequality' analysis forces an examination of energy in all its forms, not simply of oil. Light Arabian crude may be the world's marginal energy source at present. It may be the world's present energy price marker. It may be the commodity whereby the most important fraction of monopoly capital built the structure of world domination. Nevertheless, oil is probably not now, nor ever was, the prime energy source for most of the earth's people, who use wood, grass, dung and, if they are lucky, peat or coal. Even in the rich world of what Africans call the 'wabenzi' (those who ride in Mercedes-Benz motor cars — or Cadillacs, Coronas or Concordes), oil is not the only energy source, nor will it long remain the prime source. And it was not the energy source which powered the rise of capitalism — coal did that. As the oil companies buy up coalfields and uranium deposits, thereby transforming themselves from oil monopolists into energy monopolists, it becomes clear that what are needed are predictions of the total energy balance, not merely predictions about oil. For example, in 1976 Europe burnt wood which totalled 6 million tons of oil equivalent, that is, the equivalent of 10 per cent of Britain's North Sea oil production.[6] By asserting the totality of human existence, the 'inequality' analysis usefully stresses the need to include all energy forms in the calculations.

However, if the logic of the 'inequality' argument is followed through, its inadequacies become apparent. It does not explain where inequality comes from, beyond psychological concepts like 'greed'. It does not explain the historical forces which produced the present system, and it is at its most inadequate when dealing with remedies or predictions. For example, merely exhorting North Americans to consume less energy neither changes the nature of capitalism, nor averts a possible crisis. Condemning energy inequality on grounds of morality has as much effect on an energy crisis as the Salvation Army has had on crises of alcoholism or unemployment. One hundred years after Marx, methods of analysis are required which go beyond John Stuart Mill's 'equality' and beyond the egalitarianism of the French Revolution. This means that the analysis of energy questions must be firmly fixed in the analysis of capitalism, not in utopian desires for equality. If there is at least a serious possibility of an energy crisis of capitalism arising by 1988, that crisis must be understood by examining why energy is important to capitalists.

In sum, we cannot know if there is an energy crisis ahead, although the gross inequalities in energy used suggest that such a crisis may well occur. To understand this possibility, the ways in which energy serves capital must be examined.

Why Does Capital In General Need Energy?

The essence of capitalism is the appropriation by the capitalist classes of surplus value generated by the working classes in the labour process, that is, in the process where workers interact with nature to produce commodities. This generation and appropriation of surplus value is not a voluntary system where individual free agents of their own accord band together in social production to provide the goods and services which humanity needs. Rather, workers, without ownership of the means of production are forced by that fact to work for capitalists. Capitalists, in turn, do not produce goods and services to meet the needs of people: they produce commodities from the sale of which surplus value can be accumulated. These commodities need not have high use-values: 'In capitalist production what matters is not the immediate use-value but the exchange-value, and, in particular, the expansion of surplus value.'[7] Capitalist production is not concerned with utility: 'It is only concerned with demand that is backed by the ability to pay.'[8] From this lack of concern with need, and from the paramount tendency of capitalism — the competitive drive to accumulation — flows the condition of the world's workers and peasants. The 'inequality', already remarked on, is the logical result of the tendency in capitalism towards the accumulation of surplus value.

Yet capitalists cannot accumulate without struggle. They meet with continuous overt and covert resistance from workers and peasants. The methods of resistance are manifold, ranging from simple refusal to work whenever the boss has his back turned, to sabotage or even open warfare. In ruling ideologies these actions are explained by the use of words like 'laziness', 'lack of motivation', 'carelessness', and 'irresponsibility'. Open warfare is explained by saying that the Irish navvy, African miner, or Mexican fruit-picker is 'naturally violent, barbarous, uncivilized, rough, and aggressive'. Workers and peasants are, of course, no more or less 'inherently' lazy or violent than any other human beings. Their 'carelessness' and 'aggression' are the logical result of their class positions in which they are denied the full fruits of their collective labour. Far from being irresponsible, their resistance to capital is both sensible and necessary. It is this struggle which is the power plant of history — thus any analysis of an energy crisis which is taken out of the context of class struggle is hopelessly inadequate.

It is not only workers who are overt or covert revolutionaries, struggling to transform society. Capitalists themselves are among the most successful revolutionaries in history. In the three or four centuries of capitalism they have totally transformed human society not once, but many times. They have established an ongoing revolution, that of technology. The key weapon of the capitalist revolution, and the key weapon of capital in its struggle with the working classes, is the machine. Capital's need for energy cannot be understood until capital's need for machines has been understood, because energy is simply one input into the mechanized production of commodities. Whether the commodity is transport, produced by people using motor cars, or whether the commodity is cluster bombs, produced by people using other machines, energy is no more than an input. Energy may appear in mechanized production as light, as heat, as motive force, or, at some other frequency, as radio waves: but it is never more than energy. Energy (by which is meant here inanimate energy) is not human and therefore cannot create value. Only people at work create value. Energy without working human beings is irrelevant in terms of value. Important though energy may seem compared to most other means of production, energy can be nothing other than a 'raw material' means of production. It is only from capital's need for machines so that it can win the class struggle, and from energy's special relation with machines, that energy receives its particular importance.

The value of mechanized capitalist production of any commodity or aggregation of commodities may be written down in Marx's familiar equation,

$C = c + v + s$. The value of total capital, C, breaks down into the value of machinery and raw materials, including energy, used up in production, c; the value of the workers' labour power paid for in wages, v; and the value of the surplus generated by the workers and accumulated by the capitalist, s. Over time, class struggle affects all three magnitudes. Workers try to force up v by compelling capitalists to pay higher real wages, without diminishing the size of the labour force. Put another way, workers try to increase the socially necessary labour time needed to reproduce their labour power, i.e. they try to increase their standard of living. Capitalists, by contrast, try to minimize v and/or to maximize s, the surplus value extracted. To minimize v they require an industrial reserve army of unemployed.[9] To maximize s they have to increase the productivity of the workers.

Historically, the major method of increasing labour productivity has been the introduction of machinery. Using machinery, capitalists can produce the same surplus as before, using less 'living' labour. In this way the ratio s/v is increased, and the diminished value of v means that the industrial reserve army of unemployed is increased. Alternatively, the same number of workers can be employed at the same wage rates, but because of the higher productivity the surplus extracted is increased, and again, therefore, the ratio s/v is increased. But whenever additional machinery and raw materials are employed relative to the workers employed, the ratio c/v increases. Marx termed this ratio 'the organic composition of capital'. He further suggested that because of the need to use machinery to increase labour productivity so that surplus value would be expanded, the dominant trend would be for the organic composition of capital to increase, as capitalists use relatively more and more 'dead' labour, embodied as machinery and raw materials, and relatively less and less living labour.

Dead labour in the shape of machinery has another advantage over living labour. It does not talk back. It does not go on strike. It does not steal. It does not resist the designs of capitalists. By contrast, it can be used to control the class struggle, to increase the degree of ownership at the point where capital most needs that ownership: the point of production. Machines control the labour process for capitalists. Hobson wrote:

> Machinery can also register and regulate the expenditure of human power. Babbage well says, 'One of the most singular advantages we derive from machinery is in the check which it affords against the inattention, the idleness or the knavery of human agents.'[10]

Capitalists, therefore, use the disciplines and skills of machines as substitutes for the withdrawable skills and calculated indisciplines of their class enemies, the workers.[11] Another way to explain the use of machinery is to look at the working day. The workers spend a certain time producing the commodities necessary to feed, house and clothe themselves and their families. This is the labour time socially necessary for reproduction of the work force. The remainder of the time is spent producing a surplus for the capitalist. This surplus can be increased by lengthening the working day, so that more time can be spent producing for the capitalist. Such increased surplus value is called absolute surplus value. A second way of increasing surplus value is to have the workers produce more in less time, usually by means of machines, so that the socially necessary labour time is diminished, and relatively more time is spent working for the capitalist. Increased surplus value obtained by this method is called relative surplus value. It is in the creation of relative surplus value, using machinery, that capitalism is at its most revolutionary. There is a finite length to the working day (which sets clear limits to any increases in absolute surplus value) but the increase in speed of production (which is at the root of increases in relative surplus value) has seemed to have almost no boundaries in recent history. 'The production of absolute surplus value turns exclusively upon the length of the working day; the production of relative surplus value revolutionizes out and out the technical processes of labour and the composition of society.'[12] In short, by using machinery, capitalists tend to increase the organic composition of capital, c/v, in order that relative surplus value may be expanded and in order that relative over-population, i.e. unemployment, may increase.[13]

This brief survey of the basic economics of mechanization has indicated that capitalists increasingly use machinery to dominate workers and to increase capital accumulation. What has this to do with energy? Simply, while machinery does not necessarily need inanimate energy, most modern machinery is totally and increasingly dependent on such energy. Historically, increases in both absolute and relative surplus values have required increased energy inputs. Take the case of a simple energy form, light. To lengthen the working day, thus increasing absolute surplus value, light has generally had to be artificially provided. For example, one of the earliest and most productive uses of, first, the arc lamp and then the incandescent bulb, was in docks and harbours around the world, to enable the lengthening of the working day of stevedores loading ships. Today the concept of night work or overtime soon disappears when power is cut, even in those few factories which are not otherwise dependent on energy to any serious extent. In addition, lighting is used to increase relative surplus value by increasing labour productivity. Take the example given by the British Electrical Development Association: 'Better lighting leads to higher productivity and yields a very good return on the outlay.'[14] An independent test carried out in 1948 on a rayon-weaving mill for five weeks over 16 looms established that the net gains due to better lighting were as follows:[15]

Value of increased output per loom per annum - £101.00
Net increases in profit per loom per annum - £32.00
Increases in weavers' wages per loom per annum - £8.4s.

Wages increased, but profits (however defined) increased more, and the value of ouput more still. By the introduction of lighting machinery, c was increased, v probably remained the same or marginally increased,[16] and s

increased significantly. In Marx's terms, c/v and s/v increased: but neither could have been achieved without increased use of energy.

What applies to light used in production applies equally to other energy forms like heat, motive power, or radio waves. Capital increasingly needs energy as it uses more machinery to protect its ownership of property (e.g. through the use of light); to control workers; to control production; to de-skill production processes; to speed up production; to speed up transport, etc. Above all, capital needs more energy as it uses more machinery to increase relative surplus value while decreasing working class power in the process of class struggle. Because capital needs machinery to expand the accumulation of surplus value, and because capital needs machinery to 'substitute' or control workers in struggle, capital therefore needs energy. Energy drives capital's machines; it melts the metals to produce them; it transports the workers and materials; it measures and controls production; and it even heats workers' houses with less labour today than hitherto, thus cheapening the cost of labour power. In all, energy powers the ongoing technological revolution whereby capital has been winning the class struggle.

South African Mining: A Case Study

There is sufficient information available about one industry for a brief case study to be made demonstrating the relationship between class struggle, energy use, and increased organic composition of capital. The South African gold-mining industry may seem at first to be a special case, because of its division of labour by means of skin colour. However, most or even all of the productive work is done by black workers, and the labour process is a straight-forward exercise in the mining and crushing of hard rock from extreme depths. The rock's hardness and the nature of the product do not change over time. Provided the increasing depths and changing ore grades are borne in mind, gold-mining offers a relatively simple production process to study.

In the years since the Second World War there have been at least two periods of heightened class struggle between the mineowners and the hundreds of thousands of black workers who drill the rock: major conflicts occurred in 1946 and in the mid-1970s. Both times the response of mineowners to major worker offensives was the initiation of research into radical mechanization of the mining process, and both times the mechanization required large increases in energy consumption.

In August 1946 over 60,000 miners went on strike.[17] They were rapidly smashed by the forces of the state and by the mineowners. The survivors were back at work within six days. They had been demanding wages for underground work in line with surface industry wages, which had been allowed to rise so that the war effort would not be disturbed by strikes.[18] In 1946 mine wage increases were prevented by the use of police repression, always capital's ultimate line of defence. However, the mineowners were sufficiently jolted to seek to increase labour productivity by further mechanization, so that fewer miners could be employed albeit at higher individual wage rates.

Harry Oppenheimer, heir apparent of South Africa's biggest mining group, wrote to a mining engineer in New York asking for research assistance concerning mechanization. He explained to his New York colleague that 'natives on unskilled work in industries close to the mines are being paid much higher wages than natives in the mining industry'.[19] In addition, post-war inflation was putting pressure on the standard of living of the miners, resulting in the organization of workers: 'The position has become increasingly difficult through the continual increase in the prices of commodities and the scarcity of foodstuffs, and these factors, you will readily understand, have created a fertile field for propaganda by agitators and communists.'[20] Oppenheimer wanted 'further mechanization in order to economize on native labour'.[21] This would make higher wages possible for those miners still employed, and a more docile work force would result. 'If fewer natives were used, wages could be raised, and the suggested solution is to cut out manual labour as far as possible, and mechanize to the fullest extent.'[22]

Oppenheimer's New York colleague did not, in the event, help him substantially with mechanization, but the letter clearly sets out the strategy and its motivations. The gold mines were already partially mechanized, as the speakers at a special meeting of the Chamber of Mines made clear after the strike. The mineowners emphasized that they had not been neglecting their duty to mechanize production. The main speakers at the meeting were the President of the Chamber of Mines and, significantly, Dr. Bernard Price, Resident Director of the Victoria Falls and Transvaal Power Company, which supplied the vast bulk of the energy consumed by the mines. Price told the meeting that 'the consumption of electrical energy per native per annum had risen by 175 per cent during the 25 years from 1920 to 1945, an average increase of 7 per cent per year.'[23] Both labour productivity and energy use had increased. 'The consumption of electricity per ton milled rose by 100 per cent in the same period.'[24] This showed that machinery was increasingly being used. Price said, 'This striking increase is much greater than can be accounted for by the steadily increasing depth from which hoisting and pumping have taken place, and it amply confirms your contention, Mr. President, that mechanization has already been installed very extensively in the working of the mines.'[25]

Nevertheless, Oppenheimer's goals had been set and further mechanization was possible in the medium term. The new mines of the Far West Rand and of the Orange Free State, largely developed by Oppenheimer's companies, were laid out on a more highly mechanized basis. This was a small contributory factor in the coal and electricity crisis which South Africa experienced in the early 1950s because the new energy demands had not been sufficiently provided for. Complicated load-shedding schemes were set up to save electricity in the mines. The problem was only solved by the completion of new coal mines and power stations. Over the next two decades mechanization continued, but real wages did not rise until the very end of the period. Therefore, for most of these years, the increased mechanization and resulting increased labour productivity meant higher surpluses for the mineowners in their competition with other capitalists. In other words, competition between capitalists to accumulate was perhaps more important in causing some mechanization than the immediate conflict with workers. The workers had been put down by sheer force, which proved sufficient to hold down wages. The violence of the crushing of the 1946 strike, coupled with the increasingly refined controls embodied in the apartheid system, meant that real wages did not significantly increase until the gold price rises of the 1970s.

If workers did not seem to benefit by the mechanization, the mineowners clearly did. Productivity gains were substantial. For every 10 kilograms of gold produced in 1950 10 men were employed and 99,000 kilowatt-hours of electricity were used. In 1975, by contrast, for every 10 kilograms of gold produced only 5 men were employed, but 180,000 kilowatt-hours of electricity were used. The amount of gold produced depends on the grade of ore mined, however, and in 1975 higher grades were being mined than in 1950. Work done must therefore be measured in tons of rock treated. The index of tons of rock milled per black worker employed rose from 908 in 1947 to 1,000 in 1955 and 1,122 in 1974. At the same time the index of electricity consumed per black worker employed rose from 604 in 1947 to 1,000 in 1955 and 2,145 in 1974.[26] Much of this represents increased depths of mining, but at the same time it represents a significantly increased degree of mechanization, and of the organic composition of capital.[27]

Despite even these increases in mining mechanization, by the middle 1970s renewed class struggle meant that more machinery was needed. As the tide of liberation rolled across the Portuguese colonies and South Africa's other buffer states, the employment of workers from these areas became more risky. In South Africa the miners, like most other workers, felt more able to demonstrate their power, or at least to disrupt the mines and the compounds. A form of resistance developed in which workers went on strike, rioted and destroyed mine property while fighting among themselves. Between 1973 and 1976 1,043 mineworkers were injured and 178 killed by the police or by other workers in the South African mines.[28] The authorities responded first with violence. Police troops armed with machine-guns quelled the uprisings. The next response, which was also a response to the price rises which had resulted from the 1973 energy crisis, was to raise wages in an attempt to attract more black South African miners. In this way it was hoped that more peaceful conditions might prevail, and that the need to employ workers from the liberated areas would be diminished. The third response was the same as that of Harry Oppenheimer after the 1946 strike—a mechanization programme was initiated by the Chamber of Mines. The reasoning was very similar to that of 1946:

> Labour everywhere is becoming used to continually improving working conditions. To pay for this, labour needs to be made more productive than manual labour will allow. That means more mechanization.[29]

In the event, further mechanization of gold mining has so far proved to be difficult because of a world capital squeeze on South Africa, because of the intransigent technological problems of cutting very hard rock in stopes that are four kilometres below the surface, and, ironically, because of the increased costs of energy for making and powering the machinery. At the same time that the mineowners wanted to use more energy, powering more machinery operated by less labour, the world price of energy increased four-fold. As South Africa moved into recession, the mineowners were able, instead, to take advantage of the traditional defences of capital, which are depression, unemployment and violence. Despite this, the longer term response to the increased worker power of the 1970s is still mechanization, which will inevitably require further energy inputs. Because the South African goldmines obtain most of their energy from local coal, they may even at first be partially protected from an oil-based energy crisis, if it occurs.

The assumptions of this simplified case study are that, as Dr. Bernard Price suggested, increased energy consumption per worker is an index of increased mechanization, and that increased mechanization, as well as increased energy consumption, in turn means an increase in the organic composition of capital.[30] If these assumptions hold, then the case of the South African goldmines since the Second World War has demonstrated that class struggle among capitalists and between capitalists and workers has led to increases in the organic composition of capital, while energy use has also increased.

But an important question still remains: in general, must energy consumption always increase when the organic composition of capital increases because of class struggle? The answer is no, because of technical change. It should be possible to design energy-saving machinery as well as labour-saving machinery. Given sufficient inventiveness there is no reason why energy consumption should not decrease for a significant period of time, despite the increase in c/v, as machines are made more energy efficient. Hence the world's economists now call for conservation, and they try to measure energy efficiency by means of coefficients comparing growth of energy consumption with growth of the gross national product. Whether there will be an energy crisis therefore depends, among other things, on increases in energy efficiency. But the historical record suggests that sufficient energy conservation is highly unlikely. The tendency for c/v to increase has been accompanied by a tendency for energy consumption to increase also. Incentives to conservation in most countries are as yet very small. Inventiveness and research are expensive. They will not be undertaken unless they seem profitable. Competition between capitalists within a country and between capitalist states means that the cheaper short-term alternative of energy consumption, rather than energy conservation, will be used wherever possible. In Edith Penrose's words:

> The demand for oil seems to be highly inelastic even at current prices and very likely at somewhat higher prices . . . . It seems politically impossible for governments of some large industrialized importing countries to induce

their peoples to accept rapidly enough appropriate economic adjustments.[31]

To summarize what we have argued so far: There is no trustworthy estimate of the world's energy sources available, although there must be some finite limit to them, especially to the cheapest (that is, least labour demanding) of them, like oil. At various points in human history transitions have been made from one primary energy source to another, but insufficient information is available to predict accurately when the next transition might occur. The analysis of world energy inequality shows not only that most people are already in a state of energy crisis, but also that the advanced capitalist states consume so much energy that a crisis of transition may well occur fairly soon. The analysis of capitalist production shows that the organic composition of capital tends to increase, and that as capitalists need more machinery, so they need more energy. The use of more machinery but less energy is not impossible, but is to be discounted in the short or medium term as a major energy saving factor. Above all, energy use and mechanization are determined in the complex process of class struggle. Competition between capitalists, and strife between the principal classes of labour and capital, together determine energy consumption levels. The effects of competition and primary class struggle on the organic composition of capital and on energy use were outlined in the case study of the South African gold-mining industry. At the world level, it is arguable that energy is so useful to capitalists, who generally need to increase the organic composition of capital because of competition and class struggle, that the world seems highly likely soon to reach a point of transition from the less labour demanding energy forms to more labour demanding forms. *In short, an energy crisis of transition from cheap oil to other energy sources is likely because of the nature of capitalism.* To answer the main question posed in this section: capital, in general, tends to need increasing amounts of energy because of the tendency for the organic composition of capital to increase.

Why Do Energy Capitalists Need Energy?

A fundamental tendency of capitalism, then, is toward the employment of more dead labour, embodied in machinery, while employing relatively less living labour. Dead labour requires energy to power it. By monopolizing the supply of the least labour-expensive energy form (oil), the world's largest capitalist companies have created their structure of world domination, articulated through the West's immensely powerful state apparatuses and defended by the state-owned means of destruction. In recent years the monopoly has been further removed from the attentions, both of potential newcomers to the market and of the mass of the world's industrial workers, by the marriage of the companies to the new capitalist families and states of the Middle East. The cost was high for the industrial West in terms of oil price rises, and it was even higher for the non-industrial countries of Africa and Asia in terms not only of price rises, but also of class formation and wars in and around the oil states. But the new partnership — Western oil companies and Middle Eastern capitalists — have benefited enormously; they have accumulated wealth on a scale totally unprecedented in history. Much of this wealth was translated into machines of war, located both in the hands of the Western great powers and in those of the Middle Eastern states. The fundamental problems leading to war in the Middle East remain unsolved and inflammable.

The energy capitalists have a special need for energy, beyond the requirements of their increasing organic composition of capital. *They need energy because it is their special commodity.* They accumulate and re-distribute capital gained from the production, transformation, transport and sale of energy. Their major goal is to control all energy supplies to other capitalists, and to restrict the flow of those supplies so that prices are stable and have an upward tendency. Conscious of the possibility of a transition from oil to another prime energy source occurring sometime in the next 50 years at the most, the oil companies are rapidly transforming themselves from oil monopolists into energy monopolists, despite the attention of the anti-trust forces of the United States of America. They are buying up coal and uranium deposits, either overtly or covertly, around the world. Direct ownership of deposits is not always necessary, because it is generally in the interests of all energy suppliers to act together as monopolists. The energy companies must fear any prospect of uncontrolled change from the sources they control to other energy forms, especially renewable forms like solar and geo-thermal energy. If the energy companies do not control the supply and price of solar energy panels, for example, then their monopoly on energy supply is diminished It may be that part of the present resistance to further oil price increases comes from the oil companies' present lack of influence over the substitute energy forms which would become viable if existing energy-form prices rose.

What does the energy capitalists' special need for energy mean for the likelihood of an energy crisis? Their control of energy supplies is as much based on ownership of technological research ability as on the threat of use of the means of destruction. They play a continuous game of brinkmanship in the interplay of price rises, technological research into substitute sources of energy, and the bringing on to line of new oil fields such as those recently revealed in Mexico and the Sudan. Simply, a crisis could result if they get their arithmetic wrong. Sheikh Yamani of Saudi Arabia warns that a further sudden oil price rise could have grave consequences of instability, so that the answer is 'a gradual period of upward prices, with both consumers and producers arranging to avoid oil surpluses and/or shortages, to create price stability'. [32] Is this to reckon without the essentially unplanned, unstable nature of competitive capitalism in its struggle with workers? Perhaps, but a much respected energy economist, Maurice Adelman, clearly thinks not, when he insists that market mechanisms will prevent sudden crisis: 'We are never going to run out of oil and gas, but rising prices will gradually force them out of more and more markets.' [33] In reply, Anthony Sampson wisely questions whether, in the light of their past history, OPEC and the oil industry are such rational and economic organizations. [34] If Maurice Adelman bases his crisis-prevention strategy on capitalist market mechanisms, perhaps the numerous crises to be found at all stages in the history of capitalist markets are in any case sufficient indication of the likelihood of an energy crisis towards the end of this century.

Energy capitalists need energy as a commodity. Commodity markets have crisis as their chief characteristic, notwithstanding attempts at planning and control in recent years. The recent shudder in that most planned and controlled market of all, the diamond market, is a case in point. Energy's special relation with production only heightens the risks. Its importance increases the chance that the wealthy capitalist states will resort to their final solution to crisis: war. Nevertheless, Adelman could be proved right. It is conceivable that, precisely because of energy's importance, a planned transition from cheap oil to more expensive oil and to other energy sources will be achieved, so that energy price rises are slowly introduced into the system without causing instability. At present, however, it must be stressed that such a planned transition seems unlikely.

How Would an Energy Crisis Affect Relations Between Capital and Labour?

A capitalist crisis of transition from less labour-expensive energy forms, like oil, to more labour-expensive forms, like coal, tar-sands, uranium and renewable sources, seems therefore to be likely, but is by no means a certainty. What does this mean for class struggle?

Class struggle can at one and the same time both 'cause' an energy crisis and be the major area where the 'effects' of that crisis occur. The one point on which everybody, including the World Bank, seems to be agreed is that energy prices will show an upward trend. This is logical, because of capital's general need for more energy. Humankind will have to turn from less labour-expensive forms of energy to more labour-expensive forms, unless a major technological breakthrough in energy conservation is achieved. The debate would seem to be whether the price rises will occur smoothly, as in Adelman's scenario, or suddenly by crisis, as I have tended to argue. Yet whether or not the transition is smoothly planned or takes the form of a crisis, one thing is clear. If energy prices increase, and if energy-efficient technologies are not developed rapidly enough, then capitalists will find it more difficult to increase the organic composition of capital. It will be more difficult to raise labour productivity by the use of more machinery; it will be more difficult to control workers, to speed up production processes, to cheapen the cost of labour power, and, in general, to increase relative surplus value. In short, if energy prices rise substantially, capitalists will be less secure in their battle against workers, and capitalists will need to find other ways of increasing their competitive advantages over one another.

If capital becomes less able to control workers by mechanization, then deeper lines of defence will have to be used. Inflation, depression, unemployment, and higher degrees of 'discipline' or force at the workplace, are already in evidence. Put simply, depressed economies consume less energy. It seems logical that, as energy prices rise, higher levels of the flow of unemployed through the industrial reserve armies will become the norm, especially in Africa, Asia and Latin America, but also elsewhere. Further, as capitalists and capitalist states find it more difficult to increase their competitive advantages by mechanization, they are likely to attempt to gain new advantages by the increased use of force, which may well result in local or more general wars. If the transition to higher prices takes the form of a sudden crisis, these tendencies towards greater unemployment and war will be increased. Capitalism has immense and well demonstrated abilities to maintain its hold on society by means of unemployment or war. These abilities will again be used. The relations between the Western powers, China, and the Soviet Union are beyond the scope of this chapter, but there too the risks are immense, given the nature of the 'balance of nuclear terror', and the general prevalence of war in the twentieth century.

For workers, however, if capital is less able to control them by using machinery, the period of energy price rises presents an opportunity to take advantage of capital's weakness. The 'energy crisis of 1988', therefore, promises to be a period of heightened workers' struggles, and the potential exists for working class victory despite, or even because of, depression, unemployment and war.

In conclusion, it must be stressed that the 'energy crisis of 1988' may turn out to be a myth. This does not affect the main purpose, however, of this essentially suggestive chapter, which has been to pose some of the necessary questions and outline some methods of answering them, based on an analysis of capitalism. Whatever happens in the short term — even if a really vast new oil field sufficient to power capitalism for a significant period is discovered — it is still suggested that the methods of analysis used in this chapter will be more useful than the present conventional approaches.

References

1.   M.A. Conant, *International Energy Supply: A Perspective from the Industrial World,* New York, The Rockefeller Foundation, 1978, *passim.*
2.   Speech at St. Anthony's College, Oxford, May 1978.
3.   'World oil shortage in next two decades is unlikely', *Financial Times,* 25 May 1978.
4.   Ibid., and M. Tanzer, *The Energy Crisis,* New York and London, Monthly Review Press, 1974, p.129.
5.   E. Penrose, 'Choices for the oil exporting countries', *Middle East Economic Survey,* vol. 21, no. 3, 16 January 1978.

23

6. *The Economist,* 25 March, 1978.
7. K. Marx, *Theories of Surplus Value,* London, Lawrence and Wishart 1969, vol.2, p.495.
8. Ibid., p. 506.
9. K. Marx, *Capital,* London, Lawrence and Wishart, 1974, vol.1, p.598.
10. J.A. Hobson, *The Evolution of Modern Capitalism,* New York, Walter Scott Publishing Co., 1912, pp.72-3.
11. For a recent concrete examination of the use of machinery to control work see H. Braverman, *Labour and Monopoly Capital: the Degradation of Work in the Twentieth Century,* New York, Monthly Review Press, 1974, *passim.*
12. K. Marx, *Capital,* vol.1, op.cit., p.477.
13. At a sophisticated level there are problems in Marx's treatment of the organic composition of capital and the industrial reserve army. In this initial exposition of the role of energy in capitalist production these have been ignored. See M.C. Howard and J.E. King, *The Political Economy of Marx,* London, Longmans, 1975, pp.196-203.
14. British Electrical Development Association, *Lighting in Industry,* London, B.E.D.A. n.d., p.1.
15. Ibid., p. 3.
16. Whether 'v' increased in this particular case depends on factors such as the rate of inflation and the relation of the specific money wage to the general value cost of reproducing labour power at the time.
17. For an excellent analysis of this crucial strike, see D. O'Meara, 'The 1946 African mine-workers' strike and the political economy of South Africa', *Journal of Commonwealth and Comparative Politics,* July 1975.
18. H.F. Oppenheimer, Anglo-American Corporation of South Africa, to F. Searls, Newmont Mining Corporation, New York, 7 September 1946, (Johannesburg, Anglo-American Corporation Records, Box 728, File: Mechanization of Mines 1946-1953).
19. Ibid.
20. Ibid.
21. Ibid.
22. Ibid.
23. 'Effects of irresponsible demands', *Mining Survey,* November 1946, p.3.
24. Ibid.
25. Ibid.
26. A.R. Mullins, 'Power supply to the mining industry', *Transactions of the S.A. Institute of Electrical Engineers,* January 1953, pp. 12-14.
27. Figures and indices calculated from Chamber of Mines, *Annual Reports,* 1946-1976.
28. D. Horner and A. Kooy, *Conflict on South African Mines, 1972-1976,* Cape Town, S.A.L.D.R.U., 1976, p.29.
29. 'Gold mining sows a R100 million seed', *Mining Survey,* October 1974, p.17.
30. The relation between the technical composition of capital and its organic composition is not necessarily simple and direct, but for purposes of exposition it is assumed here to be so. See the reference in note 13 above.
31. E. Penrose, 'Choices for the oil exporting countries', op.cit., p.8.

32. A Sampson, 'Huge questions about oil', *International Herald Tribune*, 6 July 1978.
33. Ibid.
34. Ibid.

3. The Energy Crisis
Mohssen Massarrat

1. Preface

Of all the manifestations of the crisis of capitalism, the so-called 'energy crisis' has probably received the most publicity in recent years. Correspondingly, there has been a great deal of confusion about the real causes of this crisis. Some commentators immediately connect the 'energy crisis' with the conflict in the Middle East; others glimpse behind the crisis the conscious political action of the U.S. government, aiming to strengthen the position of the dollar. While the reactionary mass media make reference to the 'oil sheikhs' and actively stir up racial hatred by attributing the calamities of capitalism to other nations, certain socialists see the causes of the 'energy crisis' in the existence of the multinational oil firms. Behind the conscious propaganda of the former, and the speculations and illusions of the latter, the real underlying causes necessarily remain hidden.

There is no doubt that the 'energy crisis' of 1973-74 was triggered off by the OPEC states' drastic increase in the posted price of oil. There can also be no doubt whatsoever that as a result of this increase the OPEC states were able to increase their revenues by about 80 to 90 billion dollars during the same year. An enormous redistribution of the mass of value on the world market has therefore taken place in their favour.

But how could the posted price suddenly be increased fourfold? What was the source of this enormous mass of value which has now been suddenly appropriated by the OPEC states? What is the basis of the power which enabled these states to act in this historically unique fashion?

To answer the first two questions we must briefly outline the specific process of the formation of value and price and the specific mode of operation of the law of value in the extractive sphere, to which energy production belongs. Regarding the third question, we must investigate the relationships between those states, or more precisely those classes which participate on the world market in the distribution of the mass of profits of the world energy sector. In the present essay the results of the author's investigations have been summarized in rather a concentrated form. Sections 2.3 and 4.1 are taken with minor alterations from a work by the author originally published in German at the beginning of 1974.[1] Sections 4.2,5 and 6 are from an extensive investigation concluded by the author in November 1977 (also published in German).[2] For reasons of space numerous questions raised by such a complex problem have had to be omitted here. It is thus unavoidable that the author has had to refer frequently to his previous work.

2. The Dual Modification of the Law of Value in the Sphere of Raw Material Production

In Volume 3 of *Capital* (Chapter 10) Marx derives the operation of the law of value by abstracting from all forces external to capital. In part six of the same volume, where he derives the 'transformation of surplus profit into groundrent' and thus his theory of rent, Marx is really dealing with the modified mode of operation of the law of value in the spheres of production of agriculture and extraction, which are immediately dependent on nature.[3] In these spheres the law of value is subject to a dual modification: by the impossibility of generalizing the productivity of labour, which in this sphere depends on the power of nature (a circumstance which therefore limits competition); likewise, groundrent sets limits to competition (in all cases where the land and the soil, viz. sources of raw materials, are subsumed under groundrent). This essay will examine in detail both these forms of the modification of the law of value, as this is the only way in which the basic categories necessary for a comprehensive treatment of the economics of raw material production in the energy sector can be derived.

2.1 The First Modification of the Law of Value
The real causes of an increase in the productivity of labour and the possibilities of generalizing these productive powers in one sphere of production have been extensively dealt with elsewhere.[4] We know that under normal conditions a higher productivity of labour springs from capital itself, either because 'capital is used in greater than average quantities' or because 'better methods of labour, new inventions, improved machinery, chemical manufacturing secrets, etc., in short, new and improved, better than average means of production and methods of production are used.'[5]

Further, this higher productivity of labour can be generalized within a particular sphere, and can therefore be transformed into the average productive power of labour which is applied in the sphere. The market price, viz. the general price of production (cost price plus average profit), of commodities in the sphere is regulated by the individual prices of production of those capitals which produce significant portions of the commodities. Capitals producing in better conditions therefore utilize a productivity of labour which is higher than average; they thus realize a surplus profit, as their individual price of production is below the general price. Capitals producing in conditions less favourable than the average in the same sphere are not in a position to realize the average profit, as the individual price of production of their commodities is above the market price; therefore, sooner or later, they have to cease production.

If supply and demand are in equilibrium, or if there is only a short-term deviation of demand from supply, the market price is not regulated by those capitals in a sphere of production which produce in the worst conditions, but by those which operate in average conditions. Because conditions of competition exist, the capitals which produce in average or favourable conditions can, by extending their share of the market, completely cover the existing social need for commodities from this sphere in the short term. Thus they can replace the capitals producing in the worst conditions, which squander social labour.

In contrast to the conditions of competition in spheres such as industry, the productivity of labour cannot be generalized in the spheres of production immediately dependent on nature: therefore the market price cannot be regulated by the price of production of commodities produced in 'average conditions'. In the sphere of extraction the material basis of the higher productivity of labour is the power of nature, which allows certain capitals to gain a greater surplus value from the productive power of the labour they utilize — assuming that all the capitals operating in this sphere have the same average organic composition. Therefore the higher productivity of labour in the extractive sphere does not arise from capital, but:

> It arises from the greater natural productiveness of labour bound up with the application of a force of Nature, but not a force of Nature that is at the command of all capital in the same sphere of production . . . . On the contrary, it is a monopolizable force of Nature which, like the waterfall, is only at the command of those who have at their disposal particular portions of the earth and its appurtenances.[6]

Capitals which utilize a productivity of labour linked to an exceptionally favourable natural force obtain a surplus profit which, from the standpoint of the creation of surplus value, is in no way distinct from the usual surplus profit. Yet the exceptionally favourable natural force is not itself the source of surplus profit:

> . . . the natural force is not the source of surplus-profit, *but only its natural basis, because this natural basis permits an exceptional increase in the productiveness of labour.* In the same way, use-value is in general the bearer of exchange-value, but not its cause.[7]

The essential distinction between the extractive and industrial spheres, therefore, is the fact that in the former the higher productivity of labour cannot be generalised because the determination of its material basis is given by nature and independent of capital. *Therefore the first modification of the law of value is expressed by the fact that limits are set to the competition of individual capitals to raise the productivity of labour and generalize it by increasing their share of the market in the sphere (with a corresponding tendency to lower the regulating market price).* In this sphere the competition of individual capitals consists only in acquiring a monopoly in a particularly favourable material basis of the productive forces given by nature, in order to secure a permanent surplus profit by excluding real competition.

On the one hand, the natural basis of the productive forces — whether this is the land and the soil or mineral raw materials — cannot be reproduced at will. Therefore the share of the market of individual capitals in the commodities of this sphere depends on the extent to which individual capitals have a monopoly over the quantity and quality of the natural basis of such commodities. On the other hand, it is only as a result of an extraordinary accident of nature that the most favourable conceivable material conditions for the production of a raw material, whether in one particular location or in several parts of the globe, are present in unlimited quantities. As a rule, the material basis of raw material production occurs in relatively limited quantities and is distributed over the globe with decisive differences of both quality and location. The greater or lesser, higher or lower, quality of a raw material, which is ultimately reflected economically on the market, is a result of the chemical composition of the raw material, the natural conditions of its production, its transportability, and the conditions of its material processing. It may be taken as a proven fact that crude oil as a source of energy, compared to coal for example, displays considerable advantages in all the respects mentioned.

These material conditions, given by nature, for the production of raw materials have the following consequences for the production of surplus value. The materials' individual price of production produced by individual capitals in one sphere, e.g. the energy sector, differs depending on whether these capitals exercise a monopoly over the poorer or the better quality natural source of the raw material. The fact that a raw material's individual price of production varies with quality and location does not make any difference if the monopoly over the total disposable sources of this raw material is dominated by one single capital. *The question here is: what actually regulates the market price of raw materials in this sphere?*

But to completely satisfy social needs — nationally and internationally — for a particular raw material, raw materials of the same kind must, according to our assumptions, be produced at individual prices of production. We have seen that, in industry, capitals with unfavourable conditions of production dissipate social labour, and are thus driven from the market by capitals with average or favourable conditions of production. This is because there are then no external limits to the extension of the latter's share of the market. But we have also seen that, in the extractive sphere, the applied higher productive forces of labour cannot, because of their natural basis, be generalized.

In these conditions, the lowest productivity labour applied in the extractive sphere by capital produces as much surplus value as does socially necessary labour. This is only the case when the most complete satisfaction of social needs requires the production of raw materials found in qualitatively or locationally unfavourable situations which affect the productivity of labour. But this means that the capital which utilizes the lowest productivity of labour must aim for the average, the normal, profit, and that therefore the individual prices of its commodities must at least correspond to the market price. *Therefore, as distinct from the industrial sphere, the market price in the extractive sphere is regulated by the individual price of commodities produced in the worst conditions.*

Thus, if the social need for the products of the sphere rises, so that production of qualitatively or locationally even more unfavourable raw materials becomes unavoidable, the market price will tend to rise. This is because materials whose production price is higher than the individual price of production previously regulating the market price are now needed. Hence the market price must rise to such an extent that the average creation of surplus value is possible even in the production of raw materials under the least favourable conditions.

By contrast, if the social need for a raw material declines, or new, more favourable conditions (in terms of quality or location) are discovered, the capital which previously operated in the least favourable conditions (and whose commodities therefore had the highest production price, which regulated the market) no longer realizes the average profit. This is because the competition of the capitals operating in better conditions now forces down the market price to the individual price of production of those groups of raw materials in the sphere whose production still meets society's needs. In the changed conditions, the productivity of labour previously utilized by capital in the worst conditions proves to be socially squandered labour. For this reason, such capital is excluded from the market.

In all these conditions, the market price of the raw materials is in every case regulated by the individual price of production of raw materials produced in the least favourable conditions. Capitals producing this group of raw materials obtain only the average profit. The other capitals, producing under the most favourable conditions in the sphere, whose individual price of production is therefore lower than the market price, obtain a more or less large surplus profit in proportion to the favourable natural quality and location of the raw material over which they have a monopoly. These surplus profits accrue independently of whether the raw material sources are subsumed under landed property or not. Landed property can, at most, effect that transformation of surplus profit into groundrent, a circumstance which depends on the historical relation of capital to landed property. We will discuss this in more detail later.

2.2 The Second Modification of the Law of Value
In the above analysis of the first modification of the law of value in the extractive sector, we have assumed that there are no limits to the competition of the capitals in the sphere for the acquisition of new, more favourable sources of raw material. These capitals carry on their competitive struggle by permanently trying to get access to raw material sources of higher quality.

As we have described above, there were only limits to competition in so far as the capitals utilizing a higher productivity of labour cannot generalize this within the sphere. We now drop this assumption, and start from the premise that the natural basis of raw materials is subsumed as a whole under landed property, which, as a factor external to capital, therefore prevents capital from having an unrestricted choice of the natural basis of its production. This thus sets limits to the competition between capitals for raising the productive power of labour by utilizing more favourable natural bases.

Landed property excludes from production the particularly favourable natural basis of raw materials until a tax or toll is paid for the permission to utilize this favourable natural resource. The competition of capitals for a monopoly in the more favourable natural basis enables landed property to force up these tolls, which will be paid as long as capitals can give up the whole *surplus profit* to landed property and still obtain the normal average profit.

In these conditions there is no incentive for capital to increase the productivity of labour by utilizing qualitatively or locationally more favourable natural bases of raw materials, as the extra profit to be gained is ear-marked for landed property. Therefore, landed property is a barrier to capital, as it prevents the abolition of factors counteracting competition so that an increasingly more advantageous natural basis of production can be utilized. *Landed property thus again modifies the law of value in the extractive sphere in order to prevent capital from transcending the first modification.*

2.3 The Transformation of Surplus Profit into Groundrent

If the whole natural basis of raw materials is subsumed under landed property the surplus profit is transformed into groundrent. Marx distinguishes two essentially distinct forms of groundrent: *differential* and *absolute* groundrent. In the above-mentioned case where the surplus profit arises from the difference between the individual price of production of a single capital and the general price of production in the sphere, we are dealing with *differential rent:*

> . . . it is evident that this rent is always a differential rent, for it does not enter as a determining factor into the general production price of commodities, but rather is based on it. It invariably arises from the difference between the individual production price of a particular capital having command over the monopolized natural force, on the one hand, and the general production price of the total capital invested in the sphere of production concerned, on the other.[8]

By contrast, *absolute groundrent* is determined by landed property in the natural basis of raw material which is in every respect the most unfavourable, but is utilized by capital. Capital still utilizes this comparatively dubious, most unfavourable natural basis because with the given relationship of supply and demand it can still create an average amount of surplus value. But this average surplus value from capital does not cause landed property to place at the disposal of capital the natural basis it commands, however bad it is. Landed property excludes this natural basis belonging to it from production until it receives a fee. This will not happen until the social need for this raw material exceeds the supply in the long term and the market value, and with it the market price therefore rises above the general price of production of the capital generally employed in the sphere. This difference between the market price of the commodity in question and the general price of production is then (as a particular form of surplus profit, of the natural monopoly profit which enters into the price of the commodity) transformed into absolute ground rent by being appropriated by landed property.

As we have seen in our discussion of the Marxist theory of absolute ground rent,[9] landed property can only be effective in capitalist society and operate as a barrier to capital if the material basis of a commodity subsumed under landed property for which a social need exists is available to a relatively limited extent. *If, on the other hand, the natural basis of this commodity in the extractive sphere is available in unlimited quantities, as for example is sea water as the natural breeding ground for fish, then the competition of the landed proprietors − if this natural basis is generally subsumed under landed property − leads to a tendency for ground rent (both differential and absolute) to fall, and finally to the ⁓omplete abolition of landed property as a barrier to capital.*

3. The Law of Value and the Energy Sector

The basic theoretical assumptions demonstrated above now allow us to take a step nearer to dealing with the real problem, i.e. the analysis of the specificity of the formation of value and price, of competition etc., in the energy sector. It is clear that the energy sector must be seen not on the national level but internationally, since the market price for the products of this sphere, like the products of all spheres of production immediately dependent on nature, can in general only be derived in an international context. For the sake of simplicity we shall abstract from the modification of the law of value by currency mechanisms and consider only the effect of both the modifications of the law of value demonstrated above which have an immediate effect on the production process.

The carbon-bearing sources of energy − crude-oil, coal, natural gas, oil shale − in so far as they occur in nature in a use-value form, differ fundamentally in form, chemical composition, and physical and chemical properties. The only thing they have in common in terms of use-values is that they all contain carbon. If we include the most important non-carbon sources of energy, such as nuclear energy, thermo-dynamic sources of energy, reservoirs, etc., then there is not even a material property common to all forms of energy sources. What in general determines that these sources of energy are commodities on the market is that, like every commodity, they possess exchange-value. Their particular determination, and their second common property as commodities, is that they are related to each other *in the context of exchange-value,* because they are all different use-value forms of one and the same commodity.

Sources of energy that we initially abstract from by-products only have an exchange-value because they are the material bearers of one and the same form of commodity (energy), which is eventually transformed into heat under the various technical processes for changing materials. Therefore the value, and thus the market price, of a definite mass of the above-mentioned sources of energy, is a result of how much energy (expressed in calories) they eventually supply and how much it costs to separate the thermal energy from its material bearer.

In order to present clearly the mode of operation of the law of value in the international energy sector, we omit all those forms of energy sources which, because of their relatively small share in providing energy for the world, are of

Figure 1
World Consumption of Primary Energy, 1960-1969*

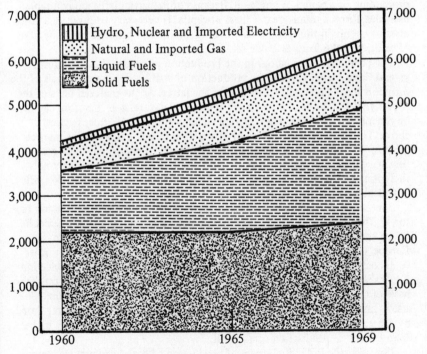

* In million metric tons of coal equivalent.
Source: United Nations, *Statistical Papers,* Series 1, No. 14/St/Stab/Ser I/14;
World Energy Supplies 1966-1969, Table 1 S.6.

little significance and which have at present no influence in determining the value and price of energy sources. This includes all energy sources which do not contain carbon; as well as oil shale and natural gas. As Figure 1 shows, this leaves two main sources of energy in the world today — coal and crude oil.

It would be quite correct to assume that, as a particular use-value form of energy, crude oil displays considerable advantages compared to coal in all respects, from its immediate production to its transformation into thermal energy. In addition, the by-products of crude oil find numerous uses in all sectors of industry; but to get rid of the residues of coal requires actually additional costs.

Let us omit all the advantages of crude oil compared to coal in processing, and the highly valuable by-products from oil, and merely consider the mass of calories which crude oil and coal contain, respectively, as the main determinant of the market value and market price of both forms of energy source. Even then we must still admit that the individual price of production (cost price, including transport costs, plus average profit) of a tonne of coal, expressed in terms of the mass of calories it contains, is several times the individual price of production of a tonne of crude oil. Because of its particularly unfavourable use-value form, a much greater mass of capital is necessary to produce a given mass of energy in the form of coal than is required to produce the same mass of calories in the form of crude oil.

The productivity of labour in the production of crude oil is, therefore, several times higher than in the production of coal, as the material basis of the former is more favourable than that of the latter. As the material basis of the productivity of labour in the sphere is given by nature, and therefore cannot be generalized, the same laws operate which were derived under Section 2 above. Thus the individual price of production of coal regulates the market price for all other carbon-bearing use-value forms of energy sources because, firstly, coal has the highest price of production in the sphere and, secondly, there is a great demand for coal on the international energy market. We will now deal with the first of these factors.

Sources of energy are in practice related to each other by a conversion factor.[10] This indicates a connection in terms of value which must also exist between them in reality. Furthermore, the average market price of oil in Europe — even before the 'energy crisis' — was almost four times that of its total costs of production, transport, processing and distribution (see Section 5.1, Table 2, below); this proves that the market price is not formed on the basis of the actual costs of production (the individual cost price) of the oil itself. Instead, it is obvious that the market price of oil in Europe is regulated by the actual production costs of European coal, which is many times higher than the actual production costs of oil.

However, the individual prices of production of coal from various regions are quite different, just as the individual prices of crude oil from various areas also reveal significant differences. The individual price of production of crude oil in the Persian Gulf and in Africa, for example, is considerably lower than that of North American crude oil. Not only is the quality of the former higher, it also contains on average less harmful impurities such as sulphur, etc., and more CUs [See note 10] (therefore in terms of CUs the production costs are lower). Furthermore, on the basis of the favourable conditions given by nature, the extraction of crude oil in the Persian Gulf and in Africa takes place in a more or less natural fashion at the earth's surface. The amount extracted for every well is up to a thousand times higher than it is in North America.[11]

In its turn, the individual price of North American coal is lower than that of European coal.[12] Here, too, the difference in the prices of production can be attributed to the difference in the natural conditions of production. The impurities in American coal (e.g. the ash content) are less, and the heat content is therefore higher than that of European coal. Thus the individual price of production of American coal (i.e. price per CU) is less than that of European coal. Further, the main deposits of American coal occur in a very suitable geological form and near the earth's surface: thus in comparative terms its production requires a smaller mass of capital than European coal which occurs in a less suitable geological form deeper under the earth's surface. In addition, the productivity of labour is higher in the American mines — this springs from capital itself. The technological level of production, and thus the organic composition of capital, is higher in the American than in the European mines.

The average individual price of production of European coal is so high that it would long ago have been driven out of the market by American coal, and to an even greater extent by crude oil, had not its production been maintained by the 'socialization of losses'; either directly through the nationalization of the coal mines as in France and Britain, or indirectly in the form of subsidies to the industry. Numerous mines would have had to close and immense masses of capital (and therefore social labour) would have been annihilated because capital could not produce the average amount of surplus value, since the individual price of production of single capitals was above the general price of production regulating the market. Only the intervention of the state and political considerations have, in the most important European coal-producing states, prevented the closure of even more productive plants. By contrast, the capitals producing coal in America do manage to create an average amount of surplus value and therefore realize the average profit to be found on the market.

The individual price of production of American coal regulates the market value and market price of all sources of energy, inasmuch as its individual price of production obtains precisely the average profit. Therefore, although other sources of energy (like Europe) produce coal, and although they contribute to the energy market, their individual price of production is even higher than the individual production price of American coal. The market price of energy sources is not determined by the individual price of production of European coal because, from the standpoint of capitalism, the labour expended in this sphere is wasted labour and thus cannot be remunerated by capitalist society. Given that European coal can in general only be produced if subsidized by the state, the market price for energy sources in the sphere is regulated as if European coal were non-existent in the energy market.

If we aimed to illustrate the *exchange-value relations* of the main energy sources on the world market — crude oil in the Persian Gulf and North America, coal in North America and Europe — and to show by means of a graph the relation between the market price for energy and the individual price of production of the respective energy sources (all converted to CUs, on the basis of the analysis given above), the following picture would result:[13]

Figure 2
Exchange-value Relations of Main Energy Sources on World Market

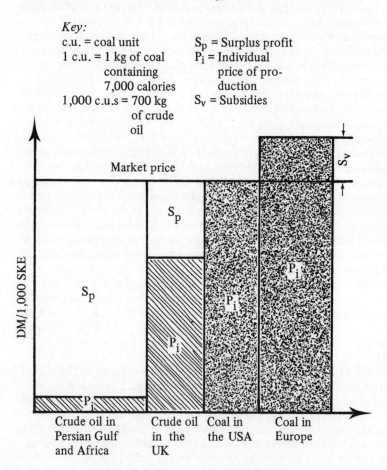

Key:
c.u. = coal unit S_p = Surplus profit
1 c.u. = 1 kg of coal P_i = Individual
       containing   price of pro-
       7,000 calories   duction
1,000 c.u.s = 700 kg S_v = Subsidies
       of crude
       oil

As Figure 2 shows, the productivity of labour in the energy sector is highest in the Persian Gulf and lowest in the European coal mines. Capitals which utilize the higher productivity of labour in the Persian Gulf obtain enormous masses of surplus profit,[14] since, as we established in Section 2.1 above, limits are set to competition in the extractive sphere by the fact that the higher productivity of labour, resting on a more favourable natural basis, cannot be generalized. Thus the socially necessary labour employed in the sphere, and therefore the market value and market price, only falls to the extent that it is possible to increase the *average* productivity of labour in the sphere through means arising from capital itself.

But, at first glance, the real development in the energy sphere seems to contradict this first modification of the law of value in the sphere of extraction. For the market price of the most important energy sources (price per CU) has remained constant for a long period — certainly this is true from the 1950s until recently.[15] In real terms, given the general devaluation of money, it has even fallen, although as we can see from the graph in Figure 1 and from Table 1 society's need for energy has increased enormously.

From the Marxist standpoint, this development means a huge increase in the productivity of labour. We shall see that such an increase cannot arise from capital. It also suggests a sharpening of competition in the sphere. How did this development take place? Has the first modification of the law of value in the energy sphere been abolished? What are the conditions of this abolition? Table 1 contains a partial answer to this question:

Table 1
Development and Structure of Consumption of Primary Energy

Source of Energy	*World*				*Western Europe*				
	1960		*1970*		*1960*		*1970*		
	Mill. CUs	*%*	*Mill. CUs*	*%*	*Mill. CUs*	*%*	*Mill. CUs*	*%*	
Coal & other solid fuels	2,116	46.0	2,263	31.0	509	56.9	423	28.0	
Oil	1,610	35.0	3,285	45.0	286	32.0	877	58.0	
Gas	598	13.0	1,241	17.0	10	1.1	91	6.0	
Hydro	276	6.0	511	7.0	89	10.0	106	7.0	
Nuclear	–	–	–	–	–	–	15	1.0	
Total	*4,600*	*100.0*	*7,300**	*100.0*	*894*	*100.0*	*1,512*	*100.0*	

* Excluding nuclear.
Source: 'Gegenwartige und kunftige Probleme der Energieversorgung', Studie 7, Esso-AG, Hamburg 1973.

We can see from Table 1 and from Figure 1 that, with the continual rise in world energy requirements, the structure of distribution between the main energy sources has constantly changed. The share of solid fuels, and therefore of coal, in world energy production has continually fallen (although its absolute production has remained almost constant); and the share of liquid fuels, and thus of crude oil, has continually risen. There has been increased competition between capitals producing different energy sources, as a result of which the capitals producing crude oil have been able to considerably enlarge their share of the market in the total production of energy at the expense of the capitals producing coal.

Therefore, the first modification of the law of value in the energy sphere has actually been abolished by the fact that those capitals which utilize a higher productivity of labour because of the more favourable natural basis of their productive forces have considerably enlarged their share of the market. *From the standpoint of the law of value, the effect of the capitals which utilize a higher productivity in the sphere, thereby enlarging their share of the market, is the same as if the average productivity of labour itself in the sphere had been increased.* The consequence of this, as was apparent for decades in the energy sphere, was a tendency for the market price to fall. The underlying reason was that, as a result of the continual fall in the average socially necessary labour in the sphere, the market value tended to fall.

While, on the one hand, therefore, the general price of production regulating the market in the energy sphere has fallen, the individual price of production of those capitals producing coal has remained constant, or at least in Europe has not fallen so far that they could have produced an average amount of surplus value without direct or indirect subsidy from the state (as in England, France and West Germany: cf. Figure 2).

This is only a partial answer to the question posed above. For, on the one hand, the supplies of natural sources of crude oil (for the time being the most favourable natural basis for the productivity of labour) are limited in the sphere, a limitation which is today more concrete than for any other natural raw material. On the other hand, the raw materials of the world, including sources of crude oil, in whatever form and wherever they occur, are subsumed under landed property. It is clear that the particular form of landed property in the sources of raw materials is not private property but, as a rule, communal ownership. The ruling class as a whole is therefore the indirect proprietor of the sources of raw material, and the relationship of these sources to landed property is regulated by means of the state which represents this class.[16]

But the relationship of capital to landed property is only the *form* in which private property of the sources of raw materials distinguishes itself from communal property, just as it is only a change of form when private property in agricultural land goes over to state property:

Landed property is thus negated from two sides; the negation from the side of capital is only a change of form, towards its undivided rule. (Groundrent as the universal state rent (state tax) so that bourgeois society reproduces the medieval system in a new way, but as the latter's total negation.)[17]

The formal transformation of landed property, and the transformation of private property into the property of the state which represents capital, does not mean the abolition of the particular relationship of landed property to capital. In these conditions, groundrent is transformed into 'general state taxes', but is not abolished. We have seen elsewhere that this particular relationship, in which landed property operates as an immediate barrier to capital, can only be completely abolished if the limitation of the land and the sources of raw materials is completely abolished.[18]

Given the limitation of the conditions of production immediately set by nature, and assuming that these conditions of production are subsumed under communal property, the proprietor state of a society is related to capital as the real proprietor, although the state essentially operates as the ideal total capitalist in this society. *It follows, therefore, that on the level of the world market landed property, even if it is state property, only sets limits to the capital operating on landed property if the state which appears as the ideal total proprietor is at the same time far from appearing as the direct representative of that capital.*

But how is it that, in practice in the energy sector, landed property in the sources of crude oil does not operate as a barrier to capital, and therefore does not set limits to the competitive struggle of individual capitals in the sphere, seeing that the production of crude oil has increased at the expense of coal? Further, we have to ask under what conditions landed property as such cannot be effective in modifying the law of value (as derived in Section 2.2 above).

This set of questions can only be answered in connection with an analysis of the historically specific inter-imperialist class relations and the transformations they are subject to in the oil industry.

4. Class Relationships within Imperialism and their Transformation on the World Market

4.1 The Historical Relationship of Capital to Landed Property: The Origin of OPEC

Two essential forms of landed property are to be distinguished — the old form of landed property in pre-capitalist society, and its modern form in bourgeois society:

By its nature as well as historically, capital is the *creator* of modern landed property, of groundrent; just as its action therefore appears also as the dissolution of the old form of property in land. The new arises through the action of capital upon the old.[19]

In the explanation above, we have always assumed that we were dealing with the modern form of property when discussing landed property as a barrier to capital. For only with the development of the capitalist mode of production in the spheres of production subsumed under landed property is landed property in a position to appropriate as groundrent a section of the surplus value produced:

> In so far as commodity-production and thus the production of value develops with capitalist production so does the production of surplus-value and surplus-product. But in the same proportion as the latter develops, landed property acquires the capacity of capturing an ever-increasing portion of this surplus-value by means of its land monopoly and, thereby, of raising the value of its rent and the price of the land itself.[20]

Capital and modern landed property are dialectically related to each other. Capital, itself the product of the destruction of the old relations of landed property, creates modern landed property and transforms it into its opposite: 'Capital arises out of circulation and posits labour as wage labour; takes form in this way; and developed as a whole, it posits landed property as its precondition as well as its opposite.'[21] Once it is fully developed with capital as a whole on a national scale, modern landed property must be abolished as a barrier to capital if, historically, capital as a social relationship still capable of development is to establish itself.

In fact, capital initially abolishes landed property as a barrier on a national level. This process occurs by capital historically transcending the limitation of the conditions of production immediately given by nature: it overcomes national barriers and for the first time creates the capitalist world market (to be distinguished from the already established world trade market). It operates on this market, in which the land, the soil and sources of raw material are available to a relatively unlimited extent. If these are available at an international level to a relatively unlimited extent, national landed property ceases to operate as a barrier to capital (see Section 2.3). But it must be stressed that this will only happen if capital manages to overcome the barriers to accumulation in the form of landed property on an international level. *To this extent the subsumption of international landed property under capital as a historical condition of its development is the reverse side of capital's initial negation of national landed property.*

International landed property was, in our view, subsumed under capital during the second half of the 19th century either by a process of direct annexation or colonization, or indirectly by the incorporation of the economy which rested on landed property into the world market ruled by capital.[22] Under these special conditions, when capital is in a position to have unrestricted use of the relatively unlimited conditions of production given by nature, it doesn't have to give up the entire surplus profit to landed property.

Capital's profit is only limited to the extent that it must utilize a part of the obtained or expected surplus value to establish the general conditions of production. This includes not only an infrastructure and administration indispensable for capitalist production, but the costs of the reproduction of the forms of rule resting on the pre-capitalist relationships of landed property. For, the particular relationship of capital to landed property in which the latter does not operate as a barrier to the former can only exist as long as the pre-capitalist relationships of class and landed property can be maintained.

For their part, the ruling classes of pre-capitalist societies, as the indirect exclusive proprietors of the national land, and sources of raw materials of these societies, are quite satisfied with a payment from capital for utilizing their landed property as the natural basis of its production. This is a kind of pre-capitalist groundrent, on which their power and domination has rested since time immemorial.

It is clear that this payment, this groundrent, has nothing whatsoever to do with capitalist groundrent created by capital itself; and that this tribute paid by capital to landed property constitutes only a small portion of real capitalist groundrent, of the surplus profit obtained by capital as a whole. In so far as pre-capitalist landed property does not operate as a barrier to capital, it in no way excludes the land or raw material sources from production in order to force up groundrent. Thus capitals in the sphere of raw materials production, including the production of energy sources, can compete with each other by employing increasingly favourable natural bases for their production in pre-capitalist societies. Assuming that more favourable natural bases of raw material production are actually present to a sufficient extent in pre-capitalist societies, individual capitals can do this by increasing the productivity of labour employed by them and by attempting to force down their individual price of production. *It is therefore clear why in the sphere of energy production, although the natural basis of production is limited and is subsumed under landed property, the former appears to capital to be unlimited; and why therefore competition can take place in the sphere and the law of value operate.*

It is also clear why, for several decades, it was not landed property, and in the case of crude oil production the countries providing crude oil, but capital (and thus the multinational oil companies) which could determine the volume to be produced, the market price and even the amount of the groundrent to fall to landed property. The question now is the following: how and in what conditions has a clear change of tendency in the relationship of capital to landed property in the case of crude oil production begun to manifest itself since the beginning of the 1970s?

We have explained above that only landed property as a pre-capitalist form remains subjected to capital and therefore it does not operate as a barrier to the latter. From this standpoint it is possible to derive the direct interest of capital in maintaining pre-capitalist forms of rule which rest on landed property. This direct interest of capital also reflects itself historically in the decades of unconditional support given by imperialism to despotic forms of rule in those pre-capitalist societies rich in raw materials.

For a whole epoch it was possible for capital to maintain the forms of rule resting on pre-capitalist relationships of landed property by means of political intervention and military force whenever there was a danger of the dissolution of the old conditions. But what capital cannot and does not do is hinder the dissolution of pre-capitalist relations of production and the development of the production of capitalist surplus value. This is because capital itself is the real cause of the destruction of pre-capitalist landed property, as well as being the immediate bearer of the capitalist mode of production into pre-capitalist societies.

At the turn of the 18th century when capital penetrated into the agriculture of England, and later into that of colonies, it initially destroyed pre-capitalist landed property as its condition and transformed the former into its opposite. To draw an historical parallel over 150 years later, capital in the international sphere is now destroying the pre-capitalist landed property of societies rich in raw materials and forcibly transforming it into its opposite.

Once capitalist surplus value production has established itself as the determining form of production in formerly pre-capitalist societies, and once the class relationships have been fundamentally transformed, then the ruling class ceases to be satisfied with the fact that it places at capital's disposal the natural basis of production of raw materials which it owns. It ceases to be satisfied merely with tribute from capital, once its own power rests on the production of surplus value. It begins to put an end to the indiscriminate exploitation of national raw materials by capital, especially foreign capital. It tries to stop the competitive struggle of capitals to increase the productivity of labour by utilizing at all costs a more favourable natural basis, and in this way attempts to have an influence on the formation of the market price in the particular sphere concerned.

The ruling classes of these societies, as the actual proprietors of the sources of raw material, themselves begin to determine the amount of tribute paid to them. They force up the tribute to the amount really owing to them as landed proprietors in the capitalist world system (the entire surplus profit obtained by capital as a result of utilizing a more favourable natural basis of production). *Provided that quite definite political conditions obtain, then the competition of capitals to acquire particularly favourable natural sources of raw materials will ensure that the entire surplus profit obtained by utilizing these natural sources is transformed into capitalist groundrent and is appropriated by the proprietor state.*

The transformation process (described above) of the old relationship between capital and pre-capitalist landed property into a new relationship between capital and the modern landed property it created began a long time ago, and we are only now experiencing its consequences. The change in the relationship between the multi-national oil companies and the oil-rich societies is therefore neither the result of the particularly clever politics of a few Harvard graduates in the oil-providing countries, nor the result of the bad foreign policies of the U.S.A. Nor is the last Arab-Israeli War of 1973 in the Middle East itself the real cause of this change of tendency, as it is simplistically presented by the bourgeois press and politicians. Rather, it is the result of the development of capitalism in the oil-rich societies themselves. The War only accelerated the change of tendency.

Of course, we cannot conclude from this that the capitalist mode of production has already established itself in all these societies. Nor can we conclude that with the development of national capitalism these societies have already become completely independent economically and politically. Further, we cannot conclude that the most capitalistically developed societies must automatically play the leading political role in the upheaval of relations between the multinational oil companies and the oil-providing countries. Too many factors play an influential role for the relationship of economics to politics to be reduced to this simplistic picture.

Among such influential factors, for example, are the particular internal political structure, the level of political and military dependence on imperialism, and the dependence of the other sectors of the national economy on the world market. Further, the particular balance of forces between the socialist states and the capitalist states, as a real power relationship, cannot be left out of account. This is a factor which has a decisive effect not only on the function of a single state in this process of transformation, but also on the overall change of tendency in the relationship of the oil-providing countries to the multinational oil companies. This relationship of forces and the real power of the socialist states has, it is true, neither brought about nor given rise to this change of tendency; but it has favoured its development and, right from the start, prevented the use of military force by imperialism to counteract this tendency.

Libya, one of the least capitalistically developed countries supplying crude oil, has, next to Algeria, played the leading role in bringing about the change in the relationship between the multinational oil companies and the countries supplying crude oil, and not only in its pricing policies. Again, Iran, next to Saudi Arabia the most capitalistically developed country, has acted as a brake.[23] At the same time, it is clear that Libya could only play the leading role in the negotiations between the OPEC states and the oil companies because the objective conditions for a change of tendency in the most important OPEC states were already present. Sooner or later these states would themselves have had to take similar steps, as was shown by the foundation of OPEC itself — the institutional condition of a necessary change in the old relationship between the multinational oil companies and the oil-supplying countries. Thus, if the Libyan government had tried to take the same measures before the establishment of OPEC as it has since 1971, it would in all probability not have succeeded.

Historically the first attempt to bring about a successful change in the relationship between world capital and landed property during the present period is that of the national bourgeoisie in 1951 in Iran. The dissolution of the pre-capitalist relationships of property and production was very far advanced in Iran, and the national bourgeoisie under the leadership of Dr. Mossadegh threatened the interests of imperialism, and its domestic allies at that period (the class of large Iranian landowners), with its nationalization of all BP's oil installations. But by means of an externally organized economic boycott and internal conspiracy, imperialism was able — just as it was in Chile in 1973, although at a qualitatively different level — to prevent the national bourgeoisie from taking power. This first attempt failed because the objective conditions in the other oil-producing states for transforming the relationship between world capital and landed property were still completely lacking at that time.

Before concluding this section, we still have to look at the logical consistency of the historical development of the relationship between capital and landed property. First of all, we must draw together what has already been said in relation to this question. Capital itself, as the destroyer of pre-capitalist relations of landed property, first develops on a national level and creates modern landed property on this same level. It then transforms this landed property into its own opposite. National capital abolishes this antithesis by making itself into world capital. The other side of this abolition is the suppression of pre-capitalist landed property on the international level. In this way, the original relationship between capital and landed property is historically reproduced, but this time on the international level and with the difference that now, because capital is already a finished product, pre-capitalist landed property represents the condition, not of its origin, but of its further development. But this further development on an international scale presupposes the destruction of pre-capitalist relations of landed property — a process which has accelerated in the present period.

Once the capitalist mode of production is established in all pre-capitalist societies, the old pre-capitalist form of international landed property is transformed into its modern form. In this way, the old antithesis between landed property and capital is reproduced historically, but this time on the international level. *It also follows from this historical relationship between capital and landed property that this antithesis, because it is now fully developed, can only be abolished with the capital relationship itself.*

4.2 Wage Labour, Capital, Landed Property and the Dual Character of the National State on the World Market

The above explanation attempted to establish the development of modern landed property as an economic power and as a barrier to capital on the world market. The emergence of organizations like OPEC and the International Energy Agency (I.E.A.), which include exclusively oil-owning states and capitalist, oil-consuming states respectively, makes it seem that two groups of states representing the interests of either landed property or capital confronted each other.[24] The real relationships are quite different.

Just as on a national level *capital* in reality exists in single capitals, *landed property* in individual landed properties, and *wage labour* in the wage workers of one factory, so likewise these exist on the world market in their individual fractions: as *national capital, national landed property,* and *national wage labour.* The classes of landed proprietors, the bourgeoisie and the working class relate to each other directly on a national level as independent political powers. Outside the national state, this relationship is quite different. On the world market this relationship is modified by the nation state, as these classes constitute themselves in the context of their specific local, historical and cultural peculiarities. Regarding the explanation of the relationship between capital and landed property as it really presents itself on the world market, what follows is not that the 'international bourgeoisie' meets the 'international class of landowners'; it is rather that nation states which represent national capital and national landed property as an organic unity, confront each other politically and economically. The antithesis between capital and landed property on the world market does not mean that states split into two essentially different groups which must line up at one or other of the two poles of this antithesis. *Instead, this antithesis appears as a contradiction established within every individual state. This also determines the dual character of the state, insofar as a landowning state is at the same time a capitalist state, and a capitalist state is a significant landed proprietor owning sources of raw materials.*

If, however, the nation states subject to such a dual determination join forces within opposing institutions such as OPEC or I.E.A., which represent and defend exclusively either the interests of landed property or the interests of capital, then in one case the interests of landed property, and in the other the interests of capital, prevail as the *decisive* interests of the nation state. This explains why the institutions of landed property on the world market were historically created by the countries of the 'Third World', and those of capital by the developed capitalist countries. Thus the interests of capital in the 'Third World' countries are marginal on the world market, in view of the less developed level of capitalism in such countries by comparison to landowning interests, as important producers and exporters of raw materials. In contrast, the interests of landed property in the developed capitalist countries scarcely come into consideration, given the high level of development of capitalism in these countries, even though in absolute terms they may have at their disposal greater sources of raw materials than in other countries.

The determination of the real antithesis between capital and landed property on the world market, which manifests itself in the dual character of nation states, helps to explain some important aspects necessary for the analysis of class relationships. *The contradiction between the divergent economic and political interests of the landowning states of the 'Third World' and of the O.E.C.D. states which occurs on the world market is not an antagonistic contradiction. Capitalist landowning states of the 'Third World' are organic components of the world market.* The national capitals of countries such as Chile, Iran, Indonesia, Nigeria, Zaire etc. are, despite their local independence, the least developed individual parts of international capital, just as the barbaric military dictatorships of these countries represent merely the localized domination of imperialism. True, the national capitalist classes of the countries of the 'Third World' are, on the one hand, as the landowning classes of their countries in a position to utilize their landed property for the appropriation of groundrent. Therefore they can redistribute surplus value in favour of their national accumulation fund. But on the other hand, as a component of the international bourgeoisie, they are forced, in view of the associated dangers for capitalism, to recognize and take into account the limits of their power. Similarly, the developed capitalist states are forced to recognize the sovereignty of the nascent bourgeois classes in the countries of the 'Third World', which they themselves have brought into being; they are forced to make concessions to them, given their mutual interests and structural inter-dependence.

The organic and structural coincidence of both blocs means that we are *not* dealing with economically and politically homogeneous, monolithic unities. Instead, both blocs are characterized by internal contradictions which arise from distinctive national interests. These interests also explain the varying positions of the states which are within both blocs. Mexico, as a capitalist country of the 'Third World' and an oil proprietor on the world market, can flirt with the O.E.C.D. states (especially the U.S.A.), instead of joining OPEC, as long as its capital interests outweigh those of its landowners. If this country becomes an important oil-exporting country, as has in fact been predicted, it will have to stop wavering between its landowners and capital and instead join the land-owning states of OPEC. Algeria and Libya, whose national economies have not yet been completely subordinated to the conditions of the world market, can for precisely this reason occupy a radical position within OPEC in relation to further increases in the price of oil. Iran, whose national capital is an integrated component of world capital, occupies a radical position as an oil proprietor, but at the same time, in regard to the intensification of the crisis of the capitalist world economy, ultimately resigns itself to a moderate position which is compatible with the interests of capital. [Publisher's note: this chapter was completed before the Iranian Revolution of 1978-79.]

In my opinion the contradictions within the O.E.C.D. states are even sharper. The U.S.A. commands extensive natural sources of almost all raw materials and is thus the most significant landowning state in the world as a whole. On the world market, however, its capital interests far outweigh its landowning interests, as it has scarcely any significance as a raw materials exporting country, while as an exporter of capital it occupies by far and away the most important position. The relative independence of the U.S.A. in the provision of national raw materials, and the function of the American state in providing the most effective political and military representation of the interests of capital on the world market, explains why its government adopts a radical position in all confrontations with the landowning states of the 'Third World', not excluding the use of force. On the other hand countries like Canada, South Africa, and Australia, which are amongst the important raw material exporters in the bloc of the O.E.C.D. states, often seem to stand closer to the positions of the landowning states in safeguarding their interests, especially in the discussion of the 'New International Economic Order'. Further, it is quite conceivable that O.E.C.D. states like Norway, and probably England, which in the near future will be transformed into important oil exporters on the basis of North Sea oil, will leave the O.E.C.D. (or even the E.E.C. in England's case) and join OPEC. But this will only happen if, in the longer term, they can more effectively represent their total national state interests by their power as an oil-landowning state. (For further analysis see Section 6 below.) Such a change of position by England, including even only a verbal willingness to join OPEC, must finally destroy the last illusions of naive anti-imperialists about the actual character of such institutions as OPEC.

Finally, the constitution of international landed property, and thus of the relationship between capital and landed property, on the world market also has decisive consequences for the workers' movement and its strategy. In the economic and political conflicts between nation states on the world market resting on the antithesis between capital and landed property, the national working classes are hopelessly subjected to the nation state interests of one or other class — the capitalist or the landowning class. The national working classes can only represent their specific class interests when they create their own international economic and political institutions, which oppose the power of capital and landed property in an *independent and unified* way. The constitution of the working class as an international class, overcoming national limits, is also the essential precondition for abolishing the power of the classes of capital and landed property, and therefore of abolishing the contradiction between these classes on the world market. Thus the manifold determined contradictions on the world market have reduced themselves to the contradiction between the class of international capitalists (landowners) and the international proletariat, of which the proletariat of the countries of the 'Third World' also forms an organic component. Thus the material basis for anti-imperialist policies that involve alliances with the non-proletarian classes in the countries of the 'Third World' was dissolved long ago. In the interest of a consistent anti-capitalist strategy on a world scale, attention must be paid to this new development.

5. Surplus Profit from Oil: its Sources, Distribution and Redistribution

5.1 The Structure of the Market Price for Oil: The Sources and Forms of Surplus Profit from Oil (Groundrent, Surplus Profit from Capital, Petroleum Tax)

It is of fundamental importance to distinguish between the posted price and the market price for oil. Before the 'energy crisis' of 1973-74 the posted price for oil was fixed by contract between the multinational oil companies and the oil-producing countries. This price was used as the basis for calculating the taxes and royalties (groundrent) to be paid to the producing countries.

On the other hand, the market price for oil is in fact determined on the world market in competition with other sources of energy. As the data in Table 2 show, an average market price for crude oil realized on the European energy market in 1972 prior to the 'energy crisis' came to four times its posted price.

Table 2
Breakdown of an Average Price of a Barrel/Ton of Crude Oil as paid by
the consumer in Western Europe*

	First Quarter 1972	
	$ per barrel of crude oil	*$ per ton of crude oil*
Average host government take (taxes and royalties)	1.75	12.25
Average consumer government take+	5.60	39.20
Average cost of industry operations (production, transport, refining, marketing/distribution, incl. downstream corporation taxes)	2.70	18.90
Average industry margin (for reinvestment and distribution to shareholders)	0.35	2.45
Weighted average gross proceeds per barrel/ton of crude	*10.40*	*72.80*

*Countries include United Kingdom, France, Italy, Benelux, and Sweden.

+This item does not, in reality, consist of duties charged on energy as such. A large proportion of this form of taxation represents a recoupment of financial burdens assumed by the community at large for the benefit of road transport.

Source: O.E.C.D., *Oil: The Present Situation and Future Prospects,* Paris, 1973, p.176.

What has been proposed and defended theoretically in Section 3 above is that the actual market price for crude oil is governed by the individual cost of production of coal on the world market. This hypothesis will now be argued in more detail and empirically substantiated.

Figure 3
Oil-producing Countries' Share of Posted Price and Groundrent for Crude Oil,
1970-1974*

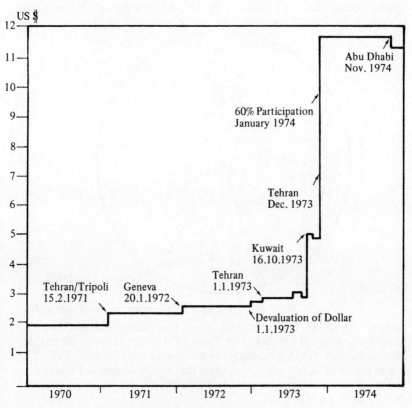

* In U.S. $ per barrel for Arabian light 34° A.P.I.

Source: Jonas, R., and Minte, H., *Petrodollar*, Bonn 1975, p. 32.

* In U.S. $ per barrel for Arabian light 34°A.P.I.
Source: Jonas, R., and Minte, H., *Petrodollar,* Bonn 1975, p. 32.

In the year 1972, approximately only one-quarter of the average market
price for crude oil (then $ 72.80 per tonne) consisted of the total actual costs
incurred. The difference between the market price and costs, i.e. the
remaining three-quarters of the market price ($ 53.90 per tonne), was appro-
priated by the oil-producing countries, the oil companies and the oil-
consuming countries in the form of groundrent, surplus profit and petroleum

49

tax respectively.[25] Figure 4 below shows a similar structure for the market price of petroleum products as Table 2 above.

Figure 4
Share of Costs, Taxes and Profits of Producing Countries and Oil Companies Compared, in ultimate consumer price for petroleum products

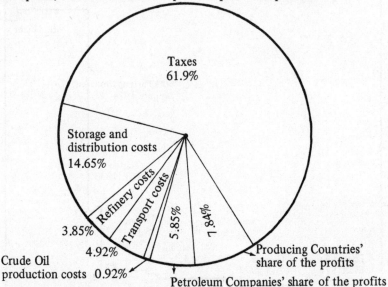

Source: Burgbacher, Fritz, 'Aktuelle Ol-und Energieprobleme und ihre mogliche Losung', in *Gluckauf 110,* Essen 1974, p.63. The negligible difference in the data on the components of the market price for oil in Table 2 and Figure 4 are probably a result of the fact that Figure 4 takes as its basis a market price which also includes, besides petroleum tax, the other usual taxes – sales tax, V.A.T. etc.

The data of Table 2 and Figure 4 respectively lead one to conclude that the market price levels for petroleum and petroleum products respectively are not determined and regulated by their individual cost prices (production costs). At the same time, the relatively high profits appropriated by the oil companies and the oil-producing countries can in no way be ascribed to arbitrary actions based on their collective political power, given that, as the development of the listed prices for petroleum shows,[26] even before the international 'energy crisis' both the landowning states and the oil companies were in competition to some degree. Even less can the levying of petroleum taxes on imported crude oil at the unique and unprecedented level of $ 39.20 per tonne – i.e. at 54 per cent of the market price of $ 72.80 per tonne (cf. Table 2) – be explained as a voluntaristic act on the part of the governments of the oil-consuming countries, since this tax,[27] unlike all other forms of taxation, is not as a rule imposed by a single country but by all the West European oil-consuming countries.[28] Until now it has not been levied sporadically but on a regular basis ever since crude oil was first imported into West Europe. Table 3 illustrates this in relation to West Germany; in all the years before the 'energy crisis' the level of petroleum tax was almost twice the import price of crude oil.

Table 3
Development of Crude Oil Imports, Petroleum Tax, Import and Market Prices of Crude Oil in West Germany, 1954-1975

Year	Crude Oil Imports (million tonnes)	Total Petroleum Tax (million D.M.)	Petroleum Tax per tonne (D.M. per tonne)	Import Price Arabian Light c.i.f. (D.M. per tonne)	Market Price (D.M. per tonne)
1954	5.98	0.810	135.4	85.0	220.4
1956	8.00	1.510	188.6	96.0	284.6
1958	10.89	1.822	165.3	93.5	258.8
1960	23.27	2.664	114.5	85.3	199.8
1962	39.56	3.699	93.2	76.3	169.5
1964	51.84	6.071	117.2	74.9	192.1
1966	68.81	8.016	116.5	66.9	183.4
1968	85.70	9.875	115.2	67.8	183.0
1970	98.79	11.512	116.8	68.3	185.1
1971	100.23	12.417	123.8	78.2	202.0
1972	102.60	14.227	138.8	71.7	210.5
1973	110.49	16.589	150.2	81.9	232.1
1974	102.54	16.052	158.0	213.3	371.3
1975	88.41	17.121	193.0	216.9	409.9

Source: Massarrat, M., *Weltenergieproduktion,* op. cit., ch. 13.1.

The fact that petroleum taxes can be levied independently of time and place by all the oil-consuming countries of Western Europe proves that these taxes are an economically determined component of the actual market value, i.e. the market price, of crude oil. This price must, therefore, also be explained in terms other than a mere political act of the oil-consuming countries dictated by national considerations.

The market price component appropriated by the oil-consuming countries' petroleum taxes could have been appropriated instead in the form of additional groundrent or extra profit by the oil-producing countries or the oil companies respectively, because it existed independently of the oil-consuming countries. However, the reason why this component has been appropriated precisely by the oil-consuming countries and not by the landowning countries or the oil companies is explained in detail elsewhere.[29]

Petroleum taxes, we must conclude, are not the cause of the unusually high difference between the cost price and the market price of crude oil but, on the contrary, are the consequence of this great difference. The oil-consuming countries are able to levy such high petroleum taxes on imported crude oil because even then this source of energy remains able to compete with other energy sources which are scarcely taxed at all. Coal is an example — its market price can be realized on the world market despite higher petroleum taxes. Finally, what has been argued above for the unusually high petroleum taxes also applies to the existence of groundrent for oil-producing countries and the extra profit of oil companies.

It is clear from the above arguments that the oil-producing countries, the oil companies and the oil-consuming countries, by means of groundrent, surplus profit and petroleum tax respectively, have all taken a share in the margin between the actual costs of production and the actual market price of crude oil. We shall now analyse the different components of the actual value of crude oil.

On the level of abstraction used in Section 3, the value relationships between different energy sources were considered exclusively with regard to the thermal energy contained within them. The uniform market price represented graphically in Figure 2 expresses the market price of the thermal energy contained in various raw materials. In examining the actual value of energy resources, however, further factors must be taken into consideration. In addition to thermal energy, crude oil also contains valuable by-products such as motor fuel, naptha, lubricating oil, bitumen, etc., which can be extracted from it with considerably less effort than from coal. On the basis of the results summarized here[30] the structure of the value of crude oil can be subdivided according to its origin, distribution and appropriation.

The basis of crude oil's market value is the value of the thermal energy it contains, given that crude oil products are used essentially to produce thermal energy.[31] The value of thermal energy contained in crude oil (measured in CUs) is, as proved above, determined by the value of the thermal energy in the same amount of coal. This most important component of the market value of crude oil shall be termed V_{CU}. The production of thermal energy based on oil requires less expenditure of effort than such production based on coal.

A definite amount of CUs in the form of crude oil as an energy resource represents *per se,* therefore, a higher value than the same quantity of CUs in the form of coal. This difference is precisely equivalent to the differential amount of effort necessary to convert both energy resources into thermal energy. This component of the market value of crude oil shall be termed V_c. Finally, we term the value components of the market price of crude oil which constitute by-products as V_{bp}. The actual market value of crude oil (V_{co}) consists of:
$V_{co} = V_{CU} + V_c + V_{bp}$ (cf. Figure 5).

Figure 5
Structure of Market Value of Crude Oil by Origin and by Distribution and
Appropriation

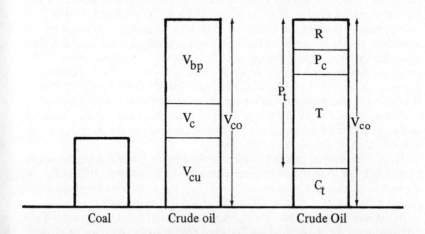

Both factors, V_c and V_{bp}, also explain why the actual market value of
crude oil as a raw material, as will be shown empirically below, is considerably
higher than the market value of coal, although the production costs of the
former are considerably lower than those of the latter. The market value of
crude oil (which, as illustrated above, is made up of various components), is
one side of the analysis. The other side is the distribution of the mass of value
embodied in crude oil between various classes, countries etc. *The market value
is determined by economic laws of the value-formation process in the world
energy sector, and the distribution of the amount of value embodied in crude
oil arises from the historically determined power relations of different classes
in the capitalist world market.*

We shall denote the value component in the form of machine depreciation
and the use of materials, as well as in the form of wages in production, transport, refining and marketing, as total cost price C_t. The difference between the
market value and the total cost price of crude oil is total profit — P_t. This is
distributed among oil-consuming countries in the form of petroleum taxes —
T; among the oil companies in the form of company profit — P_c; and among
oil-producing countries in the form of royalties and taxes — R. Hence the total
quantity of value, V_{co}, embodied in crude oil is divided as follows:
$V_{co} = C_t + P_t = C_t + T + P_c + R.$

5.2 Distribution and Redistribution of the Surplus Profit from Oil
An analysis of the structure of the market price for oil and a detailed explanation of the source of total profits (normal profit plus surplus profit) allows us

to demonstrate empirically the development of the distribution and appropriation of surplus profit from oil. In the struggle over the distribution of surplus profit from oil, the posted price acquires decisive significance. Up until the end of the 1960s the multi-national oil companies were able to keep the share of the oil-producing countries' groundrent as low as possible by means of the low level of the posted price for oil which was, in fact, dictated by them. With the formation of modern landed property (as already explained in Section 4) and given that the oil-producing states of the 'Third World' were able for the first time in history through the setting up of OPEC to organize their *de facto* monopoly power as owners of the most profitable oil wells in the world, they were able to transform the posted price for oil into the economic lever for the redistribution of surplus profit from oil.[32] Thus by drastically increasing the posted price for oil, the OPEC countries were also able to increase significantly their share of the groundrent as a proportion of the surplus profit from oil. The 'energy crisis' of 1973-74 must therefore be seen as the result of a change in class relations on the world market and as the result of the struggle for the redistribution of the surplus profit from oil.

The actual scale of this distribution of the surplus profit from oil between groundrent $-$ R $-$ of the oil-producing countries, company profit[33] $-$ P_c $-$ of the oil companies, and petroleum tax $-$ T $-$ of the oil-consuming states before and after the 'energy crisis' of 1973-74 will now be examined.

In the interests of a uniform empirical portrayal of the development of the distribution of the mass of oil profits, numerous conversions must be made when we use empirical sources.[34] It has to be emphasized that this fact makes it essential to consider the calculations that follow as only relatively accurate. However, in no case is there a serious discrepancy between individual data taken from various sources and the results enumerated below which are systematic, cover a long period, and are the outcome of the utilization of extensive data.

Here we shall limit ourselves to a comprehensive outline of the results for all components of the surplus profit from oil. These results have been calculated in detail elsewhere.[35] Table 4 and Figure 6 present a synopsis of the development of the average shares in the surplus profit produced from one tonne of crude oil of the oil-producing countries (in the 'Third World'), the oil companies and the oil-consuming states.

The data from Table 4 and Figure 6 allow one to draw the following important conclusions: (i) In the 1960s, with the reduction in the real world market level of energy prices, the surplus profit from oil also fell. This is an indication of and additional evidence for the heightened form of competition between capitals in this period in the world energy sector; (ii) After the tremendous leap in the posted price of oil after 1973, the oil-producing countries appropriated a groundrent actually higher than the total surplus profit which in 1972 (before the 'energy crisis') had been created by the production of one tonne of oil and appropriated by all the parties concerned. This fact shows particularly clearly the real aim of the oil-producing countries, which was by means of posted price increases in 1973-74 to appropriate the entire oil surplus profit as groundrent.[36] The fact that the oil companies continued to appropriate surplus profit after 1974, and were in fact able to increase it in absolute terms, is due to structural changes in the world energy market after 1974, as the result of which the actual value and price levels of the energy sources also increased.[37]

Table 4
Structures and Components of Surplus Profit from Oil (OPEC average values)

Year	Groundrent		Company Profit		Petroleum taxes in importing countries		Total Surplus Profit from oil	
	$ per ton	%	$ per ton	%	$ per ton	%	$ per ton	%
1945	1.82	-	4.90	-	-	-	6.72	-
1950	2.16	11	4.95	25	12.40	64	19.50	100
1955	5.50	11	5.39	11	39.90	78	50.79	100
1960	4.88	12	5.49	14	28.60	74	38.97	100
1962	4.99	15	5.70	17	23.20	68	33.89	100
1964	5.75	14	5.62	14	29.40	72	40.77	100
1966	6.04	15	6.05	15	29.00	70	41.09	100
1968	6.29	15	6.16	15	28.80	70	41.25	100
1970	6.26	15	6.14	15	29.00	70	41.55	100
1971	8.17	17	5.94	12	35.20	71	49.31	100
1972	10.14	17	5.69	9	43.30	74	59.13	100
1973	14.64	18	8.67	11	55.70	71	79.01	100
1974	63.02	46	14.09	10	60.80	44	137.91	100
1975	62.78	42	13.22	9	74.20	49	150.20	100

Source: own estimates. See Massarrat, M., *Weltenergieproduktion,* op. cit., ch. 16.

Not all the participants have been able to appropriate increased surplus profit shares from each tonne of crude oil produced in the 'Third World'. The advanced capitalist oil-consuming countries of the O.E.C.D. (excluding the U.S.A. and Canada) could, of course, only secure surplus profit on that part of the annual crude oil production of the OPEC countries which was actually imported by them. As for the surplus profit of the oil companies, it relates only to that part of production which they controlled in their concessionary areas. This is also the reason for the difference between the share-out of surplus profit obtained per tonne (see Table 4) and the share-out of the surplus profit which the oil-producing countries, the oil companies, and the oil-consuming countries have been able to appropriate *in toto* (shown in Table 5).

Figure 6

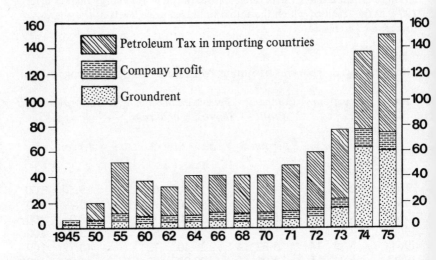

Table 5
The Development in the Distribution of OPEC Oil Profits between Oil-
producing Countries (OPEC), Oil Companies, and Major Oil-consuming
Countries (O.E.C.D.)

Year	OPEC oil-producing countries		Oil companies		O.E.C.D. oil-consuming countries*		Total	
	$ mill.	%	$ mill.	%	$ mill.	%	$ mill.	%
1945	133	-	359	7	-	-	492	-
1950	391	16	895	37	1.123	47	2.409	100
1955	1.569	18	1.536	17	5.689	65	8.794	100
1960	2.180	20	2.453	23	6.181	57	10.814	100
1962	2.658	21	3.023	24	6.781	55	12.462	100
1964	3.770	20	3.683	19	11.598	61	19.051	100
1966	4.792	20	4.799	20	14.654	60	24.245	100
1968	5.940	20	5.815	20	18.115	60	29.870	100
1970	7.343	20	7.204	19	23.342	61	37.889	100
1971	10.798	22	7.847	16	29.997	62	48.642	100
1972	13.908	22	7.808	12	41.119	66	62.835	100
1973	22.691	23	13.428	14	58.602	63	97.721	100
1974	95.601	53	21.377	12	62.715	35	179.693	100
1975	85.277	50	17.952	11	68.531	39	171.760	100

* Excluding U.S.A. and Canada.
Source: Massarrat, M., *Weltenergieproduktion,* op. cit., ch. 16.

The drastic reallocation of surplus profit derived from oil in favour of the OPEC oil-producing countries becomes evident from the fact that after the 'energy crisis' the groundrents of these countries could be increased more than 40 times compared to 1960, whereas the oil companies' surplus profit and consuming countries' petroleum taxes over the same period only increased approximately 8 and 10 times. Figures 7 and 8 below illustrate particularly clearly this redistribution of the surplus profit derived from the total amount of oil produced in the oil-producing countries.

Figure 7
The Development of the Absolute Distribution of the Surplus Profit Derived From Oil

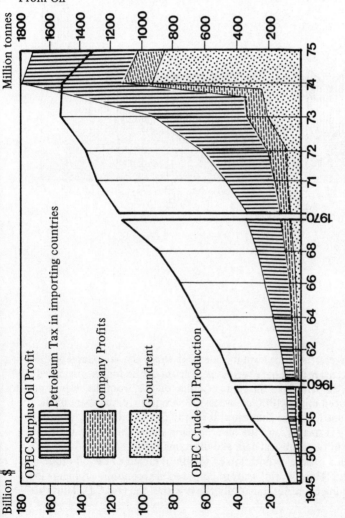

Source: Massarrat, M., *Weltenergieproduktion*, op. cit., and Table 5

Figure 8
The Development of the Relative Distribution of the Surplus Derived From Oil

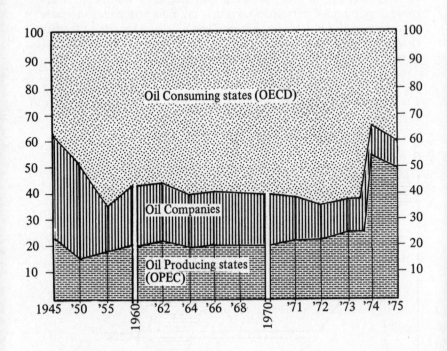

Source: Table 5

Because the present price level for energy is above the value level of the energy market, after the 'energy crisis' petroleum tax no longer originated in total, but only in part, from the value of crude oil (i.e. from the surplus profit from oil produced in the OPEC countries). Consequently, the share of the oil-consuming countries in the total surplus profits from oil after the 'energy crisis' in reality is smaller, and the oil-producing states' share actually higher, than is shown in the empirical data and diagrams above.

Clearly such a drastic reallocation of wealth in favour of the oil-producing countries of the 'Third World' leads to considerable economic problems for the oil-consuming countries, especially those within the O.E.C.D. Thus this re-allocation signifies for the developed capitalist countries the withdrawal of a part of the surplus value hitherto at the disposal of their national aggregate capital and a decrease in its average rate of profit. *During the drastic withdrawal of surplus value thus described, which was brought about by the currency crisis of 1973-74,*[38] *the decline in the rate of profit induced by this withdrawal of surplus value (at the very least) considerably intensified the ongoing crises of capitalist production.* By contrast, this reallocation of wealth has contributed to a considerable boom in (for the most part capitalist) production in the oil-producing countries and above all to the militarization of these countries. Both their balance of payments surpluses and their currency reserves increased rapidly at the same time.[39]

In considering the objective driving forces of the laws, and therefore possibility of, redistribution of wealth within the capitalist world, it is immaterial whether the masses of value recently appropriated by the OPEC countries are merely consumed as revenue, or used for the development of the productive forces or spent on armaments and militarization, or even whether they are partially fed back again into the main centres of capital accumulation by means of direct recycling.[40] Therefore we shall not discuss this any further.

6. On the Relationship of OPEC to O.E.C.D. Countries And Contradictions Within These Blocs

By drastically increasing the posted price for oil at the end of 1973, the OPEC countries were able to increase dramatically the share of groundrent accruing to them from the total surplus profit. However, as has been pointed out above, they by no means succeeded in transforming the *total* amount of oil surplus profit into groundrent. Nevertheless, this *could* be achieved by bringing the posted price up to the level of the actual price of oil on the world market. To block this, the consumer countries in the O.E.C.D. had to use their own 'monopoly' as chief consumers of OPEC oil to oppose the latter's monopoly inherent in ownership of the oil wells. Moreover, at the end of 1974, they set up the International Energy Agency (I.E.A.), the real function of which, in the first instance, was to abolish the competition between the consumer states which had been unleashed after the 'energy crisis'. The Agency's long-term aim is to enforce a *uniform strategy* for the defence of 'common interests' with regard to OPEC. The tasks of the I.E.A. laid down in its international energy programme leave no doubt as to its real function. These tasks include guaranteeing the supply of oil to all member countries, co-ordinating measures to reduce consumption, establishing an information system on the oil market, and the drawing up and implementation of a long-term co-operation programme for a more rational use of energy and for the production of alternative sources of energy.[41]

An institutionalization of the economic and political power of the O.E.C.D. countries *vis-a-vis* OPEC proved to be all the more urgent as soon as it became clear that the organized monopoly power of the oil companies would be decisively weakened by the institutionalized countervailing power of OPEC, and would be completely eliminated as a power factor in economic and political relations between the oil-producing and oil-consuming countries once OPEC states completely nationalized the companies. By completely excluding the monopolistic enterprises of the oil companies and forcing them out of the oil-producing countries, the OPEC countries brought themselves into direct contact with the oil-consuming countries. (See Figure 9)

Figure 9
Structural Relationships Between Oil-producing Countries, Oil Companies and Oil-consuming Countries After the 'Energy Crisis'

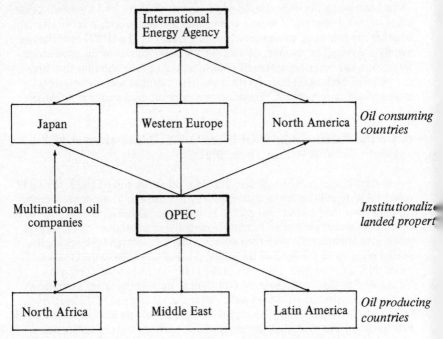

Figure 9 shows the complete change in position of the oil-producing countries of the 'Third World' and the total reversal of relationships on the world market. If at one time the monopolistic concerns of the multinational oil companies unilaterally determined the amount and posted price of crude oil against the interests of the oil-producing countries,[42] today it is, on the contrary, the latter which jointly and independently fix the amount to be produced and the price of their crude oil through OPEC. The oil companies have lost their monopoly hold over the oil-producing countries; as individual capitals in production, refining and marketing, they now have to be satisfied with normal profits in both oil-producing and oil-consuming countries. But the present position of the O.E.C.D. countries on the world energy market is still not comparable to the hopelessly weak position in economic and political terms of the oil-producing countries. The O.E.C.D. countries have at their disposal developed national institutions including tariffs and petroleum taxes with which they can set limits to the monopoly power of OPEC even without the I.E.A.

The O.E.C.D. countries are strong, even if the OPEC countries, because they own the oil wells, are in the position to take the offensive and enforce still further increases in their groundrents by reducing the quantity and increasing the price. The O.E.C.D. countries can react to this on a purely economic level by reducing their consumption and by increasing petroleum tax or custom tariffs — i.e. defensively — so long as they are not in a position to drastically increase production from alternative sources of energy. This concentration of forces is quite different, however, if beyond economic levers the military and political power of the O.E.C.D. countries is also taken into consideration. Even if the U.S.A.'s threat of force against the OPEC countries can be disregarded, it is nevertheless undeniable that the O.E.C.D. countries have decisively counteracted the economic monopoly power of OPEC, ultimately by massive political pressure on individual OPEC members. In this way they have successfully threatened the OPEC monopoly by fostering splits in the OPEC ranks. The ruling class of Saudi Arabia has proved itself in this sense to be a particularly important ally of O.E.C.D. countries within OPEC.[43] When one group of OPEC countries grouped around Iran announced a 30 per cent increase in the posted price for oil from 1 October 1975,[44] Yamani, the Saudi Arabian oil minister, firmly rejected it and pleaded instead for the freezing of the price.[45] By threatening to leave OPEC, increase its production and offer its oil at a cheaper rate on the world market than the other OPEC states, Saudi Arabia succeeded in keeping the increase down — officially to 10 per cent, but in reality to 6.8 per cent.[46]

Saudi Arabia's conduct finally led to an open, if temporary, split at OPEC's oil-price negotiations in December 1976. Against a majority of 11 out of 13 member states which voted to increase the oil price, Saudi Arabia, together with the United Arab Emirates, supported a mere 5 per cent increase in the oil list-price for the whole of 1977.[47] In our opinion, Saudi Arabia's policies contradict in every respect national interests, even those of that country's ruling classes. A small increase in the oil price means that, compared with the other OPEC countries, Saudi Arabia either secures less profit for the same amount of production or must increase production to realize the same returns. Saudi Arabia's OPEC policy can in our view, notwithstanding other arguments,[48] only be explained by the political pressure of O.E.C.D. countries, especially the U.S.A. Admittedly, the ruling class of Saudi Arabia is by no means the sole ally of imperialism amongst the OPEC countries. However in contrast to the Persian bourgeoisie, which is structurally even more closely allied with imperialism, it can be much more easily induced to adopt a 'more moderate' attitude towards the O.E.C.D. countries. In contrast to Iran, Saudi Arabia possesses enormous oil reserves, and, as the world's leading oil exporter, amasses incredible foreign exchange reserves which, given its relatively small domestic market (approximately 8 million inhabitants), it cannot transform into productive capital at a national level. The crucial weakness of OPEC has its roots in the specific conditions of Saudi Arabia. This weakness also allows the Saudi Arabian ruling class to pursue a divisive policy among the OPEC countries.

Thus the ruling class, in for example Iran, can easily present itself as 'anti-imperialist' by denouncing their Saudi Arabian class brothers as lackeys of imperialism.[49] It is clear that the present rulers of Saudi Arabia will not stand their ground on such a policy in the long term, if only for domestic reasons. In all probability, therefore, they will increasingly adapt themselves to the policy of the majority of OPEC states.[50] Notwithstanding this situation, bourgeois commentators rejoice at discovering in each difference amongst these countries 'an irreparable breach', a final 'break-up of the oil cartel'.[51] In their joy, however, they completely overlook the fact that, in relation to the world energy market, the split among the O.E.C.D. countries is significantly deeper.

In fact, the differences in national energy policies among the O.E.C.D. countries are more serious than those among the OPEC states. The contradictions among the O.E.C.D. countries originate from their specific national conditions. Roughly speaking, a total of four groups of countries should be distinguished from one another:

Firstly, countries which dispose of no energy resources worth mentioning, such as Japan, Italy and Denmark. This group has, on the one hand, an interest in keeping the price of oil as low as possible. On the other hand, in view of their strong material dependence on the OPEC countries, they are prepared to put up with oil price increases.

Secondly, countries which in the main are able to supply the majority of their requirements for solid fuels by means of national resources, but are dependent on the world market for their oil. This applies primarily to the West European countries – France, West Germany and the Benelux countries. They have an interest in as low a list-price for oil as possible. But they also seek to keep the share of their own (considerably more expensive) energy production as high as possible in relation to national energy requirements by artificially increasing the national price level for energy.

Thirdly, countries like the U.S.A., and to some extent Canada, which dispose of unlimited energy resources of all kinds, and which are not in principle dependent on the world market in material terms. But, on account of the rising costs of domestic energy production in the 1960s, these countries increasingly imported crude oil from OPEC countries. To fulfil the conditions necessary for crude oil to be produced from the most unproductive national oil sources at a profit, the U.S.A. is definitely interested in a relatively high price for crude oil. Nevertheless, it appears as a declared enemy of an increase in oil prices and can even afford to threaten the OPEC states with the use of military force, given its relative independence in meeting its energy requirements from national resources.[52]

Fourthly, countries like Britain and Norway which because of North Sea oil will in the near future, in addition to meeting their own energy requirements, also export oil (certainly as far as Norway is concerned).[53] These countries have absolutely no interest in a fall in the price of oil. On the contrary, they will endeavour to contribute to increases in oil prices in so far as they are more and more transformed into significant European crude oil producers. Instead of playing at price-breaking *vis-a-vis* OPEC on the world market, which many naive bourgeois politicians expect, Britain and Norway are more likely to side with OPEC against the O.E.C.D. countries; indeed they might even join them if they were to find that this was in their long-term national interest.[54]

The differentiation of national interests outlined here makes it clear how fragile the united front of the O.E.C.D. countries is on the world energy market in reality. In fact, because of its specific national interests, France did not even originally join the I.E.A.[55] The divergent energy policy interests of the O.E.C.D. countries were already revealed in 1975 by the so-called Kissinger Plan in which a uniform minimum price (f.o.b.) for crude oil was to have been fixed.[56] The U.S.A. as the largest crude oil producer among capitalist countries wanted, by fixing a minimum price for crude oil, to provide security for profitable domestic energy production. The majority of O.E.C.D. countries, hoping instead for a drop in OPEC oil prices, had to put up a fight against this plan.[57] In addition, it is hardly surprising that Britain, as the largest future crude oil producer of Western Europe, was decisively in favour of a minimum price for oil. At the same time the British government insisted that it would not allow itself to be represented by the E.E.C. but only by its own delegation at the International Energy and Raw Material Conference held in Geneva in December 1975.[58] This would have meant a split in the common front of the I.E.A. states and would have decisively weakened the position of the I.E.A. in relation to OPEC. Only by a massive change of position, especially by the West German government, could Britain initially even be 'drawn back' into the common front. This was achieved at a certain cost, though – in return, the majority of O.E.C.D. states agreed to the minimum price of $17 a barrel demanded by the U.S.A. and Britain. Thus these O.E.C.D. countries lacking in oil accepted a principle that put the oil-rich countries of the group in a position to pursue OPEC policies within the O.E.C.D. in the future![59]

This quarrel among the O.E.C.D. countries broke out at a time when Great Britain was producing approximately 25 million tonnes of crude oil and only supplying a small part of its own oil needs. Britain's break with the I.E.A. can certainly not be averted once the planned production for 1980 of approximately 200 million tonnes has been attained.

References

1. Massarrat, M., "'Energiekrise" oder die Krise des Kapitalismus', in *Probleme des Klassenkampfs,* no. 11/12, 1974.

2. Massarrat, M., *Weltenergieproduktion und Neuordnung der kapitalist-ischen Weltwirtschaft: Eine Analyse der Weltarbeitsteilung und der Neuaufteilung des Reichtums in der Welt,* Campus — Verlag, Frankfurt/Main, forthcoming.

3. In our opinion, the significance of the Marxist theory of rent has until now received only limited recognition. In Marxist literature its applica-tion is usually limited to the concrete investigation of the relationship of capital to groundrent in the sphere of national agriculture. But the Marxist theory of rent extends far beyond this realm. It remains, there-fore, the most appropriate starting point for investigating the relation-ship of capital to groundrent on the international level and for deriving the modification of the law of value on the world market in all spheres of production dependent on nature. This essay provides a model for applying the Marxist theory of rent: without a knowledge of this theory it would not be possible to derive the essential causes of the so-called energy crisis. In my opinion the Marxist theory of rent is also the most soundly based theoretical foundation of the classical world division of labour.

4. Massarrat, M., 'Zur Problematik der gleichen Mehrwertrate und Kritik der Marxschen Theorie der absoluten Grundrente.' This essay, in which the author critically discusses the acceptance of the equal rate of surplus value and the Marxist theory of absolute groundrent, is to be first the subject of an internal discussion, and will only be published at a later date.

5. Marx, Karl, *Capital,* Vol. 3, Lawrence & Wishart, London 1974, p.644.

6. Ibid., p.645.

7. Ibid., p.647ff; my emphasis.

8. Ibid., p.646

9. Cf. on this point: Massarrat, M., 'Zur Problematik der gleichen Mehrwertrate', op. cit.

10. For example, the concept 'coal unit' (CU) expresses the average energy content of one kilogram of coal, which equals 7,000 calories. A CU is frequently considered as merely a technical statistical magnitude, but in reality it is economically based. The energy contents of one kilogram of various sources of energy converted to CUs are: natural gas — 1.471; crude oil — 1.429; natural gas — 1.286; coal — 1.0; lignite — 0.286.

11. The extraction of crude oil per well per day yields on average only 2 tonnes in the U.S.A., but between 500 and 1,900 tonnes in the Near East.

12. The actual production costs per tonne of crude oil and coal in various regions of the world in the Sixties were approximately as follows: Near East crude oil, $0.54; Libyan crude, $2.16; Venezuelan crude, $4.21; USA coal $7.40; West European coal $15.00. Cf. Massarrat, M., *Weltenergieproduktion,* op. cit., chapter 8.3.

13. This graph does not so much depict the distribution structure of the main energy sources according to kind and region, viz. the relation of

the individual prices of production to the regulating market price according to absolute magnitudes, as give their connection in terms of exchange value. Our aim here is very much to make the connections of the energy market visible at the level of abstraction. A new reconstruction of this picture on the basis of precise data would be an empirical problem.

14. See note 12 above.

15. Thus in the period between 1950 and 1969, the posted price of oil per barrel in the Persian Gulf rose from $1.75 to only $1.84, the price in East Texas from $2.65 to $3.20, while the average coal price per tonne in the U.S.A. rose from $4.84 to $4.99. The price of European coal (B.R.D.) in the same period rose from 36.00 to 72.63 deutsch marks per tonne; that is, it almost doubled. This is why the market share of coal as a source of energy fell between 1960 and 1970 from almost 57 per cent to only 28 per cent (cf. Table 1). For further details on price trends in the world energy market, see Massarrat, M., *Weltenergieproduktion,* op.cit., chapter 10.4.

16. This statement does not apply to the European societies in which the dominant pre-capitalist property relationship was private property in land (including sources of raw materials). But it does apply particularly to the Oriental Asiatic societies in which communal property in land was the dominant pre-capitalist property relationship, and where the transition to the capitalist mode of production took place without the development of private property as the dominant relationship in landed property.

17. Marx, Karl, *Grundrisse,* Harmondsworth, Penguin 1973, p.279.

18. Massarrat, M., 'Zur Problematik der gleichen Mehrwertrate', op.cit.

19. Marx, Karl, *Grundrisse,* op.cit., p.276.

20. Marx, Karl, *Capital,* vol.3, op.cit., p.638.

21. Marx, Karl, *Grundrisse,* op.cit., p.278.

22. In my opinion, this is a very important approach for explaining imperialism and for analysing the development of the world market and the world division of labour. It has been further developed in Massarrat, M., *Weltenergieproduktion,* op.cit., chapters 4-7.

23. In this context, the price trend in crude oil is typical of the different roles of Libya and Iran. 'Until the Tehran Agreement in late 1973, which roughly doubled the price per barrel to $11.65, the Libyan posted price had risen very sharply: from $2.55 per barrel in 1971 to $8.925 on 1 November 1973. At the same time the price of one barrel of Venezuelan oil rose from $2.09 to $7.26, of Nigerian oil from $2.42 to $8.31, of Arab oil from $2.55 to $5.17 and of Persian oil from $1.72 to $5.046.' *Frankfurter Rundschau,* 29 December 1973. Yet even the Tehran Agreement to raise the price of oil to $11.65 per barrel was, shortly before, preceded by an increase in crude oil prices by Libya to over $15. While Libya was always in the forefront of the OPEC states in placing demands on the oil companies and raising the price of crude oil, and while the other OPEC states always had to follow, the Shah was continually making appeals to call a halt. As the trend of prices for Persian oil clearly shows, he himself showed the way as 'a good example'.

24. In our opinion, this appearance is also the real cause of the fact that even

Marxist scientists, basing themselves on this antithesis, have been led incorrectly to characterize the New International Economic Order as anti-imperialist: 'The conception of the "New International Economic Order" is in fact essentially *anti-imperialist*. In its essence, it is directed against the dominating structural element of the present capitalist world economic system: the great multinational monopolies. This conflict opens up real perspectives.' Schilling, Hartmut, 'Die kapitalistische Entwicklung in der ehemals kolonialen Welt unter den gegenwartigen Bedingungen der allgemeinen Krise des Kapitalismus und weltwirtschaftlichen Strukturveranderungen', in *Asien, Afrika, Lateinamerika, Heft 2, Berlin (DDR) 1976, p.172.* In our opinion, such an evaluation of the real nature of the landowning states is basically false, as it lends itself to being used to legitimize the co-operation of the 'really socialist' countries (with the People's Republic of China at their head) with reactionary regimes in the Third World.

25. In contrast to the majority of West European countries, the United Kingdom levies on imported oil an import duty instead of a petroleum tax; the level of this duty corresponds approximately to the average level of the petroleum tax of the other West European countries. In the U.K. this import duty fulfils the same function as petroleum tax.

26. Cf. Massarrat, M., *Weltenergieproduktion*, op.cit. ch.10.4.

27. Petroleum tax must be classified as a special tax. Petroleum products are also subject to sales tax and value added tax (VAT).

28. The petroleum tax of DM 138.9 per tonne (cf. Table 3) levied in West Germany in 1972 in fact corresponds approximately to the West European average.

29. For further details see Massarrat, M., *Weltenergieproduktion*, op.cit., ch.15.1.

30. For detailed proof and empirical description see ibid., ch.13.1.

31. If the structure of the utilization of petroleum products were altered so that they were produced essentially for the chemical industry, then the basis of the value and price formation process would no longer be determined by the specific conditions of the production of thermal energy, but rather by those of the chemical industry.

32. On the genesis, function, and the change in function, of the posted price for oil on the world market see Massarrat, M., *Weltenergieproduktion*, op.cit., chs.15.1 and 17.3.

33. Company profit P_c includes in addition to the normal profit from the capital of oil companies, which is related to the average rate of profit in the centres of capital accumulation, also the oil companies' share of surplus profit.

34. Thus for example, there is the conversion of amounts of crude oil produced from long tons and barrels into metric tonnes, and from production per day to production per annum, and finally the conversion of the revenue of OPEC countries, most quoted in national currencies, into U.S. dollars for the whole period under study.

35. See Massarrat, M., *Weltenergieproduktion*, op.cit., ch.16.

36. 'Studies undertaken have shown that the OPEC countries must earn at least $7 per barrel of exported crude oil, considering the costs of alternative sources of energy. In addition it was necessary to increase the list

price of standard crude oil (Arabian light) to $11.651 per barrel. This was also agreed upon by the six OPEC ministers [of the Persian Gulf region] on 22 and 23 December 1973.' Izadi Hassan, *The Recent Changes in Crude Oil Prices and its Development* (in Persian, National Iranian Oil Company, Tehran 1975, p.21. Izadi is the director of the marketing and export department of the National Iranian Oil Company.

37. Hence it follows that petroleum tax after the 'energy crisis' is no longer in its entirety a component of surplus profit derived from oil. For further details on this see Massarrat, M., *Weltenergieproduktion,* op.cit., ch.17.3.

38. Thus, for instance, the O.E.C.D. countries in 1974 showed a trade deficit of $37.5 billion (compared with a surplus of $2.25 billion in 1973). *Die Zeit,* 18 January 1975. For a detailed analysis of the monetary effect of the reallocation of wealth, see Rummert, Hans-Joachim, 'Die Olpreiserhohungen 1973-74 in ihren Auswirkungen auf die Einkunfte der Forderlander' in *Gluckauf 110,* Essen 1974, p.406ff.

39. The trade surplus of the OPEC countries in 1974 amounted to $55-60 billion. The currency reserves of these countries have increased almost tenfold from 1970 ($5 billion) to 1974 ($46.9 billion), ibid. See also Jonas, Rainer and Minte, Horst, *Petrodollar,* op.cit., p.72.

40. For further details on the institutions and mechanisms of petrodollar recycling, see ibid., p.78ff.

41. *Frankfurter Rundschau,* 19 November 1974; see also Jonas, Rainer, and Minte, Horst, *Petrodollar,* op.cit., p.71.

42. For further details see Massarrat, M., *Weltenergieproduktion,* op.cit., chapter 15.3 and particularly figure 31.

43. 'My country which possesses the largest oil reserves in the world', emphatically proclaimed the Saudi Arabian Crown Prince Fadh, 'will not be the cause of a weakening in the capacity of humanity to live in stability and prosperity. In view of this lofty aim, commercial considerations cease to exist and consequently the methods which are used to increase or lower oil prices will likewise disappear.' *Frankfurter Rundschau,* 1 April 1975.

44. *Frankfurter Rundschau,* 20 May 1975.

45. *Frankfurter Rundschau,* 2 June 1975.

46. *Frankfurter Rundschau,* 4 October 1975.

47. *Frankfurter Rundschau,* 18 December 1976.

48. Harry Schleicher attributes the differing price policy conceptions of the OPEC countries exclusively to 'national egoism'. *Frankfurter Rundschau,* 1 October 1975.

49. This happened in the Persian daily papers, *Rastachis, Ayandegan, Keyhan* etc., after the OPEC negotiations of December 1976. See also *Frankfurter Rundschau,* 21 December 1976.

50. Thus Saudi Arabia eventually had to raise the price of oil on 1 July 1977 to the OPEC level of $12.70 per barrel. After this date OPEC tendered its crude oil once more at a unified price. *Frankfurter Rundschau,* 5 July 1977. Compared to this step, no particular significance can be attached to the 'equivalent achievement' of the remaining OPEC states in renouncing in their turn a 5 per cent price increase on 1 July 1977.

51.   So, for example, Harry Schleicher in the *Frankfurter Rundschau,*
      1 October 1975; Jens Friedemann, *Die Zeit* 24 and 19 December 1975.
52.   Thus in January 1975 former U.S. Secretary of State Henry Kissinger
      'did not on principle rule out an armed conflict over Middle East oil',
      Frankfurter Rundschau, 4 January 1975. A few months later, the U.S.
      Defence Secretary also repeated this threat, ibid., 2 April 1975. Cf.
      'Krieg gegen die Olscheichs?', *Der Spiegel,* 13 January 1975.
53.   Total current oil reserves in the North Sea which could be produced at a
      profit are estimated at 2.2 billion tonnes. Crude oil production from the
      North Sea should increase to 150 million tonnes annually by 1980 (as
      compared with 2 million in 1973 and 46 million in 1975-76). Ruddiger,
      G., 'Das Ol und Gaspotential der Nordsee', in *Braunkohle,* Dusseldorf
      1974, book II, p.335.
54.   Given the structural crisis of British capitalism, which the British Govern-
      ment hopes to 'overcome' by means of North Sea oil, such a radical
      change of position — while at the moment still unimaginable — ought
      directly to suggest itself.
55.   The position of France can be explained primarily by the fact that the
      French national oil corporation C.F.P. was only partially nationalized in
      Algeria and Iraq. (The C.F.P. in 1970 produced 665,000 barrels in these
      countries; its share of production in 1975 still amounted to 271,000
      barrels. *OPEC Annual Bulletin,* 1975, p. 38 ff) Also relevant is the fact
      that it signed long-term agreements with the OPEC countries after the oil
      crisis to ensure the supply of its national needs. By not joining the I.E.A.
      the French government was presumably also pursuing the aim of appear-
      ing as a 'neutral' mediator in negotiations between O.E.C.D. and OPEC
      countries.
56.   *Frankfurter Rundschau,* 5 February 1975.
57.   'Energieagentur gegen Ol-Mindestpreis', *Frankfurter Rundschau,* 10
      March 1975.
58.   *Frankfurter Rundschau,* 8 October 1975. Callaghan, at the time British
      Foreign Secretary, remarked apropos of this: 'It would suit me if a
      common energy policy was achieved in Europe, whereby of course it
      would have to be taken into consideration that our interests result from
      different circumstances. We are bulk consumers but will also become
      bulk producers. From 1980 we will be completely independent as re-
      gards energy supplies, i.e. in oil, coal, natural gas and on a smaller scale
      in nuclear energy — a really enviable position.' *Die Zeit,* 17 October
      1975.
59.   Disappointed, the bourgeois journalist Michael Jungblut anticipated that
      the minimum price for oil would have the following consequences:
      'Once the instrument of a minimum price has been generally accepted
      there will be numerous possibilities of gradually increasing it. The
      British could repeatedly block collective decisions within the E.E.C.
      with trumped up arguments and change their mind by allowing them-
      selves to be bought off with an increase in the guaranteed price.' *Die
      Zeit,* 23 January 1976.

4. Oil and the State: A Study of Nationalization in the Oil Industry

Petter Nore

It is by now almost a truism of Marxist thought to point out that there has been a dramatic increase in the role of the state in modern societies. But even within this general trend, the speed with which the state has intervened in the oil industry remains, by any standards, exceptional. While ten years ago the state in the main oil-exporting countries played virtually no role in the running of the oil industry, by the late 1970s that industry has been or is in the process of being nationalized. This chapter aims to understand the origin and meaning of this state intervention in oil.

There are two opposite interpretations of the recent nationalizations. One claims that nothing fundamental has changed in the relationship between producer states and imperialism. Dependence and imperialist domination have simply taken on new forms. The other interpretation sees the nationalizations as part of a struggle waged by the people of the Third World against imperialism. We find neither of the two interpretations convincing.

Our alternative explanation combines an analysis of long-run trends in modern capitalism with the special historical forces that have affected the oil industry as a whole from the late 1960s onwards. We will then examine the consequences of these developments for the companies and the producer states, concentrating in particular on what it has meant for the process of capital accumulation in the producer countries.

Surplus Profit in the Oil Industry

To facilitate such an analysis we must briefly outline the special features of oil production. Oil production gives rise to large permanent financial surpluses in excess of 'average profits', which we will label 'surplus profit'. This surplus profit is divided between producer states that receive it in the form of rent, the oil companies that earn 'excess profits', and the consumer countries that collect their share in the form of indirect taxes on oil consumption.

The origin of this surplus profit is two-fold. Normally, in capitalist production, it is the most productive of the production processes within an industry that becomes generalized and that, in due course, determines the average price of production (production costs plus the average rate of profit) for commodities in the industry. This is not the case in oil production because the most productive wells with respect to production costs, quality, and location are fixed in supply and cannot be generalized in the same way as the technologically most efficient process in manufacturing industry. There is, for example, a strictly limited number of oil wells in the world which yield sulphur-free oil at 15 cents per barrel. We therefore need to modify the reference point for pricing in the oil industry so that the price of production does not relate to the average production conditions, but instead to the marginal production conditions within the industry. Because marginal producers lack access to 'average' fields, they would always earn less than the average rate of profit, and would therefore go out of business. Social demand would not, as a consequence, be satisfied. This analysis explains the existence of differential rent in the oil industry. Differential rent originates because oil is of different qualities and is found under widely different conditions. Middle East production costs are around 15 cents per barrel while North Sea production costs vary between $2 to $6 per barrel (1977). The extra return earned by Middle East producers is differential rent.

A further modification to the notion that the price of oil is related to the average price of production of oil must be made if we look at oil as only one type of energy, measured in any appropriate energy unit. (One such unit is a coal unit which equals 7,000 kcal.) In this perspective it is the marginal production unit not of oil, but of energy as a whole, which constitutes the basis for the final price of oil to the consumer. The final price for oil (when indirect taxes are included but when we abstract from particular market conditions like monopoly) will therefore be above the price of production of oil, but equal to the price of production of the marginal energy producer on a world scale, measured in energy units. (For a further discussion of this point see Masserat, Chapter 3 of this volume).

We have, so far, discussed the reasons for the existence of the total surplus profit in the oil industry. But a second question arises: how is this surplus divided? Historically, the largest share of surplus profit has accrued to the importing states. The remainder is shared between the producer country and the oil company. It takes the form of absolute rent when the state, as a landowner, manages to extract rent for the marginal oil well in operation. The origin of this absolute rent is a result of the historical strength of the landowning class (in our case the state) which forces capitalists using its land to pay a rent, even for the marginal land. This is because all property under capitalism is under the proprietorship of an owner who must be paid a revenue for the use of the property. This focuses attention on a political element in the determination of absolute rent. Absolute rent depends on the struggle between the owners of a non-reproducible property and the producers of commodities.

Such an understanding of absolute rent is necessary in view of the shortcomings of Marx's treatment of the concept. Marx's definition of absolute rent was closely related to the conditions prevalent in agriculture, which, in the 19th century, was an activity with a low organic composition of capital accompanied by a lot of uncultivated land. Oil production is clearly an industry with a high organic composition, which inevitably destroys Marx's justification for average rent. It is not enough to argue, as Murray does, that 'average rent charged by the owner of a marginal plot in mineral production is the absolute rent of agriculture and not in the mineral sector. Agriculture sets the limits for other land uses'.[1] This is because oil production takes place even where there are underground mines, which do not rule out a simultaneous agricultural use of the land. Furthermore, talking about the 'agricultural use' of offshore oilfields is clearly nonsense.

If the surplus profit is captured by the oil company, it takes the form of monopoly profit. The reason the oil industry has historically tended to have a high level of concentration and (hence) been able to appropriate a monopoly profit, is due to its character as a 'natural monopoly' and its great strategic importance. This has been well documented elsewhere and will not be discussed in any detail here.[2]

The Historical Background

The recent nationalizations must firstly be seen as a confrontation over the distribution of a given amount of surplus profit between the producer states and the oil companies. (We will disregard the importing states for the moment.) Secondly, the nationalizations emerged from a confrontation at the level of production, as the producer states, the companies and the U.S. government all struggled to increase the total amount of rent in the oil industry. Both of these objectives were achieved by what we choose to label a process of reorganization of the industry in the shape of increased state involvement and nationalization. The term 'reorganization' is preferred to 'restructuring' which implies a change in the actual process of production.

The exporting countries wanted a reorganization of the industry because they felt their share of the rent was too low. Only 8 per cent of the final cost to the Western consumer of a gallon of petrol was (in the late 1960s) made up of taxes received by the exporting countries.[3] During the late 1960s and early 1970s we also saw how the OPEC countries continuously fought for an increase in the general price level of oil. A price rise would have increased not only their share, but also the absolute amount of oil rent to be earned from oil production. The desire of the producer states to increase the rent that they controlled became particularly clear around 1970. The countries which initially pushed hardest for nationalization, and which first secured a larger share of the rent — namely Iraq, Algeria, and to some extent Libya — also had the most explicitly 'development-oriented' ruling classes. Hence they had an urgent need for additional oil revenues.[4] The complex relationship between a higher absolute price of oil and the process of nationalization will be explored in more detail later, but a direct link was thought to exist between the Algerians' fight for higher prices in the early 1970s to provide money for their development plans and their quest for nationalization of the oil industry.[5]

This instrumentalist view of nationalization goes against official OPEC statements which stressed that nationalization did not take place for fiscal reasons, but rather for reasons of 'control'. But 'control' is an open-ended and ambiguous concept. If it means 'control over the volume of production', this is simply a prerequisite for the maximization of the present value of oil production from an oilfield, computed in social terms. Hence it is the same as maximizing the state's share of the surplus profit.

For the oil companies an increase in the general price level of oil was also of great importance, not least because they had seen their distributional share steadily diminish over time. This was partly as a result of a higher level of taxation by the oil-exporting countries which it was difficult to pass on to the consumers in a situation which throughout the 1960s was characterized by a global excess supply. The diminished share of the companies was also due to a threefold challenge to the majors in the oil market: the rise of the 'independents' following the U.S. import quota system in 1958; the emergence of important state oil corporations in Europe, like Italy's E.N.I., which tried to outbid the concessions offered by the majors; and the increase in Soviet oil exports to the West. The combined expression of all these factors was a drop in the profit per barrel for the majors.[6] The reduction was only partly overcome by a sharp increase in total production. Profit rates for U.S. direct foreign investment in the petroleum industry dropped from a 30 per cent return in 1955, to 14.7 per cent in 1963, and an all-time low of 11.1 per cent in 1969.[7] The majors' return on net assets in the Eastern Hemisphere dropped from above 18 per cent in 1957 to level out around 11 to 12 per cent from the mid-1960s onwards.[8] These figures are partly contradicted by a number of studies of the majors' profitability in the Middle East.[9] However, the Middle East studies may be somewhat unrepresentative because the companies had an incentive there to transfer their profits up-stream, showing a high rate of return to crude oil production. The incentive was the provision that the total amount of tax which was paid to exporting countries could be subtracted from total corporate profits and thus decrease the companies' tax burden in their home countries.[10]

The shortcomings of these rates of return for the companies first became clear when oil exploration and production moved into high-cost areas (such as Alaska and the North Sea) in the late 1960s. The industry was used to financing itself to a very high degree, but the profit rates earned at the time were insufficient to finance these new investments internally. As a result, the companies had a clear interest in reorganizing the industry in such a way as to increase their profits from the early 1970s onwards.[11]

However, for our explanation of the wave of nationalizations to make sense it is necessary to explain why the companies were so opposed to price increases before 1970. It is possible to argue that the companies changed their pricing strategies partly at the instigation of the U.S. government,[12] whose interest in encouraging higher oil prices from 1970 onwards is discussed in more detail later.

In sum, therefore, by 1970 there was a widely perceived recognition that higher crude oil prices were needed. In this context nationalizations were necessary. Increased state involvement and nationalizations can be understood as a necessary by-product of an increase in prices. The companies knew that if they raised prices on their own, the reaction in the West would have been politically intolerable. It had to be the producer states who were seen to be raising the price of crude oil. For this reason the companies were willing to accept higher state ownership and in the process to formalize a *de facto* change in the upstream fiscal structure. In return, the companies could get higher prices and were guaranteed a stable business environment. The Tehran and Tripoli Agreements of 1971-72 did exactly that. As far as the companies were concerned the nationalizations were therefore partly a result of an already existing crisis in the oil industry. A director of Shell later wrote about this period: 'It was becoming clear that the role of government in oil matters must necessarily grow if a crisis was to be avoided'.[13]

It is also possible that there was a more defensive corporate strategy behind the actions of the companies. They understood that, in order to achieve long-run stability of supply to feed their downstream activities and to provide a guaranteed outlet for their technological expertise, the companies might have to opt out of direct ownership altogether. Such a move would have the additional advantage of removing the politically sensitive question of ownership as a source of friction between the companies and the producer states. By the legal device of state ownership, the demands of economic nationalists appeared to be satisfied.

The third party with an interest in increasing prices was the U.S. government. From 1970 onwards the U.S. clearly pressed for an increase in the general price level of crude oil. Oppenheim shows how the U.S. government's actions were interpreted by the oil producers as a desire for higher prices,[14] a point of view that has also been forcefully put by Chevalier.[15] It was thought that such a rise would make a number of indigenous production wells in the U.S. commercially viable and therefore help the U.S. to achieve a higher degree of self-sufficiency in oil as well as directly increasing the profitability of the U.S. oil companies.

The push towards higher prices was also related to inter-imperialist rivalries. The U.S. government saw that an increase in crude oil prices would deliver a serious blow to its industrial competitors in Western Europe and Japan.[16] The problem for the U.S. was that prices finally increased far more than originally anticipated, (due to some extent to exogenous events, notably the Yom-Kippur war).

Due to the peculiarities of the oil industry — both its extremely high organic composition of capital and the high rent element in the final price — it has been relatively easy for the companies to 'buy off' oilworkers with high salaries and create a type of aristocracy of labour. While the history of oilworkers' struggles has yet to be written, current information suggests that the labour force in the oil industry has played only a relatively minor role, specifically in demands for a reorganization through nationalization. This does not, however, mean that the class struggle is irrelevant for an analysis of the oil industry. Oil production often has deep-seated consequences for accumulation conditions as a whole in a producer country, and struggles over oil policies are often fought out on a national rather than on an industrial level.

We have outlined why there was a simultaneous drive by the producer states, the oil companies and the U.S. for a reorganization of the oil industry. It is important to see that it was not a conspiracy that brought oil prices to their present levels or opened the way for the reorganization of the industry. Rather, these events were outcomes of the historically specific circumstances sketched above.

What was the outcome of this process of reorganization? The interests of the three parties were contradictory; not all of them could be fulfilled simultaneously. Incompatibility of interests was also manifest within the ranks of each interest group. There was, in particular, a deep split over the nature of increased state involvement between the OPEC 'radicals' — Algeria, Iraq and Libya — on the one hand and the Saudis on the other. Following the first OPEC resolution on participation passed in 1968 the Saudis, led by their Oil Minister, Yamani, sought a 20 per cent participation in the Aramco fields in Saudi Arabia. Both the OPEC resolution and the Yamani initiative must be seen in relation to the alternatives that were presented at the time. In December 1968 Algeria took over 51 per cent of Getty's operating assets, and nobody believed that it would stop at that. Simultaneously, the tougher attitude of Iraq was making itself felt. Iraq relied mainly on the French and the Russians to implement an increasingly nationalistic oil policy. If generalized, this policy could have spelt disaster for Western companies' long-run access to crude.[17] Yamani presented his version of participation as a direct challenge to the radicals' concept of state involvement, and as the best possible solution for the Western companies once some kind of change was regarded as inevitable. He argued strongly that a full radical nationalization process and a break with the companies would become inevitable unless his notion of participation was launched as an alternative.[18] The companies were not immediately convinced by Yamani. They held out as long as possible, reaping profits, reorganizing their operations and negotiating to get the best possible deal with respect to the level of compensation. It has also been suggested that the companies held out in order to give some credibility to Yamani's demands.[19] As we shall now see, the form that nationalization eventually took in Saudi Arabia and in most of the producer countries was very much within the framework that Yamani had suggested from the late 1960s.

The Outcome of Nationalization

Today the oil-industry is nationalized or in the process of being nationalized in all the most important exporting countries. Of the 13 OPEC countries only Gabon has less than a 50 per cent share of the ownership of its oil. Otherwise ownership ranges from 55 per cent in Nigeria and 60 per cent in Abu Dhabi to 100 per cent in Indonesia, Iran, Iraq, Qatar and Venezuela. Kuwait has also fully nationalized its oil if we disregard the marginal production from the Neutral Zone. In Saudi Arabia, although the Aramco owners still retain a 40 per cent equity share, they in fact operate as though the long-awaited 100 per cent government take-over terms, already agreed in principle, have been effected. A rough indication of this increased move towards state ownership of oil is provided by Table 1.[20]

Table 1
Control Over Production of Oil*

	1963	1968	% of output 1972	1974	1975 (first half)
Majors	82.1	77.9	73.0	32.3	30.2
State Oil Companies	8.6	9.0	12.0	60.8	62.3
Others (mainly Independents)	9.3	13.1	15.0	6.9	7.3

*Excluding communist countries and North America.

OPEC fixed the companies' profit margins per barrel from 1 January 1975 because the companies were earning 'unacceptable' levels of profits in the wake of the quadrupling of prices (from late 1973). This increase had given the companies a much higher absolute profit margin per barrel. Under the regime of government participation which was in force at that time, the larger the amounts of equity oil which the companies lifted, the larger their profit, which in some cases reached $4 per barrel.[21]

But even when a fixed margin of 22 cents per barrel was introduced, this did not mean that all surplus profit at the level of extraction was decisively divided in favour of the producer states. The reason for this is that there is no unambiguous definition of nationalization. The most important distinction among the various forms of nationalizations is related to the existence of a state oil corporation. If the producer state has a state oil corporation capable of extracting the oil itself (like Sonatrach in Algeria), then the situation is fundamentally different from the case where the state has to rely on the international industry to carry out this task (as in Abu Dhabi or Saudi Arabia).

A situation of full legal nationalization where the producer state is forced to hire technology from the industry may, therefore, turn out to be less favourable in terms of division of surplus profit than, for instance, an arrangement with less than 100 per cent government participation but where the producer state controls an effective state oil corporation. The division of rent therefore depends upon the exact terms of the technological or service contracts which are negotiated in the wake of the nationalizations and which differ dramatically from case to case. Caltex, main operator and purchaser of Indonesian crude, initially charged $2 per barrel for such services,[22] while the post-nationalization agreements in Venezuela, Kuwait, Iran and Saudi Arabia envisage a 'service payment' of between only 15 and 20 cents per barrel for the lifting of the crude.[23] This fee is to be paid to the companies merely in return for the supply of often low-level technological knowledge, since after nationalization the producer states themselves undertake and pay for all new investments. Theoretically, a nationalization that brings about an increase in production costs per barrel through technological inefficiencies will also diminish the amount of rent which accrues to the producer state.

In addition to the above considerations, the present system of fixed profit margins is not operating effectively. The average profit margin reported for sale by the majors in the Rotterdam spot market was, in 1976, $1.15 per barrel[24] which is a far cry from the 22 cents originally envisaged by the OPEC countries. Because most crude still flows through the integrated network of the majors, the spot market could be said to be 'unrepresentative', but it is still an indication of the perennial problem that producer countries have always encountered in assessing the downstream situation of the companies. As long as the vertically integrated companies process a substantial amount of the crude through their own organizations, it is virtually impossible to determine how much this is 'worth' to them.

The companies' slow recapture of upstream profits can be read directly from Shell's profitability structure. While 1975 saw 20 per cent of their profit at the level of extraction, in 1976 this figure had increased to 30 per cent (but both are well below the pre-1973 figures).[25] It therefore seems that formal nationalization of the industry is not a sufficient condition for the state to capture the full amount of surplus profit at the level of extraction unless the state also controls a state oil corporation of average international efficiency which has access to and/or an extensive knowledge of the downstream markets.

We have so far ignored the existence of downstream activities. While in principle it is possible to distinguish financial results upstream and downstream, it is more difficult to do so in a concrete analysis due to the vertically integrated nature of the industry. There was even a time when the companies themselves did not know their own division of profit between the different activities. But with the principle of 'federalism'[26] gaining force such an assessment is now getting easier.

The OPEC countries have tried to expand into the downstream export markets. In this process they have clashed directly with the companies which, in the wake of being excluded from direct upstream ownership since 1973, have increasingly been forced to rely on their downstream activities in order to make a profit. The companies, which historically earned the major part of their profits upstream, after 1973 adjusted their product prices in such a way that profits, to a much greater extent, were earned downstream.[27] It is therefore crucial for the companies to maintain both their present ownership and control over downstream activities and to secure stable long-run supplies of crude. Given the present trend, the companies need not fear that the exporting states will manage to displace corporate downstream hegemony. In both refining and retailing, the movement towards state control has been very much slower than has been the case in extraction. Table 2 shows how the relative importance of the majors in refining has not been unduly affected by the recent waves of nationalizations.

Table 2
Control over Oil Refining Capacity (in %)*

	1963	1968	1972	1974	1975 (first half)
Majors	65.3	60.9	55.8	50.1	48.4
Governments	13.6	16.0	17.3	20.3	21.0
Others	21.1	23.1	26.9	29.7	30.6

Source: See note 20.
*Excluding communist countries and North America. OPEC's refining capacity is today estimated at no more than 7 per cent of world total.

Table 3 shows how retailing also still remains dominated by the majors. This is because it has been notoriously difficult for any company, let alone a new entrant from OPEC, to establish itself in the retail market for refined products.

Table 3
Control over Oil Marketing Capacity (in %)*

	1963	1968	1972	1974
Majors	62.6	55.6	53.8	45.4
Governments	10.6	13.6	15.4	19.2
Others	26.8	30.8	30.8	35.5

Source: See note 20.
*Excluding communist countries and North America.

One way into downstream markets for the oil-producing states may be through government-to-government deals which bypass the majors altogether. This development has started, but in a very modest manner. Following an initial wave of panic-deals in 1973-74 the number of such deals has now stabilized. The most important is probably a five-year, $6.5 billion bilateral deal between Brazil and Iran whereby Brazil is to buy 25 per cent of its oil imports from the National Iranian Oil Corporation (N.I.O.C.). Similar but much smaller deals have also been concluded for a number of other producer countries. But taken together these bilateral agreements are still insignificant compared with the 70 per cent of the world's crude trade that flows through the companies' integrated operations. The producer countries can also try to establish joint marketing with the majors to gain access to the downstream markets in the consumer countries. But so far no such agreements have been made.

The final downstream activity which potentially can be taken over by the producer states is the petrochemical industry. Over the last few decades this has been one of the world's fastest growing industries with a present world market of $100 billion.[28] Western Europe and the U.S. today control 70 per cent of the total output of the industry, compared with 5 per cent of all Third World countries combined. Much of this output is controlled by the oil companies. In the U.S. alone the companies control 75 per cent of the basic, 50 per cent of the intermediate, and 25 per cent of the final markets for petrochemical products.

Plans already exist for the construction of petrochemical plants in the oil-exporting countries, but so far very few projects have actually been started. The ambitious plans that were originally formulated for the export-oriented petrochemical and refining industries in the OPEC countries have been halved[29] since 1973 in the face of cost over-runs, construction lags and the current product surplus in international markets. Such plans might collapse even further if petrochemical imports were excluded from the major markets by means of tariffs, as has happened in the past.

Given the importance of the downstream activities for the companies, we can better understand why guaranteed supply contracts have been negotiated in the wake of all major oil nationalizations. These contracts constitute the key element in all nationalization agreements, as they help the majors to maintain a stable flow of raw materials which, in conditions of maximum predictability, ensures an optimal utilization of their downstream installations. Supply contracts make up more than 70 per cent of the world's international oil trade. For the five U.S. majors no less than 80 per cent of the volume of their combined liftings is in accordance with agreements with the producer countries which are effective for periods longer than five years.[30] These contracts represent nothing but a *de facto* continuation of the former vertical integration of the oil companies, following the potential threat posed by the nationalizations to this integrated structure.

We can conclude that legal ownership and control over only one stage of what is a vertically integrated industry clearly does not lead to a guarantee that all surplus profit from oil production will be captured by the producer state. The present nationalizations also perpetuate the producers' dependence on the majors' downstream markets, an extremely important potential weapon in the hands of the companies. This weapon was effectively used against Iran in 1953 when, after nationalizing the oil industry, the country managed to sell a mere 103,000 tons of crude over a period of three years. This was equivalent to one day's output before nationalization.

Where does this then leave us? As has been made clear, for nationalizations to be successful they must be accompanied by a number of other policies. These policies are not implemented in many producer states. In a preface to Shell's 1976 Annual Report, the Chairman, Sir Frank McFadzean, made the point that the Group's 17 per cent return on average net assets was 'a further indication of the ability of Shell companies to adapt to the fundamental changes imposed on the industry in recent years'.

The ability of the companies to live and prosper in this situation is due to a number of factors. The producer states may have dramatically increased their upstream 'take', but there is no indication that this has been at the expense of the majors because the total amount of surplus profit in the industry increased in the wake of the quadrupling of the oil prices. As already indicated, it was largely surplus value from the rest of the economic system which financed the increased rent of the producer states.

The extensive use of joint ventures in the industry is a second indication of how closely linked the companies and the producer states really are and underlines their mutual dependence. In particular, it shows the producer states' dependence on the companies' downstream activities. These joint ventures are not only restricted to oil. The nationalization agreement in Saudi Arabia states that ARAMCO will become a consultant and partner in the Saudi economic development plan.

Finally, the ability of the companies to survive is seen by their move towards becoming energy corporations, a development which was anticipated in the late 1960s and has recently been accelerated.[31] The purchase by the oil companies of coal, uranium and oil-shale deposits ensures them future access to sources of energy.[32] A number of these resources are to be found in politically 'secure' areas, which could yet again provide the companies with the prospect of controlling the whole integrated production structure. For instance, 60 per cent of all present U.S. coal reserves are owned by the U.S. oil industry.[33] The purchase of such new interests requires substantial amounts of internal finance, which may explain the time pattern of the oil companies' profit maximization. A short-run maximization of profit in present activities may signify a wish to get out of crude production with a maximum amount of money to finance new investments.

The results of the process of reorganization of the oil industry are by no means uniform but differ from country to country. Which of the three participants which sought the reorganization of the industry will in the end be hegemonic, and what form this reorganization will finally take, partly depends upon the peculiarities of the class struggle and the composition of class forces within each country. There can be, for instance, little question that the situation in Saudi Arabia today is infinitely more favourable for both the companies and for imperialism in general than is the case in Iraq and Algeria.

Effects on Accumulation

We will now examine what the new situation in the oil industry has meant for the accumulation conditions within producer countries. The point of departure for such an examination must be that the oil-producing states now control a larger slice of the world's total surplus value than before. There has been a change in the geographical distribution of surplus value on a world scale, something that is clearly brought out in Table 4.

Table 4
Distribution of World Oil Revenues (in $ billion)

	1970	*1972*	*1974*	*1975*
OPEC revenue (net)	7.9	15.2	110.7	115.8
Net income, 30 largest oil companies (incl. U.S.)	6.5	7.0	16.4	11.5

Source: *Petroleum Encyclopedia,* 1975; Chase Manhattan, 'Financial Analysis of group of petroleum companies', various years.

There are two different methodological starting points for such an investigation. We can either assume that the state represents a rent-receiving landowner; or alternatively that the state is a capitalist. We will examine these approaches in turn.

i) The State as Landowner

Our investigation has so far assumed that the oil-producing states, in a theoretical sense, represented a landowning class that has seen a transfer of surplus value, in the form of rent, in their favour. (This is also the theoretical framework adopted by Masserat in Chapter 2.) This perspective has important consequences for how we view the effect that the present reorganization has had on world capital accumulation.

On the most abstract and general level it can be argued that if all surplus profit is captured by the landlord then capital accumulation will not take place at a maximum rate. This is because the oil companies will not be motivated to look for the lowest-cost resource if all they will be left with at the end of the day is a 'normal' rate of profit. But in the present-day world we have already shown how the companies continue to appropriate part of the *surplus* profit. So it is impossible to argue that the present situation represents any barrier to accumulation if we accept the state-as-landowner theoretical perspective. Furthermore, the existence of such a barrier to accumulation is not exclusively an empirical question, but also represents a theoretical problem whose final acceptance depends upon whether one accepts that the state can be seen conceptually as a rent-receiving landlord.

Secondly, to draw on a historical parallel from the 19th century, it is clear that the existence of a strong social class whose income was based on rent did constitute an impediment to the development of the capitalist forces of production at that time because rent did not enter the circuit of self-expanding capital. The confrontation between the British landowning class and the emerging capitalist class over the question of the repeal of the Corn Laws in the

1840s was a manifestation of this struggle. It was only by breaking down the obstacles related to the existence of agricultural rent with the political defeat of the landlords that capital could expand. Marx described this process exclusively in relation to developments within the nation state. What is new in our context, if we accept this perspective, is that the international companies face nation states which, while they may formally be seen as landlords, also represent the hegemonic classes within their own social formations — be they a weak national bourgeoisie (Norway), a feudal royalty (Saudi Arabia), or a bureaucratized stratum of state capitalists (Iraq).

The action of nation states in the oil industry is therefore a reflection of the development of the productive forces within their own countries. So while capital, in historic terms, needed to break down the forces related to rent, the very same forces now reassert themselves, albeit on an international level and in the guise of nation states. One can make out a fairly straightforward case why this is so. While capital first had to deal with obstacles to capital accumulation on a national scale, such obstacles now express themselves internationally, partly as a result of the uneven development of modern capitalism. For instance, the extent to which the internal situation in Nigeria represents a barrier to capital accumulation is partly a result of Nigeria's integration into the international capitalist system, which has made the country into an extreme example of a weak comprador state. (See Turner in Chapter 10 for a description of this process; and for a similar example with respect to Iran, see Clawson in Chapter 8.)

To further clarify the importance of this barrier to accumulation we must distinguish between different OPEC countries. Countries like Saudi Arabia and Kuwait use a large percentage of their oil revenues either for luxury imports or investments in property and treasury bonds in other countries, both of which in no direct way increase total social capital. This use of the oil rent is a reflection of the lack of development of the productive forces, as well of the composition of the ruling classes, in these two countries. For instance the reluctance of the Kuwaiti ruling class to industrialize fully reflects their fear of the political consequences of such a process. The need to import labour, which especially in the skilled sectors is Palestinian labour, could in the long run upset their own political power.[34]

Iraq and Algeria are the most typical representatives of another set of countries in which the oil revenues are almost totally invested in development projects. This tends to increase the amount of social capital in these countries. This developmentist policy, which expresses itself through an industrialization process undertaken almost exclusively by state enterprises, is again a reflection of the correlation of forces within these countries and the aims and aspirations of the state bureaucracies which in some of the countries (especially Algeria) are influenced by their history of anti-imperialist struggle. The extent to which the present situation constitutes a barrier to overall world accumulation, therefore, depends on the division of the oil revenues between these different types of states.

Having completed an analysis which sees the state as a rent-receiving landlord, we must nevertheless conclude that we do not find this theoretical framework satisfactory for dealing with the problem of accumulation. We have avoided the common error of arguing that, as long as a landowning class receives all the surplus profit, this will automatically be used for 'unproductive' expenditure and hence slow down capital accumulation. Instead, we have concentrated on the particular correlation of class forces within a country as a determinant of how the rent will be spent. But one major weakness remains. In a number of oil-producing countries the state itself has become the single most important capitalist. This is partly a result of its role in the industrialization-process, but also through the formation of state oil corporations. As a consequence, the income from oil no longer accrues to the state in the form of taxes like 'manna from heaven'. The state's income is increasingly earned by a state oil corporation. It is to the consequence of adopting this perspective of the state as capitalist that we now turn.

ii) The State as Capitalist

Let us now regard the state not as a rent-receiver but rather as an entity acting as an individual capitalist through its state oil corporation. The confrontation in the oil industry is then no longer mainly between capitalist and landlord, but between state capital and private capital. But why is there a strong tendency towards this productive kind of state intervention in the oil industry, and how can we understand the emergence of state oil corporations on a world scale?

Oil is no ordinary commodity. It is the most important source of energy in capitalist societies and therefore plays a distinct and crucial role in the process of capitalist accumulation. From supplying 21.5 per cent of the world's energy supply in 1940, oil accounted for 67.2 per cent in 1974.[35] It is indeed possible to argue that the post-war boom has been based on the fact that ample supplies of cheap energy have been widely available. As Geoffrey Barraclough says, 'If communism . . . equals Soviet power plus electrification, neo-capitalism equals US power plus cheap oil.'[36] One set of figures is sufficient to indicate how the accumulation process during the post-war period became increasingly energy intensive, which meant an increasing reliance on oil. Whereas between 1870 and 1950 G.N.P. *per capita* in the U.S. rose sixfold and involved a mere doubling of *per capita* energy use, between 1950 and 1973 energy growth *per capita* actually exceeded the *per capita* growth in production.[37]

The operation of the capitalist system is totally dependent in the short to medium run on a steady supply of oil. A total cut-off in the supply of oil would bring the accumulation process to a halt with the same certainty as if the supply of labour power were withdrawn. It is for these reasons that we label oil a 'strategic' commodity: a commodity which is an input to more than a critical number of goods, and which does not have any short to medium run substitutes. Because of its central role in the accumulation process, the state takes a particular interest in strategic commodities. A capitalist state with the responsibility of establishing, maintaining and reproducing the conditions of capital accumulation has little choice but to ensure the security of supply of such goods. This argument explains, especially for oil importing countries, why there has been a tendency towards the establishment of state oil corporations.

To understand the creation of state oil corporations in *exporting* countries, we must turn to the increased socialization of the productive processes in the oil industry. Concretely this means that the necessary capital investment to produce oil is in many cases so vast that no single unit of private national capital is large enough to undertake investment on the necessary scale. For example, in the Norwegian case the demands for capital to explore and develop the North Sea fields has been far in excess of what could be raised and managed by Norwegian private capitalists on their own.[38] This was particularly the case until 1972, because according to Norwegian law at that time oil in the ground could not be used as collateral by oil companies to obtain finance. But even after this law was changed, the situation remained virtually the same. For instance total gross investment in Norwegian industry and mining in 1974 totalled Kr.7.4 billion[39] compared with an expected yearly average investment on the Norwegian Continental Shelf for the coming years of Kr.8.3 billion.[40] To raise such amounts of finance and undertake investments on this scale was simply beyond the organizational capacity of the Norwegian bourgeoisie.

If the numerous state oil corporations in the producer countries were allowed to operate as if they were private units of capital (Brazil's Petrobras, which now is diversifying internationally, is but one example), then capital accumulation would not be affected. The only novel element in such a situation *might* be that the surplus profit would remain within the producer state and in this way would support a process of 'modernization' either directly by positive discrimination in favour of national suppliers of 'spin-offs', or indirectly by the use of oil revenues for more general industrialization purposes.

If, on the other hand, severe restrictions were put on the operations of such state companies, either by limiting their access to capital or by forbidding them to operate internationally, then barriers to accumulation *would* result. Whether such constraints are put on a state oil corporation would depend upon the specific historical circumstance of each producer state and in particular on the strength of the technical-administrative or comprador sector in the state apparatus which might gain from the existence of an unconstrained state oil corporation. For instance, the Indonesian state oil company Petromin was able to operate in the mid-1970s in a virtually unconstrained manner as a comprador institution. It did not use its independence to accumulate, but to squander funds (almost bringing down the Indonesian regime in the ensuing financial collapse). Its behaviour was related to the lack of central state control and the relative autonomy of the top echelon of compradors within Petromin.

At this point we must add two qualifications to our analysis. We are only witnessing the *beginning* of an important trend towards state capitalism in the oil sector. While countries like Mexico and Algeria have state oil corporations which are fully capable of finding and extracting oil, this is not the case for countries like Gabon, Nigeria, Saudi Arabia or the United Arab Emirates. Whether or not a country has a state oil corporation at all (or one that does not only exist on paper) is again a function of the specific historical circumstances of each producer state, in particular of the internal correlation of class forces and of its mode of integration into the world capitalist system. (For an analysis of why Nigeria has a weak state oil corporation see Turner, Chapter 10 in this volume, and for why Norway has a strong one, see Nore, note 43 at the end of this chapter.)

Secondly, while the state may play an increasing role in the oil industry, the interests of the state and the private sector in a number of oil-exporting countries are extremely difficult to separate from one another. Our assertion that there is an increasing productive state role in the industry may therefore lose some of its force in cases like Iran, where the income earned by the state oil corporation tends to get appropriated directly by private individuals. This situation is drastically different from that in countries like Norway where, given the nature of the capitalist state, no such direct appropriation is possible.

These two qualifications notwithstanding, the trend towards productive state involvement in the oil industry is here to stay. Consequently an analysis of the conditions of accumulation must take this as its starting point. Marxists have been reluctant to see the state as a capitalist and instead have concentrated on the state as a rent collector or landlord pure and simple. The tendency to regard state ownership of productive industry as atypical is not accidental: Marxist theory is weak when it comes to analysing such phenomena.[41] Hopefully this contribution will stimulate a discussion of the state as capitalist.

Conclusion

The reorganization of the oil industry has been a unifying theme throughout this chapter. We have traced this process of reorganization, which was a response to a crisis in capital accumulation from the late 1960s onwards. In the end the crisis was overcome by raising the price of oil. The move took place in conjunction with a change in the legal forms of ownership. The result has been a more stable and profitable business environment for the oil firms and a redistribution of surplus value on a world scale in favour of the producer states. The extent to which this has also laid the basis for a process of capital accumulation for the producer states depends to a large extent on the peculiarities of the social formation in each oil producing country.[42] It has been argued that the most useful perspective to adopt when analysing the new situation is to view the producer state, not as a rent-receiving entity, but as itself a capitalist.

References

1.   *Capital and Class*, No.3, p.117.
2.   P. Nore, 'The international oil industry and national economic development', in S. Picciotto and J. Faundez, *Nationalizations in Third World Countries,* London 1979.

3. *OPEC Bulletin,* September/October 1969.
4. Especially in Algeria it was clear that the aim of nationalization was intimately related to the country's development plans. According to Madelin, *Oil and Politics,* London 1975, p.154: 'From 1969 onwards it was clear that Algeria was seeking complete "recovery" of its sources of production, in order to obtain full possession of the proceeds from them, for the purpose of financing very large investments under the First Five Year Plan.'
5. J.M. Chevalier, *Det Nye Spill om Oljen,* Oslo 1973, p. 101 argues: '. . . concerning the [problem of] prices, it was only by a process of nationalization that the Algerians could get control over the surplus so that it could serve the development of the country'.
6. Net profit per barrel in cents, 1957-75

	1957	1958	1959	1960	1961	1962	1963	1964
Government 'take'	78.1	75.7	76.5	70.8	70.0	70.9	75.1	75.2
Company profit*	77.1	60.3	58.4	56.5	54.3	53.1	56.3	43.2

	1965	1966	1967	1968	1969	1970	1971	1972
Government 'take'	76.4	77.0	79.7	82.8	83.9	86.0	126.4	134.0
Company profit*	41.8	41.1	36.9	39.9	35.6	33.0	33.5	28.0

*Relates to whole integrated operation
Source: 'Energy memo', First National City Bank October 1969, January 1973 and January 1975.

7. N. H. Jacoby, *Multinational Oil,* New York 1974, p.248.
8. Majors' return on net assets in Eastern hemisphere, 1957-71

1957	1958	1959	1960	1961	1962	1963	1964
18.6	15.0	13.8	13.9	13.2	13.1	14.1	11.1

1965	1966	1967	1968	1969	1970	1971
11.2	11.5	10.7	11.7	11.1	11.2	12.3

Source: 'Energy memo', First National City Bank July 1975.

9. C. Issawi and M. Yeganeh, *The Economics of Middle East Oil,* New York 1962, p.112, computed that the companies' rate of return on Middle East investments (as opposed to the overall eastern hemisphere, which included all downstream activities in Europe), measured as net income as a proportion of total net assets, averaged 67 per cent in the period 1948-60; A.A.Q. Kubbah, *OPEC, Past and Present,* Vienna 1974, estimated an average rate of 79.2 per cent for 1970 based on data from the U.S. Dept. of Commerce.

    There is however no doubt that there were fluctuations in the companies' rate of return. For instance in the aftermath of the Tehran agreement they experienced a significant increase in their profit margins which undoubtedly accelerated the producer states' demand for a fuller control over their operations. A similar upturn followed the Arab-Israeli War of 1967. But our point is that *these movements were nevertheless superimposed on a downward trend of profitability.*

10. This concession made the oil industry one of the lowest taxed industries especially in the U.S. Exxon, for example, paid an effective 11.2 per cent

of their net earnings in U.S. taxes in 1973 – *U.S. Senate Hearings: the Committee on Multinationals* (The Church Committee) p.13. This concession was partly in order to avoid double taxation, but was also used by the U.S. government in the 1950s as a method to increase its aid in an indirect manner to the Arab countries (ibid., p.2, Introduction).

11. The companies just assumed that the future investment in the industry would be provided from retained earnings. Hence it followed almost automatically that the industry wanted higher prices (and hence higher profits) once it was expected that production costs would drastically increase. According to the *Petroleum Press Service* (August 1971, p.212), higher prices were inevitable to produce 'the enormous quantities of oil needed to satisfy demand in the 70's and 80's . . . [which] would have to be sought for and developed in more and more difficult places . . . . The rise in prices will have to be greater than the rise in costs, because of the need for larger earnings.'

12. Such an 'external' explanation seems reasonable when it is remembered that companies do not care about the absolute price of a good as long as it is sold. (But with the high price elasticity of oil products this seems to have been no problem.) Companies are more worried about profit margins. According to the chairman of Shell Transport and Trading, 'Pressure from the producing countries on costs is something we can learn to live with, provided we are not at the same time denied freedom to move prices in the market, so as to maintain a commercial margin of profit' (quoted in *PPS*, June 1968, p.202).

13. G. Chandler, 'Oil, prices and profits'. (Discussion Paper No.13, Foundation of Business Responsibilities, London 1974), p.4.

14. Writing in *Foreign Policy*, Fall 1976, p.24, he stated, 'Since 1971, the United States has encouraged Middle East oil-producing states to raise the price of oil and keep it up'.

15. Chevalier, op.cit., pp.160-1.

16. *The Economist*, 7 July 1973, under the title 'The phoney oil crisis' voiced the suspicion that the U.S. had capitulated only too readily to the OPEC demands for an increase in oil prices because such an increase would slow down the Japanese economy. Japanese exports were outcompeting American goods at the time and its economy was more vulnerable to rises in the price of oil than any other nation.

17. The agreement which was concluded between INOC and the Russians in July 1969 to develop the huge North Rumaila fields was undoubtedly such a threat.

18. Speech at the *Financial Times'* North Sea Conference, London 1972, reproduced in full in *Middle East Economic Survey*, 22 September 1972.

19. J. Stork, *Middle East Oil and the Energy Crisis*, New York 1975, p.195.

20. Tables 1, 2 and 3 were all computed by Shell and presented by J.E. Hartshorn to an Oxford seminar on 'Integration and disintegration in the petroleum industry', Winter 1976.

21. The companies' buyback price for Arabian $34°$ light was $7.10 per barrel compared with the posted price of $11.50.

22. *Financial Times*, 15 April 1976.

23. *Financial Times* special supplement, 'Saudi Arabia', 17 April 1978, p.19.

24. P. Odell at the *Financial Times'* North Sea Conference, London 1976;

Conference papers, p.88.

25. According to a Wood McKenzie study on Shell, quoted in *Petroleum Economist,* May 1977.

26. By 'federalism' is meant a system in which each subsidiary of a major company has to show a profit on its own. For example, when B.P.'s marketing subsidiary in Italy turned out to be a loss-maker, it was sold.

27. Dillar Spriggs, Executive Vice-President of Baker Weeks & Co. Inc., declared to the Church Committee on Multinationals that the oil companies had even shifted their profits downstream between 1971 and 1973 in anticipation of producer state ownership. While profit margins per barrel of final products were 30 cents on average in 1971, this had been increased to 90 cents by the spring of 1973 (Hearings, 30 January 1974, pp.56-61, part 4).

28. This information, as well as what follows about the petrochemical industry, is taken from an unpublished paper by Professor Stobaugh to a seminar in the series 'Integration and disintegration . . .', op. cit., 10 February 1976.

29. U.S. Senate Committee on Energy and Natural Resources, *Access to Oil – the United States Relationship with Saudi Arabia and Iran*, Washington D.C., U.S. Government Printing Office, December 1977.

30. Ibid.

31. According to First National City Bank's *Energy Memo,* January 1967, '. . . the intensity of competition between fuels will make it important for companies to consider setting a foot in more than one camp . . . In the future, increasing attention may be paid to their [the companies'] access to diverse types of energy'.

32. Total U.S. coal reserves are estimated to be in the order of one trillion six hundred billion tons, equivalent in energy terms to 12 times total proven world-wide oil reserves. 'Petroleum, raw materials and development: Memorandum submitted by Algeria on the occasion of the special session of the UN General Assembly', Sonatrach, Algiers 1974, p.160.

33. Ibid., p.163; see also Chevalier, op.cit., p.142.

34. For a good analysis of the political repercussions of the industrialization process in the Persian Gulf, see F. Halliday, 'Migration and the labour force in the oil-producing states of the Middle East', in *Development and Change,* No. 8, 1977, pp.263-91.

35. G. Foley, *The Energy Question,* Harmondsworth 1976, p.64.

36. G. Barraclough, 'The great world crisis, I' in *New York Review of Books,* 23 January, 1975.

37. Ford Foundation Report, quoted in ibid., p.22.

38. A high degree of socialization of production can also mean that the time before any profit can be realized is so long that private capitalists refuse to invest in the project. Infrastructure is an example of such a commodity.

39. Norwegian Statistical Office, *Statistical Yearbook 1976,* p. 58. The figure excludes all investment related to oil and gas production but includes investment in nationalized industries.

40. Extrapolated from H.E. Anonsen, 'Financing the North Sea', Paper given at the Offshore North Sea Conference, Stavanger 1976, p.2.

41. See Nore in *Picciotto & Faundez,* op.cit.

42. Note that throughout we have only discussed the effect of the present

reorganization in the oil industry on the accumulation process in the producer countries and said nothing about how it effects conditions in the system as a whole. But as long as there are no problems at the level of circulation, it should not matter in the long run where new capital is injected into the circuit of capital. So the conditions of accumulation in the system as a whole should not change drastically as a result of what has happened in the oil industry. This is especially so because the initial problems related to the recycling of petrodollars now seem largely to have been overcome. The OPEC countries' current account surplus, which was $67.8 billion in 1974, tumbled to an estimated $18 billion in 1978, while total OPEC borrowing on the international capital market reached $5.6 billion in the first six months of 1978 alone (Mr. Ali Jaidah, OPEC's General Secretary quoted in *Financial Times,* 30 September 1978).

43. P. Nore, 'The relationship between the international oil companies and the Norwegian state over North Sea oil 1965-74', Ph.D., C.N.A.A., London, June 1979.

5. Oil Exploration Strategies: Alternatives for the Third World

Michael Tanzer

This paper deals with a topic on which I have written and worked for many years as an economic consultant to governments of underdeveloped countries and states in the United States.[1] This topic has enormous implications for the future of many underdeveloped countries, and not least for Puerto Rico. Accordingly, the focal point will be the potential and actual role of governments of underdeveloped countries in the area of oil exploration and development, and the lessons that can be drawn for Puerto Rico.

The implications I will derive for Puerto Rico are set against the following general factual background: (1) Preliminary surveys carried out by the Puerto Rican government of the area off the northern coast of Puerto Rico suggest good chances of finding oil, possibly in very large quantities. (2) An expenditure in the neighborhood of $10 to $20 million is required for several wells to test and confirm or disprove these possibilities. (3) Given this situation the Puerto Rican government is presently considering a production-sharing concession for a major U.S. oil company, under which the company will pay for the exploration and, if successful, get a share of the oil found as its reward.[2]

Against this background, which I will discuss in more detail later, I want to make clear from the beginning my conclusion that such a course of action by the Puerto Rican government, particularly under the terms being considered, would be a tragic and possibly irreversible error for Puerto Rico. Rather, as I will show, what would make far more sense, from many points of view, would be for the Puerto Rican government to pay for the exploration itself, and, if successful, keep for the country *all* the benefits of any oil found.

To explain this conclusion, I will first discuss the range of government oil-exploration policies in underdeveloped countries, the theoretical reasons why 'doing it yourself' generally makes most sense for the governments concerned, and the experiences of some countries which have done so. I will then examine how these practical experiences might be applied to Puerto Rico. Finally, I will conclude with a brief discussion of the broader implications of a government oil-exploration effort, particularly as they relate to the potentials for overall economic development of Puerto Rico, and to the vital question of the country's future political status.

Turning to the general question of the present practices of underdeveloped countries in the oil exploration area, we find a wide range of approaches. At one extreme there are countries where the state is essentially a passive tax collector, turning over the risk of oil exploration and full control of such exploration and development to private foreign companies, in exchange for a share of the profits from the sale of the oil, which remains in the control of the foreign companies (the 'state tax-collector role'). In the middle are the countries where the state essentially becomes a partner with private foreign companies on the basis of the companies putting up the funds for exploration, and if oil is found the production is shared on some basis between the company and the government — a plan similar to that being considered by Puerto Rico (the 'state production-sharing role'). Finally, at the other extreme there are the cases where the state itself bears the risk of exploration, retains full control over exploration and development, and gets 100 per cent of any oil found (the '100 per cent state-control role').

If we were to characterize today's underdeveloped countries by these roles, we would probably find that the passive tax-collector states are the smallest number, the production-sharing states the largest number, and the 100 per cent state-control cases an intermediate number. However, this static headcount would be misleading in an important sense because, looked at dynamically in terms of historical development, we would see that the passive state role is more or less rapidly dying out, having been largely replaced by the production-sharing role, and that in crucial countries the 100 per cent state role is itself replacing the production-sharing approach.

At the risk of some oversimplification, I would argue that the tax-collector role was a product of colonialism, the production-sharing role a product of neocolonialism, and the 100 per cent state-control role is a product of a drive for economic independence in the underdeveloped countries. Thus, while until the 1960s the passive tax-collector role was the dominant form, the countries which still accept this role tend to be extremely weak countries which are virtually colonies. The production-sharing approach, which was popularized by Indonesia in the 1960s, while progressive in form, was in substance often similar to the passive tax-collector role. This is because while the state got some of the oil itself rather than just the money profits, often the state simply sold back its share of the oil to the companies and ended up in the same position. The 100 per cent state-control approach, of which there are examples going back many years, has begun to gain greater influence in the underdeveloped countries, particularly since the jump in oil prices following the 1973 OPEC price revolution, and the consequent huge effect that oil, or the lack of it, has had on underdeveloped countries.

Why are more countries now turning to a 100 per cent state oil-exploration effort? There are a number of reasons, but among them I would like particularly to discuss the increasing spread of knowledge concerning the workings of the international oil industry, and in particular the beginning of the erosion of myths about the oil industry — myths which, being highly profitable to the companies, are perpetuated by them and by some international agencies in order to deter governments of underdeveloped countries from entering the oil industry, and exploration in particular. In sum, these myths are that only the big international oil companies possess the technology and capital necessary to carry out oil exploration and development and can afford to risk failure. I think it is particularly important for Puerto Rico, at this point in history, to understand why these are myths, and false, so I would now like to discuss them briefly.

As to myth number one, that *only* the big oil companies control vital exploration *technology*, the facts are that in today's world, most oil-exploration efforts, both onshore and offshore, are *not* carried out by the big international oil companies, like Mobil or Exxon, but by smaller specialized drilling firms which sell their services to anyone, usually for a flat fee and not for a share of the profits.[3] While it is true that in the underdeveloped countries these drilling firms work to a large extent for the big oil companies, this is so because the governments of these underdeveloped countries usually leave the control of exploration to the oil companies under the production-sharing arrangements. What is more relevant, however, is that any government which is willing to pay the going market rate for these drilling operations can obtain them without recourse to the big oil companies, and without giving up a share of production or profits. (And, I might note, this is also true of pre-drilling exploration, such as geological and seismological surveys, which in the case of Puerto Rico were carried out by the government's hiring Western Geophysical Company, and not by a big oil company.)

As to myth number two, that *only* the big oil companies have the *capital* necessary for exploration and development, this falsehood exists because of a failure to recognize that while very large amounts of capital are required for finding *and developing* an oil field, only a small part of these funds (perhaps 5 per cent or less) is needed for the truly risky function of exploration.[4] The great bulk of the capital required is for development of an oil field once found, and this is not a risky job. Moreover, given the great value of oil in the world today, oil in the ground is an extremely bankable asset, and the necessary development capital can easily be raised by loans, on quite favourable terms. Such loans, as we shall see, can be obtained from international agencies, commercial banks, equipment suppliers, or countries and oil companies that are anxious to secure future supplies of crude oil.

As for myth number three, that *only* the international oil companies can *afford the risk* of oil exploration, this falsehood exists because of excessive concentration on the cost of exploration, with little attention being paid to the benefits. Whether or not a risk is worthwhile, or affordable, as the oil companies know so well, depends not only on the costs but also on the possible benefits, and what resources can be diverted from other uses to take the gamble. If, by way of a not-so-hypothetical example, $10 million has to be spent on exploration, and the chance of finding a one-billion-barrel field worth 1,000 times the oil exploration investment is one out of two, surely no rational person would say the country cannot afford the risk. After all, any country — no matter how small — has some resources available which it could shift to such an exploration 'gamble'. In the case of Puerto Rico, which though a small country has a Gross National Product far greater than many larger underdeveloped countries, is it not worth the gamble of less than one-tenth of one per cent of the government's annual budget to finance a venture which could give the country a huge boost in its economic development?

Further, it should also be pointed out that exploration is not an all-or-nothing thing, but a series of steps seeking information, which can be cut short if the initial information indicates that prospects are dim. Thus, if four wells cost $10 million, but the first two give very bad results, then you can cut your losses by ending exploration, and hence your actual risk capital will turn out to be much less than the maximum.

Finally, on the queston of what Puerto Rico can 'afford', one must also ask whether the country can afford to give up control of a large share of its oil resources to a giant multinational company which has many interests all over the world. This is particularly important because in today's world oil is a scarce resource whose value is often far greater than its market price. This may be particularly true for a country which might hope to use oil as a basis for further industrialization — a point I will return to below.

By way of footnote to this topic of the possible state role in oil in underdeveloped countries, I should also point out a very fundamental reason why many of them have not moved beyond production-sharing agreements, even where they have penetrated these myths. And that reason is the historically very strong opposition of the international oil companies backed by their powerful home governments, and international lending agencies like the International Monetary Fund and the World Bank, to state companies entering into the oil companies' highly profitable business.[5]

Now, having examined some of the reasons why it is possible for governments of underdeveloped countries to move into 100 per cent state roles in oil exploration, I would like to give some specific examples. There are a number of countries in which the government has set up a state oil corporation which carries out oil exploration, either with its own personnel, or through contracting for such services on a fee basis. I will discuss briefly three illustrative examples: Mexico, India, and Vietnam. Mexico is of interest because it has a long history of 100 per cent state control of oil; India is a case study of a government shift from production-sharing to 100 per cent state control in the offshore area, and the benefits it has reaped; Vietnam is an example of a war-torn country new to the oil industry which in only two years has leaped ahead to develop a pioneering approach to 100 per cent state control.

Petróleos Mexicanos, or Pemex, the country's state oil company, was born in 1938 when the Mexican government nationalized the oil industry because of its arrogant refusal to accept the sovereignty of the government.[6] Pemex, which started as a struggling operation, inherited some old refineries and a declining oil-production sector; it faced almost universal hostility from the powerful oil companies and their home governments, which attempted to boycott and strangle it from the beginning. Nevertheless, despite continuing hostility from these sources, Pemex built in its first three decades an enviable record in the oil-exploration area.

According to some calculations I made about ten years ago, at a time when crude oil was selling at around $2 per barrel, Pemex had invested, between 1938 and 1966, an estimated $600 million in exploration efforts, finding seven billion barrels of oil reserves worth approximately $14 billion, or $24 in oil found for every $1 invested, with all of the oil and its profits going to the country. In more recent years Pemex has far outstripped even this performance, finding huge new reserves onshore and offshore, which are officially put at 14 billion barrels but unofficially estimated as high as 60 billion barrels.[7] Where once the big foreign lenders boycotted Pemex, now they fall all over each other to make loans for oil development, on very favourable terms.[8] Indeed, one of the ironies of the present situation is that those forces in the United States which continually scoffed at Pemex's efforts and called it a 'failure', now look to Pemex as a possible saviour from OPEC, hoping that it will provide the United States with a major supply source which might undermine OPEC's power.

The enormous monetary value of the oil which Pemex has found, through its own drilling operations carried out by Mexican personnel, has clearly been far greater than Pemex's exploration expenditures. All profits were kept within the country. Equally important, however, Pemex as a state oil company played a major role in helping to promote the growth of Mexico's economy, through such means as selling oil at low prices, encouraging indigenous production of oil-field supplies like steel pipe (which in turn helped develop a steel industry in Mexico), producing petrochemicals which aided agriculture, and even providing social services such as roads, schools, and water systems for some of the poorer rural regions.

The second country to be discussed here is India, which is one of the poorest countries in the world, with a per capita income of about $100 per year. Surely India would seem to fit the myth of a country whose government cannot afford the risk of exploring for oil on its own, yet it has very successfully carried out such exploration at great benefit to the country.

The background to this story is that there has been a long struggle in India during the post-Second World War period over the extent to which the government could carry out oil exploration on its own, as opposed to granting concessions to foreign companies.[9] In particular, India was strongly pressured by the foreign oil companies (inlcuding Exxon and Mobil), their home governments (particularly the United States), the World Bank, and the International Monetary Fund to leave oil exploration to the private companies. As a result, even though hardly any exploration was carried out by the companies, which at that time had huge reserves in the Middle East, the government did relatively little in the oil-exploration area, although it had some success with onshore drilling directly carried out by government personnel. However, in the more technologically difficult offshore area, the conflicting pressures resulted in delay and indecision, until the 1973 oil price jump forced the country to take action. In 1974 the government compromised by awarding two production-sharing concessions to foreign oil companies, and reserving one area for the state oil entity, the Oil and Natural Gas Commission (O.N.G.C.).

The result of that decision is that the O.N.G.C. found a major offshore oil field (the 'Bombay High'), while the two private company groups, after some unsuccessful drilling, have now ceased operations. As for the Indian government's efforts, the sequence of events was as follows.[10] The government bought what is called a 'jack-up rig', which is the simplest and cheapest kind of drilling platform suited for shallow waters up to 250 feet. (This is the same kind of rig, I might note, which would be adequate for drilling in the shallow waters where there are promises of oil offshore Puerto Rico.) The rig was built in Japan, and the Indian government hired a U.S. offshore drilling company to operate it and also to train Indian nationals to carry out this work in the future, on a fee basis. The cost of buying the rig was probably about $25 million, while the management and training fee was in the neighborhood of $1 million per year.

Five exploration wells were then drilled between mid-1974 and mid-1975, and these wells 'proved out' a field estimated to contain in the neighborhood of one billion barrels of oil, worth at today's prices about $14 billion. The total exploration costs (allowing for the fact that the Indian government did not have to buy the rig but could have rented it, and hence only a part of the investment should be charged to the one year's effort) was probably in the order of $20 million. Thus, by 'risking' $20 million in exploration expenditures, the government found oil worth more than 500 times as much, all of which now belongs to the country. Surely no other area of economic endeavor offers such tremendous potential return for such relatively small outlay!

The development expenditures to bring the Bombay High field into full production — about 200,000 barrels per day by the early 1980s (an amount which will be worth about $1 billion per year at today's oil prices) — are estimated at about $600 million in total. While this is a great deal of money for India, as it would be for Puerto Rico, the country has had no trouble obtaining loans on very favorable terms for such oil development purposes. Even the World Bank, which has historically resisted making loans to state oil companies because it favored private capital in the oil area, has made its first such loan to the Indian government, of $150 million, at 8.2 per cent per year.[11] One can rest assured that, had World Bank money not been available, other private capital would have been eager to fill the gap — as evidenced by the fact that the Indian government recently got its first commercial bank loan (at 'a mere 1 per cent above the London Interbank Offered Rate'), based partly on its newfound oil reserves.[12]

The Indian government also has been able to help 'self-finance' the oil-field development, and thus to reduce the need for loans, by a technique which might also be applicable to Puerto Rico. This is to bring the field quickly into production by loading the oil onto tankers at sea and carrying it to shore. This serves the dual purpose of not having to hold up production until an expensive pipeline from the offshore field to the land can be completed, and also providing a cash flow to help pay for the pipeline. Thus, while the pipeline being built is to be finished by mid-1978, the Indian government, by starting production in mid-1976, will have achieved production of 50,000 barrels a day by that time. It will have produced several hundred million dollars' worth of oil before the pipeline is completed, which is more than enough to pay for the entire cost of the pipeline! By way of footnote, this initial success has stimulated the Indian government to additional exploration, and thus far it has found at least one more promising offshore oil field.[13]

Finally, the experience of the Socialist Republic of Vietnam since the end of the war in 1975 illustrates how quickly an underdeveloped country can develop a highly advantageous and sophisticated approach to offshore oil exploration. Essentially the Vietnamese undertook an intensive investigation of the realities of today's international oil industry. As a result, the government has established a two-pronged approach to offshore oil exploration. This has dramatically reversed the previous situation under the Saigon regime which had awarded concessions offshore South Vietnam to foreign companies on terms highly disadvantageous to the country.

While details of the Vietnamese government's arrangements have not been made public, reports from the business and petroleum press indicate the following pattern.[14] First, the government appears to have reserved some of the most promising offshore areas for its own exploration efforts, to be undertaken at its own risk, with technical services and financing from Norway. According to *Business Week,* this involves a $45 million credit package, from a consortium of Norwegian oil companies and banks backed by the Norwegian government, consisting of $9 in aid and $36 million in a fifteen-year loan at a 'very low interest rate'; Norway is also building an offshore exploration training center in Vietnam.

Second, the Vietnamese government is negotiating arrangements for exploration in other offshore areas in the form of service contracts with state oil companies of Western European countries which are particularly anxious to obtain assured longterm supplies of crude oil – notably, Elf-Aquitaine of France, ENI of Italy, and Deminex of West Germany. These service contracts reportedly provide that the companies will take the risk of exploration and get the right to buy up to 45 per cent of any oil found at 7 to 10 per cent below world market prices. On that basis, after deduction of costs, Vietnam would end up with 95 to 97 per cent of the oil profits, and the foreign state oil companies 3 to 5 per cent.

The preceding analysis gives us a quantitative background to show just how bad Puerto Rico's proposed strategy of granting offshore concessions to major oil companies would be for the island. While all concession agreements have to be carefully analyzed because the details can often be more crucial than the widely publicized general terms, as I understand the situation in Puerto Rico, based on published reports, any concessions given out would be along the following lines. Up to 40 per cent of the production would be used to cover investment and operating costs, while the remaining 60 per cent would be divided equally between the government and the oil company, with the company paying a 50 per cent tax rate on its share of the profits.[15] In effect, then, after deducting all costs the government of Puerto Rico would get only 75 per cent of any net profits and the oil company would get 25 per cent.

Moreover, taking the Puerto Rico concession terms as indicated, let us further assume that an exploration expenditure of about $10 to $20 million could prove out, as in India, a one billion barrel field, requiring a development expenditure conservatively estimated at $1 billion. On this basis, some rough calculations would yield the following conclusion: First, by giving out a concession to private oil companies, and 'saving' $20 million, at today's prices the government would be giving up to the oil companies over the life of the field profits of about $3,000 million, or some 150 times the company's risk investment in exploration! And, if the field turned out to be larger than India's, which is quite possible, the companies might take out 1,000 times their risk investment. Surely this would be a classic case of Puerto Rico being 'penny-wise and pound-foolish'. This is especially true because apparently the results of the preliminary surveys offshore Puerto Rico (for which, it should not be forgotten, the Puerto Rican government has already spent $5-$6 million) are highly promising and suggest that the risk here is considerably less than it was offshore India.

It is also important to note another drawback to a production-sharing concession. Aside from the fiscal consequences, the fact is that in the first five years or so of production, about 70 per cent of the oil produced goes to the companies to use as they choose while in later years more than 50 per cent will go to them.[16] Since, as mentioned earlier, oil in the future may be more valuable to those who possess it than its mere market price, this loss of control of the oil could be a serious blow to Puerto Rico.

Finally, by way of conclusion, I would like to point out that to an outsider it would seem that the whole question of the possibilities of oil existing in Puerto Rico, and how it should be best exploited, has very important implications not only in the economic area, but also as regards the future political status of the island. First, and perhaps most basic: one of the most obvious prerequisites for a truly economically independent country is a viable economy. Just as obviously, if there are large quantities of oil which belong to Puerto Rico, this could go a long way toward laying a foundation for such a viable economy — something which I assume would be desired by both supporters of independence and statehood alike. At the same time, if a large part of that oil is not under the control of Puerto Rico, then this clearly weakens the role that oil could play in promoting economic independence.

Second, and related: if, for example, Puerto Rico were to become the 51st state in the United States, there would be other implications in terms of the use of any Puerto Rican oil. For one thing, such oil could easily become caught up in the whole process of regulatory law in the United States aimed at ensuring that there should be no interference by the individual states with the free flow of commerce among the states. Thus, it might come to pass that as a state, Puerto Rico would be unable to ensure that its oil was used within the island or for the benefit of the island — a situation that Texas and Louisiana have feared will occur with declining oil and natural gas production on the mainland. Moreover, there is also the whole complex question of oil taxation, and what the different possibilities would be if Puerto Rico were independent, or a state, or something else, and if the oil produced were under a production-sharing agreement.

Because the issue of oil has so many vital implications for Puerto Rico's future, it seems to me that the island has a great need to obtain as much knowledge as possible and to analyze carefully all the possibilities before it takes steps such as giving out concessions to big international oil companies — steps which may prove to be irreversible for legal or practical reasons.

The two things which seem to be most urgently needed are greater knowledge about the international oil industry and greater knowledge of what oil resources may exist in Puerto Rico. To meet these needs, it is important to develop within Puerto Rico a capability to provide this knowledge, without taking steps which will prejudge the future, and limit future options. Toward this end, Puerto Rico might consider the fact that some eighty underdeveloped countries have set up state corporations exclusively concerned with oil, whose activities range from actually carrying out exploration and development to at least putting the country in a position to negotiate better concessions from the oil companies.

In the final analysis, in the world of today, just as war is too important to leave to the military, so oil is too important to leave to the private oil companies. This fact is being recognized in strongholds of private enterprise like Western Europe and Japan, as well as in Canada where the government has set up an integrated state oil company to do everything from exploration and producing oil to operating refineries. Even in the United States itself, where the power of the big oil companies is greater than anywhere else, the federal government is now proposing to get into the business of oil exploration by contracting for drilling on the outer continental shelf.[17]

If the goal is to have all oil resources in Puerto Rico used for the maximum benefit of its people, then it is extremely important not to be stampeded into hasty action now, such as giving out self-destructive and irreversible concessions. Whatever oil may exist in Puerto Rico has been there for millions of years, and if it takes another year or two to develop the capability of dealing with it in an effective way, the oil will still be there.

References

1.   See Michael Tanzer, *The Political Economy of International Oil and the Underdeveloped Countries*, Boston, Beacon Press 1969, chapter 10 (this book is referred to hereafter as *Political Economy of International Oil*); Tanzer Economic Associates, Inc., *Alaska's Prudhoe Bay Oil: Profitability and Taxation Potential* (A Report to the Alaska State Legislature,

9 January 1976); Tanzer Economic Associates, Inc, *Impact of Increased Taxation on Oil Exploration and Development in Alaska* (A Report to the Alaska State Legislature, 25 March 1977).

2. The chances of finding oil off the north coast of Puerto Rico have been estimated to be as high as 50 to 85 per cent. For a summary of the debate on this issue, as well as other facts on the situation, see Robert Friedman, 'Will Puerto Rico get the best deal?' *San Juan Star,* 18 January 1977.

3. For preponderance of ownership of offshore rigs by independent drilling companies, see *International Petroleum Encyclopedia: 1976,* pp.290-298; for discussion of how rare major oil company ownership of land rigs is, see *World Oil,* October 1977, pp.43-46.

4. See, for example, the experience in India, discussed later in the text, where exploration was about 4 per cent of total costs.

5. See Michael Tanzer, *Political Economy of International Oil,* especially chapters 4,8,10,17 and 18.

6. Unless otherwise noted, this analysis of Pemex's earlier role is drawn from ibid., chapter 22.

7. For official estimate, see *The Oil Daily,* 21 September 1977, p.4; for potential reserve figure, see *Petroleum Economist,* June 1976, p.233.

8. See, for example, *Platt's Oilgram News Service (Platt's),* 29 September 1977, p.1.

9. For more details on this background, see *Political Economy of International Oil,* chapter 18.

10. For data on the Indian government and its Bombay High oil field see *New York Times,* 18 January 1975; *Petroleum Economist,* June 1975, pp.223-225; and *Oil Commentary* (New Delhi), 1 December 1974; 15 January 1975; and 1 February 1975.

11. *Petroleum Intelligence Weekly (PIW),* 11 July 1977, p.9.

12. *Business Week,* 3 October 1977, p.56.

13. *PIW,* 11 July 1977, p.9.

14. See *Platt's,* 22 March 1977, p.1; and 12 July 1977, p.1; *Petroleum News: Southeast Asia,* August 1977, p.12; *PIW,* 7 November 1977, p.8; and *Business Week,* 28 November 1977, p.54.

15. *Platt's,* 20 May 1976, p.2.

16. Assuming the investment costs are recovered in the first five years of production.

17. See *World Oil,* September 1977, p.23.

6. Trinidad and Tobago Oilworkers' Statement Against Texaco Worldwide

Oilfield Workers Trade Union

Editors' Note: *What follows is an unedited reproduction of a pamphlet published by the Oilfields Workers Trade Union (OWTU): 'In defence of our members and the people of Trinago against global Texaco — exploiter of our labour and natural resources' (San Fernando, Trinidad, 1978). Note also that, unless otherwise stated, currency used is (except for oil prices which are quoted in U.S. dollars) Trinidad and Tobago dollars. One U.S. dollar equals approximately two Trinago dollars.*

Introduction

Comrades, the battle of Beaumont Hill is once more underway. Already, Global Texaco has started its attack against the Union, the workers and the country.

They have been shedding crocodile tears and saying "we are losing money, we are in a poor trading position." Imagine the world's fourth largest Company, and the only major Oil Company who reported an improved financial year in 1977, saying they are losing money!

They are pursuing this line in order to achieve two objectives — get the workers to accept a small wage increase, and secondly, to get the Government to reduce its taxation on the Company. In light of this strategy to further their rip-off in Trinago, we must stand resolute in our demands. The equation here is simple — the less Texaco pays its workers, the greater their profits.

But what is at stake in these negotiations is even larger than just the retention of wealth in our shores. Texaco is one of the biggest supporters of the wicked, evil and racist system of apartheid in South Africa. Their refineries help to make Vorster's murderous war machine self-sufficient, and their use of facilities such as Pointe-a-Pierre to serve as transhipment ports for arms to South Africa makes them guilty of the murder of our black working class brothers and sisters fighting for their freedom in South Africa.

We, therefore, as self-respecting black workers, must take on our international responsibility in these negotiations. A defeat to Texaco here in Trinago, is a victory for the liberation armies in Southern Africa. If we fail in our international responsibility, then, we should hang our head in shame, for we would be assisting Vorster and his gang of criminals in shedding blood.

The incident on the waterfront where thirteen (13) comrades were suspended for refusing to tie up a ship with LPG bound for Antiqua — one of the major transhipment centres for South Africa bound arms — must be seen in this light. Those thirteen (13) comrades are part of the worldwide struggle against apartheid which is being highlighted in this United Nations year of anti-apartheid. It is against this international background that we fight our negotiations battle, and we must never forget it. That is why we have included some information on the policy of Texaco on racism and apartheid in this booklet.

Nationally, we must also view the Texaco negotiations as a battle for our livelihood, and for our very lives. Texaco has been threatening retrenchment if the Union does not lower its wage demands. We denounce this as terror tactics being employed by Texaco in their bid to squeeze the last drop of blood from Trinago.

The OWTU remains firm in its position — there must be no retrenchment in the Oil Industry! No right thinking person who sees all the petro-dollars in our country could accept that Texaco is losing money. Texaco can and must pay! There is no question about that. It is, after all, the oil workers' labour that is providing our country with all the petro-dollars today — and the oil worker, like any other worker, deserves to be paid for his labour.

All of us know that the Texaco negotiations is a time when the ruling class looks to attack the workers and the trade union movement. Texaco already have fired several salvos — dismissal of Safety Officer VICTOR SINGH, suspension of Branch Officer, GLEN WALCOTT, the suspension of the entire pump department, and now the suspension of the thirteen waterfront workers.

In 1978, when we see our country being raided by greedy multinationals who seek to get a piece of the action, we must recognise that failure to stop Texaco in its diabolical plot will mean a freer entry to these shores by these corporations. We, in the OWTU, alone can be counted upon to defend the national interest against Texaco.

In order to provide comrades with another weapon in the battle we now face, we have printed in this booklet all the facts and arguments substantiating our claim that Texaco is making a profit. We have also included the justification of our wage claim.

These positions reflect extensive research into the international oil industry, into the operations of Texaco, and into the way in which Trinago fits into the designs of the giant oil companies.

This work was done by none other than our comrade, Dr. Trevor Farrell, lecturer in economics and a specialist in petroleum economics. Our position is true and correct. Texaco, in its attempt to sidestep their responsibility to the workers, has been singing another song. But once comrades read and study this document carefully, they will be able to expose Texaco's half-truths and white lies.

Comrades, our struggle is a class war — the workers against the capitalists.

In that war, there can be no letting up. If we fail, our children and our children's children will never forgive us. Our freedom, dignity and self-respect is at stake. Let us move forward to victory.

Our Position on Texaco's Operations in Trinago

We have studied with interest the Company's statement on its position as expressed by Mr. Cabral. As best as we can make out, the gist of the argument appears to be that (a) the Company is losing money; (b) that its tax burden is extremely onerous; (c) that its costs of production are relatively high, partly as a result of this tax burden; (d) that its competitive position is weak; and (e) that this position should not be further eroded through increased costs. Therefore, the Company is currently seeking tax relief from the government of this country, and therefore too, it believes it to be desirable to restrain wage increases due to our workers.

Undoubtedly, this argument on the part of the Company will confuse many — including some of our own workers. For after all, this Company has maintained in the past that its profitability and ability to pay ought not to be an issue in industrial negotiations on the question of wages. It has been stated that profits vary, and wages do not. Therefore, the one cannot reasonably be linked to the other.

On the other hand, however, we on this side have consistently maintained that the Company's profitability and ability to pay are indeed a proper and even vital issue to be considered in negotiation on wages. In our much-ridiculed statement of case in 1975, we stated: "When a Company's profits are low or falling, its management never scruple to enter a plea of inability to pay as an excuse for not meeting what may be legitimate and justifiable wage claims on the part of their employees. Correspondingly, it is only fair that in periods of high and rising profits, profits and ability to pay be explicitly taken into account."

We on this side are prepared to be consistent in maintaining the position we have taken over the years. Consequently we have studied in detail Mr. Cabral's statement. We sought to discover whether the Company might not after all have had a valid argument on the importance of restraining our Union's wage claims.

Gentlemen, we must be frank with you. Detailed study of the Company's statement has convinced us that the argument put forward is substantially without merit. To be candid, we found the statement strewn with fallacies, misleading and confusing statements and what might well be termed disinformation — we are a little uncertain why we should have been told some of the things in the statement.

We are fully aware that there are those in the Company who are convinced that the Union and its advisers on these matters are ignorant, naive, motivated by strange political lusts or even just stupid. We are equally aware that there are locals in the Company's management structure who are eager to share these views.

Whatever the belief-system guiding those in the Company, we on this side believe very firmly that it is possible for us all to reason together and for us to look at the facts objectively and dispassionately. We believe that this approach is particularly important for those of us here who profess to be truly concerned about our country.

At the outset it is necessary for us to be clear about, and keep in our minds, three fundamental points. The first is that Texaco Trinidad Inc. is not an autonomous, individualistic entity operating on its own. It is one segment of a whole and can only be made sense of in relation to that whole. Second, it is necessary to recognise that Texaco, second largest of the US oil companies, plays an integral role in the organisation and conduct of American (and Western) politico-economic strategy. Third, we must be coolly clear about the nature of the historical relationship between the rich, white metropolitan countries of the North and the poor, black countries of the Southern Hemisphere.

Let us now look at Mr Cabral's statement on the loss position of the refinery, and at his arithmetic. He says:

> The major crude we refine is Arabian Light, so let us take this as a typical example. Arabian crude is sold at US $12.70 by Saudi Arabia and is known as the 'marker' crude for pricing in OPEC. Freight from the Middle East adds 95 ¢ to this, resulting in a landed cost of US $13.65 at Trinidad. When this crude is fully refined, that is allowing cat cracking, alkylation, platforming, etc. at a cost of US $1.03 per barrel, it yields products worth at Caribbean postings only US $13.93 versus a cost of US $14.78 resulting in a loss of 75¢ / bbl.

Fallacy No. 1 – The refinery is in a loss position

The argument here is straightforward. The Company makes a case using the economics of refining Saudi Arabian crude as an example. This crude has recently accounted for about 40% of refinery throughput. It is, therefore, in fact an excellent choice of example.

It is stated that "this crude is sold at US $12.70 by Saudi Arabia and is known as the "**marker**" crude for pricing in OPEC". The argument then goes on that freight from the Middle East to Trinidad adds 95¢ US to the cost of this crude, resulting in a landed cost of US $13.65 at Trinidad. Next, the cost of **full** refining of this barrel is added. This is stated to be $1.03 US. This should add up to $14.68 US (it is put at $14.78 in the text – presumably an error). Since, it is argued, the value of the product derived from this barrel is only $13.93 US, the result is a loss per barrel of 75¢US.

There are several things wrong here. First of all, we are **not** told that 34° Arabian Light (i.e. Saudi crude) is **not** bought by Texaco at $12.70 US. If someone ignorant of the workings of the international oil industry were to check any of the several journals or other sources which provide price information, he would indeed see a price of $12.70 US next to Saudi 34° crude. This price, however, is the '*state sales price*'.

From the point of view of a Company like Texaco there are **four** relevant prices for this (or any other) Saudi crude. The first is the tax-reference price. This is $13.66 US a barrel, and is the price on which tax is computed. The tax reference price is not the market price, but is the price set by the Government of a country to determine only the taxes to be paid per barrel of oil produced. The second is the state sales price. The third is the *'buy-back'* price and the fourth is the tax-paid cost of equity crude.

What has happened is that in Saudi Arabia (and some other Arab countries) the Government has nationalised some part of the oil industry. In the case of Saudi Arabia, the nationalisation is as yet incomplete so that the agreement is that 60% of the oil produced belongs to the Saudi Arabian oil company (Petromin) and 40% belongs to a private company called Aramco. Aramco is in fact a consortium of companies who share the costs and profits. These four companies are Texaco, Exxon, Gulf, Mobil.

The state sales price ($12.70) is, therefore, the price that the Saudi Arabian Company sells on the **world market**; the buy-back price is the price that Aramco buys back oil from Petromin; and the tax paid cost price is the price that obtains for the 40% oil produced and owned by Aramco.

What is this tax paid cost? It is composed of two elements. The cost of production plus the taxes paid to the government. The cost of production of Saudi Arabia light is 25 ¢ US per barrel (according to the *Petroleum Economist*, April 1977, page 157). The true 'price' at which Texaco obtains crude from Saudi Arabia is, therefore, a 'weighted average' of the buy-back price and the tax-paid cost of equity crude. We estimate the tax-paid cost of a barrel of Arabian light at $8.40 US. and the buy-back price of this crude as $12.70. Therefore, the Company's claim that it has to buy Saudi crude for the Trinidad refinery at $12.70 is false. The true cost to the Company is $10.98.

Just this is enough to change their supposed *'loss'* figure of 75¢ a barrel to a profit of 97¢ US per barrel. Who is Texaco trying to fool? Do they really believe that we in the Oilfields Workers' Trade Union are today totally ignorant and unsophisticated about the workings of the international oil industry?

But even this profit figure of 97¢ US per barrel understates the real profit. There are more fallacies and misleading claims in the Company's propaganda. First of all, the freight charge claimed ignores the fact that much of the crude moves in the Company's own bottoms (tankers), and that Texaco like all the other majors has increasingly used its tankship operations, which are generally incorporated in tax havens (e.g. Panama and Liberia) to hide and accumulate profits. Therefore, in the figure of 95¢ a barrel cited for freight, a large profit element is hidden.

How much profit may be thereby hidden? We are not in a position on this side to be precise. But at the end of 1976, we do know that freight in a VLCC from the Persian Gulf to the Caribbean was 63¢ US per barrel. Over the course of 1977, tanker rates have not risen. The tanker market has been characterized by continuous and widespread surplus capacity. Thus the *'hidden'* profit here may be anything in the order of 30¢ US per barrel.

Furthermore, the cost figure of $1.03 US per barrel for full refining (catcracking, alkylation, platforming, etc.) is totally misleading. For in fact with a fuel oil output of over 50% of the cut of the barrel, the barrel is certainly not *'fully refined'*. In other words it does not cost Texaco $1.03 US to refine each barrel of oil that passes through the Pointe-a-Pierre refinery. Some percentage, a relatively small one, of each barrel is fully refined and will, therefore, cost $1.03. But the oil that is **not** fully refined (e.g. the more than 50% that is fuel oil) does **not** cost $1.03. It costs considerably less.

Again, we cannot simply accept the figure of $13.93 US as the value of product deriving from the barrel of crude under discussion without qualification. Texaco has used an output mix heavily weighted in favour of fuel oil with a comparatively small proportion of the light ends. Residual fuel oil, we all know, is the lowest valued of the four major cuts of the barrel. It can be demonstrated by a simple linear programming exercise that this output mix given the pattern of product prices is non-optimal from the point of view of a refiner concerned to maximize his profits. Texaco could then, if it wanted to, improve its revenues significantly by altering the composition of its output.

Furthermore, all of Texaco's locally produced crude oil (37 mbpd) is refined at Pointe-a-Pierre. This oil does not cost Texaco $12.70 or $10.98 (US). The price here would be the tax paid cost and is considerably lower than the cost of the Saudi oil and freight charges. So on locally produced crude, Texaco in fact makes a super-profit.

What we are saying here is that fuel oil is the cheapest product of a barrel of oil. Gasoline and petrochemicals are far more expensive and profitable. If Texaco decides to produce so much fuel oil that is Texaco's problem. It could easily produce more profitable products, thereby improving its financial position. The reason that Pointe-a-Pierre produces fuel oil is because of the global policy of Texaco. It suits Texaco International to produce fuel oil, regardless of the consequences to Trinago.

Our position then is that we do not accept the Company's claim that money is being lost on its Trinidad refining operations. Profits are clearly being made as we can see. The question is simply where Texaco chooses to show these profits. Because, as we are all here quite aware, as an integrated organization Texaco has considerable leeway to distribute profits among its various cost centers by use of transfer prices amongst other things. And we are all also fully aware that the Company has never hesitated to use this leeway. As far as we are concerned, far from the Company making a loss of 75¢ per barrel, it is enjoying a profit of at least 97¢ US per barrel, and this may, by our own rough estimates of the profits hidden in freight charges and the degree of obfuscation in the cost figure cited, reach as high as $1.64 US per bbl.

Fallacy No. 2

A second, fundamental argument contained in Mr. Cabral's statement is that the refining industry in general is in bad shape. It is contended that Texaco Trinidad is running at an uneconomic level of 57.1% capacity. Various industry and financial publications are quoted to show that refineries in

Western Europe, the United Kingdom and Panama are operating below capacity. It is pointed out that the refineries in the Netherlands Antilles are also in a loss position. The general impression conveyed is that economic conditions with respect to refining operations outside the US are bleak, that Texaco's refineries in Trinidad, Panama and Western Europe all face these depressing conditions and that to survive it is imperative that we here in Trinidad seek to maintain our competitive edge. To do this, it is argued, it would be necessary to hold down costs.

On page 4 of Mr. Cabral's statement it is said that: "Our ability in Trinidad to survive this period will be dependent on cost of operation as we are fighting to supply the same markets with similar raw material costs and only the most economical will be able to compete. Any major increase in costs at Trinidad will obviously further weaken our already weak competitive position."

The implication is that wage increases ought to be held down. Further, the Company states, and we know, that it is negotiating with government for tax relief. Therefore, the proper elucidation of the Company's case here is important not only for our workers, but also for the national interest.

The questions at issue are three:
1. *Is the refining industry in fact in bad shape?*
2. *If so, why is it in bad shape?*
3. *Will the reduction of wages and taxes here in Trinidad in fact enhance Textrin's competitive position and its ability to survive this critical period?*

To answer these questions it is necessary to recognize that the white West has crafted up and is slowly operationalizing an elaborate strategy to reduce or eliminate their dependence on the non-white oil-rich countries, and to break the leverage that the OPEC countries have so painfully gained on the trade in their most important natural resource.

The decline in throughput levels in Caribbean refineries is the result of deliberate US Government policy — it is part of a long-range strategy of which the oil majors are all well aware (including Texaco) and in which they are actively and enthusiastically participating. No cost reductions on our part, no waiver of wage or tax increases will alter the course of this policy or its effects. The stakes are too high. In fact, the Caribbean refining industry as we have known it, if the Carter administration has its way, is doomed to disappear. It will simply no longer be needed.

Gentlemen, would you permit us to explain? The Caribbean refining industry consists of some nine refineries in six different geographical locations, with a daily capacity of about 3½ million barrels. Except for the refineries in Venezuela which were built at the government's insistence, all the others were built by the Companies as off-shore refineries, i.e. they were built as refineries on little islands offshore the US designed solely to supply US needs.

The Caribbean refineries were organized, the Caribbean oil industry was organized, not to serve local needs but the needs of white America. The refineries are orientated towards the production of residual fuel oil for the

East Coast of the US. The New England states of the US account for over 65% of US consumption of residual fuel oils. 80-90% of this has traditionally been imported generally through the Caribbean refineries.

In other words, just like our agricultural production was organized to serve not our needs, but British needs, so our oil industry is organized to serve American needs. In agriculture we grew sugar and cocoa because that is what Britain wanted of us. We did not grow food for ourselves, we did not even engage in secondary processing of the sugar and the cocoa. It is the same thing with oil. We specialize in producing residual fuel oil, the lowest valued of the major products because that is what the US East Coast needed.

When the US passed the CLEAN AIR ACT in 1963, designed to keep America's air clean, the Companies responded by putting desulphurization plants in their major Caribbean refineries. Texaco put one in Trinidad to keep America's air clean. All you have to do now is to think about air pollution in Point-a-Pierre by contrast and what Texaco has done about it, or water pollution in what used to be the Guaracara river and you can see whose imperatives Texaco responds to.

What is happening now is that just as when the Europeans developed beet sugar, they no longer needed cane and left us to languish in our stupidity, so too the Americans are coming to no longer need us to refine residual fuel oil to keep their homes warm, and are, in consequence, preparing our demise.

We know that there are nationals who will not believe this. There are those, placed in 'responsible' positions who believe that white foreign Texaco really cares about them and will not pull out from Trinidad leaving them to find work as they can. There were locals in BP's management structure who believed the same thing prior to 1969. During slavery, as those of us who recently read *Roots* or saw *Drums* would have had vividly brought back to mind, the house slaves often made the mistake of forgetting that they too were black slaves and they consistently paid the penalty of this error.

What the US has done is to set up an 'Entitlements' system. After 1973 foreign crude prices rose sharply over US prices, the US Congress, determined to cushion the effects of high oil prices on their citizens, introduced controls on domestic oil prices. '*Old*' oil is maintained at fairly low prices. '*New*' oil (discovered after 1973 or increased production above old levels) is priced nearer world levels, and so is oil from '*stripper*' wells.

The result is that refiners who had throughputs based on old oil or significant proportions of old oil would enjoy a cost advantage over those whose runs were based wholly or mostly on more expensive imported crudes. The Federal Energy Agency set up an entitlement system in 1974 under which refiners using old oil had to pay for '*entitlements*' to do so and those using imported oil received '*entitlements*' or rebates.

This system was designed to do two things — to ameliorate the cost advantage '*old*' oil engaged over '*new*' and imported oil when refined. Second, to encourage American refiners to refine more crude rather than importing product. A refiner who had refineries in both the Caribbean and the US, say, found that if he refined the crude in the US he got a rebate of some $2.30 a barrel (up to March, 1976) and paid a lower import fee than if he brought in product. Therefore, it turned out to be to his advantage to refine the crude in the United States. This encouraged the US refineries to run at full capacity while discouraging the Companies from refining large amounts in non-US refineries.

Amerada Hess by reason of its position in the US Virgin Islands was the only Caribbean refiner to receive entitlements. (Since the US Virgin Islands are considered US territory, the refinery would get the same concessions as a refinery located in the States). On the complaint of NEPCO in the Bahamas the entitlements program was modified — the so-called 70/30 program. Under this, domestic refiners producing fuel oil for the US East Coast had their entitlements reduced by 50%, and importers of residual fuel oil received a 30% entitlement.

This reduced but did not eliminate the advantage given to the US refineries. The reason was simply that the Caribbean refineries are needed for a few more years. The result is as desired. US refiners are producing at full or near full capacity. All Texaco's twelve (12) US refineries are operating at maximum capacity. How do we know? Because Texaco's President John McKinley, has said so. So Texaco is transshipping crude to its US refineries rather than refining in the Caribbean which it could do if it wanted. We see this trans-shipment taking place on a large scale right here at Pointe-a-Pierre where the large super tankers (VLCC's) transfer their cargo to smaller tankers which can dock at the shallow US ports.

The US refineries were traditionally reserved for producing the most valuable products. Between 1964 and 1974 for example, 45% of output was gasolene, and only 7½% residual fuel oil. (Compare the Trinidad output mix which is the exact opposite). Now the US refiners are producing much more residual fuel oil.

US policy is to:
(a) Conserve energy
(b) Expand US oil production especially offshore
(c) Switch to alternative energy sources
(d) Reduce imports
(e) Destroy OPEC

This policy will result in the liquidation of the Caribbean refining industry as we know it. By 1985, if the Carter Plan succeeds, US demand for imported residual fuel oils could drop all the way to zero. They have begun as we have seen to utilize their domestic refineries more fully and to produce residual fuel oil at home.

Relatedly, they are expanding and upgrading domestic US refining capacity. In line with this, Texaco is spending $500 million US (*Petroleum Times* 20th Jan.) on its Port Arthur and Louisiana refineries. Next, they are switching utilities to coal. This is a major plank of the Carter strategy. They are seeking to reduce energy demand and they are planning to reduce imports. The falling throughput levels being experienced in Caribbean refineries are due to these reasons, and not to anything about local costs.

So the decline in employment and output of the Curaco and Aruba refineries has nothing to do with being expensive compared to the Hess refinery or the US refineries. It has to do with the economic and political strategy of the giant oil companies and the Carter Administration.

Furthermore, we would be fools to hold down wages and taxes here, all of us in the hope that we will make Textrin more *'competitive'* and boost back up its throughput levels. American policy directions are sufficiently clear. Residual fuel oil produced in the Caribbean will be by 1990 like sugar is today.

The US is also planning to expand its own production of energy (including oil) dramatically. As far as petroleum goes, the problem is that much of this will have to come from the Outer Continental Shelf. This will require heavy investments. This is the reason why the oil companies have such important stakes in continued high oil prices, and in high profit levels. If you observe, Texaco which has about 47-49% of its assets located in the US has over the last five to six years invested about 65% of its capital back in the US. The Companies are moving to the *'safe'* areas of the developed world.

We on this side are, therefore, led to reject the analysis offered by Mr. Cabral of the reasons for the depressed conditions of Caribbean refineries and his implied solution of holding down wages and taxes here. Whether the government will be naive enough to misunderstand the dynamics of the oil industry is an open question. We here do not believe that tax reductions are in the national interest. If anything, taxes should perhaps be raised a bit. Trinidad is coming to the end of its usefulness for Texaco.

Texaco, we predict, will soon be quietly abandoning its traditional role here. Texaco Trinidad Inc. as it is today, if maintained, will be the Caroni Limited of 1985. We must get what we can before white America has finished sucking the orange dry and proceeds to spit it out.

In Conclusion

In concluding, gentlemen, let us say that we find the Company's arguments unconvincing and misleading. What the Company has offered us on wages is unacceptable. The Company claims losses. Yet it is remarkably generous with its top officers. We have noted that its directors and officers got a 19.3% increase for 1976 alone, and that it did not scruple to raise Mr. Granville's pay (the Chairman of the Board) from $521,975US in 1975 to $651,036 in 1976 — an increase of 25%. They could hardly be serious about doing badly with increases like that.

Furthermore, we also note that Texaco's net income for the third quarter 1977 was $247.8 million or 15.6% higher than the third quarter 1976 — the highest quarterly gain for the five US majors and that Texaco reported a 49% gain on its foreign operations for the first nine months of 1977.

This is an impressive but understated picture of profitability. For we know too that faced with the angry threats of horizontal and/or vertical divestiture in the US Congress after 1973, the Oil Companies embarked on a quick and largely successful search for ways to reduce and hide their true profits in their accounts. We may note three successful techniques:

1. *The change from FIFO to LIFO inventory accounting. This was adopted by Texaco in 1974.*
2. *The expensing rather than capitalizing of exploration expenditures. (This elegantly reduces both net income and assets).*
3. *The charging off as 'losses' due to 'nationalization' large sums from net income.*

We also want to say that we cannot accept the device of implying losses or a poor financial position by citing tax-takes per barrel whether as percentages or as gross amounts. Taxes per barrel are irrelevant to profitability. In Mr. Cabral's example where his rum manufacturer was left with 5¢, we would be wrong to agree that his operation was very marginal before we know how much capital he had invested in the operation. If he made 5¢ and had invested 5¢ then he would have enjoyed a 100% profit and we on this side would say he was doing very well indeed.

Nor do we accept the claim that Texaco has had to put more money into Trinidad than they took out, and that they have not engaged any dividends for the last three years. Dividends is probably the least important channel used by Texaco to extract money from our country. The Company has a multiplicity of ways, including its very potent use of transfer prices. Some of the channels, e.g. the processing fee arrangement, are so subtle that they never appear as channels at all, because they are embedded in the institutional structure of the Company's operations. And, furthermore, at particular periods any business has to put in more than it takes out e.g. investment programs − current capital expenditure has to be related to future income streams over many years and cannot be compared with current income. That is like comparing mangoes and oranges.

Finally, we do not believe that we have very much of a role to play in Texaco's future, nor they in ours. We do not believe that we have a refining capacity of 450 mbpd in this country and that given projected crude shortages we will need Texaco to provide access to crude. The refining capacity here in Pointe-a-Pierre is Texaco's, not Trinidad's. It was put here for their needs, not for ours. Our country's needs do not call for refining 450 mbpd. We need capacity for only some 250 mbpd, crude production of 200,000 barrels per day, a different (higher-valued) composition of products, a petrochemical complex, linked to certain identifiable secondary manufacturing industries. These are our country's needs. We will be both shortsighted and idealistic to believe that Texaco is interested in serving our needs.

Texaco, gentlemen, has exploited this country long and well. It will soon have no more use for our country or for any of us, house slaves or field slaves. The least it can do while it is here is pay its workers a decent wage. And this is the demand that we are reiterating here today.

Justification of Our Wage Claim

The OWTU is asking 120% wage increase but in the spirit of compromise and in order to save time we are prepared to settle for 100%. We are making this claim after a full, detailed and careful assessment of the economic situation of the country, the Company (in both its local, and global manifestations) and the international petroleum market. The key consideration that arises is the question of achieving economic Justice for oil workers and for their country. There are in all six (6) factors or issues on which our case is based:

(1)   The essential contribution of oil workers to the economy of the country and the wealth of the Company.
(2)   The impact of inflation in eroding the workers' real wages.
(3)   The impact of projected inflation.
(4)   The increase in the workers' productivity.
(5)   Modern industrial relations practice in terms of employee welfare.
(6)   The beneficial impact of the settlement demanded on the country's welfare.

1. The Essential Contribution Of Oil Workers To The Country's Economy And The Company's Wealth

The first consideration that must be taken into account is the condition of general prosperity being enjoyed by this country, other oil-producing countries and the international petroleum Companies. This prosperity is based on oil, the oil produced by the workers.

According to the Trinidad and Tobago Government's official statistics, by 1976 the oil industry accounted for 48.3% of this country's Gross Domestic Product; that is, oil workers were responsible for producing almost half this country's wealth. Furthermore, oil (adjusted to exclude oil under the processing agreement. The reason why we exclude oil under the processing agreement is that this is oil that Texaco imports from itself and exports to itself in a transaction that has nothing to do with the national level of imports and exports. It is purely intra-company trading and the prices of the imported oil and the price of the exported product and hence the value of imports and exports is determined according to the dictates of Texaco's head office) by 1975 accounted for 81% of this country's exports. That is, oil workers were responsible for $81 out of every $100 worth of this country's exports.

From recurrent revenue of $476 million in 1973, the Government of Trinago, by 1977, received $2.2 billion of recurrent revenue — again predominantly contributed by oil and the oilworker. The value of the oilworkers' production and contribution to the economy grew by 62% between 1974 and 1976, and as a result between 1974 and 1977, government revenue increased by 81%. This country's current prosperity is built on oil — oil which cannot be produced without the workers. We believe that in consequence they must enjoy a fair and just share of this prosperity.

In the same way, Texaco and the other large integrated petroleum companies have enjoyed fabulous increases in their wealth position over the last few years due to developments in the international oil industry and the production of oilworkers. Again elementary justice demands that the workers who have laboured to help produce this prosperity should enjoy a fair share of it.

2. Inflation And The Erosion Of Real Wages
The first duty of any economy is to provide its citizens with their basic material welfare. In a system based on the extensive division of labour and on a commodity economy, people's ability to obtain their basic material welfare is based on their ability to earn a living wage. Therefore, for every specific enterprise or industry, the first responsibility is to provide its employees and their dependents with a living wage. After all, the primary purpose of production and output is MAN.

A living wage, however, once achieved, has to be protected, maintained and enhanced as prosperity advances. The key enemy to the maintenance and protection of the worker's wage is inflation. Hard-won gains are eroded, the worker's real wage is diminished. It is intolerable that the worker's real wage be suffered to be eroded by inflation — inflation for which the worker may bear no responsibility.

This is precisely what has happened to the wages of the oil worker since the starting date of the last agreement, February 1975. While the present agreement ends in February 1978, data on inflation is at the time of writing available only up to December 1977. In February 1975, the cost of living index stood at 241.2 points. By December of 1977, it had advanced to 326.6 points — an increase of 85.4 points or 35.4%.

In the last agreement signed by the Company and the Union, a highly inadequate C.O.L.A. [cost of living allowance] formula was imposed on the workers. This formula provided for a 3¢ per hour wage increase for every complete five point rise in the cost of living. This means that there were 17 complete five point rises up to the end of December 1977 and the C.O.L.A. received as a result would amount to 51¢ an hour.

We have studied the complex of wage rates in the 1975-78 agreement. The median wage in this complex was estimated to be in 1975 between $3.86 and $3.80 per hour. On this basis, the C.O.L.A. formula compensated the average wage earner for a 35.4% inflation with a 13.4% wage increase. (The actual range of compensation was spread between 9.6% for the high wage in the complex to 14.8% for the low). As such, using the median as the appropriate measure of central tendency in this case, it means that the worker's real wages have been eroded by 22% over the 1975-78 period.

To restore the worker's real wage, then, 22% of the 1975 wage is needed. This works out to 14.7% of the 1977 wages. On this basis then, we are asking for an increase of 14.7%.

3. Expected Inflation
It takes no special skill to forecast that current real wages will also be subject to erosion over the course of the next agreement. This, however, is unacceptable.

The living wage, measured in real terms, of our members cannot be subjected to the unconscionable erosion of inflation for which they bear no culpability. Their wages must be protected.

Now over the last year for which full data is available (October 1976 to October 1977) inflation was 10.57%. We can extrapolate this rate over the next three years. This gives us a likely **under-estimate** of expected inflation. In the international economy right now, as countries bottom out of the 1974 recession and growth momentum picks up, inflationary pressures are beginning to mount. Therefore, 10.57% a year is a likely under-estimate.

Nevertheless, on this basis inflation compounded over the next three years will amount to at least 35.18%. Now, the C.O.L.A. formula on the last agreement compensated for approximately 37% of the inflation. (By contrast, the previous COLA in the 1972-75 agreement compensated for only about 15% of the inflation in these years).

Anticipating an improved C.O.L.A. formula we estimate an expected improved protection of 50% compared to the previous 37%. On this basis then, we claim an increase of 17.59% as a hedge against future inflation. We stress that this is a likely under-estimate of future inflation and a possible over-estimate of the protection that a new C.O.L.A. formula can be expected to provide. Nevertheless, in an effort to characterize our claims by a spirit of conservation and moderation our claim here is held down to 17.59%.

4. The Increase In Labour Productivity

It is widely accepted that a key factor in determining wage increases should be the increase in productivity experienced in the enterprise or the industry. In both the United States and the United Kingdom, for example, official government policy has for many years now sought to link wage increases with productivity increases on a point for point basis. The basic reason for this is that such a link ensures that labour gets a fair share of increases in the value of the output it participates in creating.

In the present situation, however, the same people who have traditionally advanced this argument when productivity increases were of the order of 2% and 3% a year find themselves embarrassed when, as in the oil industry, due partly to market conditions, productivity increases are quite large. Suddenly, one is treated to all kinds of ignorant and nonsensical **obfuscations** on the part of those who are no longer happy with the implications of their previous arguments. We reject this kind of inconsistency and hypocrisy. If productivity is put forward as the key factor in wage increases when it is of the order of 2% a year, and this is philosophically and economically justifiable, then we cannot change the argument when we find a situation where productivity increases by 20% or 200% a year.

The philosophical and economical basis for linking wage increases to productivity increases is, however, eminently reasonable. It is the one way to ensure that one factor does not appropriate more of the benefits of increased productivity than other co-operant factors. It maintains the proportionate income distribution between factors and, on an economy-wide basis, it does not result in a stimulus to inflation. To claim that in supporting this well-known principle of wage determination, the Union is thereby advocating retrenchment when prices and productivity falls is sheer nonsense. We are advocating no such thing. It is nothing more than a fact of life that when prices and productivity falls, companies seek to reduce costs. To recognise this is most certainly not tantamount to advocating it.

The adjustment is made in any of several different ways. The wage bill may be reduced through retrenchment, leaving wage rates unchanged. To recognise this is, we repeat, not to advocate it. In fact, we would deplore it. (See for example the Fed Chem full page advertisement in the *Trinidad Guardian* in December 1977). Another method of adjustment is to change the factor proportions in the industry by increasing capital-intensity while leaving the size of the work force and the wage rate unaffected. Output may thusly be expanded rather than contracted. If this sounds strange, it is not. It depends simply on the elasticity of demand for the company or industry's output. Again, the composition of output may be changed, or other elements of cost reduced. Finally, the complex of wages rates may in rare cases be indeed reduced. If this sounds strange, again it is not. Precisely this happened a couple of years ago in the United States airline industry where Pan Am workers and pilots assented to pay cuts on the request of management. Again we repeat we are not advocating any of these modes of adjustment. We are simply saying that adjustments do in fact take place. This is why the linking of wage increases to productivity increases is in fact a practical proposition for running a business. To those who doubt, all they have to do is consult capitalist US and UK experience over the last ten years.

Productivity in the Texaco Trinidad Case: In 1974, Texaco employed 2,534 workers in crude production and 4,296 in refining according to our data. In 1975 crude production employment declined to 2,335, in 1976 to 2,287 and in 1977 to approximately 2,218. Employment in refining moved from 4,296 in 1974, to an estimated 4,371 in 1975, 4,282 in 1976 and 4,149 in 1977 (estimated). (These figures were all obtained from official sources).

Using the published data on Texaco's own crude production and official prices to value this out-put we find that whereas, in 1974, each Texaco worker engaged in crude production produced out-put valued at $75,030 TT, by 1977 each such worker was producing out-put valued at an estimated $126,427.92 TT. Over the three years (1975 over 1974, 1976 over 1975, 1977 over 1976) productivity thereby increased by 68.5% in the Texaco case. (We ignore refining because the existence of the processing agreement makes true value added in the refinery almost impossible to estimate). Therefore, on the basis of productivity increases, and in line with internationally accepted practice, we claim a wage increase of 68.5%.

5. Modern Practices In Terms Of Employer Welfare

Our total claim so far is, therefore, for a 100.8% wage increase. There are other considerations bolstering this claim and even more. In a modern world, even in capitalist countries, it is increasingly accepted and understood that enterprises have a social responsibility which begins with ensuring and enhancing the welfare of their employees. It is a matter of enlightened self-interest that employees who are well taken care of materially and psychically are going to be happy, highly motivated and productive people. There are several American social-psychological researches which demonstrate this and Japanese and Swedish experience rightly confirms it.

It has taken root among American companies as well. However, it is not good enough for foreign multinationals to look after the welfare of employees in their home country only. ALL EMPLOYEES MUST BENEFIT. We are not impressed with Texaco's comparative performance on the issue of employee welfare not even in its home country.

What do we mean? The new approach to employee welfare among American multinationals is exemplified by IBM. According to *Newsweek,* November 21, 1977, page 82, "Not only does IBM pay its 300,000 employees generous salaries and cover their medical bills, it also counsels, trains and entertains them, supports their favourite charities and helps with their children's education, and uniquely among American corporations, it virtually guarantees its workers life-time job security."

The report in question continues (page 83): "In all, IBM spends an estimated $2.3 billion a year, about 14% of its 1976 gross revenues to keep its people happy. 'It's good business', says chairman Frank T. Cary. 'The more satisfied your employees are, the better they will perform' (Please note carefully.) "What do employees get for IBM's money? Practically everything. Like most large companies (sic) IBM underwrites a generous pension plan, supplies group life insurance and covers most medical expenses. But its fringes far transcend traditional benefits packages.

For employees who adopt children, for instance, IBM pays for up to 80% of the related costs, and it rebates the tuitions of those who want to go back to school to prepare for a second career after retirement.

IBMers can put their children in IBM day-care centres, stay at IBM hotels (called "homesteads") jog on IBM tracks and play tennis on IBM courts. The company operates three dollar-a-year country clubs for workers and their families and runs a vast network of schools and training centres where employees can study everything from computer programming to international finance".

We believe that this is the path that Texaco must take. After all, it is a bigger wealthier, older company than IBM. Furthermore, we insist that these kinds of benefits, this modern emphasis on employee welfare, is not just to be provided for mainly white, metropolitan employees. We in Trinago work just as hard to produce wealth for the Texaco system as does Texaco's metropolitan employees. Consequently, the approach to employees welfare demonstrated by the IBM case and advocated by us, must apply in the same way as to the Company's metropolitan employees. As a start, therefore, we are insisting that Texaco provide its Trinidad workers with a decent wage and the decent fringe benefits they are demanding.

6. The Benefits To The Company

Sixthly, our case is presented with full cognizance that we are dealing with a foreign Global Corporation exploiting our country's non-renewable natural resources. This country's economic transformation depends critically on its ability to harness the benefits from its oil resources and direct these to the satisfaction of its citizens' welfare and to the development of new lines of activity against the day when our oil and gas run out. For we all know that despite all Texaco's protestations to the contrary, they don't give a damn about our country's welfare. What little they give is what we wring out of them and what they believe it is expedient for one reason or another to provide. And the day that Trinidad is of no more use to Texaco, we all know that they will up and leave, just as BP did in 1969.

Furthermore, we are mindful that that day when Trinidad is of no more use to Texaco, and its home country, may be fast approaching. We are aware that there is a complex, subtle and carefully orchestrated plot afoot to vitiate the effectiveness of OPEC and ultimately to break it up. This is operating on three levels – the economic, the political and the diplomatic. Furthermore, it is not prudent for us to give this plot, in which all the large petroleum multinationals are playing key roles, every chance of success.

One aspect of this which we are also monitoring is the proposed new US energy policy which may have the effect of rendering Texaco Trinidad's operations, concentrated on producing residual fuel oil, irrelevant and unnecessary with consequent serious repercussions on the local economy and on employment. Texaco is an integral part of all these plans, and the people in its global head office will be well aware of the truth of what we are saying, whether the local people and our government are aware or not.

Given the extreme seriousness of the situation and the future portents, it is imperative that this country maximizes the benefits it derives from the local oil industry over the next few years. This country's benefits from the oil industry are essentially two-fold: wages and tax receipts. We must maximize both of these while we can before Texaco and the other multinationals, now expressing such warm interest in our development and well-being, ruthlessly cast us aside. Now whatever is denied from us as wages largely leaves the country, since the effective tax rate is no more than about 55% (corporation tax plus unemployment levy plus withholding tax). It is, therefore, imperative that wage payments be maximized if the torrent of wealth now gushing abroad through Texaco's profit is to be stemmed somewhat.

Increased wages, as is well known by now, benefit the country through the effects of the income and employment multiplier. Finally we need spend no time disproving the old, tired and false argument that increased wages to oilworkers lead other wages upward and causes inflation. We thoroughly debunked this fallacy three years ago, and even the Industrial Court in its judgement on the OWTU-Texaco case of 1975 rejected this argument.

Summary

In all, therefore, the OWTU is claiming a wage increase of 100.8% over the next three years based on the above six considerations.

Texaco and South Africa: An Appendix

The following proposal was submitted by certain stockholders of the Company:

WHEREAS in South Africa the black majority is controlled and oppressed by a white minority which comprises 18% of the population,

WHEREAS South Africa's apartheid system legalizes racial discrimination in all aspects of life and deprives the black population of their most basic human rights e.g. Africans cannot vote, cannot collectively bargain, must live in racially segregated areas, are paid grossly discriminatory wages, are assigned 13% of the land while 87% of the land is reserved for the white population,

WHEREAS the South African system of white minority rule called apartheid has been widely condemned by the U.S. government and numerous international bodies,

WHEREAS black opposition to apartheid and black demands for full political, legal and social rights in their country has risen dramatically within the last year,

WHEREAS widespread killing, arrests and repression have been the response of the white South African government to nationwide demonstrations for democratic rights,

WHEREAS Prime Minister Vorster has openly declared his intention to maintain apartheid and deny political rights to South African blacks,

WHEREAS we believe that U.S. business investments in the Republic of South Africa, including our Company's operations, provide significant economic support and moral legitimacy to South Africa's apartheid government,

THEREFORE BE IT RESOLVED: that the shareholders request the Board of Directors to establish the following as corporate policy:

> "Texaco and any of its subsidiaries or affiliates
> shall terminate its present operations in the Republic of South Africa as expeditiously as possible unless and until the South African government has committed itself to ending the legally enforced form of racism called apartheid and has taken meaningful steps toward the achievement of full political, legal and social rights for the majority population (African, Asian, Coloured)."

Supporting Statement

As Church investors we believe that Caltex's investment in South Africa strengthens apartheid and white minority rule and, therefore Caltex should begin to withdraw.

The oil industry in South Africa is extremely strategic and the white government looks to it to provide petroleum products for the overall economy and its expanding military forces. Meanwhile, South Africa is attempting to suppress a virtual nationwide rebellion by its black population, continues to occupy Namibia illegally and recently invaded Angola. We feel that Caltex's strategic investment significantly involves it, willingly or not, in assisting South Africa's apartheid government as it pursues these policies. If South Africa's access to oil production, oil exploration and oil supplies were limited it would be a severe challenge to them.

We believe that oil refined in South Africa is sold through third parties to Rhodesia thus violating international sanctions and strengthening Ian Smith's illegal regime. Caltex says it is unable to control such third party sales.

Caltex has argued that their South African presence is a constructive force for social change. We believe that recent events indicate this claim is false and that Caltex's investment bolsters the racist status quo of apartheid.

Management's Statement

The Board of Directors recommends a vote **Against** this stockholders' proposal for the following reasons:

This suggestion that the Company abandon investments and interests in South Africa is essentially the same as the proposal to curtail expansion in South Africa which was overwhelmingly rejected by stockholder vote at the 1976 Annual Meeting.

The initiation or continuation of investments in any area is not, and never has been, intended as an indication of this Company's, or its affiliates', support for any political party or particular form of government. Investment decisions are made as such; the Company's policy, and that of its affiliates, is to avoid involvement in or interference with the political affairs of any nation. This policy does not mean that the Company is callous to conditions existing in the areas in which it operates.

Texaco believes that continuation of Caltex's operations in South Africa is in the best interests of Texaco's stockholders as well as Caltex's employees of all races in South Africa. In this regard, the continued presence of Caltex in South Africa does not constitute an endorsement of South African policies. Rather, it simply reflects the long-standing policy of carrying on commercial activities in compliance with the laws of the different countries in which operations are conducted.

In reaching these conclusions, the Company is fully aware of the present social, political and economic situation in South Africa. In Management's opinion, if Caltex were to withdraw from South Africa in an attempt to achieve political changes in that country, as the proposal directs, it would be interfering with United States foreign policy which under the law is reserved to the Government.

Moreover, such withdrawal would endanger prospects for the future of all Caltex employees in South Africa regardless of race. We are convinced that the resulting dislocation and hardship would fall most heavily on the non-white communities. In this regard, and contrary to the implications of the stockholders' statement, Caltex employment policies include equal pay for equal work and the same level of benefit plans for all employees as well as a continuing and successful program to advance employees to positions of responsibility on the basis of ability, not race.

Further, the wording of the proposal would put the Company and Caltex in the position of having to decide what constitutes "meaningful steps toward the achievement of full political, legal and social rights . . .". The impracticality of such a burden as the proposal would place on the Company and Caltex is self-evident.

7. Libya: Class and State in an Oil Economy

Ruth First

Libya, unlike Saudi Arabia, Kuwait and Iran, is not one of the largest and wealthiest oil states; nor is her political system similar. Nonetheless, oil economies impose certain characteristic forms of skewed underdevelopment on all oil-producing societies, so that Libya is perhaps as good an instance as any to serve as the starting point for an explanation of these forms.[1]

The oil economy could be seen as arising from the conditions of the rentier state. Rentier states, according to H. Mahdavy who demonstrates the case of Iran,[2] are countries that receive substantial amounts of external rents on a regular basis, paid by foreign governments or foreign concerns. Payments for the passage of ships through the Suez Canal (allowing for the operating and capital costs involved) are external rents. The same holds for payments to countries in the Middle East that have oil pipelines passing through their territories. Above all, oil revenues received by governments of oil-producing and exporting countries are external rents. The distinguishing characteristic of the rentier state is that: 'The oil revenues received by the governments of the oil-producing and exporting countries have very little to do with the production processes of their domestic economies. The inputs from the local economies — other than raw materials — are insignificant.' The turning-point in the economic history of the Middle East came during the 1950s when Anglo-American rivalry over the control of Middle East oil enabled governments in the region to appropriate a larger share of the rents that had accrued to the oil companies as profits. The public sectors in the rentier states began to receive rents on a scale that affected the pace and pattern of their economies to a degree previously unknown. These governments could thus embark upon large public expenditure programmes without resorting to taxation and without running into drastic balance of payments or expenditure problems. Since oil revenues typically increase at a spectacularly faster rate than the gross national product of local economies, the public sector of these countries expanded rapidly. The government became the dominant factor in the economy — and out of this, significantly, a special form of *étatisme* was to grow.

The analysis of the social base of this form of *étatisme* presents formidable difficulties, for not only are there knotty problems in the theorization of the state form of these underdeveloped societies, but this necessarily involves an analysis of the specific social formation penetrated by the international oil economy.

But at the more limited level of state direction of the economy and state planning strategies, the oil revenues that accrue to governments in the form of rents make possible spectacular government expenditure and thus certain features of rapid economic growth, without corresponding changes in the society at large. This is because the hallmark of the rentier state is the generation of an expensive product by an industry that employs very few people and very few local resources, so that participation in productive economic activity in the modern sector is extremely low. There is no nexus between production and income distribution, since revenues accrue directly to the government not through any production but from oil taxes which come from outside the economy. Government expenditures and development programmes become totally dependent upon oil revenues and consumption patterns become geared to the use of imported commodities.

The rentier state can achieve dramatic rises in *per capita* income without going through the social and organizational changes usually associated with the processes of economic growth. It need not train labour; it can purchase it abroad. But with technology static except in the oil industry and with little change in the country's social structures and in standards of education and training, prospects for long-run growth and development are gloomy. A consequence of the rentier state is that the usual development process is reversed – instead of the progression from agriculture to industry to services, oil provokes the growth of only the third sector (services), directly in the shape of all the ancillary services that the oil companies need: accommodation, pipelines and storage tanks, supplies to the desert and provision for the army of workers (foreign and Libyan). The tertiary sector, always disproportionate in underdeveloped societies, thus grows to elephantine proportions. Certain hallmarks of development are present in the housing, infrastructure and social services which expanded government revenue can purchase, but these signs are deceptive for levels of production everywhere, except in the oil sector, remain virtually unchanged, at least in the initial period. Oil offers industrial use in the shape of fertilisers, plastics, detergents, natural gas and the whole range of petrochemical products. But the technology, the know-how and the organization necessary for the development of these sectors of production are highly complicated for a backward economy. They can, of course, be purchased abroad.

Agriculture which, before oil, had supported the greatest majority of the population, suffers a serious reverse. Labour rushes towards the urban service sector, agricultural production declines, and a new cycle commences: the use of oil revenues to purchase food. The country remains a producer and exporter of raw materials – in this instance the heavily price-favoured commodity of oil – and it imports not only capital goods but even essential everyday commodities. Oil rents offer a semblance of prosperity, but in fact they insert Libya ever more deeply into the division of labour of the international economy.

My original work on Libya made rather central use of this notion of a rentier state and the skewed sequence of development it is invariably tempted to initiate. It remains, perhaps, a useful entry to the exercise of describing the planning tendencies adopted by the state of an oil-producing economy. At the same time, proceeding from the fact of an oil-based economy to the facts of the state's planning strategy leaves certain vital issues unquestioned. In the original work I posed certain problems: In the midst of spectacular state expenditures, were important conditions for long-run change receiving attention? Was the level of economic participation of the mass of the population being raised? Were political means for mobilizing human resources being used?[3] These still seem valid questions, but they were posed in an indeterminate, unspecific, populist fashion; and this left them confined within the development/underdevelopment problematic recently so effectively questioned. Ann Phillips in 'The Concept of Development'[4] argues that notions of development, even when espoused by the theorists of underdevelopment as an indictment of capitalism, have begged essential questions. This is because development is handled as an ostensibly neutral, technical, non-class process. There is uncritical acceptance of the concept of 'national development'. Samir Amin's model of the autocentric economy[5] — that 'normal' development should correspond to a fully autonomous capitalism — is the best-known theorized conception. This approach assumes that governments seeking to alter their relations within the international economy represent an uncontentious assembly of interests within their respective societies, each in need of a self-reliant development strategy. Questions, says Phillips, should be asked not about development, but about capitalism, class forces and politics, and this precludes any notion of 'national' development. This is a concept linked not to class analysis but to Third Worldist politics. So if the questions posed about Libya are to be sharpened, they cannot rest with any notion of a 'rational' deployment of resources in the interests of balanced rather than skewed development. They have to probe the character of the Libyan state, itself arising out of the nature of the Libyan social formation, the balance of class forces and the class struggle, and the social forces on whose behalf this state acts. Which are the ruling classes, the dominant classes? And how is the character of the state to be explained not only by domestic class alignments, but in terms of the relationship between domestic classes and the international bourgeoisie whose writ runs through the international oil industry.

The State in the Post-Colonial Society

If these are the central issues, the answers to them are locked in the growing but convoluted debate about the nature of the state in post-colonial or underdeveloped societies. For the most part, Marxist analysis of the state has been preoccupied with advanced capitalist societies. Only recently were attempts made to deal with the problem of the form of the state in peripheral capitalist society, the underdeveloped society, on a basis which acknowledges social formations in such societies to be distinct from the historical experience of advanced capitalisms. For while the industrial revolutions of the latter were the outcome of a continuous process over four centuries, a process which included exploitation of the resources of the underdeveloped world, underdeveloped societies were constrained to be export-oriented economies concentrating on the production of limited products in an international division of labour imposed by the advanced capitalisms. This dependent place in the international division of labour was consolidated in the internal social structure of underdeveloped countries.

In underdeveloped societies forcibly subjected to the needs of advanced capital, state forms were devised in the interests of metropolitan capital and the metropolitan bourgeoisies. It is from this understanding that Hamza Alavi theorized the post-colonial state.[6] He argued that, unlike Marx's primary view of the state as the executive of the bourgeoisie, the colonial state was not the organized power of one class for oppressing others, but had to exercise power over *all* indigenous social classes. To this purpose the colonial state was equipped with a powerful military-bureaucratic apparatus to exercise this domination. At independence the direct command of the metropolitan bourgeoisie over the colonial state is lifted. But its influence is by no means brought to an end; the metropolitan bourgeoisie is still present in the post-colonial society, though it is now joined by neo-colonial bourgeoisies and landed interests. Arguing from the case of Pakistan, Alavi sees the bureaucratic-military apparatus which was devised by the colonial state as being vastly 'over-developed' by comparison with the weak indigenous propertied classes. Whereas the state in the original capitalist centres is the instrument of the bourgeoisie and possesses only relative autonomy with respect to the different factions of that class, the post-colonial state (in Pakistan) is the instrument of three, partly competing, dominant classes: the indigenous bourgeoisie, the metropolitan bourgeoisie and the landowning classes. And it is this unstable balance between the different dominating classes — in what might be called the power bloc — which gives a particular autonomy to the over-developed bureaucratic-military apparatus. Alavi's argument is that the state 'superstructures' are vastly over-developed in relation to the underlying structures, and that the post-colonial state has inherited that overdeveloped apparatus and its institutional practices from its colonial predecessor.

Alavi's exposition raises several thorny issues. There is the notion of the state as 'relatively autonomous' and also 'overdeveloped'.[7] This is to conceive of the state in its most limited sense — as the state apparatus and personnel — but clearly an understanding of the nature of differing state activities and their relationship to the organization of production can only proceed in the light of an analysis of class structure and of the character of the dominant classes. It is this latter issue — the character of the dominant classes — that has proved the most intractable.

For some writers[8] the post-colonial social formation is characterized not by any balance of class forces, as Alavi argues for Pakistan, between domestic and metropolitan classes, but, on the contrary, by the frailty of indigenous classes. Where indigenous classes are weak, it is argued, the petty bourgeoisie rushes in to fill the breach. It does not possess an infrastructure of economic power before it wins political power, but it acts to transform the state into a source of economic power, and the state becomes the instrument for the installation of the petty bourgeoisie in these societies. At this point the exposition branches out into two variations. In the first, the petty bourgeoisie, very much still in the process of formation, 'swirls around' the post-colonial state.[9] So fluid is this class that it cannot be said with any certainty which factions within the petty bourgeoisie, if such can be located, achieve control of the state and place their own stamp upon events. These could act either for progressive purposes or for neo-colonial purposes. This view has elicited the critique that a theory of petty-bourgeois politics is really no theory of politics at all.[10] For the category of petty bourgeoisie is not defined in terms of social relations of production, distribution and exchange. Instead politics, having been presumed to be a manifestation of class struggle, the petty bourgeoisie is defined as a class by its political activities alone. The analysis is thus tautological: political conflicts are explained by showing their class basis in the petty bourgeoisie; the petty bourgeoisie is defined by the very political conflicts which the concept has been used to explain in the first instance. Political analysis has given way to an evaluation of the ideological drift of this or that group in power, and the attempt to analyse the character of the dominant class forces of the state has been grounded at the level of 'ideology'.

In the second variation of the theory, the faction of the petty bourgeoisie that achieves control of the state machine at independence is seen as a class in the making, a class of a new type. This is not a class that owns the means of production, but one that controls them, using state power to appropriate and control productive resources, and to serve as collective manager of the so-called public sector. It has been termed a bureaucratic bourgeoisie: a bourgeoisie by virtue of its control of the bureaucracy, the state machine.[11]

But the class character of the state cannot be discovered by an inspection of the class interests of the state bureaucracy, as Leys points out:

> One of the valuable points made by Nicos Poulantzas in his book *Political Power and Social Classes* is that it is a mistake to think that the class origins, class ties or class ambitions of the individuals who compose the apparatus of the state need be the same as those of the dominant class, or that state power reflects their own class interests, except in a secondary way. The first question must always be which class is dominant in a given social formation, since this dominance must be enforced by the state; the class character of the state is given by this relationship . . . . The class interests of the bureaucracy, whether they are congruent with those of the dominant class, or in conflict with them, are unlikely to be the determining factor in establishing or upsetting that dominance.[12]

In other words, the central question remains a structural one: in whose class interests does the state function? In post-colonial societies there can be little doubt that the dominant class is still the foreign — or international — bourgeoisie.

The difficulty is that, in resuscitating the importance of the metropolitan bourgeoisie (from the colonial to the post-colonial period), this approach could tend to cause the specificity of the state form of the post-colonial society to evaporate. Contradictions between domestic and international classes are then by-passed and politics in the underdeveloped world merely read off the manipulations of international capital, the state becoming a mere reflection of the economy. It is, of course, undeniable that the economies of the underdeveloped world continue to be dominated by international capitalism. But it is important not to neglect the particularity of the process at the level of the underdeveloped state form. For this would take us back to the theory criticised by Ann Phillips which investigates the relationships between national and international capital, but neglects the analysis of dominant classes within the underdeveloped society in their relationship with oppressed classes. The nature of the contradictions between the latter are of crucial importance, not least in the impact of state-determined development strategies which presume that the interests of the 'nation' are one.

In an attempt to cure this difficulty the distinction is made by Van Freyhold,[13] also following Poulantzas' work, between the ruling class and the governing class — the metropolitan and domestic dominant classes respectively. Unless the governing (domestic) class actually determines the process of economic reproduction in the country, it cannot be called a ruling class however large its formal power may be. While the governing class must really carry into effect the interests of the real (metropolitan) ruling class, the latter requires activist states on the periphery, which can make foreign interests profitable and which can suppress growing internal social contradictions. Derived from the Tanzanian experience, though not restricted to it, this explanation sees domestic dominant classes unable to escape their servitude to the metropolitan bourgeoisie.

The Libyan State

The Libyan state has projected itself as distinctly different. Its oil policies are avowedly not only independent of international oil interests, but even in confrontation with them. An understanding of how deep this contradiction really runs rests on an analysis of the relationship between producer states and the oil corporations over issues not only of pricing policy but, more importantly, of the organization of production for capital accumulation within this powerful industry. Within Libya state policy has been predicated on the assertion of radical social forces which were unleashed with the military seizure of power in 1969. The character of these forces, the forms in which they are organized and represented in the Libyan state and, not least, the extent to which they are likely to assert interests in conflict with those of metropolitan capital, can be tested only in a scrutiny of the social formation as a whole, seen historically in at least the most recent period.

The greater part of Libya is desert. This has throughout its history placed severe limits on the utilisation of land, with agricultural production restricted to coastal areas and the better-watered hill country. Conditions are thus not conducive to the formation of a large peasantry, one of the characteristics distinguishing Libya from the peasant societies of Egypt, Iraq, Syria and other parts of the Maghreb. In Libya, forms of social organization for production developed which were appropriate to inhospitable desert conditions. Around the oases the need for labour-intensive construction and maintenance of irrigation systems absorbed serfs, but the drying-up of the source of this labour and its interruption by the trans-Sahara slave trade undermined the economic base of these societies. Over time, and especially after the development of oil, the outflow of population to the modern sector of the economy disrupted the productive system, eventually necessitating the importation of food from outside.[14] The vast desert interior offered negligible productive surplus and made necessary nomadic organization based on small herds and self-sufficient kin (tribal) communities. (As late as 1964 the census data showed that, of every 100 people enumerated, 12 were still nomadic and 9 semi-nomadic.) Among the bedouin, discrete portions of the tribal territory, running from the coast to the fringes of the Sahara, were identified with segments of the tribal genealogy; marriage and kin ties linked the system together in patterns of mutually obligatory aid.[15] Within the tribal structure there were horizontal divisions between the majority tribes who claimed the land and water by right of conquest, and the minority or vassal tribes which used earth and water by grace of the free tribes. The core of the distinction was property rights, for the client tribes had to be granted access to land and water by their patrons, and this privilege had to be periodically renewed. Over time, because the surplus was marginal, and with near-drought conditions lasting numbers of years, the differences between patron and client tribes began to fall away. Yet while it was often difficult to distinguish between them, as late as the independence elections of 1950, all the candidates from the semi-desert areas were from the dominant lineages. The spread of the Sanusi order into the eastern interior of Libya during the 19th century provided a system of authority over and above the segmentary tribal system, and the Sanusi notables, by virtue of their control over land and water resource allocation and long-distance trade in the interior, constituted a ruling class.

Until the Italian colonization of 1911, Libya was under Turkish domination. The Turks ruled the coastal towns of Tripoli, Benghazi, Derna and Misurata, where the bulk of urban dwellers were descendants of merchants, marabouts from other parts of North Africa, or officials of the Ottoman administration. The Sanusi order in the Cyrenaica interior acted as intermediaries for the collection of taxes for the Turkish state.

The latter period of Turkish rule was marked by the expansion of maritime trade promoted by European capital, and the formation of a tiny local and largely commercial bourgeoisie concentrated in the coastal towns. The subsequent entry of capital into Libya was connected with the Italian occupation.

The Italian colonization was a demographic colonization undertaken to solve the overpopulation problems of the agricultural provinces of southern Italy, and to give Italy access to external supplies of grain and oil and strategic and trade access to the Mediterranean. The settlement of Italian peasant producers required the confiscation of tribal lands, the decimation of herds and extensive pacification exercises. From 1911 to 1934 the population declined by 13 per cent. Cyrenaica lost 90 per cent of her flocks. Italian land acquisition had totalled less than 10,000 hectares by the end of 1923, but it rose to twenty times that area in the next five years. By 1940 Italian colonizing efforts were making possible the intensive use of irrigated land. Italian colonization efforts more than doubled the farmland area under use. But it was for use by Italian settlers. In the administration Libyans were employed only in minor posts; by 1940 there were only 14 Arabs employed in the civil service in other than menial jobs. These were mostly townsmen from Derna and Benghazi, some members of Turkish families, most with a record of collaboration with the Italian system. Only towards the end of Italian rule was an attempt made to groom a new class of indigenous officials brought up in the towns under Italian rule and educated in Italian-Arab schools. This was the group ready to co-operate with the British military administration when the Second World War detached Libya from Italy's control.

Following a period of Allied military occupation, Libya became independent in 1951, out of the Cold War intrigues of the post-war period. (Perhaps out of hindsight, this independence was seen by some to be a creation of oil capital; there had been oil exploration some time before the actual oil strikes.) The political character of the newly independent state was carefully shaped under the tutelage of Britain and France. If Libya was to be insulated from the currents of Arab nationalism, the tribal structures of the Sanusi order had to be guaranteed dominance over such urban nationalist forces as were emerging. The head of the Sanusi order was installed as monarch, creating a regime whose legitimacy derived from two principal sources: the claim to religious authority exercised over the lodges of the Sanusi order and the tribal notables who presided over the allocation of grazing and water rights within traditionally defined areas. They were joined by townsmen and business families picked for their complicity with the system of political patronage.

Oil was struck in 1955. It brought about a massive inflow of capital which in turn gave rise to serious internal contradictions. The oil period opened with a series of financial scandals prompted by the *enrichissez-vous* activities of the ruling group around the monarchy. Access to government now gave access to business and financial manipulations. When foreign firms needed go-betweens for contract negotiations, they used ministers and members of parliament with influence in government departments and tender boards. The spill-off fed a Libyan private sector of real estate and property speculation; transport, catering, and other services auxiliary to the oil industry; and foreign trade. After the mid-1960s the growing group of newly-trained technicians and professionals were incorporated into the political system; many had links, of course, with the older traditional families. The ruling class that had presided over the allocation of resources in bedouin society was being fused with an emerging commercial bourgeoisie, far stronger than, though not necessarily distinct from, the older class of town merchants.

There were growing contradictions, too, at another level. The price of Libyan independence had been a state heavily committed to the West and its policies in the Middle East. This was perhaps the overt cause of the 1969 coup which overturned the monarchy eighteen years after its establishment. Ideological politics, as distinct from the politics of the tribe and the patronage of the palace, emerged slowly and tentatively as the nationalist stirrings of the Arab world began to impinge on Libya. When independence produced its first generations of university students the majority entered Egyptian universities and became involved in nationalist politics of the Nasserite or Baathist variety. Libya's first army officers were trained in the Baghdad Academy.

The coup which toppled the monarchy and installed an army regime presided over by the Revolutionary Command Council (R.C.C.) emerged from the junior officer ranks of the Libyan army. There was a highly significant pattern in the social composition of the R.C.C. group and the Free Officer Movement from which they had sprung. Only two members of the R.C.C. were members of majority tribes; the others, with one exception, came from minor tribes and poorer families of the interior or, in the case of those born on the coast, from the poorer social strata, not the traditional urban citizenry or the new rich families. It appeared to be a revolution of the oases and the interior against the large town families and dominant tribal leaders. The ideology of the R.C.C. was expressed in a denunciation of 'corruption' which, summed up in frequent diatribes, seemed to be the private acquisition, through political influence, of resources generated by the oil economy. The anti-corruption thrust was combined with Arab nationalist slogans against Western political involvement in the Middle East and Western control of the oil industry.

The Gadafi regime made important breaks with the past in some ways, though not in others. When it came to oil policy, the R.C.C. asserted Libya's control over her resources by means of two principal methods: by intervening in pricing policy and by achieving state participation in actual production. This was an important break with the policy under the monarchy of leaving the oil sector exclusively to the corporations. When it came to development policy, the state's intervention generated even more resources than the previous share of oil rent, but the use of these resources under the development strategy of the Gadafi-run state was for the greater part a continuity, though on a more extravagant scale, of the previous regime's activities. Finally, though increased state intervention in the economy generated more revenue within Libya, the military regime initiated policies calculated to freeze such formation of propertied classes that had been the product of the monarchical period. These three aspects – oil policy, the economic role of the state, and the processes of internal class formation – need to be reviewed in turn.

(i) Oil Policies

Libya's oil law of 1955 had laid the basis for an oil industry very different in structure from Aramco's monopoly of Saudi Arabia's oilfields or Basra's in Iraq, where a single giant cartel exercised control over the entire oil concession, without necessarily working it. Libya had to break into the oil business at a time of plentiful supply, and United States oilfields were operating at only part capacity. Oil companies had to be seduced to open up new fields, and Libya's oil law accordingly went out of its way to offer favourable inducements to smaller and competing oil interests. Anxious to break into the industry, independent oil companies not owned by the majors played an important part in casting the law. A ceiling was set on the maximum number of concessions and the total areas to be held by any one interest; concession holders had to surrender unused concessions after a stipulated period of time, and the government was free to offer a relinquished concession for competitive bidding once again. The law thus ensured rapid turnover of concessions and maximum competition between oil companies. The idea was to induce the largest possible number of competitive bidders to enter Libya in search of oil, and the plan worked.

The Libyan oil industry grew at an unprecedented rate. It was the first oil-producing country to exceed production of a million barrels a day in less than five years from the start of production. By the end of 1967 40 companies were operating in the country, 17 of them exporting oil. Instead of having to deal with a group-company operating as a unit, as in the older oil-producing areas of the Middle East, Libya faced a flock of individual firms, for the competitive conditions had induced both majors and independents to enter the country. By 1965 the independents were extracting just under half of Libya's total oil production. Esso, the world's largest oil company, which owns one-third of Aramco, was the largest producer among the majors in Libya; but a group of three independents, combined in Oasis (Amerada, Continental and Marathon), produced almost as much.

It was the heavy presence of the independent companies that was to give Libya its leverage over the industry. But not until the change of regime in 1969 was advantage taken of these special conditions. The closing of the Suez Canal after the Six Day War put Libya, already on Europe's doorstep, at an enormous geographical advantage. But the old regime was reluctant to take advantage of it. In the Oil Ministry the technicians were pressing for tough government action to assert its right to take part in price-fixing, but the Cabinet was in awe of the companies and felt beholden to them. Eventually the companies agreed to pay Libya (and Saudi Arabia whose oil went in part via the Trans-Arabian pipeline to the Lebanese port of Sidon) an allowance as a 'temporary' measure, and the government was conciliated. The price issue was never brought to a head. The government accepted the company's oil royalty payments 'under protest'; but these periodic protests were casually treated by the companies as annual pro forma complaints. The timid gestures and conservative thinking of a regime chronically dependent on Britain and the United States died hard. Apart from the regime's dependence on the West, the government was indebted to some of the oil companies for loans to make up deficits in the budget. During 1968 attempts to limit the wasteful flaring of gas were side-tracked, again by government pusillanimity. Negotiations with the companies over a higher price were due to open in September 1969 but there was a general scepticism that the government would hold its ground.

The new regime came to power that September, and as early as January 1970 its price-hiking strategy was launched. There was the danger that if Libya raised prices to a level higher than Gulf or West African oil, the majors would substitute supplies from these areas for Libyan oil. But Occidental, which accounted for almost one-third of Libya's output, could not shift its production, which was all in Libya. Conveniently, the Trans-Arabian pipeline (Tapline) was blocked at this time. Libya imposed production cutbacks on several of the operating companies. These were said to be conservation measures in no way related to the price issue, but then Libya seized her moment and took the companies on one by one. Occidental, as the most vulnerable, came first, and it capitulated. The others were called in their turn. The new Libyan price at $2.53 a barrel was the highest then paid outside the United States. But far from this being seen as a final settlement, Libya announced that it was merely a rectification of past injustices. In the next round of negotiations advantage was taken of the fact that Libyan oil was not only on the Mediterranean side of the Canal, a few days' delivery from Europe's ports, but was also excellent quality, low-gravity crude with good viscosity and a comparatively low sulphur content. Libya's success in asserting her own price-fixing interests prompted OPEC-directed action by all oil-producing countries, and her example acted as a prod to generalized price increases for all producers.

Libya's tough tactics were fortified by huge reserves. There was the psychological advantage held by a regime that had just nationalized the banks and whose chief spokesman was announcing that Libya could do not only without the oil companies but even without oil. Libya's case was based on already available OPEC studies on oil price-fixing, and some of it had even been prepared by the Oil Ministry under the monarchy. What was needed was a regime with a blazing sense of persecution at the hands of foreign oil monopolies and the reckless abandon with which Gadafi and his colleagues entered the fray.

Yet the higher price agreement gains of 1970 and 1971 were still within the framework of the oil industry as it had always operated. Arguments about posted price or realized price, raising or lowering the price, bonuses for quality and freight advantage, were all moves within the same circle. The companies continued to manipulate the market, to control all downstream (including refining) facilities, and company profits continued to climb steadily upwards. It was in the interests of the United States companies, which had control of the market, for the price to rise. Higher prices also made marginal fields in the United States itself more economic.

In part it was this dominance of the United States oil companies which explained the trend, which Libya now turned to, for oil deals to be made between producer and consumer state companies. The monarchy had initiated some joint ventures, though most of their discoveries had not been of commercial value. In September 1972 E.N.I., the Italian state oil company, signed a 50-50 participation agreement with LINOCO, the Libyan state oil company which subsequently became N.O.C. (National Oil Company). N.O.C. was intended to be a fully integrated oil company operating exploration, drilling, transport of crude oil, and processing through a petrochemical industry. Any future participation by foreign-owned oil companies would take the form of partnership agreements with N.O.C. In addition, N.O.C. was assigned all concession areas relinquished by foreign companies. Since 1973 the government has concluded a number of production sharing arrangements with Western companies to open new fields. Under these arrangements the foreign partner bears the exploration risk and ultimately the cost of developing commercial finds. Production is split either 85-15 or 81-19 in favour of the state.

The state share in the older companies is smaller: a 59.2 per cent in Oasis, for instance. N.O.C. as the state company is marketing some of the crude oil it gets from its participation fields, though these remain the minority oil-producing fields. The petrochemical plants being financed under the development plans are under N.O.C. control, as will be the tanker fleet also provided for in the plans — despite the slump in the tanker market.

Libya's revenue from oil has grown spectacularly, though annual production figures have been cut back. This is consistent with the regime's policy of conserving resources and seeking increased revenues rather than increased production (Libya's reserves are not high by the standards of the Gulf producers). It has been a highly successful policy — witness the fact that by the beginning of 1974 Libya was earning almost seven times its 1970 revenue although oil output over the period had dropped by half. The growing inverse relationship between increased revenue and reduced production levels can be seen for the years 1968 to 1974:

Libya: Oil Output and State Revenue, 1968-1975

	1968	*1969*	*1970*	*1971*	*1972*	*1973*	*1974*	*1975*
Libyan state oil revenue p.a. (US $ billions)	952	1.132	1.295	1.766	1.953	4.020	8.232	6.000
Libyan daily oil output (millions of barrels)	2.605	3.110	3.320	2.765	2.240	2.180	1.525	1.490

The 1974-75 slump in oil demand, and the oil companies' reaction to Libya's aggressive oil policy, led to reduced demand for Libyan oil; for the first four months of 1975 production fell to below 800,000 barrels a day. The Libyan government responded in mid-1975 by cutting oil prices. In 1976, 1.9 million barrels a day were sold. By 1977 higher production targets had to be set to pay for the government's ambitious development programmes. Thus the target for 1978 was set at 2.3 million barrels a day. This was later reduced to 2.1 million barrels a day, since it was apparent that the original target would not be met. With extravagant development plans under way, and despite handsome oil revenues, it was becoming clear that development financing would require the careful handling of oil.

(ii) The Economic Role of the Libyan State

Not that this consideration weighed with the new, or for that matter, the old regime. From the moment that oil revenues flowed, Libya's economy became one of the fastest growing in the world. In the first decade of its independence, Libya's principal exports had been esparto grass, used in paper-making, and scrap metal salvaged from the debris of the Second World War. Libya's books were balanced then only by British and American military base rentals, and the first so-called development agencies functioned under the direct supervision of Libya's foreign creditors. The average income of the population was £15 a head in 1971. As in Kuwait and Saudi Arabia, oil brought a precipitate leap from rags to riches. Suddenly this state began to amass such handsome reserves that, however profligate, the country seemed unable to bankrupt itself. But oil was now laying down the characteristic patterns of the oil economy, as seen in the drastically unequal contributions of various sectors to the gross domestic product. Agriculture shrank dramatically. Manufacturing, small as it was, also declined in relative importance, though in absolute figures its contributions to gross domestic product increased.

Sectoral Contribution to Gross Domestic Product (in percentages)

		at factor cost	*at constant 1964 prices*		
		1962	*1965*	*1968*	*1969*
1.	Agriculture	9.7	4.9	2.6	2.4
2.	Petroleum and quarrying	27.2	54.8	61.3	65.0
3.	Manufacturing	5.6	2.6	2.2	2.0
4.	Construction	7.1	7.0	6.9	5.6
5.	Electricity and gas	0.5	0.3	0.3	0.4
6.	Transportation	5.5	3.8	4.0	3.6
7.	Trade	8.6	5.1	4.6	4.1
8.	Banking and Insurance	1.1	1.4	1.2	1.2
9.	Public admin. & defence	9.7	7.4	7.4	6.8
10.	Educational services	3.2	2.6	2.5	2.5
11.	Health services	1.3	0.9	1.1	1.0
12.	Ownership of dwellings	17.2	7.5	4.8	4.5
13.	Other services	3.3	1.7	1.1	0.9
	Gross domestic product	*100.0*	*100.0*	*100.0*	*100.0*

This pattern was firmly laid during the 1960s, hardly to change in the ensuing years except to confirm itself. Whereas agriculture had been the only means of livelihood for the great majority of the population, there was, with the coming of oil, a rapid rush of migration from the countryside to the coastal towns. The rush for the proceeds of oil attracted far more people off the land than the oil industry could absorb. The result was crowded urban centres coupled with deserted farmland in many parts of the country. A side-effect was the sudden increase in the demand for food in the towns as a result of the increased urban population, the rise in consumption levels, and the extravagant consumption by foreigners in the oil industry. This might have been a stimulus to agricultural production but the low state of technology in agriculture was one of the factors that made this impossible. In any event, there were higher profits to be made in the trade and service sectors of the economy. So both capital and labour moved away from agriculture. Libya turned to world markets for the purchase of its daily food. Agricultural exports declined from a value of £L1,230,000 in 1956 to £L600,000 in 1961, and to only £L32,000 in 1968; this was not enough to pay for Libya's import of food for one-third of a single day! From here on, the circle grew even tighter. Imported food became an easy alternative to the development of domestic production. The government under the monarchy lacked the determination either to use fiscal measures to favour agricultural investment or to discourage unproductive activities such as real estate speculation. In any case, the latter was not a politically feasible step for a government that relied on the support of the growing commercial bourgeoisie. During the period 1952-62 the discovery of oil produced its greatest adverse effect on agriculture. Although the more modern farms, mainly still operated by Italians, remained in production, their relative position in the economy deteriorated.

Side by side with the decline of all the productive sectors except that of oil, there started a pattern of indiscriminate, extravagant expenditure and of giantism in planning. It began under the monarchy, but continued after the army revolution. In the first Five Year Plan, drawn up in 1963, the concentration was on infrastructural projects, and much of the expenditure of this plan laid down the foundation of an infrastructure that had previously been missing. The government was less successful when it came to human capital. It started a ruinous policy which is the temptation before every rentier state. The classic method is to offer any citizen who wanted it a job, and the state multiplied the posts in its bureaucracy accordingly. The administration was smothered with useless civil servants, workers, orderlies and watchmen. The jobs created by the state were often disguised unemployment and the salaries disguised handouts. The policy led to a serious manpower shortage in productive sectors like agriculture and building. The state absorbed manpower just when new sectors of construction and transport began to grow rapidly; this created artificial labour shortages and forced the import of manpower from outside the country.

The monarchy's Second Five Year Plan had just been launched when the Revolutionary Command Council took power. Most of the pre-revolution policies were continued, but with increased oil revenues the subsequent development plans committed the economy to even more spectacular expenditure on a huge range of infrastructural, industrial and agricultural projects. They have all been conceived, tendered and executed by foreign companies. Every ministry has its shelf of expert reports commissioned by one or other, or both, of the regimes. Advisers are falling over one another; consultants swarm all over the country. Expertise and consultancy-hire is often an adjunct of foreign policy, designed to give each of the big powers a showing, and also to spread good relations and business between a scatter of small states and so-called neutrals. The expertise in the field has this same patchwork quality. At one point several different teams were investigating underground water resources, some working the identical region, and each apparently ignoring previous work done in the field. Some advice is good, some bad, most of it goes uninterpreted and unco-ordinated. One of the technical obstacles to long-range and co-ordinated planning in Libya is that there is as yet no complete inventory of national resources. Agriculture remains the principal employment sector, yet those planning for it lack the most basic information. Virtually nothing is known of the contribution made by the subsistence sector of the economy. It is said, perhaps apocryphally, that a Minister of Planning under the previous regime complained that in the country's expectancy of miracles after oil wealth there was no time to plan. Ministries are under constant pressure to spend and have had neither the time nor the strength to prepare properly. Spending has to be seen to be done. Major Jalloud, who has been in charge of important oil negotiations and production ministries told a press conference the reason why. It was natural, he said, for any military group to produce economic and social plans for a radical change so as to convince the people and the world at large that it was not a movement aiming only at a seizure of power. This was the way army leaders could prove that they had led not a military coup d'etat but a revolution.

With each development budget, the state's financial commitment to large-scale projects has grown more spectacular.[16] A three-year 'rolling' development plan from 1972 to 1975 projected a 15 per cent growth rate in industry, agriculture and electrification. Since oil is a wasting asset, the Libyan economy has to be induced to reach conditions of self-sustained growth independent of the oil sector within a period of 20 years, it was said. Pride of place is to be given to agriculture and the building of a modern industrial sector. The next plan — for 'Economic and Social Transformation' — is to run between 1976 and 1980 and calls for a total investment of £11.5 billion. Of this sum £2 billion was due to be spent in 1976 alone. But over-allocation proved to be part of the problem; thus in 1977 little more than half the funds allocated that year to development projects had actually been spent. Bottlenecks were put down to the ambitious nature of the development effort and specifically to the shortage of labour to execute the projects.

The industrialization programme has included plans for food industries, textiles, wood and wood products, chemicals and petroleum by-products, cement and building materials, metallurgic, engineering and electrical industries, some providing not only for local needs but for export. A steel works at Misurata is to cost $1 billion; a chemical complex $515 million. Without exception the projects of the development plans involve contracting out to foreign firms, thus the $480 million power and desalination plant at Al Khoms has gone to Deutsche Babcock, and the telecommunications contract to W.G. Siemens. The costs of many of the individual projects have soared since they were initially planned, and as the development plans proceed, the rise in the cost of imported machinery and construction materials is reflected in the regular upward revision of investment allocations.

The 1976-80 Plan gives the largest allocation to agriculture, and there is continuing emphasis on the determination of the regime to reclaim the desert and transform it from barren to fertile land. The agricultural projects of the development plans are slices of Western technology inserted into the economy and, like oil, run by foreigners. The Kufra sheep-breeding project is one such instance of push-button mechanized farming in the desert. In the case of this project there appear to be no calculations about the price, ultimately, of a pound of mutton; so total is the dependence on imported technology and skilled management that the decisive factor will be the flow, not necessarily the cost, of this expertise. The policy-makers have argued that astronomic expense is no obstacle and that Libya must break its dependence on food imports at all costs. But this import dependence is being exchanged for a new dependence — on the West's advanced technology.

So while oil made Libya inescapably a part of the international capitalist system, the attempt to diversify the economy is actually perpetuating the relationship. Oil is being traded for an agricultural and industrial sector of high technology and high capital intensity, utterly reliant on the import of capital goods and skilled and managerial manpower. These sectors, by virtue of their reliance on imported technology, in fact constitute a transplanted vertical sector of international capitalist firms; they are unrelated to productive activity in the rest of the Libyan economy.

Furthermore, the development approach is characteristic of a statist style of technocratic planning. The state not only plans production, but actively intervenes in it. The great majority of the projects of the development plans are under the direction of state companies and public corporations — though these can only be executed by sub-contracting to international firms. The Gadafi regime calls its system Libyan Socialism, on the assumption that state involvement in production and socialism are one and the same thing. How legitimate this claim is involves an inspection of class relations in the Libyan social formation, and takes us back to the problem of how to theorize this kind of state.

(iii) Class Formation in Libya

The change in regime tended to freeze the process of formation of Libya's propertied classes. Under the monarchy the traditional nobility and urban commercial interests were using political influence to consolidate economic control, and an energetic and rapacious commercial bourgeoisie was emerging. The leading representatives of this class, who were the political support of the monarchy, went into exile after 1969. At the same time the Libyanization of commerce under the Gadafi regime — only Libyans are allowed to register companies and hold partnerships — provided it with new avenues. There is a marked ambivalence in the regime's policy. Its pronouncements envisage both a public and a private sector. The private sector is expected to concentrate on small, and possibly some medium-sized, industry and on retail trade. In the private sector some taps are turned off, others on. Thus in the transport sector it was decreed that no private owner should operate more than three trucks, but in the construction industry, by contrast, private capital was given a free run, and contractors and real estate investors were offered generous government loans. However, the private sector is nervous about its role and confused about the relations between the private and public sectors. (In 1969-70 when the government allocated subsidies to private investors in industry, less than a third of the allocated sum was spent.) All the major projects of the development plans, as mentioned earlier, are state undertakings under the aegis of the Industrial Corporation. There is said to be room for private industrial enterprise, but it is not clear what the regime's policy towards an emergent capitalist class is likely to be. The Charter drafted for the Arab (subsequently Libyan) Socialist Union, said that 'non-exploiting capitalists' would be tolerated, perhaps even encouraged. But what distinguishes an exploiting capitalist from a non-exploiting capitalist? It was said that exploitation would be limited by taxation, and that private enterprise would have to be synchronized with the needs of the economy, but there was little elaboration of the approach. In any event, given the scale of the industrial projects being undertaken and their massive cost, only oil revenues could possibly foot the bill. These, accruing directly to the state, make *it* the motor of the economy: there is no room for a strong indigenous bourgeoisie.

In the rural sector the change of regime also worked certain changes unfavourable to the major tribal heads and families who had been the economic and political underpinning of the monarchy. Previously, while tribal land was communally owned, its allocation for use by commoners was managed by the sheikhs. This had produced a system of patron/client relations. The first important change introduced by the Gadafi regime was to decree that land not in use was to revert to state ownership. The second, which sought to whittle away the influence of large tribal landowners, involved regulations on subsidized fodder, placing a ceiling on any individual farmer's purchase and thereby a constraint on the speculator. The purpose was to undermine the commercial activity of the tribal notables, though the exact effects are difficult to evaluate.

The system of land tenure varied considerably between the east (formerly Cyrenaica, the original domain of Sanusi power) and the west. Thus in the eastern region the percentage of tribally owned land under the monarchy was twice as high as in the west, and even this was considered an underestimate, since the 1960 census had failed to include tribal grazing land. Overall agricultural statistics produced in 1963 showed that, whereas the average farm size in the whole country was 28 hectares, in some coastal areas in the Tripoli region farms were smaller than two hectares and a third of agricultural holdings occupied only three per cent of arable land. Calculations made from the 1960 agricultural census showed that one in four landlords in western Libya owned 37 per cent of all private land, with holdings of between 20 and 100 hectares, and a third of the landed peasantry had less than five hectares each. Within the agricultural sector in western Libya, there was therefore a certain degree of class differentiation. But whereas the poor and landless had previously to turn sharecropper for the better-off landlords, with the start of the oil economy, working on the land was no longer the only source of employment. A new labour market opened, and for the people living on the land a dry year no longer meant famine or extreme hardship – there were wage labour, and even salaried, openings in the non-agricultural sector. Better-off landowners found ways to diversify their income by investing capital in the modern sector of the economy. Previously, surplus income had been invested in land or livestock; now it was likely to be invested in buildings or shops in Tripoli.

This movement of labour and capital from the rural to the urban sector was common to both regimes. The Gadafi regime instituted change in the countryside to the extent that it used former Italian settler lands for the expansion of a class of medium-sized Libyan landed proprietors. The R.C.C. promulgated a decree restoring all property usurped during the colonial period, whether agricultural land, real estate, livestock, or machinery. This was placed under sequestration to the state. A decree also banned the issue of licences or permits to Italians to practise commerce, industry, or professions in Libya. Within a month the Italians began to depart – leaving behind a number of small businesses and workshops which were put up for purchase by Libyans, and 368 farms spread over 38,000 hectares. This land was placed under the authority of a body for 'Land Reclamation and Reform'. The government was flooded with applications for the Italian farms, but they were divided into 16 projects and put under the control of Libyan agricultural managers. The first graduates of the College of Agriculture had just qualified; their postings in charge of the farms were announced over the radio. The plan was to prepare model settlement schemes for Libyans, as Italy had at one time done for her nationals. Once it had been decided which farms were economic (for they varied in size from half a hectare to 1,500 hectares) and how they would be subdivided, the lands would be planted and farmhouses built. Only then would the farmers be invited in to reap the crop and qualify for the range of subsidies and agricultural assistance. For the first 15 years the government would retain title to the land; after that it would be available for purchase. Co-operatives were talked about, but there was no consistent policy favouring them; more likely a class of farmer-proprietors was being encouraged.

So in the countryside there is now a growing yet uncertain class of medium-sized landowners heavily dependent upon state loans and assistance. This growth of a class of capitalist farmers will be slow, if not impossible, because of the capital cost of machinery and labour. As for the subsistence economy, it has experienced a steadily falling rate of productivity and a flow of unproductive rural labour to the towns. The class of propertyless rural day labourers working on private farms as well as on state-subsidized agricultural projects is largely non-Libyan, Libyans who cannot support themselves on their land tending to move into the protected urban wage economy.

Industry was late in developing and capital-intensive when it did grow, so there is only a tiny working class. The statistical department produces quarterly statistics on production and employment in 'selected large manufacturing establishments': 'large' means any establishment engaging 20 or more persons, many of these offering only seasonal work, as in canning factories. By 1970 there were only 7,306 workers in manufacturing, most of them operatives but also including 155 working proprietors and unpaid family workers. Of this total, 1,550 were in food processing factories and 1,135 in tobacco factories. Other industries in which a total of more than 500 persons were employed were textiles, chemical products, cement, and fabricated metal (though not machinery). Many of the enterprises recorded in the manufacturing sector were little more than family workshops.

The majority of industrial workers are in construction and the oil sector. By the 1970s, the oil sector itself employed just under 13,000 persons, half of these working for the concession-holding companies, and the remainder in the employ of companies providing services to the industry. The majority of the industrial enterprises inaugurated by the development plans are too new and incomplete for any conclusions to be drawn about the character of their work-force. But even with the huge expansion of industrial projects, it has been esti-mated that by the end of the 1970s industrial employment is likely to absorb no more than seven per cent of the total Libyan labour force: this is a measure of the capital intensity of the industrial projects, the low level of skill and training of Libyan manpower, and the reliance on non-Libyan manpower.

By 1972, when Libya had an estimated working population of just over half a million (of the total number in employment it was estimated that 62 per cent were wage or salaried employees, and the rest tradesmen, proprietors, farmers, craftsmen and family workers), for every six Libyans working there was one non-Libyan, and this was considered an under-estimate of the real numbers of non-Libyans employed in the economy. Later figures have put the number of foreign workers at one-third of the workforce. It is estimated that by 1980 40 per cent of the workforce will still be expatriates. The majority of Libyans work in the lower skill level occupations, and the majority of profess-ional, technical, administrative and executive workers are foreigners. The most experienced sections of the Libyan working class are in the oil industry, on the docks and in construction. The petroleum workers produce immense surplus value; but this is mediated between state and corporations, with the govern-ment refusing to permit the workers direct action in the oil industry. In March 1972 stevedores and dockers at Tripoli harbour staged a week-long strike for higher pay and better working conditions, but in the same year the government forbade strikes and sit-down protests, as well as stoppages by students in edu-cational establishments.

Towards a Synthesis

To summarize then: there is not a consistent policy against the development of an indigenous bourgeoisie, but the growth of this class is in practice con-strained by the state's own economic ventures and its direct links with inter-national capital. There is also no policy against the acquisition of private land, but there is no powerful entrenched landed class. There is a working class, but it is small and its action as a class is government controlled. There is a large and growing petty bourgeoisie, especially in the urban economy. This is the fastest growing stratum, but one difficult to analyse both because of incomplete data and because of the elusive nature of this category.[17] It includes the small manufacturers, the shopkeepers and traders of the commercial sector and the importers in the retail trade: the more 'traditional' middle class. But the largest and fastest growing strata are employed in the service sector, above all in the public sector — the so-called 'new' middle class. Unlike the traditional petty bourgeoisie, this group does not hold any capital; at the same time it is not engaged in productive labour, producing commodities, but instead carries out service and administrative functions. Under the oil economy, and especially since the advent of the military government of the Gadafi regime, these 'new' middle class strata have proliferated enormously. The lower levels of state employment have been swollen by the unskilled; this is the indulgence of an oil-rich state which can finance welfare and sheltered unproductive employment more easily than it can generate new productive sectors. At the middle and higher levels of the state bureaucracy are the newly educated and recently trained administrators, managers and technicians. Large allocations for graduate training abroad and the Libyanization of senior posts in the oil industry are providing openings for an upper layer of technical specialists and influential administrators. Short of considerably more data for an analysis of the constituent bodies that comprise the state apparatus — the military, the administration, the judiciary, the ideological apparatus and, importantly, the state enterprises — it is difficult, if not impossible, to dissect the forms in which different state structures have varying representational ties with other classes or fractions of classes.

This is not to reinstate the search for the social origins of the bureaucracy for, as has already been argued with reference to the general studies of the postcolonial state, the social origins of the occupants of government posts has little explanatory power; the critical issue is to locate in whose class interests the state operates. But to enquire into the complex structure of the state, which appears as a unity but is in fact a compound of diverse elements and structures, is to try to discover how the state mediates differing interests in the pursuit of its function, namely the maintenance of social relations for the requirements of the oil economy. For, despite the state's intervention in oil pricing policy and even its entry into the sphere of production through the National Oil Corporation and the Industrial Corporation, capitalist relations of production continue to be reproduced. The state has inserted itself into the economic sector, but without the workers themselves attaining any control over production, and with the state thus remains an institution distinct and separate from the producers.

While this much is clear, and Libyan state ownership is thus anything but socialism, nonetheless the structural class determination of the bureaucracy is extremely difficult. This could be theorized in two ways. First, it might be argued that the occupants of the state apparatus — the bureaucrats — occupy the place of ownership and possession of the means of production and exercise the powers that derive from this: exploitation and the extraction of surplus value. If these powers are those of the heads of the state apparatus, this would be to argue that the conditions of state capitalism are met[18] and would make at least the heads of the state apparatus a state bourgeoisie, a distinct class or class fraction.[19] But in the case of Libya, the greater part of the means of production is still owned by the oil companies, and the members of the state apparatus, while they may preside over the administration of state companies linked with foreign capital, do not control the terms and conditions under which surplus value is extracted nor do they benefit as a class.

The second possible explanation, also drawn from Poulantzas,[20] is to see the bureaucrats not as a class but as a distinct social category, determined by the fact that they are agents of the state apparatus and perform functions for it. It is not a matter of reducing the incumbents of the top state positions to their own class origin or membership, because the bureaucracy can have diverse origins and yet retain an internal unity and can also serve the interests of classes other than those to which they belong or from which they have originated. But, it is suggested, this social category could function as an effective social force, intervening in the political field and in the class struggle with a weight of its own, and not merely kowtowing to the hegemonic class or fraction, or to the class from which it originated or to which it belongs.

The bureaucrats run the state apparatuses and improvise the functions of the state in the reproduction of the social division of labour, more especially in the creation of ideology. Here the Libyan military, the dominant faction in the state apparatus, has developed an ideology which projects a 'third way' (Gadafi's 'Third Theory') between capitalism and socialism and which expounds a Libyan Socialism which seeks not to assert class interests within the society but to reconcile them. The 'non-exploiting' bourgeoisie is called upon to struggle for socialism like everyone else. The stress is on the need for an equilibrium between exploiters and exploited. The reconciliation of interests is done under the aegis of the state and through government initiated and government run politics. Since it is the duty of the state to initiate politics, albeit in the name of the masses, there is a distrust of the masses and their autonomous action. Politics are created from the top; the existing organizations of labour were dissolved. Populist demagogy is passionate, but it disguises the manipulation of the people by the carefully fashioned instruments of the state. At times struggle against certain interests is encouraged, even initiated, as in the Libyan cultural revolution against bureaucracy, but it is liable to be frozen when it reaches a critical mobilizing phase.

The rejection of any conception of the class structure of society and sources of conflict has led, in turn, to a rejection of the independent role of dispossessed classes, and the assertion of a populist ideology which the state ideological machine projects as the interests of all Libyans. This is, of course, nothing new in the underdeveloped world. The parallel stretches back to the Turkey of Kemal Ataturk and the populist regimes of Vargas in Brazil or Mexico under Cardenas. In each instance, in the absence of a hegemonic bourgeoisie, a state bureaucracy, sometimes but not invariably dominated by its military faction, played not merely a mediating role within a power bloc, but improvised policies for the development of the economy by the state, and even maintained its political authority at the expense of members of the power bloc. (In Turkey against the landlord class, for instance.) The goal was an industrialization policy which would alter the place of the underdeveloped economy in the international division of labour. Ataturk's vision, like that of Gadafi, was of a nationalist regime building an autarchic self-reliant economy.

In the case of an oil state this appears to be deceptively easy. But while the state may take on the role of principal investor in those sectors of the economy which are not directly owned by international capital, its relations with international capital continue to be such that it functions merely as a junior partner within the system. Compounding this disability is the second, even more important source of weakness of such a state: the groups in control of the state conceptualize 'development' as the increase in levels and extent of production, not as any change in the social relations of production and without any assertion of the need of the mass of producers for social control of the productive process. In other words, the military bureaucrats of Libya have a conception of 'development' but none of capitalism — nor, thus, of class struggle, for the Third World politics of Libya's military regime explicitly exclude this.

References

1. Although most of this chapter is based on my earlier study, *Libya: The Elusive Revolution,* Harmondsworth, Penguin 1974, I have used it as an opportunity for reconsideration and self-criticism of some of the concepts used in the original book.

2. H. Mahdavy, 'The patterns and problems of economic development in rentier states: the case of Iran', in M.A. Cook, *Studies in the Economic History of the Middle East from the Rise of Islam to the Present Day,* Oxford 1970, pp.428-67. See also Robert Mabro, 'La Libye, un etat rentier?' in *Projet 39,* November 1969, pp.1090-1101.

3. First, op.cit., pp.148-50.

4. A. Phillips 'The concept of development', *Review of African Political Economy,* No. 8, January-April 1977, pp.7-20.

5. Samir Amin, 'Accumulation and development: a theoretical model', *Review of African Political Economy,* No. 1, 1974, pp.1-8.

6. Hamza Alavi 'The state in post-colonial societies', *New Left Review,* No. 74, July-August 1972.

7. The treatment of the state as 'relatively autonomous' appears to be in danger of reifying the state as a disembodied force standing above civil society. In any case, do not all states have 'relative autonomy' — especially in periods of transition — and is it not precisely as an 'autonomous' body that the state acts to solve the contradictions of class society? The state is only 'autonomous' in that it, not a class, encompasses the necessary sphere of relations for the reproduction of the dominant classes: market form, division of labour, the complex of practical and theoretical activities by which ruling classes maintain and justify their dominance.

Classes are more or less able to organize in their interests, but are they ever organized to the extent of extinguishing state 'autonomy'? The state organizes the dominance of a power bloc which may well encompass different classes, as elaborated by Alavi, as well as different fractions of classes. So the analysis of the post-colonial state requires the identification of these classes and class fractions and the role of the state in mediating them, but this does not seem to posit any exceptional autonomy for the post-colonial state.

8. This has been argued especially for the Tanzanian case by John Saul, 'The state in post-colonial societies — Tanzania', *Socialist Register 1974* London, Merlin Press 1974. It was taken further by Saul in 'The unsteady state: Uganda, Obote and General Amin', *Review of African Political Economy,* No. 5, January-April 1976.

9. Saul, 'The unsteady state', op.cit., p.19.

10. Gavin Williams, 'There is no theory of petty-bourgeois politics', *Review of African Political Economy,* No. 6, May-August 1976.

11. The most consistent advocacy of this approach is by Issa G. Shivji, *Class Struggles in Tanzania,* Dar es Salaam 1975. An early precursor of this approach was Claude Meillassoux's 'A class analysis of the bureaucratic process in Mali', *Journal of Development Studies,* Vol. 6, No. 2, 1970, pp.91-110. Meillassoux argued that the bureaucrats in the colony were a body generated by the colonial power to cary out the tasks which could not be undertaken by the Europeans themselves, and this group was entrusted with some of the instruments of power, namely expertise. With this access to power the bureaucracy gained some of the characteristics of a social class: thus it gained control of the economic infrastructure and use of it; and control of the means of repression and hence to devices to maintain its dominance. Meillassoux added, however, that its opposite classes were not clearly defined, and he does not call this group a class outright: 'a distinction should be made between the class proper and the dependent social elements which are the outgrowth of classes, which may assume certain functions'.

12. Colin Leys, 'The over-developed post-colonial state: A re-evaluation', *Review of African Political Economy,* No. 5, January-April 1976.

13. Michaela von Freyhold 'The post-colonial state and its Tanzanian version', *Review of African Political Economy,* No. 8, January-April 1977. In making the distinction between the ruling class and the governing class, this article posits the governing class in the shape of the *nizers* (those who benefited from Africanization). These are the ministers, principal secretaries, directors of the administrative apparatus, general managers of the larger parastatals, heads of the appointed party bureaucracy and of the repressive apparatus, derived not according to their social origin (as in Shivji) but from their function, in the course of which they expand their power over submerged classes, and make themselves a viable, though very junior, partner to the metropolitan bourgeoisie.

14. Some of the historical evidence is summed up by Izabela Budzynska, 'Aspects of the study of Libya's history', University of Sussex, 1976, unpublished paper.

15. On the tribal social organization, see Douglas L. Johnson, *Jabal al Akhdar, Cyrenaica, an Historical Geography of Settlement and Livelihood,*

Chicago 1973.

16. For a discussion of general planning perspectives, see First, op.cit., chapter 9, 'The economic environment'. The latest plan is known as 'The Plan for Economic and Social Transformation 1976-1980', Libyan Arab Republic, Ministry of Planning and Scientific Research, March 1976.

17. Nicos Poulantzas, *Classes in Contemporary Capitalism,* London, New Left Books 1975, has tried to cure the vagueness and imprecision with which concepts, such as 'the middle classes' and 'the petty bourgeoisie', are used, and the tendency to lump together many different elements within an undifferentiated petty bourgeoisie. He divides these intermediate layers into two groups: the traditional and the new petty bourgeoisie. See especially part 3 of his book.

18. Poulantzas, ibid., pp.188-9.

19. This has been advocated, though rather uncertainly, for the case of Algeria. See Middle East Research and Information Project, Report No. 35, *State Capitalism in Algeria:* 'The most efficient, technically competent and profit-motivated persons were brought to the fore in the state bureaucracy and promoted as the new rulers of the society — in Algeria they became the state capitalists.' (p.26); 'They may not constitute a class in the classic capitalist sense since they do not own the means of production, but they have monopoly control over the means of production, a distinctive life-style in terms of material privileges and social contacts; and upward mobility through the hierarchy of the state organization.' (p.27).

20. Poulantzas, op.cit., pp.186-8.

8. Capital Accumulation in Iran

Patrick Clawson

Iran has been industrializing rapidly in recent years. In 1976, 2.5 million people out of a population of 34 million worked in manufacturing industry, according to government statistics. Ten years earlier, there were only half as many manufacturing workers. Manufacturing now employs up to one-quarter of the work force. This industrialization has been largely financed out of oil revenues, which were nearly $22 billion in 1976 — a ten-fold increase since 1971, a seventy-fold increase since 1961. Iran's oil reserves are sufficient for only twenty years' more production at the current rate of about 320 million metric tons a year. The Iranian government intends to build a major petrochemical industry around natural gas production to maintain revenues as oil income drops (Iran has the world's largest reserves of natural gas). It hopes that, by the time oil exports cease, the Iranian economy will have an industrial base. Already, many sophisticated consumer durables are assembled in Iran: for instance, 100,000 automobiles per year. Large industrial complexes are being built, including steel mills which will more than treble production from the 1976 level of about 1.5 million tons. The plans for future growth are grandiose. While it is likely that only a fraction of the 'planned' projects will be built, these new plants will convert Iran into an industrial nation.

This is a dramatic change for a country that only 45 years ago lacked even a single railway or paved road. But the change has *not* been reflected in the standard of living of the great majority of the population: the best paid industrial workers today still live in miserable conditions (up to 70 per cent of wages go on rent; typical housing is a room without running water to be shared by at least one family). The dramatic economic change experienced by the Iranian people has been in the relations of production: capitalist relations of production — i.e. wage labour relations, with most people forced to sell their ability to labour in order to survive while a few people control the means of production — have replaced pre-capitalist relations. Under the latter, the direct producers (the 'peasants') had a large measure of control over the means of production (chiefly the land), but had to surrender a portion of the product to the ruling classes in rent or tribute. The first major thesis of this chapter is that the emergence of capitalist relations of production has been at the root of the transformation of the Iranian economy in the

Publisher's Note: This chapter was written just before the 1978-79 Revolution that overthrew the Shah.

143

past century. Increasing oil exports, rising industrialization, changing land ownership patterns – all are basically results of the rise of capitalism.

The second major thesis is that capitalism has arisen in Iran not primarily as a result of the developments internal to the country, but because of the penetration of capitalism from the advanced countries. Before the transformation of the Iranian economy by capitalism can be investigated, some words are necessary on what is meant by 'the internationalization of capital'.

The Internationalization of Capital

Capitalism is the first mode of production to remake the world in its own image: to penetrate every corner of the globe, to transform all existing societies into capitalistic societies. Capitalism as a system is based on the accumulation of capital – by its nature, capital is self-expanding value. That self-expansion seeks to break through all quantitative bounds, to become ever greater and greater. In pursuit of more rapid and greater accumulation, capitalism is driven to expand outward, to transform non-capitalist societies along capitalist lines. The history of the 'Third World' has been the history of the outward spread of capitalism conflicting with the pre-existing modes of production. Capitalism has battered down the pre-capitalist societies; it has internationalized itself.

From a Marxist standpoint, the internationalization of capital is the framework within which to understand the 'development' of the 'Third World'. Liberal apologists for capitalism speak of 'development' as limited by internal factors, such as poor resource endowment; they implicitly maintain that the barriers to growth have been unrelated to the nature of the *world* capitalist system of which the 'Third World' is a part. In contrast, Marxist theory understands capitalism as a system which essentially reproduces *inequality* on an expanded scale. This process of uneven development on a world scale means rapid growth at some poles and stagnation or decay at others. Not only does Marxist theory understand the development of capitalism within a *world* framework; it also understands the rise of capitalism within an *historical* framework. Once capitalism had appeared in certain societies, its rise in other areas has been largely based on the outward expansion of that capitalism: in short, the internationalization of capital. The liberal theories of 'development' overlook the fundamental distinction between the origins of capitalism in Europe and its rise in the 'Third World'.

Many Marxists have incorrectly argued that the main effect of the international capitalist system on 'Third World' countries has been to prevent the growth of modern industry; i.e. that industrialization has been hampered by multinational corporations, imperialist powers, and local ruling classes allied with the imperialists (especially the 'comprador bourgeoisie'). In its strongest form, this particular Marxist theory argues that the internationalization of capital 'blocks' the development of the 'Third World'.

The substantial industrialization of some 'Third World' countries during the 1960s and early 1970s has made this 'blockage' theory less popular. The theory survives, however, in a slightly modified form: that imperialism blocks 'truly autonomous', 'independent national' development. Therefore 'Third World' governments must 'break with the world market' to be 'self-reliant' and to develop in a 'truly autonomous' fashion. This theory implies that the ability of a 'Third World' country to industrialize depends primarily on the policies of the government in power. The lack of industrialization in the 'Third World' is largely ascribed to the perfidious policies of imperialist governments and multinational corporations which force 'Third World' governments to abandon pro-development programmes. Little mention is made of the structure of the capitalist mode of production, a structure independent of the will of any government or capitalist.

Both the 'blockage' theory and the 'break with the world market' theory are profoundly mistaken in their understanding of the capitalist system. For one thing, both assume that socialists support 'development' of the 'Third World'. 'Development', in a capitalist country, is nothing more or less than the development of capitalist relations of production. The class nature of 'development' is clearly revealed in some of the synonyms that social scientists use for 'development': 'industrialization' means capital accumulation; 'formation of local elites' means the consolidation of bourgeois rule. Capitalist industrialization has brought few if any benefits to the great majority of the Third World's population: the workers, peasants and students. Nor do the mass of people benefit from a shift in power from the imperialist bourgeoisie to the local bourgeoisie, which is what 'national development' is all about. The interests of the people do not lie in capital accumulation ('development') but in socialism. Socialism is not the result of capitalist development, except that a precondition for socialism is the dominance of capitalist social relations — loosely, the creation of a working class and a bourgeoisie. Socialism come from a revolution in which the working class and its allies sieze state power and fight for socialism.

Neither the 'blockage' theory nor the 'break with the world market' theory is based on an analysis of the changing dynamics of the world capitalist system. The 'break with the world market' theory implies that 'Third World' bourgeoisies could industrialize if only they wanted to; i.e. that industrialization depends on the will of the bourgeoisie, not on the laws of the capitalist mode of production. The 'blockage' theory assumes that capitalism has no dynamic: if imperialism once blocked the industrialization of the 'Third World', then imperialism will always block that industrialization.

Capitalism is based, in fact, on the expanded reproduction of the means of production and the relations of production. The process of self-expansion of capital is not a smooth process; it moves through distinct periods, each of which is characterized by certain dynamics. The dynamics of each period give rise to certain contradictions whose resolution requires the transition to a new set of dynamics. It is beyond the scope of this article to analyse the

145

periodization of capitalism based on the dynamics of accumulation. Some
assertions will simply be made and then Iranian society looked at to see
how well the 'stylized facts' of Iranian history fit with the theoretical
framework which has been posited. The theory will in no sense have been
'proved'. At best, a framework will have been sketched which future research
might connect to the laws of capital accumulation in the advanced and 'Third
World' countries.

Capitalism in the advanced countries has passed through several stages.
There was the stage of 'modern industry', of the triumph of industrial
capitalism based on small units of capital ('competitive capitalism'). With
the concentration and centralization of capital into massive units ('monopoly
capitalism'), there came a new stage in which access to credit determined
the pace at which any individual capital could expand (with the rise of
corporations, the capital for expansion came not only from surplus value
generated internally to the unit of capital, but also from credit raised from
other sources). 'Finance capitalism' characterizes this stage – meaning the
importance of credit and therefore the credit-granting institutions, the banks.
The further concentration and centralization of capital gave rise to the
organization of production on a world scale ('multinational corporations',
'the internationalization of production'). The outlines of this new stage
in the accumulation process are now appearing.

Later in this chapter suggestions are made about how each of these three
stages in the advanced countries has affected the 'Third World'. Again, there
is no 'proof' of a systematic theory: only some insights which might be
woven together into a theory at some later date. The contention is that the
transformation of 'Third World' countries from pre-capitalist into capitalist
societies has been fundamentally conditioned by the requirements of the
accumulation process in the advanced countries; any study of the development of capitalism in the 'Third World' must, therefore, take into account
the changing nature of the accumulation process in the advanced countries.

The stages in the internationalization of the capitalist mode of production
identified above are analogous to the circuits of capital analysed by Marx in
Chapters 1 to 4 of *Capital*, Volume II. Marx explains why examination of
the circular flow of capital is essential for understanding the dynamics of
capitalism:

> Capital as self-expanding value embraces not only class relations, a society
> of definite character resting on the existence of labour in the form of
> wage-labour. It is a movement, a circuit-describing process going through
> various stages, which itself comprises three different forms of the circuit-
> describing process. Therefore it can be understood only as a motion, not
> as a thing at rest.[1]

The circuit described by capital goes through three stages: commodity,
money and production. Corresponding to each of these stages is a circuit of
capital; while all the circuits refer to the same self-expansion process of capital,
each reflects different aspects and different moments of that process. Each

circuit, for example, is characterized by the insertion of other capital at different points of intersection. In the circuit of commodity capital (see the chart below), commodities from other capitals or from non-capitalist producers can form the starting point (through purchase or plunder) or the end point (through sale). It is only by examining each of the circuits and the intersection of the circuits that capital can be understood as a social relation in motion, not as a thing at rest.

The Circuits of Capital

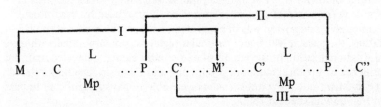

M: money
C: commodities
L: labour power
Mp: means of production
P: production

I: the circuit of money capital

II: the circuit of productive capital

III: the circuit of commodity capital

Marx analysed the circuits of capital at the level of capitalist circulation. When he came to the analysis of capitalist production as a whole in Volume III of *Capital,* he demonstrated how each moment of the circuit became fixed in particular units of capital; for instance, the conversion of commodity capital into commercial capital, a particular branch of capital as a whole. Our analysis is at a still more concrete level, for we are looking at how capitalism expands outward into pre-capitalist societies. At the concrete level, there are additional determinants which enter into the analysis; the laws set forth at the abstract level remain, however, the underlying dynamic.

The Internationalization of the Circuit of Commodity Capital

With the rise of capitalist industry in Europe, world trade developed on a qualitatively new basis. Capitalist industry enormously expanded the physical quantity of raw materials required for production. Some could not be easily produced in the original capitalist countries; for instance, some agricultural products could be more easily grown, and some mineral products more easily extracted, in other areas of the world. These 'natural' — geological and climatological — advantages led merchant capital to seek raw materials from pre-capitalist societies. The relentless search for raw materials was the prime force in transforming pre-capitalist societies into commodity producing societies, generally of a non-capitalist sort. This transformation entailed the creation of the economic categories of commodity producing society; specifically private property in land to replace the previous system of reciprocal rights and the exaction of tribute.

Iran was drawn into the internationalization of the circuit of commodity capital long after the rise of capitalist industry in Europe. The lag was not due to any technical characteristics of Iran's geography, climate or other 'natural endowments'. For instance, Iran is well suited to the production of cotton (now in fact a major crop, and easily produced by 'traditional' technology), and cotton was in heavy demand from the early 1800s on. Rather, the pace at which any particular region was incorporated within the internationalization of the circuit of commodity capital depended upon the resilience of the local modes of production and the resistance they offered to capitalist trade.[2] Capitalist traders were able to have a significant impact on Iran only in the late 1800s.

Late nineteenth century Iran was characterized by increasing exports of agricultural commodities and increasing imports of manufactured consumer goods. Agricultural production was being transformed by the rise in commodity trade, but production relations remained 'traditional'.[3] There were remnants of a communal form of settlement with individuals having more or less equal rights. The village remained the basic unit within which land was periodically redistributed. Much of the land was crown land (*khaliseh*), but the government was hardly the owner in the capitalist sense. A great deal of the crown land was removed from the direct control of the central government in the form of *tuyuls* (land assigned to individuals, theoretically as tax farms or in place of payment for services to the government). Consequently, local notables had effective control over the countryside both as 'government officials' and as landowners. The general tendency of the period was for crown land to be converted into private property: commodity production transformed the means of production into commodities as well. But commodity production, impelled by the requirements of European capital for raw materials, had not yet made its full impact. The land was subject to various claims: claims by the crown, by the landlords, and by the direct producers. The village, through its headman (the *kadkhuda*), still determined the production process and the distribution of land. The direct producers had not been stripped completely of control over the means of production; there were no potential wage-labourers, and therefore there could be no capitalist production.

One side of the internationalization of the circuit of commodity capital is the export of commodities, generally agricultural raw materials, from the backward areas. The other side is the import of manufactured consumer goods from the advanced areas. As commodity production in nineteenth century Iranian agriculture was at a low level, so too were imports, which were restricted to basic consumer goods: cotton and woollen cloth, tea, sugar, and kerosene. However these imports were sufficient to hamper Iranian artisans, and they had to have agricultural sidelines to survive. Unlike early capitalist Europe, the destruction of the artisanry in Iran was not associated with the rise of local modern industry. Foreign powers, principally Britain and Russia, prevented the erection of tariff barriers, denying the infant local industries the protection which would have allowed them to mature into fully productive facilities. A modern sugar mill was set up in Iran about the turn of the century, only to be bankrupted by Russian dumping. In this stage of the internationalization of capital, industrial capital was the dominant form in the countries which were the source of the foreign capital penetrating Iran; the Western industrialists opposed any local manufacturing because local industry would compete with imported goods.[4]

At the turn of the century there was rising Iranian opposition to foreign penetration. Direct producers (the peasants) were chafing under the increased tax and tribute burden, part of which went to foreign concessionaires. The expanding merchant class was determined to control trade, and resented the privileges of foreign traders. These two elements were mixed in with religious opposition to the growing influence of non-Muslims. The most powerful opposition to the ruling Qajar dynasty came from the large merchants who wanted the state to end the independent political power of the big landlords and thus guarantee private property. A long period of turmoil marked the final years of the dynasty. The Qajars managed to survive a successful mass protest in 1890 against the tobacco concession. The growing penetration of commodity production in the economy created the basis for a 'bourgeois revolution' led by the merchants against the landlords for the establishment of property rights, but the Constitutional Revolution of 1906 only succeeded on paper in securing bourgeois property rights. The slow death of the Revolution and the succeeding turmoil (intensified by the various armies operating in Iran during World War I) nullified any changes in the 'traditional' system of rule by local landlords.

While the Constitutional Revolution had changed the legal status of landlords into owners of the commodity, 'land', the actual transformation of social relations took place primarily under the new Pahlavi regime. Upon taking power in 1921 Reza Pahlavi built up a strong military force from the Cossack brigade he had commanded. This force was used to curb centrifugal tendencies and, more fundamentally, to alter the status of the large landed proprietor from that of a petty territorial prince to that of an ordinary commodity owner. *Bigari* (labour servitude), which had been the most onerous personal service owed to the landlord by the peasants, began to diminish. Taxation was placed on a more regular basis. An effort was made to register landholdings, a necessary precondition for the regularization of land transfers. Property rights in land were strengthened.

The Pahlavi regime did not rest content with reducing landlords to commodity owners. In the 1930s Reza Shah established many state industries, thereby furthering the spread of commodity production by increasing the purchases of raw materials and by marketing the output locally. Reza Shah aimed at more than commodity production, however; he hoped that the state industries would be the spark for the general development of 'modern' – i.e. capitalist – industry. By 1941, there were about 50-60,000 workers in some 200 modern industrial plants; about 40 per cent of them being in the 30 state plants, which were the largest and most modern.

The failure of the state-led industrialization was primarily a result of lack of ties to international capital. The establishment of local industry required the importation of foreign machinery, an expensive proposition. From the perspective of international capital, Iran was seen as a source of cheap raw materials, not as a market for machinery nor a site for potentially profitable investment. The result was a foreign exchange crisis, unalleviated by foreign loans. The internationalization of the circuit of money capital had not reached Iran, and so the country could not obtain the foreign capital necessary to establish industry. Not only was money capital lacking; there was little interest on the part of international capital in establishing capitalist relations of production in Iran – few foreign technicians and advisers (let alone direct investment) to establish industry on an all-round capitalist basis with sufficient productivity to compete given suitable tariff barriers. International capital did not regard Iran as a site for possible investment. The world economy's relation with Iran was primarily through the requirements of industrial capital in the advanced countries for cheap raw materials – via low payments to the Iranian government – and for markets for manufactured goods, without competition from local producers. Finance capital, ready to invest wherever profits are to be had and ready to create industries in favourable locations, was not yet tied in with the Iranian economy.

Only on the basis of the full development of the dynamics of commodity production – with the creation of an internal market and an economic infrastructure, as well as the rise of a class separated from the means of production – could commodity production be transformed into general capitalist production. Because this necessary precondition was missing in Iran, the internationalization of the circuit of money bypassed the country until about 1960. The prime determinant of the dynamics of backward societies is, as previously argued, the stage reached in the internationalization of capital. The appearance of new stages is also determined by the requirements of accumulation in the advanced capitalist countries. Of course, it does not follow that each stage in the internationalization process will appear simultaneously throughout the backward countries; some states may be ripe for the new stage while in others the contradications of the dynamics of the previous stage have not yet fully developed. The pace at which the new stage of internationalization will develop in any particular 'Third World' country depends in part on the resistance to international capital offered by the pre-existing modes of production. A new stage cannot appear, however, until the requirements of the accumulation process in the advanced countries make necessary a new step in the internationalization of capital.

Besides the government's actions, there was another major impetus for the generalization of commodity production in Iran during the 1930s: the increasing oil production. This rose almost nine-fold from 1919-20 to 1939-40, with government revenues nearly quadrupling. The oil industry was contributing to the expansion of the Iranian market and of the Iranian working class. The internationalization of commodity capital through oil exports was creating the preconditions for the rise of capitalist industry, which could not establish itself on a large scale until finance capital was prepared to invest in Iran. So long as industrial capital dominated the relations between the world economy and Iran, foreign capital would work against any local competitors for imported manufactured goods.

With the development of a working class in the oil industry came a trade union movement, and large-scale strikes took place in 1946 and 1951. Other social forces opposed to British influence and the Pahlavi regime also gathered strength. The growth in government employment (technicians, educators, bureaucrats) and the rise of the independent professions created a stratum of intellectual petty bourgeois. This stratum was dedicated to the ideology of 'developmentalism', for they had the most to gain from capital accumulation (through which they could end their precarious position and possibly even rise into the bourgeoisie). The merchants were also growing in strength; they allied themselves with the middle-rank clerics on a basis of anti-Westernism, anti-modernism, and anti-despotism. The alliance was partly based on reactionary ideology (especially in some of its religious elements) but also partly on opposition to the 'traditional' ruling class and 'traditional' relations of production.

In 1951, Mossadeq became prime minister, based on the strength of the popular nationalist movement. For a short time, there was an alliance between the merchants, clerics, intellectual petty-bourgeoisie, and the popular masses — a powerful combination which if it had lasted might have uprooted the old ruling class and the 'traditional' relations of production. But by 1953, the alliance had fallen apart. One reason was that Mossadeq was unwilling to move against the landlords: he did not push for land reform, a necessary step to destroy the landlords' power and win the peasants' allegiance. At the crucial moment, furthermore, the merchants and clerics shrank back from an open attack on the old ruling class. Mossadeq had nationalized the oil industry, outraging the imperialist powers who replied with a boycott of Iranian oil; at a single blow the Iranian government lost all its revenue from oil sales. The imperialists were determined to resume the flow of cheap materials. When domestic support for Mossadeq weakened in 1953, the C.I.A. organized a coup which restored the Shah to power (the Shah had not been formally deposed under the Mossadeq government, but his powers had been limited and he had fled Iran in fear of arrest).

During the period of the internationalization of commodity capital, foreign capital is determined to hold down the costs of raw materials. It therefore opposes governments such as Mossadeq's, which raise taxes on foreign trade to finance development projects. This generally implies support

for the old ruling classes, which are less dedicated to expensive infrastructural or industrial projects than are the emerging bourgeois forces. Even
when international capital later becomes interested in developing capitalist
industry through the internationalization of money capital, it generally
supports the old ruling classes, pressuring them to transform themselves into
a new capitalist ruling class rather than run the risk of stirring up popular
opposition to them — opposition which might threaten the continued rule
of international capital.

The Internationalization of Money Capital: Capitalist Relations of Production Triumphant (1953-1970)

By the time of Mossadeq's overthrow in 1953, the Iranian economy was
characterized by widespread commodity production of a non-capitalist
sort. There existed many of the preconditions for the establishment of local
industry: a local market, an adequate infrastructure (transport, utilities,
financial system, etc.), a nascent working class. Iran's relationship with the
world economy was undergoing substantial change. No longer was Britain
the main influence on Iranian policy; the C.I.A.-led coup was an indication
that the U.S. had displaced declining British imperialism. U.S. imperialism
was in its era of ascendancy, seeking to bring the entire world under its
wing through the export of capital. U.S. finance capital, interested in profitable investment opportunities throughout the 'free world', was the leading
element in the internationalization of capital; the requirements of industry
(for raw materials and markets for production) took a back seat in relation
to the demands of finance capital for the highest rate of profit. And so the
internationalization of the circuit of money capital penetrated into Iran,
transforming production relations into capitalist production in order to
realize higher rates of profit.

While the pre-capitalist relations of production had to be smashed forcibly,
U.S. imperialism hoped to retain the old ruling class through transforming it
into a new capitalist ruling class; to displace the old ruling class would create
political turmoil that might lead to mass mobilizations and possibly to
socialist revolution. Elements in the old ruling class were quite prepared to
participate in the destruction of pre-capitalist relations; the Iranian government had, after all, promoted local industry during the 1930s. The state,
under the leadership of the Shah and with the advice of U.S. experts, carried
through a land reform designed to convert agriculture and give it a capitalist
basis. It instituted a 'planning' process – meaning a public agency which
invested in infrastructure and large industrial projects as well as other
agencies which made extensive loans to private industry. The funds for these
agencies came partly from international capital: 'aid', loans from public
agencies and private banks, and some direct investment. The special circumstances of the internationalization of the circuit of money capital in Iran
lay, however, in the large oil revenue which allowed Iran to develop capitalist

relations quickly without running into the constraints facing most nations at this stage. The oil revenue was largely an historical accident: the particular use-value, petroleum, is well suited to modern industry, and this use-value is found in large quantities in Iran. Even though the the price per ton of oil was kept low, the Iranian government received large revenues from oil production: $150 million in 1956, $295 million in 1961, and $625 million in 1966.

Land Reform Destroys Pre-capitalist Agriculture
One of the major barriers facing the transition to capitalist relations of production was the hold which pre-capitalist relations still had in agriculture. Over two-thirds of Iran's population of 19 million lived in 1956 in rural areas (i.e. in villages with fewer than 5,000 inhabitants); 3.1 million people in a labour force of 6.1 million were working in agriculture. So long as such a substantial portion of Iran's population was tied to pre-capitalist relations, the process of proletarianization would be slowed, thereby hampering the accumulation that capitalist social relations makes possible. The 'traditional' ruling class would further reduce capital accumulation by using in a pre-capitalist manner the surplus product it extracted from the producers: i.e. in luxury consumption and land speculation. The landlords maintained a distinctive and expensive lifestyle, setting high standards which government officials and town merchants sought to match or surpass. 'Imports of pleasure vehicles alone amounted to over $45 million in 1959-60, while more foreign exchange was spent on silks and tailored clothing than on electrical machinery, more on jewellery than agricultural equipment, and nearly as much on perfume as fertilizer.'[5] Additional income was sunk into land speculation, which was among the most significant sources of revenue for the wealthy.

Relations of production in agriculture in the early 1960s were non-capitalist. A small group of landowners controlled much of the land. Keddie quotes the 1963 *U.S. Army Area Handbook* for Iran: 'In 1962, the Ministry of Agriculture estimated that about 15,000 villages (out of 45,000 to 60,000 villages in Iran) belonged to landlords with more than 5 villages, and the government stated that 400 to 500 large landlords owned 57 per cent of all Iranian villages.'[6] The landlords extracted surplus product from the direct producers through rent and tribute, not through wage-labour. The main form of land tenure was sharecropping. But the main group of direct producers still had some claim on the means of production: they may have owned their own tools and they had some rights to work the land. One of the pre-conditions for capitalism is that direct producers be stripped of any remaining control over the means of production and forced to sell their ability to labour in order to survive. This precondition had not been fully met in Iran by the early 1960s.

There was substantial class stratification below the landlords. The most basic distinction was between the *nasagh* (title holders) and the *khoshnashin* (landless). The latter were mostly casual labourers, but they included some

153

clerics, shopkeepers, teachers, etc. In 1960, there were approximately 1.9 million *nasagh* and farmer-owner families along with 1.3 million *khoshnashin*. As Mahdavy wrote, describing the situation in the mid-1960s:

> About 10 million out of the 15.4 million rural population of Iran belong to the poorer classes who have either no land at their disposal or have less than four hectares to cultivate. This is at the root of Iran's 'Agrarian Problem', irrespective of the ownership of land which undoubtedly aggravates the situation. The distinction between the different classes within the village community is seldom appreciated. The peasants have their own *bourgeoisie*.[7]

This 'bourgeoisie' included the heads of work teams, a category which was in theory identical with that of the owners of a pair of oxen. Other peasants had to compete for a place on the work team, usually assigned by landlord-appointed headmen; the alternative was day-labour. Some owners of oxen or other factors of production (tools, water) chose to rent these out without themselves working. In other words, there was a dynamic towards the separation of the direct producers from the means of production, and towards the concentration of the means of production in the hands of a class of non-producers. But so long as control over land remained in the hands of the 'semi-traditional' landlords, the formation of a bourgeoisie was blocked.

In 1962 the Shah proclaimed a land reform which over the next few years in effect destroyed the traditional system of production in the villages. The land reform was the most important part of the Shah's 'White Revolution' which also included a literacy corps and suffrage for women. The White Revolution was designed to win support for the Shah from the rising bourgeoisie as well as from the petty-bourgeois reformers, reducing his reliance on the old landlord class (who were, however, to be transformed into a bourgeoisie, not discarded). In the first flush of the reform, the movement went well beyond the limits laid down in the government decree. Lambton speaks of land being distributed to all the peasants in the village including the *khoshnashin*; Vieille describes an atmosphere of 'great uprising' (*jacquerie*).[8] 1963 saw open rebellion and riots in Iran's major cities. The official interpretation, picked up by the international press, portrayed these events as a sign of hostility to the land reform and to women's suffrage. There certainly were reactionary elements in the riots, especially some of the religious leaders. Even a progressive cleric such as Khomeini was opposed to the vote for women, while other clerics denounced the land reform as contrary to Islam. The main element in the rebellions was, however, general opposition to the Shah's regime, including on such issues as relations with Israel, the U.S. loans for arms purchases, and the privileges of U.S. advisers and military personnel. The Shah reacted to the riots with a heavy hand. Several thousand people were openly slaughtered. He also weakened the land reform through promulgating Additional Articles on 17 January 1963 (in what is referred to as the 'second stage' of the land reform, which was generally put into operation in 1964).

The main effect of the reform has been to create a bourgeoisie and a proletariat in the countryside. For most of the Iranian rural population, the land reform has meant proletarianization. Even in theory, the land reform was to provide land only to a minority: the *nasagh* holders living on land owned by large landlords. Nor was there in fact distribution of all the land theoretically subject to the reform (no landlord was to retain more than one complete village, except under certain circumstances). As a result, many people, in post-reform Iran, depend for a living on intermittent wage labour, along with some animal husbandry and small-scale agricultural production. These people retain many elements of their status as petty producers; they are also partly lumpen-proletarians due to their irregular employment. Yet the trend is clear: the separation of the producers from control over any means of production continues. A proletariat is emerging from the Iranian countryside.

Just as the land reform has created a proletariat from the direct producers, so it has also transformed the old landlord class into a bourgeoisie. The land reform law was generous towards the old landlords, especially in the second stage when the prices to be paid by the peasants for land were raised to the 'market' price as distinct from the tax assessment price. The law contained many provisions encouraging a shift towards capitalist agriculture; thus, any land farmed by mechanized means could be retained.

Capitalist Industry Arises with State Aid

While the destruction of pre-capitalist agriculture was the key to ending the influence of 'traditional' production relations, the establishment of industries has been the main force behind the rise of capitalist production relations. Import-substituting industrialization — local production of goods (primarily consumer goods) previously imported using foreign technology and machinery — has proceeded rapidly in Iran since the late 1950s. Rather than reflecting any 'break with the world market', this industrialization has been based on the internationalization of the circuit of money capital. Foreign finance capital has been actively promoting Iranian industrialization, from which it has expected high profits. Reflecting the interests of U.S. capital, the U.S. government has encouraged and advised the Iranian government to promote industry via economic planning, infrastructure construction, loan programmes, and the like. Industrialization in Iran has been heavily supported by the government; nevertheless, capital accumulation has been primarily by private capitalists, rather than the state.[9]

One major aspect of the state's encouragement of industry has been the activities of the Plan Organization. Despite its name, the Plan Organization has not been primarily a planning body until recently; it functioned as a separate ministry which implemented projects recommended by foreign engineers. Total Plan Organization spending was $275 million in the First Plan (1949-55), $1,085 million in the Second Plan (1956-62), $3,030 in the Third Plan (1963-68), and $8,300 million in the Fourth Plan (1968-73). Most of the projects have been infrastructural; that is, designed to provide low-cost services to private capitalists rather than produce profits on their own. The Plan Organization and other public agencies were involved in the establishment of some state-owned industries in the 1960s, generally in cases where the initial costs required a centralization of capital beyond the means of Iranian capitalists. The most notable example was the National Iranian Steel Corporation, which was established to run the steel mill built near Isfahan with a $286 million loan from the U.S.S.R. For most industrial projects, the Plan Organization's activities included feasibility studies, technical assistance, and facilitating the extension of government credit. From 1956 to 1973, about two-thirds of its funds came from oil revenues, of which it received around three-quarters.

The Plan Organization has created the necessary technical foundation for profitable capital accumulation — roads, telephones, water systems, electricity, and other utilities. The major profit-making investments have been left to private capitalists, often operating with large government loans. A whole network of government financial institutions was established from the late 1950s on to reinforce private capital accumulation. A major institution was the Revaluation Loan Fund (R.L.F.), set up in 1957 with $16 million from Bank Melli (then the Central Bank of Iran) and $48 million from the increase in the money supply due to the revaluation of gold and foreign exchange holdings when the rial was devalued. The R.L.F. provided relatively long-term credit (3 to 5 years in most cases) for the expansion of industry. Benedick has assessed the importance of the R.L.F. in establishing a new awareness of capital accumulation in industry as a means to riches:

> In future years R.L.F. may be looked back upon as a landmark in Iran's industrial breakthrough. Even more than capital, the program contributed to an aura of confidence that private companies would be encouraged. In light of earlier government approaches, R.L.F.'s psychological significance to investors should not be underestimated.
>
> There is no doubt that considerable private capital, which might otherwise have entered real estate or trading cycles or left the country, was attracted to industry. Capacity and output have in fact been augmented. Perhaps more important, an increasing recognition of potentialities of an industrial sector have been awakened, both in investor awareness of profits and in consumer interest in new products; locally made plastic kitchen articles are objects of noticeable pride by even the poorest class of Persian citizens, who may only have entered the monetary economy within the past five years.[10]

The long-existing government-owned Industrial Credit Bank also received a new-found importance in the 1960s. Its loans rose from $2.5 million in 1960 to $24 million in 1968 and $234 million in 1975. The government was also heavily involved in the establishment of the Industrial and Mining Development Bank of Iran (I.M.D.B.I.), a private bank set up in 1959 with $2.1 million in equity from foreign investors and $3 million from Iranians, along with loans of $5.2 million from the World Bank, $5.2 million from the U.S. government, and $26.7 million from the Iranian government. The

I.M.D.B.I. became the principal factor on the industrial scene, spreading capitalist financing practices, encouraging equity issues, and participating in nearly all major industrial adventures. I.M.D.B.I. loans utilized went from $6.7 million in 1961 to $31.4 million in 1968 and $476.8 million in 1975. Of the $2.5 billion private industrial investment in 1972, $1.5 billion was in projects receiving I.M.D.B.I. loans.

Most capital accumulation in Iran has been under the direction of capitalists from a mercantile background. Marx spoke about two paths to capitalism: the first 'really revolutionary path' of 'producers [who] became merchant and capitalist', and the second less thoroughgoing path of 'merchants [who] establish direct sway over production.'[11] The industrial entrepreneurs with backgrounds in bazaar merchant families are less 'revolutionary' in the sense that they are uninterested in revolutionizing the process of production. Factory operations are uninteresting preliminaries to the sale of the product for the ex-bazaar merchant. Such an attitude will give way under the pressure of competition; the new industrialists are being forced to learn about and invest in technical improvements. While the 'second path' capitalists (merchants who become industrialists) have established most of the large modern industries, the 'first path' capitalists (producers who become industrialists) are also becoming a major force. Starting with the R.L.F., government loan programmes have extended some loans to small producers (like artisans and people who do repairs). The sums involved have been modest — no more than 10 per cent of total funds lent — but the credits have allowed for more small-scale industry than in most Third World countries. The International Labour Organization assessed the importance of small capitalists in 1972:

> There is in Iran a well developed small-scale manufacturing sector, the largest component of which is not traditional handicrafts as is sometimes thought. It supplies a range of mass consumption goods such as foods, textiles, knitted goods and shoes, and it already supplies a range of building materials, doors and windows, as well as furniture and metal products. In addition, through feeder units, it has started supplying spare parts for large-scale industry, and it also produces the greatest part of manufactured exports. Modern technology is penetrating the small-scale sector. This development originated in the traditional metal-working industry and led to the adoption of more sophisticated technology allowing the production of spare parts and light machinery.[12]

In discussing the rise of industry in Iran in the 1960s, two further points need to be made explicit. First, the expansion of industry was closely linked with the availability of credit for investment in production equipment, physical plant, and working capital. It seems likely that without the credit facilities provided by the Iranian government there would have been much less local industry. Rising consumption needs would have been met through a further expansion of consumer good imports from the advanced countries. [Indeed the next section of this chapter details how the provision of credit (as well as other government activities to promote industry such as tariffs) was linked to the internationalization of capital.] Second, the expansion of industry during the 1960s was considerable. Given the overwhelming evidence (even allowing for the substantial doctoring of government statistics uncovered by researchers), this would seem a rather superfluous point to stress. There are those, however, who refuse to allow the facts to intrude upon their preconceived notions of how the world economy operates: they have decided that imperialism blocks the development of capitalism, especially industry, in the backward areas.[13]

Employment by Manufacturing Sector in Urban Areas of Iran
(in thousands)

Manufacturing Sector	1962	1966	1972
Consumer non-durables	*174*	*272*	*397*
Food	51	72	112
Beverages	3	3	5
Tobacco	4	4	5
Textiles & carpets	69	127	159
Apparel & accessories	33	47	94
Leather	3	3	5
Wood and furniture	11	16	17
Intermediate goods	*55*	*89*	*152*
Paper and cardboard	1	1	5
Printing and binding	3	4	9
Rubber	2	4	6
Chemicals	7	9	20
Non-metallic minerals	23	30	49
Basic metals	1	3	11
Metal products	18	31	52
Consumer durables and capital goods	*19*	*30*	*58*
Non-electrical machinery	0	4	12
Electrical machinery and appliances	2	7	20
Transport equipment	17	19	26
Miscellaneous	2	4	11
Total	*250*	*388*	*616*

Source: Ministry of Economy, *Trends in Industrial and Commercial Statistics 1972*. These figures do *not* include even all urban firms, much less rural manufacturers.

Iranian Capital Accumulation Is Limited by Foreign Exchange
The hegemony of finance capital over industrial capital in the advanced countries means that advanced capital *invests* in the Third World whenever a higher rate of profit is to be obtained, instead of treating the Third World

primarily as a source for raw materials and a market for output.

The previous stage in the internationalization process, the internationalization of commodity capital, spread commodity relations. It therefore created a precondition for capitalism, namely a group of people with no way to live except by sale of their ability to labour. Foreign money capital flowing into the Third World results in the rise of capitalist relations of production. The internationalization of the circuit of money capital is the stage in which *capital* is exported: not only capital as money, but also capital as a social relation between capitalists and workers.

In this stage in the Third World, the accumulation of capital quickly runs into a barrier — shortage of foreign exchange. The creation of capitalist industry in Iran required particularly large amounts of machine tools and intermediate inputs. Since at first only a few industries were established and since local producers of manufactured goods and semi-processed inputs had been driven out of business by low-cost imports, the requirements could be met only through further imports. Capital accumulation thus required more and more goods to be brought in. Imports of electrical and non-electrical machinery rose from $176 million in 1960 (28.3 per cent of imports) to $964 million in 1972 (35 per cent of imports); imports of metal products and chemicals more than quadrupled in the same period. 'Import-substituting' industrialization is actually quite import-intensive, the new industries requiring extra imports of capital goods. In the same way, import substitution *increases* dependence on the world economy. The Economic Commission on Latin America's vision of economic independence via import-substituting industrialization is a pipe-dream. Capital accumulation in the modern era ties countries closer together; there can be no such thing as capitalist economic independence.

While the demand for imports in the Third World increases, there is no corresponding increase in potential exports. Local industry is too immature to compete on the world market. The only source of export earnings is raw materials (including foodstuffs) in which the Third World country has a 'natural' advantage due to geology, climate, location, or other factors besides the accumulation of capital. Capital accumulation in the Third World is limited by the availability of foreign exchange. No matter how much savings are piled up by the rich, they can only be used for capital accumulation if there is sufficient foreign exchange to pay for additional imports of capital goods and intermediate inputs (since extra savings may go into real estate speculation or other forms of non-productive 'investment'). Capital accumulation can increase only if raw material exports are raised — an example of how the internationalization of capital at one stage reinforces the internationalization of earlier moments in the circuits of capital.

It was Iran's good fortune to be endowed with a raw material (petroleum) whose use-value is so suitable for capitalist industry that demand for it rose rapidly during the period when Iranian industry was increasing its own demand for imports. Despite falling revenue per ton, Iran's total oil revenue rose at almost 15 per cent a year during the 1960s (from $283 million in

1960 to $1,100 million in 1970). The increased production took few
domestic resources; employment in the oil industry has not risen since the
Second World War. Iran was therefore able to accumulate capital more
rapidly than most backward countries. It went from being one of the more
underdeveloped societies, with a significant pre-capitalist element, in the
late 1950s, to being a substantial industrial producer by the early 1970s.

The ability to overcome a foreign exchange shortage depends on inflows
of foreign money capital. In the early years of industrial expansion in Iran,
the inflow of foreign money capital largely took the form of U.S. foreign
aid. When the conditions for general industrialization had been laid, private
foreign investment began; only then did industrialization extend to the
higher technology areas where foreign investors had considerable advantages.
With the spread of tariff barriers to encompass products previously exported
to Iran, foreign investment increased substantially. Faced with the threatened
loss of markets, or hoping to gain a share of a growing and protected market,
many foreign firms responded to tariffs and other import restrictions by
setting up local production facilities.

While the data on industrial investment are too inaccurate for exact
comparison, it would seem that the foreign component has run at some 5 to
10 per cent of total industrial investment. But foreign investment has had a
significance beyond this. For one thing, overseas investors are generally
associated with local partners and receive loans from local credit institutions,
such that the projects in which they have invested undoubtedly represent
a much higher percentage of overall industrial investment. Secondly, foreign
investment is concentrated in the leading sectors – the fastest growing, the
most technologically advanced, and those with the highest entry cost. These
industries spawn a host of local sub-contractors and ancillary services. Finally,
foreign investment entails the use of advanced capitalist technology and
management practices which can do much to reinforce capitalist relations
of production. It is safe to say that foreign investment has been a leading
factor in the expansion of local industry in Iran.

Hot-House Capital Accumulation (the 1970s): Moving to the Internationalization of Productive Capital?

Between 1970 and 1974, Iranian oil revenue increased from $1,095 million
to $17,092 million. The additional foreign exchange income has funded a
long list of infrastructural and manufacturing projects which are transforming
the Iranian economy into a substantial industrial power. The rapid capital
accumulation of the last few years is due not only to increased revenues,
but also to the determination to accumulate those revenues instead of
spending them all on luxury consumption. The rise of a local bourgeoisie
has brought about the triumph of the capitalist ideology of growth ('Accumulate! Accumulate! That is Moses and the Prophets.'). 'Developmentalism – the
conviction that economic growth will solve all social problems – has a strong

appeal to the bourgeoisie of the backward countries. The petty bourgeoisie, including the intellectuals, are the strongest champions of 'developmentalism' for it is through economic growth that they hope to rise into the bourgeoisie (and it is economic stagnation which is likely to force them down into the proletariat). Armed with justifications from the intellectual petty bourgeoisie, the bourgeoisie of the backward countries have rallied around the banner of 'development' to forward their own interests against those of the bourgeoisie in the advanced capitalist countries. The most successful example of the struggle by backward bourgeoisies has been OPEC.

OPEC has functioned as a cartel — fixing prices and dividing markets in order to increase profits for each producer. The cement keeping the cartel together has been 'developmentalism'. Its success has depended not only on its internal cohesion, but on its ability to withstand pressure from those having to pay the higher prices — specifically, its ability to overcome economic, political, or military threats from the advanced countries. The price rises of the 1970s were made possible by the weakness of U.S. imperialism. Faced with a growing threat from European and Japanese competitors, U.S. capitalists supported the rise in oil export prices in 1971; Europe and Japan, dependent on imported oil, had to pay higher prices while U.S. industry did not suffer. Once the OPEC governments discovered how easily they could enforce a price rise, they kept on raising the price; the oil companies were willing partners, since their profits rose along with the price (with spectacular short-term profits due to inventory gains and artificial shortages). Realizing its increasing dependence on oil imports (and its inefficient use of energy relative to its competitors), the U.S. government sharply opposed the later price rises. But it was not able to bring sufficient force to bear to reverse them; inter-imperialist rivalry (each out for itself) broke apart all efforts at a common front among the Western powers, and talk of military intervention raised the prospect of conflict with the Soviet Union. The result was to leave the bourgeoisies of the OPEC countries with substantially higher revenues.

The increased oil revenues in Iran have been used for more than capital accumulation. There has certainly been a big increase in luxury consumption, some of which is hidden in the 'investment' column of the national income accounts under the excuse that the construction of luxury housing constitutes investment. Urban land speculation has also absorbed vast sums; this pre-capitalist form of wealth creation is among the most profitable activities in Iran. Government statistics indicate that land prices in the cities rose by about 70 per cent in 1976-77 alone. The Shah's fascination with advanced military equipment is widely known. The regular defence budget for 1976 was $7.6 billion; total military expenditure was closer to $9.5 billion or 20 per cent of G.N.P. Iran has ordered some $18.0 billion in arms from the U.S. alone in the 1970-77 period. Arms imports were $3.5 billion in 1976 (27 per cent of all imports); since deliveries lag behind orders by several years, this figure will not shrink soon even if no new systems are ordered. The Iranian military will soon be as well equipped as the West German, which is entirely out of proportion with the requirements of Iranian capitalism. While capitalists generally recognize the need for arms spending to ward off threats of revolution and of force from competitors, they begrudge each penny spent as a deduction from the surplus value available for investment. The expenditure of vast sums on the military may partly reflect the Shah's determination to dominate the Persian Gulf, thereby preventing revolution or capitalist competitors from threatening Iranian capitalism. Iran, for instance, has had up to 35,000 soldiers in the Dhofar region of Oman during the 1970s, combating a left nationalist movement. Iranian military expenditures also partly reflect a non-capitalist attitude towards the military (loosely, a desire to 'show off').

Much of the oil revenue has been accumulated, however, and this accumulation has led to a rapid growth in capitalist relations and capitalist industry in Iran. The revenues have not always been efficiently used. The Shah has grandiose plans, the Fifth Plan (1973-77) was revised in Winter 1974, with expenditures doubled to nearly $70 billion (seven times larger than the Fourth Plan). The attempt to do too much too quickly and the consequent lack of co-ordination have resulted in high costs and continuing inflation; for instance, the congestion at the ports forced the use of high-cost overland transport from Europe as well as costing $1 billion in demurrage charges in 1976 alone. Costs on major projects have escalated sharply; for instance, the cost of a petrochemical complex to be built by Iran-Japan Petrochemical Company at Bandar Manshahr was estimated at $600 million in 1974, but will run to more than $1.8 billion by the time it is completed 'around 1980'. Higher costs, coupled with no effective increases in oil revenue since 1975, have forced the postponement of many projects. Less than a year after the Fifth Plan was revised, many projects had to be postponed; the Sixth Plan, proposed in the Autumn of 1977, includes a few major investments that had not been in the revised Fifth Plan. In 1974, the National Iranian Steel Company had forecast steel production for 1983 at 14 million tons: by 1976 the target had been lowered to 5 or 6 million tons, and that may prove too high. The anarchy of capitalist production is acute in Iran.

There is no reason to expect that capital accumulation will necessarily bring benefits to the working class. The process involves no necessary tendency to raise the standard of living of the working class; in circumstances where severely repressive state policies inhibit the organization of the working class, an increasing standard of living for workers is not likely. There is a common but erroneous argument that capitalism must eventually increase workers' wages or face a limited market which will choke off growth. The increase in aggregate demand sufficient to call forth additional production rests not primarily on autonomous increases in consumption, but on increases in investment (which in turn induce an increasing consumption). Higher profits raise investment, and therefore they provide an engine for an expanding market. The enormous increase in the Iranian internal market has been accompanied by a reduction in the share of income going to workers; it has been investment and luxury consumption which have provided the growing market. Just as the accumulation of capital has not meant higher wages, neither has it meant an increase in jobs proportional to those looking for work. While the labour force grew at 2.5 per cent a year and the population by 3.1 per cent a year from 1956 to 1966, employment grew at the lower rate of 2.3 per cent. Much of the Iranian working class is employed only temporarily or seasonally; even those holding full-time permanent jobs have not seen any substantial rise in standards of living from the new oil revenue.

The growth of Iranian industry in the 1970s has been closely tied to the internationalization of money capital. Finance capital, which dominates over industrial capital during this stage of the internationalization process, regards the backward countries as areas for investment, and so it is eager to see the development of local industry which can increase the opportunities for profitable investment. In no sense is local industrialization a break with the world market, an assertion of independence from the imperialist powers, or an expression of collective self-reliance among backward countries. The industrialization of these countries is in the interests of the advanced economies at this new stage of capitalism. The local industry includes many plants operated at high profit by foreign capital, especially in the advanced sectors which are the engines of growth. Local industries provide an important market for the manufacturers of machine tools and technology. Not only do the capitalists of the advanced countries profit from the industrialization of the backward countries; the industrialization is made possible only through the actions of capital from the advanced countries. It is the willingness to invest, the toleration of tariff barriers, the political support to local bourgeoisies, and related policies, which create the necessary environment for capital accumulation in the backward countries. Without these elements, rising local incomes would translate only into increased imports of manufactured goods without stimulating local production.

Foreign investment in Iran has hitherto been directed towards production for the local market of commodities previously imported. Foreign firms often set up local manufacturing facilities to preserve a market they have previously developed through imports, but which is now endangered by the possibility of local production behind a tariff barrier (with the ever-present threat that a competitor from another imperialist country will set up local production first and thereby capture the market). These are the characteristics of the internationalization of the circuit of money capital. Finance capital looks upon backward countries as possible sites for profitable investment.

There are signs that Iran is moving beyond this stage in the internationalization process and into the internationalization of the circuit of *productive* capital, in which industry — not just investment, but industrial production — is organized on a world-wide basis. Each activity is located in the area of lowest cost production; inputs may come from a dozen countries, be assembled in yet another country, and be destined for markets in scores of states. This stage is characterized by world-wide marshalling of the necessary inputs and by the generalization of world-wide competition to all major manufactured commodities. Backward countries are brought into this stage of the internationalization process only when capitalist relations have developed widely and

163

when local industry is sufficiently mature (with a broad infrastructural base and with ample supplies of adequately skilled labour). The backward country becomes part of a world-wide production process, yet it remains backward: the product life-cycle reproduces the technological lead of the advanced countries. The backward countries remain dependent on the advanced countries for technologically sophisticated goods, particularly the means of production vital to modern industry.

The Iranian government has grandiose plans to propel Iran into this stage of the internationalization process. The Shah, the Plan and Budget Organization, and the economic advisers have all fixed their attention firmly on the need to prepare for the end of the oil era. Present production levels of petroleum in Iran can be sustained for only another 20 years or so, although natural gas will last much longer. The basis must be laid now for prosperity in the post-oil era; the government has firmly decided that the production of manufactured goods for export is the route to future riches. Industrialization based only on the national market is insufficient: there must be a source of foreign exchange earnings, and that can be provided only through competition on world markets with other capitalist producers (exports based on 'natural' advantage being insufficient). Such competition requires openness to the world market: the tariff barriers of import-substitution produce cost structures which make impossible generalized competition on the world market. Only through openness to the world market can Iranian producers reach a wide enough market to realize economies of scale which will reduce their costs to world levels. Acutely aware of these problems and eager to see Iran as a major power, the government has been pushing hard for the expansion of manufactured exports.

The core of Iranian plans to compete on the world market is the development of forward linkages from the oil industry. High priority has been given to petrochemical plants which use natural gas as a feedstock for fertilizers, basic ingredients for plastics, and the like. Iran intends to become a major producer of ammonia, nitric acid, ammonium nitrate, and urea (fertilizer). While the government-owned National Petroleum Company will produce such basic feedstocks and intermediates as P.V.C., private producers will make the more downstream plastic products; for example, I.M.D.B.I., DuPont, the Beshahr Group and the Sacka Corporation are jointly building a $440 million plant to produce polyester and acrylic fibres. In addition to the petrochemical industry, the steel industry receives high priority, based on direct-reduction technology using natural gas to convert iron into steel. The overly ambitious expansion plans of 1974 have been delayed substantially; it seems likely that all of the plants originally called for will be built, but on a much slower schedule, such that Iran will not be a major exporter by 1985 as had been hoped. Both the steel and petrochemical industries are capital-intensive; they will create few jobs per rial invested (as is true of another high priority investment, the construction of nuclear power plants). Both industries are also facing world-wide gluts. Iranian plants will be competitive only if a substantial portion of the (inflated) construction costs are 'written off'.

Government plans for the expansion of manufactured exports have so far had little success. One major obstacle has been the explosion in local demand, which has sopped up any available local production. This hothouse growth has created myriads of problems which have slowed down existing producers (e.g. power shortages and shortages of skilled labour have cut down production in many industries). More importantly, Iranian industry is not yet sufficiently mature to compete on world markets. In the next few decades Iran may well emerge into the internationalization of the circuit of productive capital on the basis of generalized industrialization. But even an optimistic article in *Fortune* about the Iranian economy and the Iranian government hedges its predictions of Iran's future: 'If oil prices stay high, the Shah has a chance of transforming Iran into a middle-rank power with a fairly substantial economy. It is . . . at least a couple of generations too soon, in terms of technology and popular education, for Iran to become a Middle Eastern West Germany.'[14]

A Concluding Overview

Iranian society went from a 'traditional' (non-capitalist) basis in the 1800s to become thoroughly capitalist — with not only modern industry and a state which fosters capital accumulation, but also with a class structure increasingly divided into two fundamental groups: those with control over the means of production and those with no means of surviving except by selling their ability to labour. The main thesis argued here has been that the rise of capitalist society in Iran cannot be meaningfully conceived outside the context of the internationalization of capital. Capitalism is the first mode of production to remake the world in its own image. The internal dynamic of capitalism (accumulation of capital on an ever-expanding scale) leads capitalists to make the world their market and eventually to develop capitalist production in all corners of the globe which they can penetrate. Capitalism did not appear in Iran primarily as the result of 'internal' developments subject to some influence from the 'foreign sector', as most conventional theories of development imply; capitalism was not the product of the inherent superiority of the market for the efficient allocation of resources. Discussion of questions like 'balanced versus unbalanced growth', 'forward and backward linkages from a dynamic sector', and the other 'problems' with which orthodox development economics shadow-boxes, makes little sense unless these questions are placed within the context of the world-wide spread of capitalism outward from its base in the first capitalist countries. Capitalism was *introduced* into Iran by the dynamic of the capital accumulation process in the already capitalist countries of Europe. From the early spread of production for the market to the most recent establishment of high-technology industry, the connections with international capital have been at the centre of the evolution of Iranian society.

Furthermore, it has been argued that the outward expansion of capitalism has not been a continuous linear process; it has gone through distinct stages, based on the requirements of the accumulation process. Elsewhere, the present author has developed the elements of a theory of internationalization — not a systematic analysis rigorously developed into a theory, but some insights which enter into the construction of a theory.[15] The schema runs as follows: with the rise of capitalist production in Europe, there came an insatiable demand for inputs into the production process. Some of these inputs, by nature of their use-values, were difficult to obtain in the original capitalist countries; capitalists therefore scoured the world for raw materials. The production of raw materials for export transformed pre-capitalist societies into commodity-producing societies, setting in motion social forces which converted the means of production into private property and which dispossessed the direct producers of their control over the means of production.

The concentration and centralization of capital in the advanced countries had meanwhile given rise to corporations and then to monopolies. In order to be able to compete, individual units of capital had to have access to large sums of money; credit became the determining factor in the accumulation process. Financial institutions, the mobilizers of credit, asserted their power over industry. Finance capital regarded the whole world as an arena for profitable investment: this was the internationalization of the circuit of money capital. Money capital flowed to the backward countries to establish industry producing for the local market. The state provided assistance with tariff barriers, etc., for the state had come under the control of the pro-capital-accumulation forces with the crushing of the 'traditional' ruling class. The conditions were being created for generalized capitalist production in the backward countries. At the same time, the concentration and centralization process had continued in the advanced countries, units of capital were now organizing production on a world scale. The result was the internationalization of the circuit of productive capital; from the backward countries, production became oriented towards the world market.

The evidence presented here from the evolution of Iranian society is consistent with the theoretical schema presented above. There has been no proof, however, that this theoretical schema accounts (in the strict sense of that word) for the development of capitalism in Iran. There has been no adequate analysis of the history of the Iranian state, the effects of the class struggle in Iran (its impact on both the economic and political movements), or many other factors which would have to be theorized and analysed in any rigorous account of the rise of capitalism in Iran. The project here has been much more limited: a particular theoretical schema has been shown to provide a framework around which the facts of recent Iranian history can be organized.

References

1. K. Marx, *Capital,* vol. 2, Moscow 1971, p.113.
2. In the 1600s under the Safavid Empire there was substantial trade in commodities in the form of raw materials for export. Silk exports ran at

four to six million pounds per annum in the mid-1600s; in 1688 silk exports were still worth one to two million pounds sterling, as compared to the five million pounds that total exports from England and Wales were worth. With the decline in the Safavids (for internal reasons; i.e. not related to the internationalization of capital), the silk trade dried up. Tribal nomadism and the lack of a strong government characterized the period from the late 1600s until the rise of the Qajar dynasty just before 1800. Surplus product was no longer appropriated and concentrated by a centralized ruling class, nor were there the preconditions for petty commodity production (e.g. private property in land); capitalist traders therefore had difficulty penetrating the local society. With the restoration of 'order' in the mid-1800s by the new Qajar dynasty, the internationalization of commodity capital began in earnest.

3. An ambiguous term chosen to avoid the debate over the applicability to Iran of such concepts as 'feudalims' or the 'Asiatic mode of production'.

4. Besides these developments characteristic of the internationalization of commodity capital, there was another dynamic at work in Iran. British and Russian capitalists each contended to secure privileges which would exclude the other. The era of free trade was on the wane. Capitalists could no longer be content with seeing an area opened up generally to capitalist trade; they had to secure that area from foreign competition through the use of state intervention, including open annexation where necessary and possible. Even areas not yet ripe for capital export and inclusion in the imperialist economy (based on the internationalization of money capital), had to be controlled lest a competitor move in and monopolize the eventual exploitation of the area. The Anglo-Russian rivalry in Iran was a classic example of pre-emptive imperialism.

5. R. Benedick, *Industrial Finance in Iran,* Boston 1964, p.14.

6. N. Keddie, 'The Iranian village before and after the land reform', *Journal of Contemporary History,* 3 (1969), p.83.

7. Ibid., p.79, quoting an unpublished paper of Mahdavy.

8. A. Lambton, *The Persian Land Reform,* London 1969, pp.98-113; and P. Vieille, 'Imperialisme, absolutisme, reforme agraire' in P. Vieille and A. H. Banisadr, *Petrole et Violence,* Paris 1974; on the riots of 1963, see N. Keddie, 'Iran: de l'independance religieuse à l'opposition politique', *Le Monde Diplomatique,* 281 (1977).

9. In 1959, the government owned about 150 plants employing 20,000 out of the 134,000 workers in manufacturing. The government has sold off many of these plants. It has invested in massive new industrial ventures which it also expects to sell off once these plants have established themselves as profitable and once Iranian investors are prepared to sink large sums into firms they do not control.

10. Benedick, op.cit., p.118.

11. K. Marx, *Capital,* vol. 3, Moscow 1971, p.334. Marx argues that the second path 'cannot by itself contribute to the overthrow of the old mode of production'.This is correct when discussing the original appearance of capitalism, but inaccurate when analysing the internationalization of capital, that is, capitalism's spread outward from an already established capitalist society.

12. International Labour Organization, *Employment and Income Policies for*

Iran, Geneva 1973, p.56.

13. There are some who identify capitalism with the 'growth of the productive forces' and then argue that the inefficiencies, cost over-runs and postponements in Iran are indications of the non-capitalist nature of Iranian society. Marx clearly demonstrated that the differences among modes of production are determined by the different relations among people in the process of production (especially the different manners in which surplus labour is appropriated), not by the character of the commodities produced. The capitalist character of Iranian society is not dependent on the construction of modern technology, but on the relations of production in Iran. Inefficiencies are endemic to capitalist production.

There is a mistaken opinion in some quarters that those who recognize the growth of industry in Iran therefore support the Shah's regime. In fact, scientific analysis of class relations in Iran is the soundest basis for the formulation of political strategy. Those who support the development of capitalism will be found to be basically with the present system (although they may deplore some of the autocratic and dictatorial policies of the Shah and may even support a 'national democratic' government); those who are opposed to capitalism and who support the cause of socialism will be found supporting the struggle to replace the present system with a workers' government (a dictatorship of the proletariat).

14. L. Kraar, 'The Shah Drives to Build a New Empire', *Fortune,* 90 (1974), p.192.

15. P. Clawson, 'The Internationalization of Capital in the Middle East', unpublished Ph.D. dissertation, New School for Research, 1978, chapter 1. One of the issues raised there is the role of the state in the accumulation process. As capitalism develops, the concentration and centralization of capital raises the amount of capital which each individual unit of capital must command in order to be competitive. At first, individuals can raise the necessary capital; then, corporations and banks are necessary; finally, the state must mobilize the capital (see A. Gerschenkron, *Economic Backwardness in Historical Perspective,* Cambridge 1966). Vast quantities of capital are necessary for modern industry. The Iranian state, as the representative of a more general capital interest, can mobilize these funds more readily than any private capitalist, including banks. The Iranian state is therefore immediately involved in any major investment decision. It is not correct to speak of 'state capitalism' in Iran, however: the state actually aids private capitalists to take over state established enterprises as quickly as possible, and the state has substantial programmes to benefit private capitalists.

A Guide to Further Reading on the Political Economy of Iran

A more scholarly presentation of the issues mentioned in this chapter can be found in P. Clawson, 'The Internationalization of Capital in the Middle East', unpublished Ph.D. dissertation, New School for Social Research, 1978, chapter

3. Full references for all data cited here can be found there.

The Internationalization of Capital

The theory that imperialism blocks the development of capitalism was eloquently stated by Paul Baran in *The Political Economy of Growth,* New York 1957, chapters 5 and 6. In a 1939 essay, Mao Tse-Tung spoke about 'the collusion of imperialism with the Chinese feudal force to arrest the development of Chinese capitalism': see Mao, *Selected Works,* vol. 2, Peking 1965, p.310. Contrast with Lenin's *Imperialism:* 'The export of capital greatly affects and accelerates the development of capitalism in those countries to which it is exported'; see V. Lenin, *Collected Works,* vol. 22, Moscow 1964, p.243.

The theory that capitalism in the 'periphery' can develop only when the ties with the world market are broken is expounded by S. Amin, *Accumulation on a World Scale,* New York 1974.

A seminal work in the analysis of the relationship between capitalism and pre-capitalist society is P. P. Rey, *Les alliances de classes,* Paris 1973. Rey demonstrates that capitalism may not immediately dissolve pre-capitalist society. Due to the resistance of pre-capitalist society to capital's penetration, capitalists may for a while preserve pre-capitalist society and extract surplus product in the form of commodities.

In spite of the explosion of self-styled Marxist writings on 'development', few authors base themselves on Marx's analysis of the laws of the dynamics of capitalism. The task at hand is to carry Marx's analysis forward to a more concrete level than is analysed in *Capital*; namely, the expansion of capitalism into pre-capitalist society. Christian Palloix has some important insights scattered through *Les firmes multinationales,* Paris 1973; and *L'Internationalisation du capital,* Paris 1975.

The Internationalization of the Circuit of Commodity Capital

N. Keddie's short essay, *Historical Obstacles to Agrarian Change in Iran,* Claremont Asian Studies no. 8, Claremont 1960, provides an excellent analysis of the evolution of the Iranian economy under the impact of trade with the West; its references to empirical sources are, however, sparse. Her account of the tobacco concession revolt of 1890 in N. Keddie, *Religion and Rebellion in Iran,* London 1966, portrays the social forces at work in Iran in the late 1800s, including the growing commodity relationships and Anglo-Russian imperialist rivalry.

On the question of 'pre-emptive imperialism', see Lenin, *Imperialism,* op.cit., p. 260ff.

C. Issawi (ed.), *The Economic History of Iran 1800-1914,* Chicago 1971, an invaluable collection of articles from primary sources and difficult-to-find secondary sources.

A. Ahmad, 'Historical Obstacles to the Development of a Bourgeoisie in Iran', in M. Cook (ed.), *Studies in the Economic History of Iran,* London 1970. This gives references to the debate over whether pre-capitalist Iran was feudal.

A. Lambton, *Landlord and Peasant in Persia,* London 1953, is a detailed account of agrarian society in the last several hundred years. Lambton discusses much more than legal relations; the character of the relations of production can be inferred from the information she provides.

An excellent class analysis of Iran at the turn of the twentieth century written by a contemporary observer is B. Mu'mini, 'Iran on the Eve of the Constitutional Revolution', *Review of Iranian Political Economy and History*, 1 (1977).

The best account of Reza Shah's reign is R. Banani, *The Modernization of Iran 1921-1941*, Stanford 1961.

The Internationalization of Money Capital

The effects of the agrarian reform of the 1960s are best analysed in Guerrilla Organization of the People's Fedaeeh, *Land Reform and Its Direct Effects in Iran*, Iranian Rural Research Series of the Iran Committee (British Section), no. 1 (1972). There are some other excellent accounts of this period: N. Keddie, 'The Iranian Village Before and After the Land Reform', *Journal of Contemporary History*, 3 (1969); R. Antoun, 'The Gentry of a Traditional Peasant Community Undergoing Rapid Technical Change: An Iranian Case Study', *Iranian Studies*, 9 (1976); P. Vieille, *La Feodalite et l'État en Iran*, Paris 1975; and P. Vieille, 'Les paysans, la petite bourgeoisie rurale et l'Etat apres la reforme agraire en Iran', *Annales Economiques, Sociales, Civilization*, 27 (1972). See also A. Lambton, *The Persian Land Reform*, London 1969. On the agrarian society just before the reform, see P. English, *City and Village in Iran*, Madison 1966.

There are a number of orthodox economic accounts of the Iranian economy since the 1950s. J. Bharier, *Economic Development in Iran 1900-1970*, London 1971, has the best data, but not much analysis. G. Baldwin, *Planning and Development in Iran*, Baltimore 1967, is an account of the Plan Organization by a member of the Harvard advisory team of the early 1960s. R. Benedick, *Industrial Finance in Iran*, Boston 1964, may be unfamiliar with Marx, but Benedick's discussion of the 'merchant to capitalist' path and the 'producer to capitalist' path follows Marx nonetheless. On the same subject, see A. Ashraf, 'Iran: Imperialism, Class and Modernization from Above', unpublished Ph.D. dissertation, New School for Social Research 1971; and W. Bartsch, 'The Industrial Labor Force of Iran', *Middle East Journal*, 25 (1971). R. Looney, *The Economic Development of Iran*, New York 1973, cites a great many government statistics of dubious validity.

On politics and general social organization, see J. Bill, *The Politics of Iran*, Columbus 1972; M. Zonis, *The Political Elite of Iran*, Princeton 1971; and E. Yar-Shatar (ed.), *Iran Faces the Seventies*, New York 1971.

Hot-House Capital Accumulation (the 1970s)

The best source of information on the contemporary economy of Iran is the *Financial Times* annual survey (28 July 1977, 21 June 1976, and 25 July 1975). The monthly London-based *Middle East* magazine is another good source. The Iranian Economic Mission to the U.S. publishes *Iran Economic News* each month. The best sources of official data are: Bank of Iran, *Annual Report and Balance Sheet;* and Plan and Budget Organization, *Statistical Yearbook*. Data are rarely available for the latest two or three years. Plan Organization, *National Census of Population and Housing November 1966*, 169 vols., has the most accurate and useful data. The results of the November 1976 census should be released in 1978 or 1979.

Two examples of authors who refuse to recognize the accumulation of capital in contemporary Iran (an accumulation of capital both as *means of production* in modern industry and as a *social relation* between capitalists and workers): A. H. Banisadr, 'Developpement de la consommation du futur et misere', in P. Vieille and A. H. Banisadr (eds.), *Petrole et violence,* Paris 1974; and T. Ricks, 'Contemporary Iranian Political Economy and History: An Overview', *Review of Iranian Political Economy and History,* 1 (1976).

There are a number of useful accounts of recent economic developments in Iran. On foreign investment, see Y. Nowshirvani and R. Bildner, 'Direct Foreign Investment in the Non-Oil Sectors of the Iranian Economy', *Iranian Studies,* 6 (1973). On the need to move to generalized capitalist production and the export of manufactured goods, see D. Avramovic, 'Industrialization of Iran: The Record, the Problems, and the Prospects', *Taghigat-e Eqtesadi,* 7 (1970). Two collections of papers presented at conferences on Iran are: J. Jacqz, *Iran: Past, Present, and Future,* New York 1976; and K. Farmanfarmaian, *The Social Sciences and Problems of Development,* Princeton, 1976. See also International Labour Organization, *Employment and Income Policies for Iran,* Geneva 1973; and J. Amuzegar and A. Fekrat, *Iran: Economic Development under Dualistic Conditions,* Chicago 1971. J. Amuzegar, *Iran: An Economic Profile,* Washington 1977, has much up-to-date information, including data from the 1976 census and from the files of Iranian government ministries; the author is an important official in the Iranian government.

9. Oil and the Penetration of Capitalism in Iraq

Joe Stork

Iraq has been one of the most militant of the oil-producing states and played a leading role in the drive to nationalize this critical commodity. Oil, in turn, has been the most important single determinant of the political economy of modern Iraq.

The first phase in the intricate history of the oil industry and its impact in Iraq can be defined as the period from the British colonial takeover after World War I to the years just after the next War. In this period oil provided the strategic motivation for British rule, which shaped the contours of modern Iraqi society and constructed the Iraqi state apparatus. The second phase, 1950-58, coincides with the increased production and export of crude oil to meet post-war imperial priorities, including the reconstruction of Western Europe. The increased production and revenue per barrel allowed the regime of Nuri as-Said to resolve the financial dimensions of its post-war crisis but undermined the political base of the regime and its colonially constructed roots in the 'proto-feudal' landlord class.

The 1958 Revolution realigned the political structure with the emerging class formations and marks the start of a decade in which the oil question is the most prominent feature of the struggle for hegemony among different fractions of the Iraqi bourgeoisie and petty bourgeoisie. The fourth and current phase can be dated from the seizure of state power by the Baath Party in 1968. The resolution of the oil question with the nationalization of the Iraq Petroleum Company (I.P.C.) in 1972-73 helped to assure the political consolidation of Baathist rule. The hike in crude oil prices over the 1971-74 period allowed the economic consolidation of the regime and gives this phase its distinctive character. The resolution of the *national* dimension of the oil question allows for redefining that question in class terms. The sharp increase in oil revenues qualitatively modifies, as it did in the early 1950s, the extent of capitalist penetration of the main sectors of the economy. This may be the basis for structural changes and class transformations that will, as in the 1950s, undermine the regime through the disjuncture of its economic base and political roots.

The First Phase

European economic penetration of the Mesopotamia region took on significant dimensions over the second half of the 19th century. The British were in the forefront, forging transportation links to facilitate the export of agricultural commodities, chiefly grains, and the import of Western manufactures. This led to a profound shift from tribal, subsistence agriculture to production for the external markets of British India and Europe, and to the transformation of the sheikh/tribesman relationship into one of landlord/peasant. Iraqi trade increased eightfold in volume between 1870 and 1914. There was a decline in the noma- dic population and an increase in the rural sedentary population as the demand for grain exports compelled the mobilization of 'surplus' labour and land. The size and number of marketing towns increased. The flood of merchandise, chiefly British textiles, destroyed local handicraft industries. Trade was mono- polized by British firms and comprador elements, chiefly from the Jewish communities of Baghdad and Basra. Tribal isolation was sharply modified and Ottoman state authority extended in the form of gendarme garrisons and forays to collect taxes and 'recruit' troops. On the eve of the British colonial conquest the integration into the world market of this territory and its ethnically and ecologically diverse population had produced severe demo- graphic and social dislocations that impoverished masses of tribespeople/ peasants and townspeople and benefited a handful of merchants and tribal sheikhs.

Mesopotamia was a minor theatre in the British campaign against the Ottoman-German alliance during World War I, but the known and suspected oil reserves of the province of Mosul (the Turkish Petroleum Company had been formed just before the War by British, Dutch and German interests) and the territory's proximity to the Persian oil fields provided all the necessary justification for maintaining a colonial presence. The character of this presence was modified by the nationalist revolt of 1920 that linked up tribal and urban resisters. The cost in British lives and money to suppress it threatened to undermine political support for this particular enterprise in London. An 'Arab solution' — indirect rule through an indigenous, dependent elite — became imperative.

The building blocks for a British-sponsored local ruling class were the Iraqi officers from the Ottoman Army who had providently sided with the British during the War and the landlord-sheikhs in the countryside. The officers came as an entourage with the British candidate for king, the Hashemite prince, Feisal. Without roots in the economic life of the towns and with no significant material wealth, they depended on the British and the sheikhs for their continued rule.

In the countryside British policy centred on re-establishing the authority of the sheikhs, which was eroding with the shift in land tenure patterns. Political and tax-levying authority was delegated. The Tribal Criminal and Civil Disputes Regulations (1916) granted the sheikhs full juridical authority and proved an important legal prop for the feudal-type social relations that developed. Under the guise of restoring the 'natural' bonds between tribespeople and sheikhs, the British ensured political tranquility and agricultural supplies for the urban population and invading forces. Sheikhs acquired private title to formerly tribal landholdings. Throughout the Mandate period their support was periodically reaffirmed by the timely remission of taxes, which steadily increased their share of the agricultural surplus (land taxes declined from 42 per cent of the total revenue in 1911 to 14 per cent in 1933).[1] An organic relationship evolved among the indigenous ruling segments as urban officials used their positions to secure vast estates for themselves and partnerships with the large merchants; sheikhs took up residence in the towns as absentee landlords and acquired interests in urban real estate and the import trade.

Foreign capital, not any indigenous ruling class, set the priorities for the new state and formulated its most intimate details through the provision of 'advisers' to the prominent ministries. The state's share of the surplus, in the form of indirect taxes that hit the poorest classes, financed the colonial state apparatus and was siphoned off directly to the British Treasury and private banks as payment for 'public works' undertaken by the British to facilitate their takeover and even to pay off the old Ottoman public debt! Sectarian, ethnic and tribal differences were manipulated to preclude co-ordinated popular opposition. The ultimate sanction for maintaining territorial unity and political legitimacy was the liberal use of R.A.F. bombers conveniently stationed outside Baghdad.

The hegemony of foreign capital was clearly reflected in the negotiations over the northern border of the country with Turkey. Both Turkey and Iraq claimed Mosul province and its oil. Mosul was important to Iraq for demographic reasons as well: without the Sunni Arab and Kurdish population of the province, the Shi'i Arabs would constitute a clear majority in the new state and weaken the already fragile base of the 'Arab solution'. Iraqi dependence on the British in resisting Turkish demands and silencing Kurdish pressure for autonomy had a price: Iraqi agreement to the concession terms laid down by the oil companies.

The main legacy of the colonial period was political. Although weak and fragmented, the new state met the primary need of foreign capital to secure the territory for its oil. Economic penetration was limited and class transformation therefore also limited. In the countryside technical improvements, notably the expansion of pump irrigation, were grafted on to the politically determined latifundist class relations, intensifying the extraction of absolute surplus value and erecting barriers to the transformation of production relations into capitalist ones. In the urban areas manufacturing efforts were few and feeble. The urban bourgeoisie was overwhelmingly mercantile and tied to foreign capital. But the construction and imposition of the state apparatus placed an almost imperceptible shift of political and economic power to the urban areas, especially Baghdad. This process included the formation and reproduction of a new urban petty bourgeoisie, operating small stores and workshops and staffing the lower levels of the bureaucracy. Dependent on the expansion of the state apparatus and the urban trading and manufacturing sectors, these elements came to articulate resentment of control by the British and the parasitical local ruling class.

The political and economic crisis that led to 'independence' in 1932 was precipitated by the sharp fall in world prices of grains, still Iraq's main export. The I.P.C. – the consortium of Anglo-Iranian, Shell, Mobil and Jersey Standard – was the only source of cash for the regime. In return for an advance on future royalties, I.P.C. demanded an expansion of their concession area from only 192 to 35,000 square miles, leading to their monopolization of the entire country by 1938. Popular resentment of these extortionist terms and the regime's capitulation, along with the imposition of new taxes on small merchants, provoked widespread strikes and demonstrations in 1931. The 'independence' granted to restore tranquility gave a freer hand to the Sunni officials around Feisal, 'but the British authorities still retained supreme power, and the vast majority of the population still possessed no power at all'.[2]

The tasks of the state did not change with 'independence'. Foremost was the need to develop and maintain the administrative machinery and repressive apparatus. (Thirty-eight per cent of the official budgets went for public security, 30 per cent for administration; only 17 per cent was available for irrigation, agriculture, public works, communications, etc.)[3] The urban ruling elements, rather than take advantage of the crisis to accomplish its historic tasks – appropriation of the agricultural surplus in place of the parasitical landlords, the establishment of productive economic relations in the towns and countryside – continued along the path of compromise with the colonial power and repression of the newly conscious strata of the petty bourgeoisie and workers in the urban areas. This fatal inclination of the regime to isolate itself from the emerging urban social forces and forge closer links with the landlords was consecrated in the Consumption Tax of 1931 (ending efforts to tax the landowners directly), the Settlements Law of 1932 (legalizing the sheikhs' landholdings as private property) and the Rights and Duties of Cultivators Law of 1933 (binding peasants to landowners and restricting the circulation of labour).

Until this point the direct impact of the oil industry was quite limited. Through to the end of the Second World War, company activity had been restricted to exploration, construction of production and transport facilities, and the operation of a small refinery on the Iranian border, processing Iranian oil for internal Iraqi needs. The total number of workers employed by the company reached 3,600 in 1938 and 5,700 in 1945, but rose to 15,000 by the mid-1950s.[4] Most were skilled or semi-skilled workers, both blue and white-collar. A strong trade union was organized after the War and the oilworkers' strike at Kirkuk in 1947 for better pay and conditions was significant in the political crisis after the War.

The sharp surge of inflation that accompanied the Second World War benefited the merchant and landlord classes but drastically hurt the rural and urban masses, including the salaried government workers and other elements of the petty bourgeoisie. The wartime environment of protection and high demand led to the establishment of small manufacturing enterprises, but few survived the post-war adjustment period. Wartime profits were 'concentrated and in hands itching to employ them in the import trade'.[5] Most companies set up after the War were trading rather than manufacturing, and most manufacturing firms were small and privately held. Thus the War produced only a slight shift in the mercantile orientation of the Iraqi bourgeoisie.

The endemic economic crisis that set in after the War and mounting anti-British and anti-imperialist militancy on a popular level produced a politically explosive atmosphere. Massive demonstrations and political disturbances were frequent. The leadership in these incidents came from the workers (under the effective leadership of the Iraqi Communist Party), notably the relatively well-paid and large concentrations of workers in the state railways, the oil company and the textile mills. A spiral of strikes, repression and demonstrations led the manager of the largest Iraqi bank to describe the situation in 1948 as 'desperate', with the regime 'helpless to stem the mounting tide of unemployment, inevitably leading to riots and a political crisis of the first magnitude'.[6]

The Second Phase: Prelude to Revolution

These same years marked the beginning of a new period of reconstruction and expansion in the industrialized capitalist countries under the leadership of the United States, calling for a rapid and protracted expansion of crude oil production and export from the Middle East. The financial dimension of the Iraqi crisis was resolved by the decision of the American oil companies to 'share' their profits with the producing regimes as part of a strategy to 'get more money into the hands of the conservative governments in the Arab world'.[7] The 1952 agreement between the I.P.C. and the government increased revenue from $1.75 to $5.50 per ton; oil revenue as a proportion of government revenue jumped from 10 per cent to over 60 per cent.

In the decade of the 1950s the crude oil extraction sector accounted for over 35 per cent of the country's total domestic production of goods and services, while employing only 0.6 per cent of the labour force. Total local disbursements, including wages, were less than I.D. 9 million in 1954. [The Iraqi Dinar was linked to the British pound sterling formally until 1959; its equivalent dollar value was $2.80.] The profits of the industry were nominally divided in half between the company and the government: in 1956 I.D. 69 million was repatriated abroad and the same amount was made available for the development plan and regular expenditures. It was used directly and indirectly to finance construction, manufacturing, trade and real estate. Beginning in the latter half of the decade the price of crude began to decline in world markets, adversely affecting the most important component of the national product. Output and pricing decisions were firmly in the hands of the company executives in New York and London.

The largest government expenditures were for dams and irrigation projects, but the unaltered latifundist social structure in the countryside ensured that benefits were confined to the large landowners who appropriated over 70 per cent of total production in the agricultural sector. The continued impoverishment of the peasants was manifested in frequent outbreaks of violence against the landlords and, more permanently, in the squalid slums of cardboard and reed huts that swelled the outskirts of Baghdad and Basra.

Agriculture accounted for nearly 21 per cent of total national production, and employed about 55 per cent of the labour force. Of the I.D. 88 million total value added in this sector in 1956, I.D. 62 million was appropriated by the landlord class and I.D. 26 million formed the subsistence income for the masses of peasants.[8] Little of the landlords' share was invested productively; immediate consumption and speculation in real estate and the import trade were the preferred means of disposal.

Manufacturing, construction and utilities accounted for 13.8 per cent of the domestic product in 1956, and 12.5 per cent of the work force. Profits amounted to I.D. 27.2 million and wages to I.D. 35.9 million (including the earnings of self-employed small shopowners). Profits in manufacturing alone, excluding the government-owned refinery, showed a 59 per cent increase between 1953 and 1956 and a further jump of 48.4 per cent by 1960.

Trade (wholesale and retail), banking, insurance and real estate accounted for 10.7 per cent of the domestic product and an estimated 15 per cent of the workforce. Profits totalled I.D. 32.5 million while wages were only I.D. 4.2 million. Trading profits increased 41 per cent between 1953 and 1956, and a further 15 per cent by 1960. For banking, insurance and real estate the profit increases were 96 per cent and 26 per cent for the same periods.

Services, including transport, communications and storage, accounted for 12.2 per cent of production and an estimated 8.6 per cent of the workforce, with I.D. 16.6 million in profits and I.D. 26.1 million in wages. The bulk of the wages were in services, the profits in transport.

The low growth of national production in agriculture and industry put the burden of meeting increased demand on imports. As a proportion of national income, imports rose from 18 per cent to 31.7 per cent between 1950 and 1957. Half of total imports in 1955 were consumer goods, and the fastest growing category was consumer durables, at a rate of 47.6 per cent a year and serving the needs of a small but growing elite.

The increased oil revenues gave the regime a new lease of life, but no efforts were made to effect structural changes in the productive or distributive character of the economy. Revenues for the regular budget came almost exclusively from indirect taxes, weighing most heavily on the poorest classes.

The impact of development spending was similarly skewed. Construction, mainly of public buildings (including an opera house designed by Frank Lloyd Wright!) made up 35 per cent of total expenditures. A housing boom, prompted in part by the influx of foreign experts and technicians and by the predilection of the Iraqi bourgeoisie for real estate speculation and over productive investments, added to the growth of construction in this period. Much of the increase in the manufacturing sector in these years was in fact in construction materials.

The structure of ownership was overwhelmingly private, with utilities accounting for the bulk of public ownership. Services were 56 per cent private, including education and health. Trade, banking, insurance and real estate were 86 per cent private, with the government represented only in the banking sector. Foreign capital was significant in all of these subsectors.

Public administration and defence accounted for 6.5 per cent of production, an estimated 8 per cent of the workforce, and provided I.D. 21.4 million in wages in 1956. (Army and police accounted for 33 per cent of government spending in 1950, 40.7 per cent in 1957). Perhaps the most important aspect of the growth of the public sector was the expansion of education and the consequent pressures to provide employment, given the unaltered traditional orientation of that system to provide training for government, professional, white-collar jobs. The budget for education increased from $2.4 million (11.8 per cent of government spending) in 1940-41 to $10.1 million (14 per cent) in 1950-51 and $36.1 million (18 per cent) in 1957-58. The number of primary schools practically doubled between 1950 and 1958 to more than 2,000; primary students went from 180,779 to 430,475. Secondary schools increased from 95 to 158 and their students from 22,706 to 51,934. The number of students in higher education was 5,338 in 1958. Neither the public nor the private sector was able to absorb more than a fraction of the graduates in this decade.[9]

Iraq in this period is a society enduring tremendous dislocations. The largest source of national wealth is under foreign control. The locus of domestic production is the agricultural sector, but there land tenure, income distribution and the sharply polarized class structure contribute to the continued deterioration of the means of production – the land – and the immiseration of the producers. There is accelerated growth in the urban centres, especially Baghdad: the oil rent and agricultural surplus are concentrated there in trade, construction and speculation. Great numbers of peasants flee the land and crowd the slums, finding even the miserable, part-time, unskilled, poorly-paid jobs there an improvement over conditions in the countryside.

There is a marked growth of a bourgeoisie in this period: an incalculable expansion in numbers, but primarily the growth and diversification of wealth and property within the existing elite, with its links to the regime, the land, commerce and, increasingly, manufacturing. This numerically small and inter-linked bourgeoisie, relatively weak in the realm of production, is counterposed to a much larger but more fragmented working class, with only some 30,000 in large-scale manufacturing (i.e. in firms employing 10 or more workers). In this period we can speak of an emerging, if still small, industrial bourgeoisie and working class. By the end of the 1950s, profits in manufacturing exceed those in trade. This newer, emergent fraction of the bourgeoisie has a different agenda than the commercial fraction with its heavily comprador character.

Between the few who are unmistakably bourgeois in their outlook and material conditions and the masses of peasants and workers is the petty bourgeoisie. Here the lines on the class map get especially blurred: the thousands of small handicraft shops that make up a huge part of the so-called manufacturing sector; the even more numerous one-person stores; the professionals and semi-professionals employed in services and the public sector, including the army; the thousands of students looking for scarce posts, but whose orientation is unmistakably towards commerce and the government bureaucracy. Much larger than the bourgeoisie itself, this class is educated, ideologically articulate, and expanding more rapidly than any other.

The opposition that developed toward the regime gathered force in the face of the pervasive and severe contradictions of the 1940s and 1950s. Broad in its potential, it included peasants, workers, the petty bourgeoisie and the small 'national' bourgeoisie. Peasant opposition remained unorganized, spontaneous, untapped. In contrast, that of the workers was well organized in vanguard sections made up of the larger trade unions and under the leadership to a large extent of the Communist Party (I.C.P.). The industrial bourgeoisie, to the extent that it can be separated from the other fractions of the bourgeoisie, had aspirations and interests not served by the feudal-like relations in the countryside and the extreme concentration of wealth and property. This was very different from the commercial bourgeoisie, whose stake in an expanding internal market and a trained and disciplined workforce was not so great. Finally, the petty bourgeoisie was similarly interested in expanded employment opportunities, growing markets, and mobility into the ranks of the bourgeoisie.

The disarticulation between the political system (a parliament monopolized by the landlords and hand-picked government supporters) and the rapidly changing social reality became untenable with the increasing pace of urban-based economic activity following the growth of oil revenues. Strikes and demonstrations by workers and students increased in tempo and severity. Repression was harsh and democratic rights systematically denied.[10] When the regime's alignment with the U.S. and Britain against Egypt led to the Baghdad Pact, this affront to Iraqi and Arab nationalism heightened the already explosive confrontation over basic democratic rights and, more importantly, the allocation of economic and political power in Iraqi society.

The opposition had formed a United National Front comprising parties that represented virtually all the emerging urban political forces. The working class was represented by the I.C.P., the largest and best organized party. The petty bourgeoisie was represented ideologically by the Baath Party, which however was of recent origin in Iraq, and this class remained organizationally fragmented. Large numbers of the petty bourgeoisie, especially students and intellectuals, supported the I.C.P.; others adhered to the National Democratic Party (N.D.P.). This was the liberal, left-of-centre party of the new 'national' bourgeoisie. (The lawyer, Kamal Chaderchi, and the industrialist and landowner, Muhammad Hadid, were the most prominent members of the N.D.P. and identified themselves ideologically with British Fabian socialism.) The last and least significant of the opposition groups was the right-wing bourgeois Independence Party.

The contours of Iraqi society by the late 1950s were the specific product of phases of capitalist penetration as modified by the particularities of the Iraqi scene, where oil production was of particular importance. The country's modern history is punctuated by political eruptions that are traceable to the dislocations precipitated by adjustment to the world market at different periods, setting the conditions of interaction betwen Iraqi social forces and foreign capital in the next phase.

In penetrating Iraq, foreign capital set up a political system hinged in the countryside on pre-capitalist relations of production that were already in the process of disintegrating. This impeded but did not halt the feeble extension of capitalist relations and means of production in the urban areas; but it largely pre-empted such relations from emerging in the rural areas. The barriers to capitalist development that foreign capital helped to erect were set up to facilitate the political control of the territory. Content with political control and unhindered access to oil, foreign capital left the direct economic exploitation of the country to the tender hands of a pre-capitalist leadership unable, unwilling, and without incentive, to develop and utilize the agricultural surplus, to innovate production and set labour free to combine with capital in any sector. Within this setting comprador commercial capital, narrowly based, could flourish without creating incentives to move towards alternative relations of production.

But Iraq's status as a supplier of crude oil after 1945 brought with it a heightened penetration by capital, directly in the industry itself and indirectly with the vastly increased state revenues. Capital's response to the potential spread to Iraq of the Iranian political crisis over Mossadeq's nationalization after the War had been fully in character: the payoff. It brought no political reforms. Conditions in the rural sector steadily worsened and the landlord's right to confiscation was extended to the right of exclusion.

Structural changes occurred nonetheless. The rent from oil accrued to the centre, was dispersed from the centre, and perceptibly accelerated the shift of economic activity and the generation of new surplus to the urban areas. The demographic data confirms the obvious. Unlike the situation in the countryside, where the pre-capitalist mode of social organization could be more or less frozen from the centre to preserve political control and enhance the appropriation of absolute surplus value by extending cultivation and intensifying the exploitation of peasant labour, the growth of urban economic activity in the sphere of production necessarily involved sharp modification of the relations of production that existed in the rural areas. Given the lack of appropriate conditions — 'free' labour, productive capital, market prospects — no half-hearted stimuli could spark an industrial revolution. The dominance of merchant capital in the cities, its comprador character, its links with the monarchy on the one hand and the landlord class on the other, the dominant role of foreign capital in the trading sector, all militated against the easy transformation of social relations. But this negative balance was challenged fitfully, chiefly by the influx of the oil rent. The 'pay-off' nourished the very revolution it was designed to pre-empt.

On one level the power of the state was enhanced by this provision of income. The repressive apparatus could be strengthened. Income could be distributed in a limited way to provide modest sinecures for potential opponents among the bourgeoisie. But this assumed the preservation of the existing balance of social forces — including foreign capital — that had been represented by the old regime. As this shifted, new forces emerging and old ones weakening, the state would have to reflect those changes. The last British political advisers attached to the ministries left in the early 1950s. Investment funds became available. 'Free labour' multiplied with the migration from the countryside and the expansion of the educational system. Market demand intensified as the labour force grew. Foreign advisers and experts infested nearly every ministry with their ideology of 'development'. The ascendant bourgeoisie, petty bourgeoisie and working classes demanded that the state represent their interests. As even the armed forces came to reflect the shifting balance of social forces, the immunity of the regime to radical alteration evaporated.

The Third Phase: The Revolution Shakes Down

Revolutions are political earthquakes in which structural strains occasionally manifest themselves. The eruption can be anticipated but not predicted. In the aftermath there is a period when a new alignment of social forces is assembled. In Iraq the open struggle for class hegemony lasted a full decade and centred on the control of the state apparatus and conflicting interpretations of the appropriate role of the state within the social formation as a whole. In the years just after the Revolution, Iraqi society was intensely politicized at every level. Parties, especially the Communists, worked to mobilize popular support for their programmes by re-establishing trade unions, peasant associations and professional organizations. The tendency over the decade, though, was for the political struggle to be increasingly restricted to competition among the petty-bourgeois groupings within the state apparatus, purposefully removed from the popular level. Conspiracies and bureaucratic manoeuvring replaced mobilization.

The social origins and political inclinations of the 'Free Officers' placed them squarely among the petty bourgeoisie. Typical of their outlook was Qassem's proposition that all classes had merged and that the regime 'will not lower the standard of the rich, but . . . will raise the standard of the poor'.[11] While all the parties, notably the I.C.P. and the Baath, had adherents among the officers, the dominant political influence on Qassem was exercised by the 'men of substance', the leadership of the N.D.P. Their programme called for the gradual restructuring of the economy under the leadership of the new urban bourgeoisie, including fiscal protection for new industries, a 'welfare state' array of social services, easy mortgages, government salary hikes, better working conditions, and regional labour exchanges.[12]

The Baath Party, reflecting its recent origin among petty officials and the intelligentsia, defined their 'socialism' as 'social justice'. This was compatible with the views of the N.D.P., but the Baath priority was a programme for Arab unity under Nasser, and identified the concept of 'revolution' with the 'reawakening Arab nation'. The non-materialist and occasionally chauvinist character of this outlook was manifested politically in a fanatical anticommunism and organizationally in the isolation of the party from contact with workers and peasants.[13]

Organizational experience lay with the I.C.P. Because of its specific opposition to unity under Nasser, it was a useful tool for Qassem in fending off pressures from the Baathists and unorganized Nasserists. The I.C.P. saw Qassem leading a 'national democratic' phase of transition, the most promising environment for building socialism. But Qassem carefully excluded the Communists from any share of state power, persistently rejected their demands for the implementation of democratic rights, and, once the Baathist/Nasserist threat was contained in the first year, moved to purge them from the state apparatus and the mass organizations and incrementally reduce Communist influence on a popular level. 'The main contradiction in Iraq in the decisive years between 1958 and 1963 was that of a national bourgeois regime which was confronting, yet at the same time relying upon, a politically conscious and radical left.'[14]

The main achievement in this period, due in no small part to the vigorous efforts of the I.C.P., was the agrarian reform programme. The political strength of the landowning class was broken. Political and economic power was restructured in favour of the urban and petty bourgeoisie while maintaining the principle of private ownership.

The question of national control over oil came to dominate Iraqi political life in the first years after the Revolution. Success in this arena was seen as a way of restructuring the economy while avoiding a direct confrontation with the class structure of Iraqi society. In Qassem's words,

> We are not combatting the oil companies to obtain an additional I.D. 7 million a year. This is not a fundamental point. We are fighting for the industrialization of our republic and the ending of our dependence on the sale of crude oil. [The resulting financial gains] will benefit all and improve the lot of the poor whose rights we came to power to uphold without jeopardizing a fair standard of living for the rich.[15]

But confrontation came at a time of declining crude oil prices, thus making the question of revenues a potent one. Price cuts in 1959 and 1960, growing out of contradictions within the oil industry itself, forced budget reductions and triggered political disturbances.

Iraqis charged that the companies were out to make an example of this first Arab oil-producing state to undergo a nationalist revolution. Iraq did, in fact, represent the most tangible and concrete threat to the unhampered control of Middle East oil by the companies. The surplus world production at that point, and the alternative sources available to the members of the consortium, put the Iraq Petroleum Company (I.P.C.) in a strong position. (The concern of the companies with the course of developments in Iraq was evident in the I.P.C. decision to appoint Jersey Standard's Harold Fisher to head their negotiating team — 'one of the industry's most experienced diplomats', who had played a leading role in the formation of the Iranian Oil Consortium after the C.I.A. overthrew Mossadeq.)

The chief Iraqi demands, in addition to the restoration and increase of revenues, concerned implementation of a 20 per cent state participation in the I.P.C. management and the Company's relinquishment of the 60 per cent of Iraqi territory it held so that Iraq could arrange joint ventures with smaller companies, as was then being done in Iran and Egypt. But the company would not guarantee minimum production or revenue levels, rejected a demand to construct refineries in Iraq, made clear it had no intention of relinquishing anywhere near 60 per cent of the concession, and denied the government any role in choosing the area to be relinquished. Qassem broke off the futile negotiations in October 1961 and two months later issued an ultimatum, Law 80, which limited the Company's rights to the 0.5 per cent of the concession actually being exploited, and reserved all rights in the other 99.5 per cent of the country to the government. The lengthy statement that accompanied the promulgation of Law 80 testified to the extent that abiding resentment of the colonial imposition of the original concession was as important as the immediate controversy in provoking the expropriation.

From this point on, the issue of national control of oil resources was the most important single point of struggle among the various political factions in the series of regimes that followed Qassem's. The Baathist coup against Qassem in February 1963 (in which the C.I.A. also collaborated and in fact supplied the Baath with the names of Communists who were later murdered)[16] did not, despite the subsequent physical decimation of the Communists, settle the struggle for political hegemony, but it did set limits on how radical the 1958 Revolution would be. The alternatives now consisted of limited reformist programmes, with shades of radical rhetoric reflecting the diverse ideological strands of the petty bourgeoisie.

None of these groupings could advocate revoking Law 80; popular sentiment would allow for no such backsliding. But Law 80 had a loophole, permitting the government to return to I.P.C., in the context of a general agreement over all pending issues, a further 0.5 per cent of the concession, including the North Rumaila fields where abundant crude had been discovered but left unexploited. Radical nationalists insisted that the Iraqi state itself exploit North Rumaila with contracted technical assistance. More moderate elements favoured returning North Rumaila to I.P.C. as the price of a 'new era' of high production and increased revenues for state expenditure and investment. The Company rejected the validity of the new law entirely and retaliated by holding down production and bludgeoned other companies (like Italy's E.N.I.) into not making offers on the expropriated area.

The question of who should exploit North Rumaila was only the most prominent. Iraqi politics from the fall of Qassem took the form of contending coalitions representing a variety of particular interests from both the private and public sectors. The 'radicals' favoured an expanded public sector role throughout the economy. The 'moderates' wanted to restrict that role to the provision of basic services and physical infrastructure. This would include the state-sponsored development of those basic industries beyond the capacity of individual entrepreneurs, but the essential character of the economy would be private.

An important locus of 'moderate' strength in the state apparatus was in the Oil Ministry and, after it was set up in 1964, the Iraq National Oil Company (I.N.O.C.). The struggle over the control of oil and the disposition of revenues was often manifest in the various reorganizations of I.N.O.C. throughout this period: the 'radicals' wanted it under the control of the cabinet, where they often held the edge; the 'moderates' favoured an autonomous body that could function like a commercial company, not be bound by civil service salary limits, and develop Iraq's oil resources in partnership with foreign private or state companies, including I.P.C.

The 'radicals' enjoyed more popular support and were frequently prominent in the many governments formed over these years, but lacked a coherent ideology and political organization. Typical of their mode of operating was the July 1964 nationalization decree affecting the large private manufacturing, trading, insurance and banking firms. An unsophisticated imitation of similar Egyptian measures, motivated by Nasser's insistence that political unity required compatible economic systems ('socialism before unity'), it was designed to co-opt leftist support behind a campaign for unity. But there was no effort to mobilize popular support. Up to the night before the announcement (on the sixth anniversary of the Revolution) President Arif and Prime Minister Yahya stoutly denied any intention of such a move. It transferred overnight the largest, most profitable enterprises to the public sector. Private capital was rooted out of productive investments, operations were disrupted and mismanaged, and no alternative 'socialist' orientation was introduced, even in the regime's loose sense of the term.

The pace of developments in the oil sector and the economy as a whole could best be described as one of 'limping paralysis'. Negotiations with I.P.C. resumed in May 1964 and an agreement was reached in June 1965 restoring North Rumaila to the Company in return for a joint I.N.O.C.-I.P.C. concession over a further 32,000 square kilometers, a guaranteed hike in production, and a cash payment of £20 million. A bumbling effort by the 'radicals' to oust President Arif in another unity bid backfired and gave the 'moderates' their strongest position in years under a regime headed by the only civilian Prime Minister since 1958, Abdul Rahman al Bazzaz, a diplomat and legal scholar. Bazzaz launched a concerted effort to 'correct' the impact of the July 1964 nationalizations with a programme of 'prudent socialism' that removed restrictions on private investment, encouraged joint ventures with foreign capital in raw material exploitation projects, and sought to restrict, even dismantle to some extent, the public sector.

The Bazzaz premiership lasted through the autumn of 1966. The assault on the public sector degenerated into a favouring of private over public initiatives and a liberal imports policy. Bazzaz's fall, like much in Iraqi politics, cannot be described in strictly ideological and class terms. His policy of compromise with Mustafa Barzani's Kurdish forces, for example, was opposed by right-wing officers who otherwise supported his economic programme. The accidental death of President Arif in April 1966 brought the politically divided officers back to the forefront.

Even in its strongest moments the Bazzaz government never felt strong enough to push through ratification of the 1965 agreement with I.P.C. It was never even formally presented to the cabinet. Oil officials favoured ratification, claiming the state could nationalize any and all the concessions when able, but that for the moment the foreign companies 'must be allowed to make a reasonable profit' and that the government's aim should be fixed on 'increasing the yield per barrel . . . that is what really counts'.[17] Indeed the technocrats had all the 'realistic' arguments on their side: the agreement did represent concessions on the part of the Company, including acknowledgement of Law 80; it would also have removed obstacles toward increasing production and therefore government revenues, and would have permitted joint ventures with other companies in the rest of the territory.

But the price — handing back to I.P.C. proven, prolific fields strictly on the basis of the majors' monopoly control of world markets — was resoundingly unpopular among politicized Iraqis, for whom the very existence of the original concession was a legacy of treachery and brute force. Popular sentiment was reflected in the views of the commentator in the nationalist journal *Arab Oil and Gas*: 'The world may well wonder how the Iraqi revolutionaries can nation-alize cases of Ceylonese tea and at the same time restore ten billion barrels of oil to the monopolistic companies at whose hands the Iraqi people have suffered so much.'[18]

Events outside Iraq destroyed the possibility of any agreement that restored North Rumaila to I.P.C. A rancorous dispute between I.P.C. and Syria over pipeline transit fees came to a head in December 1966, halting all I.P.C. Mediterranean exports and posing a severe financial threat to the Iraqi regime. The Iraqis argued privately with the Syrians for a quick settlement but felt constrained from publicly compromising their pan-Arab and anti-I.P.C. credentials.

That dispute was settled in March, but the spring of 1967 was not the best of times for coping with the assortment of political and economic issues facing Iraq. The June War between the Arab states and Israel had a shattering political impact that resounded far beyond the carnage of the battlefields. The Khartoum summit in August was an unambiguous manifestation of the realignment of political forces in the Arab world, reflecting in particular the enhanced status of Saudi Arabia and Kuwait as paymasters for the front-line states. Iraq had led the campaign for an oil embargo; government acceptance of the Khartoum decisions prompted protest demonstrations by the Nasserists of the Arab National Movement (A.N.M.) and the temporary resignation of A.N.M. members from the government. The inability of the 'radicals' to secure support for their policies in pan-Arab circles focused once again their attention on the domestic situation.

The Six Day War removed for good the slightest possibility of the return of North Rumaila to I.P.C. The parameters for possible negotiation shifted markedly to the left. Law 97, proclaimed in August 1967, prohibited the return to I.P.C. of 'any area in which a field or part of a field is situated and in which oil has been discovered'. Law 123 reorganized I.N.O.C., replacing its technocratic management with political appointees.

When the 'radicals' pushed ahead in December 1967 with an agreement between I.N.O.C. and the French Elf-E.R.A.P. company for a joint venture on some promising acreage of the revoked I.P.C. concession, the technocrats charged that the terms amounted to a 'give-away' and were far less beneficial than those negotiated with the I.P.C. in 1965. The 'radicals' defended the deal as consistent with the maximization of national control while also coping with the majors' hold over world markets. In April 1968 the government announced that North Rumaila would be exploited directly, not as a joint venture, and put out bids for turn-key contracts. Khayreddin Haseeb, a director of I.N.O.C. (and author of the 1964 nationalization measures) characterized this decision as the first step in creating 'a national oil sector independent of the foreign oil monopolies' and laying the ground work for 'the second basic step — namely to terminate the monopoly of the foreign oil companies operating in Iraqi territory and nationalize them'.[19]

The strong popular sentiment against any deal with I.P.C., to which the nationalists' success is partly attributable, set certain limits on what could be a politically acceptable oil policy; but it did not directly contribute to the formulation or implementation of that policy. The 'radicals' were politicians and bureaucrats, not organizers. Their petty-bourgeois character was reflected in their opportunistic reliance on that popular support without developing a comprehensive programme to resolve the many outstanding contradictions. There was no effort to mobilize the public for a protracted struggle with the Company. The drop in oil revenues, combined with another futile campaign against the Kurds, forced the regime to increase taxes, hitting especially those on fixed salaries and thus eroding support from those in the public sector. Communist activity among peasants in the south testified to the ineptness with which the agrarian reform programme had been carried out. Migration to the cities reached a rate of 57,000 per year. Wages in manufacturing had stagnated over the preceding five years. The overall ineptness of the regime only made the oil dispute that much more protracted and costly, as the Company played for time and manipulated internal forces. In July 1968, just after the tenth anniversary of the Qassem Revolution that had brought the diffuse petty-bourgeois and bourgeois forces to power, the Baath Party in alliance with right-wing military officers seized power in a bloodless coup.

The Current Phase

The Baath Party, in the composition of its membership and its limited ideological development, represented the lower stratum of the petty-bourgeois forces: sons of small shopkeepers, petty officials, graduates of teacher training schools, the law school, the military academies. The Party had never faced the same repression under the Arif regimes as their Communist rivals, and opposition from rival petty-bourgeois organizations like the A.N.M. was diffuse.

It was unmistakably a right-wing coup: Baathist alliances reached out in one direction only. But the mistakes of 1963 were not repeated. The non-Baathist military co-conspirators were hustled out of the country within two weeks. Aside from the notorious public hangings of 1969-70, much of the political violence occurred between rival Baathist factions. Over the course of several years all except two of the original coup-makers were eliminated. The Party consolidated itself politically by skilful manoeuvring of opponents through tactical and temporary alliances and selective but thorough intimidation and repression.[20]

This ensconcement in power of one fraction of the petty bourgeoisie brought no significant policy changes but did result in more effective implementation of existing policies. In the oil sector, for example, despite the arrest and vilification of the 'radicals', Haseeb and al Jadir, their legacy remained intact. The establishment of an Oil Affairs Committee directly under the Revolutionary Command Council in March 1970 was one of several steps taken to ensure political control of the negotiations with I.P.C. and the strengthening of the national oil company. Major decisions included the service contract with the Soviet Union for the development of North Rumaila in 1969 and the nationalization of I.P.C. in June 1972. The success of the latter campaign showed considerable planning and astute implementation by the top political leadership. This unity of purpose was probably the main ingredient of its success.

However, behind all the rhetoric of 'direct confrontation with imperialism at its nerve centre',[21] the results were remarkably like those envisaged by the Baath's predecessors. Al Jadir rhapsodized in the spring of 1968 about the 'era of the long-term contract', in which negotiations between the international companies and the national producers 'would be limited to the question of volume of sales and the price discounts . . . The dream of all producing countries to transform oil negotiations into purely commercial transactions will have come true.'[22] The present oil minister now boasts that 'Iraq is today considered as the largest direct national seller of oil in the world.' 'Our policy is based on diversifying markets',[23] he continues. And indeed France, Italy and Brazil are the largest importers of Iraqi oil today. But the major lifters continue to be the international companies, including all the former I.P.C. group except Exxon.

This 'commercialization' policy was implemented by the top political leadership of 'socialist' Iraq. In September 1971 the Oil Affairs Committee became the Follow-up Committee for Oil Affairs and the Implementation of Agreements. Marketing was later taken over directly by this Committee. Decisions concerning markets, discounts and so on are restricted to the top leadership, as is any information concerning production, exports, destinations, or purchasers. (The sensitivity of the regime to criticism on these matters is evident from the fact that from the official *Statistical Abstract*, for example, one would hardly know Iraq ever produced or exported a single barrel of oil.)

The dependence of the economy on the oil sector increased sharply following the 1973-74 price hikes. Crude oil made up 98 per cent of exports in 1975. Its contribution to total revenues increased from 52.3 per cent in 1971 to

87.2 per cent in 1976. Its share of the national product jumped from 35 per cent in 1970 to 60 per cent in 1974.

The Follow-up Committee not only directs the oil sector, but functions as the highest authority in the whole realm of economic planning. Its membership is limited to its president, Saddam Hussein, and secretary-general, Adnan Hamdani.[24] Designed to circumvent the prodigious bureaucratic procedures that beset any project implementation, the Committee can short-circuit the entire planning procedure, such as competitive bidding, when deemed expedient. It simply declares the project 'strategic' — and most of the large industrial schemes are eligible for such designation.

The oil industry in Iraq, both directly through the production and marketing of this commodity and indirectly through the provision of revenues to the state, has been a major force behind the penetration of capitalist relations in the country and the consequent restructuring of class forces. The oil sector's provision of large revenues to the regime has helped to veil its class character and to mute the class struggle internally. Without the provision of those considerable rents, the appropriation of surplus value from Iraqi commodity production in the agricultural and manufacturing sectors would pose the class question starkly and heighten the level of struggle.

Agricultural reform was at the top of the revolutionary agenda in 1958, including not only the expropriation and redistribution of land but the complete renovation of the forces and relations of production. The Qassem regime moved swiftly to break up the latifundia-type estates that dominated the countryside, and decisively accomplished the political goal of breaking the back of the landlord class. This represented a clear-cut victory for the ascendant petty-bourgeois forces. It owed most, ironically, to the strong influence of the Communists in the Ministry of Agrarian Reform and the rural peasant associations.[25] Following the purge of Communists after 1960 and their subsequent repression under the Baath and Arif regimes, the implementation of reform lagged badly. Expropriation had begun with the largest estates, as decreed: by 1966 6.3 million *donums* (out of a total of 23.3 million *donums* of privately held land) had been requisitioned; 5.1 million were finally expropriated. Much of it was 'uncultivated, and wasted by salinity, and therefore unfit for distribution'.[26] Only one million *donums* had been distributed, along with a further 1.3 million of already state-owned land. This backsliding was reversed after 1968. Law 117 (1970) limited further the maximum that could be held, eliminated compensation to the landowner, and abolished payments by beneficiaries (thereby acknowledging the extremity of peasant indebtedness and poverty.). By 1975 the total expropriated had reached 10.2 million *donums*; distribution had reached 6.2 million; 5.1 million was under 'temporary lease'.[27]

Despite improved tenure patterns, significant inequality in landholdings and rural income distribution perisists. The last agricultural survey (1971) reportedly shows that the top one per cent of landholders still owned over 22 per cent of the total, admittedly down from over 55 per cent in 1958. On the other hand, the lowest 60 per cent of peasant families still owned only 14.1

per cent of the land.[28]

There is little statistical information or independent research available for assessing significant changes in rural social structure. The combination of land expropriation and distribution, and wholesale migration to the cities, has probably reduced the number of landless peasants. The reform has created a large number of small holdings. It seems likely, however, given the information available and the experience of efforts in other countries, even under Communist leadership, that a new stratification has emerged in the countryside characterized by the rise of middle peasants who either directly, or through their leadership in the co-operatives, control much of the agricultural machinery and its use. This stratum probably includes recent Baath Party members who use their political affiliation to secure access to and control over the local means of production.

One serious problem in the agricultural sector is the decline in total arable land (by nearly 30 per cent between 1958 and 1971),[29] the decline also in actually cultivated areas, especially for foodstuffs, since 1968, and the erratic pattern of crop yields. Another is the limited progress in the establishment of co-operatives. Marketing and credit provisions, in particular, are still largely in the hands of local merchants, resulting in high credit costs and price mark-ups of several hundred per cent between producer and consumer. Poor agricultural performance, coupled with rising urban population and income, has put the burden for increased supplies on imports. Food imports quadrupled in value between 1972 and 1975, amounting to 30 per cent of all imports in that period.

The continued relative deterioration of living conditions in the countryside has produced continued large-scale migration to the cities. This sector, which still accounts for over half the active labour force (there were 2.1 million agricultural workers in 1971),[30] produced only 7.6 per cent of the country's national product in 1976. This poses a serious threat of protracted labour shortages to the regime's development plans, especially the skilled labour necessary for the capital intensive agro-industrial projects being planned and under construction.

There is a higher level of prosperity in the countryside today, although the gap between rural and urban areas has increased. This is due to the infusion of income from the central government rather than any increase in productivity. The establishment of schools, clinics, utilities and other manifestations of government presence is radically altering the traditional isolation of the rural villages, but the contradictions inherent in the structure of the economy, with its enormous dependence on oil revenues and consequent expansion of the state apparatus as a source of services and employment, are not directly addressed by the development strategy of the regime. The ruling party itself has few roots in the countryside. Early Baathist literature makes virtually no reference to the question of land reform and while the Party has attracted many people from rural backgrounds, these were typically sons of small shop-keepers and petty officials and were in any case interested in bettering their individual status rather than that of the peasant class as a whole.

Industrialization Strategy and the Manufacturing Sector

The urban focus that has characterized the Iraqi economy over recent decades has been nourished by the post-revolutionary regimes with their fixation on industrialization as the key to growth and prosperity. Industry consistently received the biggest share of development expenditures, although a low rate of implementation kept actual investment to only 20 per cent of the total. The slow trend towards the manufacturing sector accounting for a greater share of the national product, which began before 1958, continued in spite of the political uncertainty of the 1960s. Manufacturing's contribution to the G.D.P. rose to 7.9 per cent in 1965 and 10 per cent in 1973. It fell to 4.7 per cent in 1974 after the oil price hike but reached 7.1 per cent in 1976.[31] The number of large firms rose from 727 in 1954 to 1,202 in 1964 and 1,482 in 1976; correspondingly, the number of employees in large firms went from 44, 410 to 80,066 and 131,850.[32] Small manufacturing shops also increased, especially after the oil price hikes: in 1976 they numbered 37,669, employed 85,460 (including the owner/workers), had inputs worth I.D. 159 million and output totalling I.D. 268 million.

The public sector share of large firms rose from 22 per cent to 27 per cent between 1964 and 1974. Its share of workers increased from 52 per cent to 74 per cent and wages from 64 per cent to 76 per cent over the decade. Public sector inputs jumped from 55 per cent to 74 per cent of the total and output from 65 per cent to 74 per cent. 1964 set the pattern of state control of the most modern and productive components of the domestic economy. This takes the form of public sector establishments attached to state organizations under Directorates-General accountable to one, or often several, ministries for purposes of authorization, procurement and planning.

The greater part of Iraqi manufacturing consists of light industries producing import substitutes and based on local raw materials, under strong tariff protection. Food, beverages and tobacco processing accounted for about one-quarter of the firms, workers and wages; half the inputs; and 38 per cent of the output of the manufacturing sector in 1974. Textiles accounted for another 20 per cent of the large firms, 28 per cent of the workers, 17 per cent of inputs and 19 per cent of outputs. Twelve large public sector textile firms employed 1,666 workers each, on average; whereas 139 large private sector firms averaged only 35 workers each.[33] The value added per worker is higher in the private sector in these two industries, but public sector dominance in chemicals and oil products, and similar capital-intensive industries, gives the public sector on average a higher input, output and value added per firm and per worker.

One accomplishment of the current regime has been a slight reversal of the former concentration of industries in the Baghdad area. In 1968 Baghdad accounted for over 60 per cent of large establishments, 64 per cent of workers and 70 per cent of wages. By 1974 the proportion was still the same for private firms but total concentration was lower as the public sector figures were 39 per cent, 50 per cent and 54 per cent respectively. Mineral extraction projects in the north, hydrocarbon-based industries in the south, and processing plants in various provinces have helped to redress this inbalance.

The economic viability of the large capital-intensive hydrocarbon-based industrial projects that have been the centrepieces of the regime's planning strategy since 1973 is based on the projected export of substantial portions of production. The $570 million urea plant at Khor al Zubair will export a million tons of fertilizer a year, more than half its planned output. The phosphate-based fertilizer plant will export some 85 per cent of its output. The steel plant at Khor al Zubair plans to export 1.5 million tons of concentrated ore a year. The $1 billion petrochemical plant in the same area will produce 150,000 tons of polyethylene and polyvinyl chloride, and 40,000 tons of caustic soda, more than the domestic economy is likely to absorb in the foreseeable future. The capital costs of these plants run 50 to 75 per cent over equivalent costs in industrial countries, and skilled labour costs are extraordinarily high. If the raw materials (feedstocks and fuels) are not factored in at world market prices, the effect will be a subsidizing of these industries with revenues foregone from the export of hydrocarbons directly. These projects strengthen Iraq's links with the world market as a provider of intermediate-stage resources, and tend to reinforce the pattern of an economy whose export sector is the dynamic core, producing most of the value added and earning most of the revenues, but employing a small fraction of the country's labour force and dependent on the multinational corporations for capital in the form of technology and skills.

Looking at the manufacturing sector as a whole, between 1974 and 1976 we find that the number of large firms increased by 17.8 per cent (to 1,479), the number of workers increased by 24.3 per cent (to 142,740), wages increased by 66.5 per cent (to I.D. 88.4 million), inputs increased by more than 90 per cent (to I.D. 398.8 million), and output increased by 102 per cent (to I.D. 589.9 million). The private sector, however, expanded at a slightly greater rate than the public sector in all of these categories. If we add in the manufacturing firms employing less than ten workers each, which are wholly private, we find that the public sector accounts for only 43.6 per cent of workers, 50.8 per cent of inputs and 49.9 per cent of output for manufacturing, large and small. The main area of private sector growth was in the category of 'manufactured metal products, machinery and electrical equipment', in other words, consumer durables.[34]

The relationship between the public and private sectors in large-scale manufacturing is reflected in their employment and wage structures. Of production workers, the public sector accounts for 60 per cent of the unskilled, 78 per cent of the skilled, and 93 per cent of the technicians and highly skilled experts. Among non-production workers the public sector accounts for 84 per cent of those in services, 68.2 per cent in administration and marketing, and, reflecting the much smaller number of public sector firms, only 20 per cent of the high administrators. Wage scales run from I.D. 372 per year (average) for unskilled to I.D. 1,594 for highly skilled experts. Above average wages are paid by the public sector for unskilled and non-production workers; the private sector pays a substantial premium for its small number of technicians and skilled workers. There is considerable differentiation between various industries, public and private.[35]

Other Sectors of the Economy

Construction is a commodity sector that has expanded tremendously over the past few years; it currently ranks above agriculture or manufacturing in its contribution to the G.D.P. (7.7 per cent). Once almost entirely private, there is now a very large public sector component employing 76,479 labourers in 1977, far more than the total number of unskilled and semi-skilled workers in both public and private large-scale manufacturing. The average wage for ordinary labourers was I.D. 919. The prominence of the construction sector is reflected in loans by the Estate Bank, totalling I.D. 66 million in 1976. Comparable figures for the Agricultural Bank and the Industrial Bank were I.D. 13.2 million and I.D. 12.5 million respectively. Over three-quarters of this construction was buildings rather than roads, dams, and similar projects, and the greatest proportion was for residential buildings. More than half the residential buildings and three-quarters of the commercial buildings were in Baghdad.[36]

Far larger than any of the commodity sectors (except oil) are the finance and trade sector (12.7 per cent of G.D.P. in 1976) and 'other services' (10.4 per cent). An Iraqi Chamber of Commerce Report in 1973 estimated the number of retail trade firms had risen from 36,000 in 1965 to about 100,000 in 1973, and the number of persons engaged to 200,000. Official figures for 1976 claimed 77,766 establishments and 106,823 employees (nearly 13,000 of those part-time). Only 5,401 were paid employees, with an average salary of I.D. 349. Total sales were close to I.D. 730 million, more than the total value of sales of large manufacturing firms. There were also 1,532 private wholesale trading firms employing 2,719 persons.[37]

The 1973 Report complained of the dominant public sector role in domestic trade and the diminishing role of private wholesalers. The public sector relies on private retail agents who get commissions averaging 10 per cent. Public sector commercial establishments numbered 17 in 1974, employed 20,697, and had total sales of I.D. 278 million; 66 per cent of its purchases were imports. Consumer co-operatives numbered 55, but had total sales of I.D. 2.4 million, only 0.8 per cent of total public sector commercial sales. Official personnel statistics record 35,204 persons engaged in trade activities in 1977.

The largest employer is, of course, the government itself. In 1977 the number of government personnel was 580,132, an increase of more than 50 per cent since 1972 and 160 per cent since 1968. The largest employer within the government is the Ministry of Interior with 136,900 employees — almost as many as those employed by all large public and private manufacturing firms together. These figures do not include the armed forces, estimated to number 160,000 men.

The State and the Structure of Iraq's Economy

The basis for the expanding role of the state in Iraq lies in its access to some 54 per cent of the national product by virtue of its control of the hydrocarbon extraction and export sector, and in the momentum of the ruling party towards monopolization of political power over the state and of the state over society.

In the sphere of production the largest enterprises are by definition in the public sector. The structure of public and private sector employment demonstrates the strategic character of state control over the most capital-intensive and technologically advanced industries. The extension of the public sector into agriculture through the establishment of co-operatives, collective farms and agro-industrial projects will take years, perhaps decades, but the trajectory is clearly established.

In the sphere of circulation the Baath regime has established virtually complete state control over external trade, with the public sector directly responsible for some 90 per cent of imports. While the private character of domestic retail trade will probably be maintained, the state role grows through price controls, subsidies and the establishment of large wholesale and retail outlets, especially for agricultural goods. Early in 1978 the Central Organization for Pricing (under the Ministry of Trade) completed a draft pricing policy to cover production, distribution and services for the whole country, reflecting 'pricing policy's role in the reallocation of income'.[38]

Thus state ownership places in the regime's hands the appropriation of the bulk of the surplus value at the levels of production and exchange. There are several important sets of contradictions, however, that are specific to this present and projected state role.

The first concerns the fact that in none of these spheres is state control complete. Most agricultural production and even most manufacturing, including the small shops, is still in private hands. There are of course no individual monopolists, but combined with the private sector's strong role in retail trade, this keeps state control in large measure only indirect, in the form of regulations and decrees. Price controls, for example, are easily circumvented because the permitted profit levels are based on the producers' own estimates of the costs of production. The difficulty also, in controlling the labour market is reflected in the decree forbidding private firms from hiring skilled workers who have resigned from public firms. A network of private contractors with close ties to the Party and state officials functions as a channel of access for foreign firms bidding for construction projects. The predilection of state and Party officials for real estate investments is reflected in the boom in residential construction and indicative of the sizeable wealth in the hands of those occupying the appropriate offices. On a broader level the sharp rise in the production of consumer durables reflects the growth of the regime's class base, the petty bourgeoisie.

A second set of contradictions is precisely rooted in the expansion of the state apparatus itself. Each policy dilemma is dealt with by the establishment of yet another bureaucratic layer. This is reinforced by the determination of the Party that the state should serve as the employer of last resort, especially for its primary constituency, the petty bourgeoisie. The decision in 1974 that all university graduates would be guaranteed jobs in the state apparatus is one example. The Iraqi bureaucracy, like most others, is notorious for its inefficiency and incompetence, for the lack of initiative and willingness to take responsibility. The role of the Baath in the state apparatus, in the form of 'commissars' attached to the various bodies and offices, and in the pressures for job holders and applicants to join the Party, complicates an already inherently unwieldy arrangement.

This particular set of contradictions has serious implications for the future of the economy, as it affects not only the services sector but the commodity sector as well, and particularly the ability of Iraqi goods to compete abroad or at home with the manufactures of other newly industrializing countries, not to mention the multinational companies. There is presumably a high level of consciousness of this problem at the top levels of the state and Party apparatuses, but the consequences of this awareness, as reflected in the frequent productivity seminars that are organized, leads us to the third, and most serious, set of contradictions.

The character of the state is most apparent in its role as boss. The nonproletarian and anti-communist origins of the Party stand in sharp contrast to the pretensions to proletarianism by this 'dictatorship of the petty bourgeoisie'. A recent example is the decree that the public sector and its constituent parts be henceforth known as the 'socialist sector' — an indication of the seriousness of the problem and the flimsiness of the regime's ideological arsenal.

The policies of the Iraqi state towards the working class since 1968 are not noticeably different from those of regimes, like Iran under the Shah, openly in the service of capitalist development. Trade unions are set up by the state and are under the direct control of ruling Party functionaries. Free trade union organizing is forbidden. To resolve acknowledged tensions between management (public and private) and workers, a scheme of worker participation on the boards of directors of firms, and a share-out of a specified portion of the profits, has been instituted. This representation is strictly token: representatives are selected by the Party from among the workers, not by the workers themselves.

In the 'productivity seminars' already referred to, responsibility for low productivity is shared between management and workers, but there is little ambiguity in the thrust of the solutions: 1) a stress on surveillance and discipline to raise productivity; and 2) the tying of wage increases (but not bureaucrats' or professionals' salaries) to increases in productivity. The efforts by the regime to secure working class support early in its life, particularly through guarantees of job security, now hamper its efforts (as the main capitalist in the society) to reallocate labour and capital and to redefine the terms of their relationship.

The patina of proletarianism that graces the Party's ideological pronouncements peels away on close examination. In the political report of the Eighth Regional Congress in 1973, the Party rhetoricians engage in some outwardly candid self-criticism: 'most of the measures taken so far resemble state capitalism rather than socialism . . . . Industrial production is dominated by officials among whom the ratio of Party members and socialists is not high enough.' Socialism requires that the working class occupy 'effective, worthwhile positions of leadership'. But the working class is described as 'lacking in political, economic and technical consciousness' and its participation 'must be preceded by adequate political education, administrative and technical training', and the term 'working class' itself must be redefined 'to encompass new social segments while being very careful to keep the basic qualities of the class and its revolutionary nature'. The party was once more frank as to where its roots and future lay. In the National Action Charter of 1971, for example: 'While the Revolution is keen to protect the interests of the toiling masses . . . it is at the same time keen to protect the interests of the small and middle merchants.'

These contradictions merge in the arena of wage determination. Law 151 (1970) empowered the Minister of Labour and Social Affairs to form a board that would fix wages, bonuses, and 'other financial inducements'. The Board is made up of representatives from the Ministries of Economy, Planning, Industry, Agrarian Reform, Finance and the Central Bank, as well as three trade union chairmen and three private sector owners. There is increasing wage differentiation both within the working class and between the working class and the petty-bourgeois professionals who make up an important base of support for the regime. Since 1973 wages have risen considerably in all categories, but additional significant bonuses have been decreed for engineers, doctors, and the like.[39]

Perhaps the largest increase occurred in April 1974, when wage and bonus hikes were accompanied by price reductions and tax cuts. This proved a relatively simple, but not directly productive, means of distributing the oil rent increases, but further complicated the serious disparity between rural and urban living conditions. Such moves had no effect on the 40 per cent or more of the population still in the countryside. What is involved is more than a question of equity: the relative deterioration of rural living conditions promotes the depopulation of the rural areas, threatens serious labour shortages in the agricultural sector and greater dependence on food imports, and also increases pressure on the public sector to expand its non-productive employment. For the regime it exacerbates an already serious obstacle to the long-term reproduction and accumulation of capital.

Conclusion

This brief sketch of the political and economic history of modern Iraq is an effort to interpret its development in terms of the impact of the oil industry, domestically and globally, on the penetration and expansion of capitalist relations in that country. It has not been possible to deal sufficiently with the important changes in the structure of international capitalism over the last three decades. Such factors must be taken into account if we are to situate the experience of Iraq and similar societies, and develop the theoretical frame-work for interpreting this experience and projecting its future.

It is clear that despite its proclamations the Baathist regime in Iraq is by no responsible criteria socialist. Any effort to justify such a label, for example in terms of the Soviet theory of non-capitalist development, simply exposes the analytical poverty and political opportunism of such notions. At the same time the formulations of theorists like Samir Amin, which maintain that the dependency of economies like Iraq on the indus-trialized capitalist countries has simply been transferred to a higher level, seems similarly inadequate, although of greater political integrity. It seems correct to identify the petty bourgeoisie as the contemporary 'bearers of bourgeois ideology' in regimes like Iraq. But it seriously underestimates the qualitative shifts in the level of the productive forces and class relation-ships in these countries and misleadingly oversimplifies reality to maintain that the petty bourgeoisie has merely taken over the role of the latifund-ist/comprador bourgeoisie as 'transmission belt for imperialist domination'. Such an interpretation freezes a once accurate description of an historical relationship into an immutable formula. The ruling classes in countries like Iraq have clearly taken a more active and assertive stance *vis-à-vis* imperialism than their counterparts of an earlier era.

Iraq experienced a Revolution in 1958 which the local bourgeoisie proved incapable of carrying out. Because of its relative numerical strength and its historic ties to the state, the petty bourgeoisie seized the the leadership of the Revolution, almost by default, and assumed the historic tasks of the bourgeoisie, using the state — its apparatus and its access to oil rent income — to transform the political economy of the country and, in the process, transform itself into a functional bourgeoisie.

It is still not clear that this class-in-transformation is up to the task. The contradictions it faces are fundamental and cannot be bought off. The capitalist character of its 'ideology of development' will inevitably strip away its socialist garb as it becomes necessary to develop seriously the domestic productive forces to support the level of expenditure and consumption acquired in its rentier days as an oil-producing state.

References

1. Peter Sluglett, *Britain in Iraq, 1914-1932,* London 1976, p.232.
2. Ibid., p.222.
3. Walid Khadduri, 'The social background of modern Iraqi politics', unpublished Ph.D. dissertation, Johns Hopkins 1970, p.307.
4. Fahim Qubain, *The Reconstruction of Iraq, 1950-57,* New York 1958, p.143. In recruiting workers for pipeline construction the company dealt with the respective sheikhs whose territories they crossed. The tribesmen forked over at least a tenth of their wages

to the sheikhs for this 'opportunity to provide unskilled labor'. E. A. Finch, 'Social effects of the oil industry in Iraq', *International Labour Review*, March 1957.

5. Great Britain, Department of Overseas Trade, *Iraq: Review of Commercial Conditions*, London, February 1945, p.15.

6. This remark was made to the U.S. embassy and was passed to Washington in dispatch 890G.51/2-749.

7. Testimony of Ambassador George McGhee to the Senate Foreign Relations Subcommittee on Multinational Corporations, 28 January 1974.

8. These and other sectoral calculations for this period are based on K. Haseeb, *The National Income of Iraq, 1953-61*, London 1964.

9. Abdul Amir al Rubaiy, 'Nationalism and education: a study of nationalistic tendencies in Iraq education', unpublished Ph.D. dissertation, Kent State 1972, pp.92, 123-47.

10. The penal code was amended to deport 'communists', a term that included the whole spectrum of the opposition, and disband labour and professional organizations. Nuri as-Said's rigged elections in the fall of 1954 produced a familiar legislature: 49 landowners, 42 tribal leaders, 23 lawyers, 18 businessmen, and 3 physicians. For a pro-Nuri account, see ex-US. Ambassador Waldemar Gallman's *Iraq Under General Nuri*, Baltimore, 196?, pp. 3-8.

11. Uriel Dann, *Iraq Under Qassem*, New York 1969, pp. 63-4.

12. Dann, op.cit. p.54.

13. John Devlin, *The Baath Party: A History from its Origins to 1966*, Stanford 1976, pp.25-41.

14. Marion Farouk-Sluglett, 'Contemporary Iraq: some recent writing reconsidered', unpublished ms., p.19.

15. *Middle East Economic Survey (M.E.E.S.)*, 12 May, 1961.

16. Edith and E.F. Penrose, *Iraq*, Boulder 1978, p.288.

17. *M.E.E.S.*, 8 October 1965.

18. Quoted in *M.E.E.S.*, 15 October 1965.

19. *M.E.E.S.*, 19 April 1968.

20. The political report of the Eighth Regional Congress of the Party in late 1973 notes that 'the psychological state and the after-effects of the 1963 experience made any immediate large-scale purges intolerable . . . . A different method with more flexibility was required to achieve the same objectives . . . .' The Party did, the Report notes, immediately establish a 'special security branch which was called at first the Public Relations Bureau'. Composed of 'Party strugglers', it was 'meticulous in carrying out security missions ordered by the Party. Members of this branch had little formal experience in this field of work except for some aspects of Party activity prior to the [1968] Revolution [*sic*]. But they were quick to learn and prove their high calibre by liquidating external and internal conspiracies and exposing intelligence networks'. *Revolutionary Iraq*, Baghdad 1974, pp.63, 171-2.

21. *Revolutionary Iraq* (Political Report of the Eighth Regional Congress of the Arab Baath Socialist Party), Baghdad 1974, p.92.

22. *M.E.E.S.* 12 April, 1968.

23. *Arab Oil and Gas*, 1 August, 1978.

24. Hussein and Hamdani are both graduates of the Baghdad law faculty. Hussein masterminded the Party's consolidation of power after 1968 and the assertion of civilian control. He is Vice-President of the Republic and Vice-Chairman of the Party and the Revolutionary Command Council. Hamdani is a close and trusted ally. His first position after 1968 was as Director of Oil Company Affairs in the Ministry of Oil. He moved quickly to the post of Director-General of the Presidential Office, a post he continued to hold in conjunction with his duties on the Follow-up Committee. In 1976 he took over the Ministry of Planning. In one of his few pronouncements on the subject, Hamdani once observed that 'The Baath Party is not just a ruling party; it has an ideology based on rapid development of the economy in a limited period of time. For this we need large revenues.'

25. Rony Gabbay, *Communism and Agrarian Reform in Iraq*, London 1978, chapter 5.

26. Doreen Warriner, *Land Reform in Principle and Practice*, London 1969, p.90.

27. Iraq, Central Statistical Organization, *Annual Abstract of Statistics (Statistics), 1975*, Baghdad 1976, p.93ff.

28. Shakir M. Issa, 'Rural income distribution in Iraq' (mimeo), Development Seminar Working Paper No. 8, London University, School of Oriental and African Studies, March 1977, p.3.

29. Ibid.

30. K. Hameed, 'Manpower and employment planning in Iraq and the Syrian Arab Republic', in United Nations, *Studies on Development Problems in Countries of Western Asia, 1975*, New York 1977, p.31.

31. Calculated from Yusif Sayigh, *Economies of the Arab World*, New York 1978, pp.50-1.

32. Statistics from Kathleen Langley, 'The Industrialization of Iraq', Cambridge University M.A. thesis, 1961; and *Statistics, 1975, 1977*.

33. Calculated from *Statistics, 1975*.

34. *Statistics, 1977*.

35. Ibid.

36. Ibid.

37. Federation of Iraqi Chambers of Commerce, *Summary* (of Annual Report), 1973 (mimeo), pp.22-6.

38. *Baghdad Observer*, 14 January 1978.

39. For one of many such instances, see *Ath Thawra* (Baghdad), 17 July 1976.

10. Nigeria: Imperialism, Oil Technology and the Comprador State

Terisa Turner

The substantial UNCTAD literature on the transfer of technology concentrates on the technical questions of unequal information between buyer and seller, the nature of the bargaining situation, the technology package, costing and imperfections in the technology market. The assumption is that poor country governments are seriously striving to obtain technology on the best possible terms. This chapter questions that assumption and argues that, in many poor countries, the state blocks the acquisition of technology and the development of indigenous know-how. Technology transfer is first and foremost a political problem. The problem can most usefully be examined from the perspective of political economy, which I take to be the study of the formation and inter-action of social classes. This chapter examines the role of the state in the transfer of technology and know-how to the Nigerian oil industry. Part I dis-cusses the interests of oil companies, Part II examines the nature of the Nigerian state and Part III reviews the Nigerian experience in the transfer of exploration and production technology, downstream[1] project technology and oil-related expertise.

I. Oil Companies

The Nigerian oil industry is controlled by multinational oil corporations which are vertically integrated and carry out each function, production to marketing, in many countries. As an oligopoly, these large multinationals seek to maintain their levels of retained earnings and growth through non-price competition. The success of a large oil corporation depends very much on the ability of its management to co-ordinate and plan for a mammoth international apparatus. The corporation's strength also depends on exclusion of competitors, and this is especially important at the crude production end of operations since the downstream phases of the industry depend on crude supplies. In short, oil companies aim to exclude competitors, acquire sufficient crude for their inte-grated networks and acquire it at the lowest possible cost. The related objec-tives of optimizing profits, efficiency and control of the industry lead oil companies to resist the transfer of technology and know-how to parties wishing to undertake oil activities.

199

Technology for Exploration and Production

Subsidiaries of oil corporations in charge of exploration and production resemble 'brains' which organize and then contract out much of the work related to actually finding and producing crude oil. This work goes to foreign firms for several reasons. Foreign contractors are well-established, experienced and familiar. They may be owned in part or in full by the oil company or they may be based in its country of incorporation. In this situation, companies have little incentive to encourage the establishment of local contracting capacity or to patronize those contractors which exist, except in very peripheral areas such as grounds maintenance, transport, food supply or minor civil engineering. As a result, the transfer of oil technology for much of the actual operations does not occur without government intervention.

Technology connected with the exploration and production phase is not, however, monopolized and unobtainable. The government oil authorities of some OPEC (Organization of Petroleum Exporting Countries) member states have successfully separated out the various aspects of the technology 'package' and have indigenized the capacity to obtain, use and perhaps even generate aspects of technology used in the extractive phases of the industry. The case of Algeria is instructive since oil was discovered there in 1956 just as Nigeria was confirmed as an oil province. Sonatrach, the Algerian state oil corporation set up in 1963, has established partnerships with nine oilfield service firms since 1966. The terms ensure that in the period during which the foreign firm realizes its profit — about 15 years — technology and know-how are localized. By first nationalizing the technical structure serving the oil industry, Algeria was able to acquire 100 per cent ownership of the exploration and production companies by 1974 and achieve almost total control of operations. Dependence on foreign sources of essential exploration and production technology was reduced or eliminated. Sonatrach developed the capacity to hire foreign contractors to do specialist jobs.[2]

Technology for Downstream Operations

Oil comapny management resists the transfer of technology for use in the processing of crude and gas into petroleum products as part of its efforts to avoid displacement in these downstream areas. If an oil exporting government establishes an export refinery, not only do the oil companies lose a portion of their crude supply and get displaced in the refining industry, but their international product markets may be penetrated and taken over by the newcomer state oil company. This threat to market control is especially serious since state oil corporations have access to crude at no more than the cost of production and therefore can afford to engage in price competition. Consequently, oil companies strive to block entry into downstream operations. A major means of doing so is to create obstacles to the transfer of technology required in the processing of crude oil.

This is not to say that downstream technology, including tankers, pipeline systems, refining, petrochemical and natural gas plants, is not available. In the wake of the acute shortage of 1973, producer governments received downstream proposals from consumer governments, from crude-short oil companies, from independent sources of oil technology and even from the majors. In the scramble to ensure adequate petroleum supply, energy importers were willing to offer technology in exchange for hydrocarbons, a reciprocation which is fundamental to Algeria's conception of a new international economic order. But even without the special circumstances of crude shortage, some OPEC member countries have established downstream operations. For instance, as early as 1969 Sonatrach, following the examples of Venezuela and Iran, had participated with foreign firms in establishing two transport operations, one refinery and four projects for liquefying, shipping and marketing natural gas.

Know-how

Oil companies resist the acquisition of oil expertise by nationals as part of a wider company imperative to retain control of operations. Co-ordination, flexibility, size and organization of huge multinationals depend very much on communication between management at various levels. Communication usually occurs most readily among those who share a common cultural background. Reliability and loyalty are further ensured by common class and status affiliations as well as long years of corporate training and service. While the foreign oil companies do train low and medium level technical assistants, administrators and some engineers, they limit the career development of local oilmen to the extent they can do so, given local consciousness and political demands. While a few 'show-case' *indigenes* move in the top echelons as window dressing, the oil companies deliberately avoid and resist the transfer of technical know-how. Expatriates strive to remain in charge of key functions and in those jobs essential to the actual work of producing oil. For instance, the supervision of contractors and the maintenance of equipment is usually done by expatriates, when the companies have a choice.

Again, this does not mean that the transfer of know-how for the oil industry is impossible. Companies have accommodated to nationalist sentiments by recruiting and training nationals for management positions. The majors, in particular the European firms British Petroleum and Shell, do seek to minimize their losses by adapting to, or even foreseeing and guiding, social and political change while simultaneously encouraging commitment by an indigenous stratum to the institutions and values of capitalism. The majors are given strong practical inducement to be flexible by the presence of weaker independents and state companies such as E.N.I. and Elf which are anxious to offer host governments more favourable deals in order to get an edge on the majors.

Generally speaking, an oil company will train quickly and competently when convinced that the host government is seriously intending to bar expatriates from particular jobs. In the face of company resistance, governments of some oil exporting states have themselves assumed the responsibility for developing technical expertise. The Algerian example is again instructive. Sonatrach pursued a vigorous two-faceted approach to manpower development. First, government found foreign technical partners for both exploration and production as well as downstream projects. Algerians were attached directly to these projects and a great deal of emphasis was placed on learning-by-doing. Other nationals were put on crash courses in operation and maintenance of the project once it was commissioned. Second, the state oil authority initiated a long-term, well-planned programme to train technical and scientific personnel.

To sum up, oil companies resist the transfer of technology and know-how since it does not further their main concern which is to extract oil and make profits. It has thus been necessary for governments of oil exporting countries to bring about the transfer of technology through direct intervention in the oil industry itself. Many OPEC states have successfully pursued this strategy. The crude shortages and high prices of 1973 and 1974 have made it infinitely easier for producer governments to acquire technology from and access to markets in the industrialized countries.

If governments can bring about the transfer of oil technology despite resistance from oil companies, how can we explain the absence of significant progress in the acquisition of oil technology in Nigeria? Since ownership of oil is vested in the sovereign state, an explanation of the under-development and foreign domination of the Nigerian oil industry must start with an examination of the Nigerian state.

II. The Political Economy of the Nigerian State

The Development of a Comprador State

Pre-colonial commerce established in what is now Nigeria a group of middlemen who provided European traders with slaves, palm oil, cocoa and other commodities. These middlemen buyers then distributed beads, cloths, guns and other valuables to the primary suppliers in the interior. Local merchant princes and the agents of European and American trading houses constituted a bilateral oligopoly which operated through coastal trading 'factories'. The need to rationalize and regulate this trading relationship led to the imposition of colonial administration in the late 19th century. British colonial rule in West Africa was partly the result of competition among European powers. But locally, too, there was a need for infrastructural investment, notably for transport to evacuate export crops on a large scale. Commercial interests also needed open trading routes through unsettled territories. They needed the means of enforcing contracts, and providing for credit, for protection of title to property and for the exclusion of non-British interests which threatened to encroach on the area.[3] Lugard's system of 'indirect rule' involved locals who were either traditional rulers or British-appointed 'chiefs'. These officials depended on the colonial authorities for their income and status. They acted as intermediaries between the British and the local population, maintaining order and supervising extractions. This small stratum of commercial and administrative interests co-operated with colonial concerns in establishing British trading companies firmly throughout the region. As documented by Bauer,

The net effect of the pre-World War II foreign investment policies was to displace indigenous African entrepreneurs while strengthening the position of the expatriate trading firms. This trend was intensified with regard to trading activities when the Statutory Marketing Regulations were applied during World War II.[4]

In 1960 political independence was conceded to a moderate faction of the stratum of Nigerians who had advanced in education and commerce to the limits allowed by the colonial trading firms and administration. In Wrigley's view, Nigerian nationalism was '. . . almost synonymous with Nigerianization and appropriation of the white man's jobs'.[5] In the first five years of independence (1960-65) it became clear that politics, rather than entrepreneurship, was the more attractive avenue open to Nigerians for the accumulation of funds. 'Government was conceived more as a vehicle for distributing bounties to the faithful than as an agent of economic development,' according to A. Ayida, in 1977 secretary to the Obasanjo government.[6] Political entrepreneurs in official positions diverted state and marketing board funds to their personal and party use. Robin Cohen observed that

> Where finance on any scale was available to Nigerians, it was closely linked to the capture of political power by elite groups. Companies were indeed often run as extensions of a political party while, conversely, access to political power, particularly at the Regional level, was used as a means to finance private investment, or more usually, private consumption.[7]

With decolonization the way was open, in theory at least, for the development of capitalist production with the assistance of the state. However, the state lacked the autonomy and cohesion necessary to regulate the relations between local and foreign capital in order to give Nigerian production a firm, independent footing.[8] Instead, local businessmen continued to act as middlemen for foreign firms which expanded to add the assembly of 'import substitutes' to their traditional activity of trade. The new federal and regional governments actively sought foreign aid, credit, loans and investment capital. This incorporated Nigeria more firmly into the economic system of the West at the expense of local petty commodity producers and artisans. The expansion of middlemanship into import-substituting industrialization did correspond with the embryonic beginnings of a 'state economic bureaucracy' charged with managing the economy and the industrial projects involving state participation. But in the pre-1966 period this group remained small, scattered and subordinated to administrators and politicians. The import-substitution phase of the early 1960s is more usefully understood as a post-independence accommodation and multilateralization of foreign commercial activities than as the initiation of capitalist production, which remained insignificant.[9] Similarly, the Nigerian interests which formed links with foreign capital invested in import substitution activities are, in my view, more usefully considered as extensions of the middleman class than as a new class of dependent or national capitalists. By

1971-72 oil income had dwarfed import and excise duties which, along with export duties on agricultural products, had been the main source of state revenue. As the state became more dependent on revenues from oil companies, the economic importance of export crop farmers as producers of surplus and state funds declined sharply.

From independence Nigeria has been governed by a neo-colonial comprador state which lacks coherence and stability. The description 'neo-colonial' is useful as a means of indicating that, in the transition from colonialism to independence, political power was transferred to a regime based on the support of social classes linked very closely to the foreign interests which were formerly represented by the colonial state. Compradors[10] are those professional intermediaries who organize the access of foreign traders to the local market. Nigerian middlemen constitute a comprador class. Representatives of this class occupy government posts and control the state. For the purposes of this discussion, these state officials will be called bureaucratic compradors, partly to distinguish them from their private sector counterparts, middlemen, but also because they perform a comprador function. The Nigerian state itself constitutes a significant market for foreign goods and one which has expanded with the inflow of foreign exchange earnings from oil. In addition, the state has some jurisdiction over virtually all economic interaction between foreign firms and the final consumer.

Specifically, compradors are state officials who use their public offices for personal gain. Illicit income is derived largely from kick-backs on government financial transactions, usually involving the purchase of goods or services from foreign firms. Bureaucratic compradors may also receive considerations for taking actions favourable to foreign firms or refraining from making or enforcing provisions unfavourable to foreign firms. Large numbers of civil servants do not occupy positions from which they can influence government policy or expenditure although they may support their superiors' comprador activities or even engage in minor corruption on their own behalf. It is also possible that officials of state, whether politicians, military officers or civil servants, in positions of influence over spending may refrain from enriching themselves. But this is unlikely due not to any generic venality but to the pervasive dynamic of a corrupt system already in operation. Since international firms compete for sales through offering inducements to buyers, whether private or state,[11] the pressure on individual bureaucrats, especially in the absence of a politically mobilized public, is virtually irresistible.

Middlemen and compradors are often closely linked, with the latter seeking on retirement from public office to enter commerce financed by the wealth accumulated while working in the state. Not all compradors support the involvement of private Nigerians in official transactions. In sectors of the economy over which the state has established monopoly jurisdiction, private middlemen are usually excluded and direct deals are arranged between foreign firms and compradors. On the other hand, compradors may favour a continued role for middlemen in government purchasing. The position of a particular comprador on the powers of the public and private sectors has to do not only with the particular financial and economic fields he is involved in, but also with his position in the civil service hierarchy and therefore his ability to influence spending decisions.

To summarize, compradors can be divided into 'statists' who exclude the private middleman from state transactions with foreign firms and 'collaborators' who join with private middlemen in carrying out these transactions. The comprador nature of the Nigerian state derives from its overall orientation towards facilitating commerce, from its domination by representatives of the local middleman class, and from the intermediary role its officers play between foreign salesmen and the local (state and final consumer) market. It is this last feature which leads to the state's incoherence and instability. Since control of state office confers access to funds as well as to power and patronage of other kinds, competition for these posts is intense. In the political party era, competition escalated into conflict and the rules of the political process were overridden. According to Williams, 'the state proved incapable of regulating factional competition for money and opportunities for profit, since it was itself the major source of money and opportunities for the indigenous bourgeoisie and their clients.'[12] The military takeover in 1966 conferred increased power on civil servants and made it easier for them to exclude middlemen from government transactions. Nevertheless the influential commercial class successfully resisted state encroachment in most sectors of the economy.

Technocrats
The coups of 1966 and the subsequent civil war enabled the technical, professional and modern managerial personnel in the civil service to exert more influence than they had done during the political party period. By the early 1970s a technocratic stratum proper began to emerge in connection with implementing the state's new policy of economic nationalism. In contrast to comprador administrators in the ministries, technocrats in the state corporations appeared relatively uncorrupt, more nationalist in outlook and more concerned with broad national principles of development. For the purposes of this discussion, technocrats are those state officials whose ability to influence decisions derives from their technical knowledge and specialized experience and whose jobs involve reducing national reliance on foreign goods and services. The contrasting orientations and behaviours of technocrats and compradors can be explained by reference to differences in their training, jobs, and roles in production or commerce.

The Second National Development Plan (1970-74) announced the state's intention to promote indigenous private capitalism and to establish public control over the 'commanding heights' of the economy. Dozens of state corporations and agencies were set up to implement this policy. Each had a budget, a purpose, an interest to defend and members of staff who, because of their training and productive function, behaved differently from comprador state officials. It is estimated that, of the total public sector employment of 1,009,600 in 1975, the Federal and State Civil Service combined accounted for about 312,000 or 30 per cent while the statutory corporations accounted for about 160,000 or 16 per cent.

Technocrats share a similar social background with compradors and are usually five to ten years younger. Members of the two groups come from families who could afford to pay school fees. Their fathers are prosperous farmers, school teachers, clergy, merchants, clerks and in a few cases, professionals and traditional rulers, especially from the North. Compradors were among the first Nigerians to secure university education, usually in liberal arts or humanities and often in British universities. With a few earlier exceptions, those Nigerians who were destined for senior positions in the state had graduated and joined the civil service by the mid-fifties. These first beneficiaries of the policy to Nigerianize the civil service were in relatively powerful positions by 1966 and in most cases under forty years old. In contrast to this group, technocrats tend to be younger and have received technical or science-based education, often in the United States and Nigeria as well as in European institutions. Many have held jobs in the private sector in Nigeria and abroad. Because of differences in training, age and exposure to British culture and, in the case of early administrators, British supervision, technocrats tend to be less Europeanized and less afflicted by the psychology of dependence[13] than are compradors. Technocrats joined the civil service later than did their senior administrative colleagues since colonial officers in professionally-oriented posts departed later than did generalist administrators. Furthermore, state expansion into the economy was a post-1970 phenomenon. For the most part technocrats joined various state corporations and public agencies in the late sixties and early seventies and are between the ages of 25 and 35.

The bulk of these technically-skilled professionals were hired to put into effect the military's new policy of state intervention to foster capitalist economic development. Technocrats' jobs involved combining technology, finance and managerial skills in a commercial organization to produce a tangible result — for instance, a steel mill in the case of the National Steel Authority. The division of labour in such an economic agency requires an interdependence among specialists, the success of which is measured in terms of actual production and in terms of profits. Individual technocrats, by virtue of their technical training and, for some, experience in industry, are accustomed to using rational, impersonal and universal criteria in making decisions and in assessing their own accomplishments. Professional standing, and therefore job mobility within and between the public and private sectors as well as abroad, depends on getting results which in turn depends on co-operation with other technocrats. Technocrats are relatively uncorrupt, not because they possess special moral qualities, but because their function is to replace national dependence on foreign firms with local capabilities. In contrast, comprador officials, who control the new parastatals from their senior positions in the ministries, are reinforcing dependence on foreign capital through organizing the access of foreign firms to the local market and to local resources. This difference in relationship with foreign capital is the source of tension between technocrats and compradors within the state.

What is the nature of the relationship which technocrats have struck up with foreign firms? Are they seeking a better deal for nationals? Are they similar to an aspiring national bourgeoisie which has capital and is seeking to gain a foot-hold in the local economy, by unseating metropolitan capital which has seized the profitable opportunities? Are they radical nationalists seeking development without revolution under an anti-imperialist, populist leader who has established unity under a technocratic state? Are Nigerian technocrats the forerunners of a revolutionary vanguard or an authoritarian repression? These questions are bound up with the extent to which technocrats are able to fulfil their formal responsibilities of transferring technology and establishing public and state capitalist production. Until research and developments unfold, it would be rash to make assumptions about the capacity of technocrats to bring about basic changes in the relations between the local economy and foreign firms. The jobs which technocrats fill were created in response to a set of ideas about 'development', not in response to demands by an incipient class of productive entrepreneurs nor even on the crest of a wave of economic nationalism.[14] Whether technocratic efforts to realize the objectives of 'development theory'[15] have had any impact on Nigeria's political economy and in particular on the nature of the Nigerian state is a question which awaits investigation. The following discussion of technocratic initiatives in a compra-dor oil administration suggests that technocrats share certain features with 'would-be' national bourgeoisies, namely the command of capital and the desire to replace foreign firms, but that they lack an indigenous base and are overshadowed by the comprador-middleman class.

The Nigerian government has been concerned with making oil policy only since 1967. Attention was focused on oil when Nigerians trained by the companies joined the civil service during the period of industry shutdown as a result of the civil war, also because of OPEC's prominence and due to the relatively free hand which civil servants were accorded in policy making after the 1966 coups. In the 1967-76 period the comprador section of oil admini-strators has been concentrated in the oil ministry. Bureaucratic compradors are also found in the large number of ministries which have some influence on oil policy. These include Internal Affairs, Industries, Trade, Economic Develop-ment, Finance and Education. Technocrats have opposed the comprador faction from a base first in the Ministry of Finance, and then in the oil corpor-ation, which is a parastatal body, and ultimately in the Federal Executive Council. In the late sixties the Ministry of Finance began to review financial agreements with the oil companies. Influenced by the attention OPEC was devoting to the problem of increasing oil revenues, the Ministry of Finance spearheaded the entry of the Nigerian state into policy-making for the oil industry. The oil companies, but also the Ministry of Mines and Power, resisted the encroachment of the Ministry of Finance's Petroleum Section into what had hitherto been their sphere of interest. Technocrats in the Ministry of Finance continued to oppose compradors in the oil ministry, as well as the oil companies, until 1972-73 when the technocratic faction began to express itself through the state oil company established in 1971 but staffed only in 1973. This shift in the technocrats' institutional base coincides with the evolution of policy emphasis from income to industry control.

III. The Nigerian State and the Transfer of Technology

Technology for Exploration and Production
Technology for exploration and production can be transferred both through direct state involvement in the work of exploring for and producing crude and through the establishment of indigenous oilfield service companies. Neither step has been taken.

The Policy of Participation: In 1969 a Fact-Finding Mission Report proposed that government participate in exploration and production companies.[16] Technocrats centred around the permanent secretary of the Ministry of Finance, Abdul Atta, advocated participation. They emphasized the need for systematic renegotiation of company agreements to give the state an undivided interest and the need for a state oil corporation to administer this interest. Through the active operational involvement of a national oil corporation, Nigeria would acquire the technology necessary for finding and producing oil.

In seeking reform, the technocrats contrasted their proposal for co-ordinated operational participation with the haphazard shareholding pattern which prevailed at the end of the sixties. Prior to 1969 the government had a 50 per cent shareholding in the British Petroleum-operated refinery in Port Harcourt and a participation option with the Italian state oil company Agip. These piecemeal efforts did not arise from an organized strategy of nationalization. Nor were state interests handled systematically:

> . . . what we have in Nigeria may be aptly described as 'acquired financial interests' with most of their attendant rights and benefits mortgaged for free. To even confuse the situation more, most of these interests are dispersed among several other semi-independent bodies such as the State Governments and even the interest of the Federal Government is handled by different ministries. But what is worse, however, is that the different representatives of national investment act in accordance with what they feel rather than in concert within the framework of some guiding principles.[17]

Between 1968 and 1971 officers in the Ministry of Finance and supporters scattered through the state apparatus campaigned for the adoption of a clear-cut policy, strategy and instruments for direct involvement in oil exploration and production. They argued that it was a central policy of OPEC, which Nigeria had joined in July 1971, and that it made good financial sense. Technocrats carried out their campaign among officials of state on this and other aspects of oil policy by the means available to them under a military regime. In general, the objective was to influence the permanent secretaries who ruled their respective ministries and made decisions in the Federal Executive Council. Reports, minutes and memoranda were written. Seminars, colloquia, conference tours and briefings were organized. Speakers, consultants and OPEC representatives were brought in. As long as technocrats had access to such institutions of decision-making as the Petroleum Advisory Board and the Federal Executive Council, they argued their cases there. Personal lobbying is perhaps the most important form of campaigning. The press and oilworkers' unions or other sections of the public were rarely enlisted and campaigning outside state, personal and informal channels was almost non-existent.

The technocrats' arguments were received with scepticism, especially in the oil ministry. However, the comprador element was unable to counter the technocratic case for the financial benefits to be gained from participation. By 1970 the Federal Executive Council had adopted the technocratic policy in principle. This policy commitment was stated in the Second National Development Plan (1970-74) in terms of '. . . active state participation in mining operations'.

The Nigerian National Oil Corporation: By N.N.O.C. Decree No. 18 of April 1971, the Federal Executive Council created the Nigerian National Oil Corporation, '. . . to engage in prospecting for, mining and marketing oil and in all other activities with the petroleum oil industry'. The new parastatal was an offshoot of the Ministry of Mines and Power which appeared reluctant to allow N.N.O.C. to develop the capabilities necessary for accomplishing the duties with which it was charged in the decree. The oil ministry opposed the growth of a potentially competing organization and one which would control much of policy making by virtue of being the source of data on the local and international oil industry. The permanent secretary of the oil ministry drafted the decree which established N.N.O.C. He was chairman of the corporation board. N.N.O.C. was limited to making expenditures of only N100,000 ($160,000) without the approval of the Federal Executive Council, after clearance by the Board and the Commissioner for Mines and Power.

The corporation's only real independence from the oil ministry followed from the requirement that a General Manager be appointed by the Federal Executive Council on the advice of the Commissioner for Mines and Power. But N.N.O.C.'s chief executive post remained vacant. Compradors in the oil ministry maintained ultimate control and prevented the pursuit of active government-led technology transfer in the area of exploration and production. *Participation:* The state acquired participation interests before the oil corporation was staffed and put into operation. The interests were of a formal and legal nature: they did not entail active state involvement in oil operations. These acquisitions were made smoothly. But gaining participation in the concessions of established majors through renegotiation was a more difficult step. Delays and drawn-out negotiations finally ended in June 1973 when government acquired a 35 per cent undivided interest (effective 1 April 1973) in Shell-B.P. which accounts for two-thirds of Nigerian production. By June 1974 the state had 55 per cent undivided interest in all producing companies.

N.N.O.C. was activated in July 1973 to handle the government interest in Shell-B.P. and to sell crude in a tightening international market. But the corporation was not allowed to become a full operator. With technocrats concentrated in the state oil corporation and compradors in the oil ministry, and given the relationship between the two, the stage was set for factionalism and deadlock. The Ministry of Mines and Power resisted operational involvement by the state in foreign oil companies. Technocrats refused to approve the ministry's version of an operating agreement. An operating agreement specifies the terms of the organizational merger of the two parties which have an undivided interest in the exploration and production projects in question. Dissent within the government has resulted in the failure to sign an operating agreement as late as 1978. Oil companies continue to function without direct Nigerian state involvement.[18]

The oil corporation staff has been limited to approving the operating budgets of its producing partners and providing 55 per cent of the funds. In the cases of the smaller companies — Agip and Elf — N.N.O.C. is beginning to participate in some technical decision-making. But the major producers, Shell-B.P., Gulf and Mobil, are operating on their own. The oil ministry defended non-involvement with an array of arguments centring around efficiency and manpower shortages and has prevented intervention by oil corporation technocrats.

It is clear that the policy and type of corporation accepted by government in 1971 were formal concessions to the campaign mounted by technocrats, but ones which bear little resemblance to the technocrats' conception or OPEC models of active intervention in the oil industry.

Oilfield Services: During the period in which there was controversy over the advantages of participation itself, the question of the indigenization of oilfield service companies remained in the background. The 1969 Fact-Finding Mission Report recognized the need to set up local consulting, engineering and construction companies in partnership with international oilfield service firms. Such contracting operations would be subsidiaries of a state oil corporation.

Although technocrats urged that the state participate in oilfield service firms along the lines of the Algerian example, comprador policy makers set aside this area of the oil industry for the local private sector. The oil ministry announced that the state would encourage private Nigerian businessmen to set up partnerships with foreign firms to cater for the needs of the exploration and production industry. It was envisaged that private local contractors would become established and the state would patronize them and require that oil companies use these local services.[19] The policy was unsuccessful.

To summarize, between 1968 and 1978 very little progress was made in the transfer of technology for exploration and production activities. Oil companies have continued to spend abroad for contract work and have managed their local operations without government involvement. Little has changed in Nigerian oil beyond a much larger transfer of money from the companies to the state. The government remains very much a passive tax collector.

Compradors within the oil administration have succeeded in dominating government oil affairs, in suppressing a potentially competitive parastatal and in serving their own and company interests. The policies of the oil ministry have not advanced the ability of the state to act independently in matters of oil. For instance, in 1976 Shell-B.P. produced one and a quarter million barrels, or 60 per cent of the 2.07 million barrels of oil produced each day. The company generated over half of federal revenues.[20] Yet this vital subsidiary is operated almost totally by expatriate management and professional staff who employ foreign contract firms. The state has no capacity to keep the oil moving in the event of deteriorating relations with the Anglo-Dutch concern. Technocrats who advocated and sought to bring about the transfer of technology for finding and producing oil were overriden by a company-comprador alliance. This structure of interests is detrimental to the growth of self-reliance. Rather than enhancing political and economic independence, the state has increased its dependence on foreign capital in the form of oil companies.

Technology for Downstream Operations
In 1978, after 20 years of exporting oil, Nigeria processes only enough oil to satisfy about half of internal demand. State downstream activities are limited to two refineries (160,000 b.p.d.) and shares in one of the seven marketing subsidiaries of foreign oil companies which distribute products in Nigeria. Although a great many oil projects have been discussed by government since the late 1960s, none have been implemented, apart from the 100,000 b.p.d. Warri refinery in 1978. As a result Nigeria is the world's third largest exporter of crude but has yet to begin processing it in any significant way. In addition ninety-eight per cent of associated natural gas is flared.

The absence of downstream technology transfer underlines the extreme problems which beset the realization of oil projects in Nigeria. These problems are not based on the monopolization of technology for processing crude oil. It has been the experience of Nigeria and other OPEC members that once government takes a firm decision to establish an oil-based project, companies compete to supply technology or enter partnerships. Downstream project implementation in Nigeria is ridden with problems because of the competition among state compradors and private middlemen for opportunities to profit from the transaction in which technology is purchased and installed.

The Commercial Triangle: The state acquires much technology via a triad of state comprador, Nigerian middleman and foreign supplier. The purchase of technology involves channelling public funds to foreign firms. Local compradors and middlemen seek to divert and claim a percentage of those funds.[21] The stakes are high since each project runs into hundreds of millions of dollars. It would be no exaggeration to say that contemporary Nigerian politics are dominated by efforts to appropriate oil money. In many cases compradors in the state need the assistance of Nigerian middlemen in order to secure their percentage of contract awards and their cuts from land deals. Since these transactions place a premium on trust, it is not unusual for there to be kinship or at least language links between compradors and middlemen.

How does the commercial triangle work? Competing foreign suppliers hire local agents. These agents or middlemen vie with each other for access to government officials who can influence, and care to profit from, the successful award of a contract. Since there are usually several foreign firms competing

211

to supply materials, expertise or some aspect of the technology package, the triangle of foreign businessman, local private middleman and state comprador may be repeated many times. The larger the number of state officials involved in making decisions, the more triangles are formed and the more intense is the competition. This dynamic is at the basis of regional competition over location of projects. It leads to delay in agreeing to undertake a project and to inflated costs of often inappropriate technology.[22]

State compradors maximize their own advantage by closing off participation in decision-making wherever possible. For instance, compradors in the oil ministry succeeded in removing oil project decisions from forums such as the Petroleum Board and the Federal Executive Council and thereby effectively reduced competition from other triangular interest alliances. Compradors seek direct deals with foreign technology suppliers. However, the strength of the middleman class rules out the exclusion of private Nigerians except in those cases under direct military sanction. Compradors in oil-related ministries and agencies struggle to gain and maintain control over oil projects. Well-placed individual compradors strive to bring downstream projects within their personal grasp. This dynamic fosters secrecy, closed decision-making and the wide dispersal of responsibility for the oil industry among government branches. The varied and substantial costs of this approach to the transfer of downstream technology can be discussed in turn.

Downstream Integration: Virtually all oil companies have organized or seek to organize their operations so that crude production dovetails into transport, refining and marketing. The decision to become vertically integrated, as well as to pursue horizontal and product integration is normally due to a combination of two factors: a desire to find profitable investment outlets for current revenues, and/or a desire to reduce the instability or riskiness of future profits. Vertical integration became characteristic of the international oil industry,

> . . . as independent companies which were to find large quantities of crude oil had to integrate forward into refining and marketing in order to have outlets for the crude, particularly in times when there was a glut of crude. On the other hand, independent marketers and refiners found it necessary to integrate backward into crude oil production in order to have assured supplies, particularly when there was a scarcity of crude. Thus, vertical integration became the rule in the industry so that today virtually all large oil companies operate at every level of the industry.[23]

If the Nigerian state oil corporation was meant to become a viable oil company, its formal control of over a million barrels of crude a day since mid-1974 would be followed by forward integration into refining and marketing in order to have secure outlets for the oil. In addition, time-action imperatives favour integration, as do considerations of efficiency and profitability. Oil is a viscous, inflammable liquid which cannot be stored cheaply. It must flow constantly from well to consumer. Again, the organization which is producing crude from a set of oilwells is best-placed to collect and commercialize gas that is produced in association with this oil. Consequently oil activities are usually organized in an integrated way under the control of a single, centralized organization which can perform the complex task of co-ordination. A final reason for integration is that the duplication of scarce expertise which follows from the dispersal of oil-related projects is particular inefficient in under-developed countries such as Nigeria.

Compradors throughout the Nigerian state did not favour an integrated oil corporation. The operation of the commercial triangles through which compra-dors seek to transfer downstream technology would be seriously impeded by the centralization and integration of the oil industry. This is not to say that the move from a comprador bureaucracy to a technocracy necessarily eliminates corruption: it may mean more centralized, organized corruption. Technocrats in the oil apparatus have urged that downstream projects be centrally planned, executed and operated: compradors have presided over their dispersal.

Cost Inflation and Inappropriate Technology: A second drawback associated with the comprador approach to the transfer of downstream technology is the delay in project initiation caused by competition among 'triangles' of compra-dor, middleman and foreign supplier. These delays are very costly, especially since 1973 when oil equipment was hit with sky-rocketing inflation. The cost of downstream oil technology increases by more than one-third in each year.[24]

Inter-triangular competition leads not only to delays but to deadlocks. Because the prevalent 'winner-take-all' attitude results in virtual inaction, the Federal Executive Council has experimented with package decisions which contain something for each influential group. It was possible for the Council to approve the building of a second domestic refinery at Warri when commit-ment to a system of uniform oil product pricing and the construction of a third refinery at Kaduna were included in the package. In this way work could begin in 1977 on a second refinery which had been needed in 1973 and proposed as early as 1968.

The purchase of technology through compradors and middlemen pushes its cost up and increases the possibility of acquiring inappropriate systems. Local businessmen who act as intermediaries have no expertise qualifying them to choose and promote a particular supplier. As a result, local middleman-comprador teams are susceptible to the full range of malpractices and mistakes identified in the literature on technology transfer. If the buyer is both ignorant and well-funded, the foreign supplier has what amounts to a free hand in executing the sale. He is limited only by the conditions which Nigerian techno-crats are able to impose. But technocrats have had little influence in situations which ensure a role for local middlemen in the transaction. The technocratic cadre's call for direct government-foreign supplier deals has received little attention.

Economic Dependence: The final cost of the operation of commercial triangles follows from the fact that they bring about the transfer of very little techno-logy. Since the Nigerian state has failed to transfer downstream technology, oil companies continue to supply local and regional oil product markets. Supply has been erratic and gas/kerosene shortages endemic. Six of the Nigerian

213

marketers – Shell, Mobil, British Petroleum, Agip, Elf and Texaco – belong to multinational oil firms which also have producing-subsidiaries in the country. The government's failure to require an adequate supply of petroleum products as a condition for the export of Nigerian crude is a typical instance of policy incoherence and economic dependence. With responsibility for oil widely dispersed, the state suffers a tremendous loss of bargaining power. Rather than withhold permission on one matter until compliance is secured on another, the state itself is riddled with division as foreign firms pursue their particular interests. This disorganization limits the state's exercise of sovereignty.

In January 1976 the state was responsible for selling its full 55 per cent share of production. The government must either find secure crude markets such as those offered by export refineries producing for guaranteed product markets, or must rely on the oil companies to take the oil. Given these alternatives, the government's 1974 decision to scrap participation in a large Caribbean export refinery for the U.S. market indicates a choice to continue to rely on oil companies to market government crude.

To summarize, technocrats in the oil administration have had little influence over the transfer of downstream technology. Compradors were able to move projects and personnel outside the centralized scope of the oil corporation, even after N.N.O.C. had carried them past the feasibility stage. Technocrats were often isolated from each other: they were working on logically interdependent projects which were bureaucratically separated through interministerial competition. Technical decisions on project location, choice of contractors and selection of processes or equipment have been open to challenge from compradors who occupy senior positions in the state structure.

Technology for downstream projects has not been transferred as a result of the coincidence of oil company resistance, competition among triads of foreign technology suppliers, private middlemen and public compradors, and the struggle to profit from project location and the diversion of public funds. Oil companies benefit in that they continue to obtain their crude requirements since no oil is diverted to local processing plants. A few compradors and middlemen divert sometimes fabulous amounts of money. Technocrats in the oil administration have little power. The Nigerian people have lost the most.

In the Nigerian case, the recommendation that the state should exclude middlemen and centralize the process of buying technology ignores political reality. The state itself is dominated by compradors who as a group profit from the pattern of technology acquisition. In many cases they depend on middlemen to conclude their deals. As a result of the competition among commercial triangles, opportunities are missed, costly delays are incurred, inappropriate choices are made and the benefits of centralized, co-ordinated planning and operation are foregone. A further cost is the instability which follows from the unbridled competition for profit among the compradors charged with carrying out the transfer of oil technology.

Know-how
Labour force development is the most important aspect of any programme for

technology transfer. But in Nigeria, little progress has been made. This situation reflects the lack of serious state commitment to involvement in the oil industry, either in exploration-production or in refining and other downstream activities. Ironically, however, the major reason given by compradors for state inaction is the lack of adequate manpower.

By 1968 Nigerian university graduates could no longer be certain of employment in the civil service or in the private sector. A demand for Nigerianization — the replacement of expatriates in the private sector — was raised. In this atmosphere oil technocrats criticized the unorganized and unsatisfactory manner in which training for the oil industry was being carried out.

> The complete absence of proper directives and co-ordination by the Government of the individual training efforts of the oil companies helps to render the position more haphazard and disorganized . . . it becomes manifestly clear that oil companies are not enthusiastic about the training of local personnel to take over the jobs of expatriates, and such training should never in fact be left to their own initiative and control.[25]

It was recommended that the transfer of oil-related know-how be pursued (i) as the responsibility of government, (ii) through a centralized authority, and (iii) according to the dual strategy of crash training in order to staff particular projects and long-range training through petroleum institutes. Comprador response through the oil ministry and ultimately through Council decree was fragmented and fell short of the technocratic strategy for developing Nigerian oil expertise. This unco-ordinated reaction followed logically from comprador reluctance to commit government to a role in oil. Without involvement there is little need for strong cadres of oil personnel. But demand from individual Nigerians, the expectation that the state provide education, the requirements of oil companies for low and middle level personnel and the general concern to appear on a par with other OPEC member countries were among the factors which influenced even the comprador oil administrators to take piecemeal steps towards training Nigerians and placing them in oil-related jobs.

In 1975 it was clear that government's policy of Nigerianization had failed. The 1969 Petroleum Decree specified that at least 60 per cent of managerial, professional and supervisory categories, and 75 per cent of the total senior staff be Nigerians by January 1970 at the earliest, and by December 1978 at the latest. Nigerianization was to be enforced through checks on expatriate entry into the country by an Expatriate Quota Board and through a 1972 requirement that oil companies gain oil ministry approval before terminating the employment of a Nigerian on the senior staff. These measures did not encourage company management to promote Nigerians into positions directly related to oil work or into jobs of significant managerial responsibility. Nor did the state's takeover of majority financial control, 55 per cent participation by June 1974, bring about any change in the pattern of expatriate domination of top positions in exploration and production. Annual returns published by the

Ministry of Mines and Power on the employment of Nigerians and non-Nigerians in the exploration and production companies show no steady improvement in the decade between 1964 and 1974. Nigerians constituted 20 per cent of the top level (management and professional) in 1963-64, and ten years later reached an all-time low for peacetime of 17 per cent in 1973-74.[26]

The government's policy of leaving oil companies in charge of transferring technical know-how to Nigerians has borne little fruit. Companies can buy expatriate quotas when turned down by the Expatriate Quota Board; they can frustrate and induce Nigerian senior employees to resign when promotions to responsible positions are due. But more important, the Nigerianization law has never been seriously enforced. Those jobs falling within the categories to be dominated by Nigerians — management, professional and supervisory — are not identified. As late as 1978 companies, government and employees were without definitions of the jobs which were supposed to be filled by Nigerians. In the absence of precise specifications, oil companies can realize their goal of maximising the number of expatriates in their organization by structuring and naming positions in a suitable way.[27]

In 1975 Nigerian employees in one of the most strike-ridden[28] of the exploration and production companies requested that management (i) define the jobs falling within each of the categories listed in the 1969 Petroleum Decree, and (ii) report on how the company planned to comply with the law by 1977 when its oil mining lease would be ten years old. Management informed the oilworkers that the enforcement of Nigerianization terms was a matter for settlement between management and the oil ministry and did not concern employees.

Training efforts have been as laissez-faire as has been the approach to localization of staff. Some scholarships have been awarded by government and companies, a petroleum training institute is operating in Warri and a small, financially constrained department of petroleum engineering at Ibadan turned out its first seven graduates in 1975. None of these efforts are co-ordinated in such a way as to identify needs, select students, train and then place them.

The effective transfer of know-how: The few instances of effective transfer and absorption of oil expertise have come about through struggle, usually against the comprador oil administration and company management. Four examples can be cited. (i) Most important is the experience of Biafrans, many of them ex-Shell-B.P. and Safrap employees who ran an oil industry including production, refining and distribution, under blockade conditions in order to fuel and provide munitions for the Biafran war effort. This achievement has contributed to demystifying oil technology and expertise. Its impact is not fully felt at the national level since it was central to the anti-federal campaign. Since the civil war, research on lubricating oils and local crude characteristics has been carried on in the Anambra (formerly East Central) State. This work has been discouraged by the federal oil ministry. (ii) The near-complete Nigerianization of the Port Harcourt refinery was the result of a campaign by Nigerian refinery staff, representatives of whom became members of the

Refinery Board after the 1966 military coup removed political appointees from the Board. These technocrats succeeded in extending state ownership from 50 to 60 per cent and revising the operating agreement with British Petroleum. (iii) Individual Nigerians in the foreign oil companies have made slow progress towards positions of technical responsibility through determination and by being 'twice as good'. An oilworkers' union is pressuring management to comply with the Nigerianization law. (iv) Finally, the National Oil Corporation has trained energetically since 1973 and has over 200 qualified oil personnel who have little prospect of gaining working experience.

The Manpower Shortage Myth: In their struggle to obtain know-how, techno-crats and oilworkers have challenged and disproved a pervasive oil company myth about efficiency, experience and the need to rely on expatriate know-how. This myth is widely used by oil companies and compradors as a rationale for the domination of oil activities by foreign firms and expatriate personnel. Company spokesmen argue that oil industry technology is highly sophisticated and very specialized. Therefore, its mastery requires many years of experience in the oil industry proper. Lengthy experience is linked to operating efficiency. If Nigerians are promoted too rapidly, the argument goes, the company's level of efficiency will suffer. As a result government oil income will be threatened as well as the national economy and the security of the state. Although all the statements are open to question and bear no necessary relation to one another, the manpower myth finds wide and uncritical acceptance and is affirmed and disseminated by state compradors.[29] The failure of the Nigerian state to establish control over the oil industry is excused, rationalized and even 'explained' by reference to the absence of competent local personnel.

To sum up, the transfer of know-how to Nigerian oilmen has been blocked by oil companies and by state compradors. This stance is a spin-off of comprador-company resistance to local involvement in exploration-production and downstream activities. Technocrats, acting independently, have been able to transfer some know-how in limited spheres. Some success has followed from actions taken by private Nigerian oilworkers and by technically-competent individuals. Nigerianization remains an explosive issue in the oil industry since it highlights and questions the contrast between well-paid expatriates and less well-paid Nigerians.[30] Oilworkers, technocrats and sections of the public are becoming critical not only of the expatriate firms, but of the state, as a result of the regime's failure to enforce Nigerianization laws.

Conclusion

The comprador nature of the Nigerian state prevents it from organizing the transfer of oil technology and, more broadly, from initiating the development of capitalist production. In Nigeria the comprador state is based on, and often its officers merge with, the local commercial class. Middlemen are more numerous and influential as a result of the oil boom, the policy of import substitution and the state's policy of intervention to foster economic development. As government expenditure and bureaucracy grew, the numbers of bureaucratic compradors establishing triangular relations with middlemen and foreign suppliers increased. The logical ally of the technocratic cadre, a local capitalist class of producers, does not exist in Nigeria. Without such support, technocrats lack significant influence in the Nigerian state. The comprador state is unsteady because it has been unable to override specific capitalist interests in favour of broader considerations of national policy. Comprador authority within institutions of state derives from the senior and usually administrative positions held by members of the group. Professionals and technocrats have been in subordinate posts in the bureaucracy since the colonial period. They are unable to impose rational methods and national objectives on the state in the face of the overwhelming strength of the traditional comprador elements within the civil service.

Technocrats are a relatively rootless group. As a professional stratum, they are based not on indigenous social categories but in institutions inspired by a set of ideas deriving from theories of 'development' and 'modernization' along capitalist lines. Technocrats in the oil administration are marginally more influential than those elsewhere due to their knowledge of the world of oil and to the support they receive from OPEC policies and from oil technocrats in other exporting countries. But perhaps the base most notable with respect to the future actions of Nigerian oil technocrats is those oil companies which seek to compete with the firms which have hitherto enjoyed comprador favour. Although the colonial links between Shell-B.P. and the state persist, they are becoming more costly. The oil industry as a whole is beset with instability, with a limping infrastructure and with the possibility that techno-cratic criticism might feed more radical sentiments. Oil companies may prefer to deal with a Nigerian state in which technocrats have a more weighty role, and one in which oil is managed by a sector clearly isolated from the rest of the state apparatus. Oil technocrats may be amenable to co-existence with the foreign oil industry on more organized and nationalistic terms, especially if companies support them in resolving the 'non-antagonistic'[31] contradiction between themselves and compradors.[32] Since such a transformation of relations within the state would occur without corresponding developments among social classes, it is likely to be effected and maintained by authori-tarian means. In this scenario, technocrats become the functionaries of a repressive corporate state which may at the same time espouse populism and nationalism.

At present the significance of technocrats within the state is largely political: they are well placed and motivated to criticize comprador policies and thus provide aspiring rulers with reasons for unseating the in-group. On the face of it, oil technocrats resemble strata which seek to become a national bourgeoisie. But the scope and force of technocrats' oil policies are more probably symptoms of their powerlessness than indications of their commit-ment to replacing foreign oil companies by an integrated state corporation. However, some technocrats — aware of the expanding power of the comprador class and of the need for political support if their policy conceptions are to be realized — have left the civil service for political work. What technocrats do in the future depends largely on how other classes inside and outside Nigeria develop. Currently they are a professional group which is critical of comprador behaviour. The middleman-comprador alliance has thus far been successful in suppressing the technocratic faction within the state. Along with this suppression goes the possibility of any significant state-led transfer of oil technology.

Postscript

Although there are strong supporters of technocratic-led capitalist accumulation in Nigeria, commercial capitalists continue as the dominant class and compradors remain in charge of the state. Three developments since this chapter was written appear at first glance to have increased technocratic power. First the oil ministry, a comprador stronghold, was dissolved by decree in April 1977. The state oil corporation, where technocrats are concentrated, was renamed the Nigerian National Petroleum Corporation. On paper, oil activities were centralized under production-oriented state capitalists.

The second boost to technocracy in oil is external. Multinational oil corporations, their governments, and institutions such as the World Bank, have devised a new strategy for mineral exploitation. Stable profits require state involvement. Foreign firms prefer joint ventures. The U.S. government's Overseas Private Investment Corporation insists on host government equity in those U.S. multinational oil projects it insures. Multilateral organs assemble 'packages' of finance, technology and markets which tie up corporate-country interests. Resource-rich governments find it virtually impossible to extricate themselves from these complex networks with their multiple ramifications. In short, contract renegotiation is no longer on the cards. But states must be technically equipped for joint ventures. An essential prerequisite to stabilization through state involvement is the existence of a public corporation staffed by competent technocrats. Thus, technocratic dominance in the Nigerian state may suit the interests of some foreign oil companies.

Third, external support for state capitalists over compradors has mounted in the midst of world recession. There is need for international economic growth, yet barriers to trade, consumption and production abound. The industrial powers look to OPEC countries as key sites for expansion. Technocrats are charged with capital accumulation in OPEC states. At the September 1978 annual meeting of the International Monetary Fund and World Bank, U.S. Treasury Secretary Blumenthal stressed the importance of 'middle-income countries' such as Nigeria. The industrial countries must ensure that these countries can obtain the capital they need to expand their economies, he said. 'To sustain this flow [of credit], he added, 'the borrowing countries must demonstrate they can use this capital productively, and that they can maintain an encouraging investment climate.' International creditors from whom Nigeria has borrowed heavily in 1977-78 can be expected to back technocrats in the state apparatus.

However, developments in Nigerian oil, and in the broader political arena, confirm that compradors continue as the dominant faction of the Nigerian bourgeoisie. Nigerian oil policies actually reduced taxes on companies in 1977 as an incentive for more exploration. There is no indication that companies responded to higher profits with intensified efforts to find oil. And ironically, the Nigerian state which owns 55 per cent of oil operations has overriding responsibility to initiate exploration itself. Other concessions to oil companies in 1977-78 included lower oil prices (when production plummeted due to the new North Sea and Alaskan supplies), conformity to the major producers' timetable for the L.N.G. project, and granting more expatriate work permits. 'Revenue permissiveness' in the Warri refinery project with Italy's Snam Progetti is phenomenal.

More important in giving free rein to compradors is the legalization of political activity in 1978. The comprador class has grown rapidly as oil revenues provide more opportunity for commerce, but also due to the experiment in return to civilian rule (which had been originally cut off by the coup-makers of 1966). In 1979 Nigeria's military regime presides over elections. Hundreds of aspirants to state office are aligned with middlemen to swell the ranks of the comprador stratum. The stakes are big, as oil revenues and an expanding bureaucracy offer extensive opportunities for patronage. The multiplication of commercial triangles can lead only to more corruption, more instability and a rapid return to military rule.

References

1. The processing and handling of crude oil are often referred to as downstream activities since after oil leaves the well, it is flowing 'downstream' to the consumer.

2. Carlos Anez, 'The Transfer of Petroleum Technology in Algeria' (Science Policy Research Unit, University of Sussex, 1975; mimeographed). I am indebted to Carlos Anez for making available data collected for his thesis on technology transfer to the exploration and production phase of the oil industry.

3. In this section I have relied on Gavin Williams' analyses of the Nigerian political economy. See his 'Class relations in a neo-colonial economy', in P.C.W. Gutkind and P. Waterman (eds.) *African Social Studies: A Radical Reader*, London, Heinemann 1978; and 'Nigeria: a political economy', in G. Williams (ed.), *Nigeria: Economy and Society,* London, Rex Collings 1976.

4. P.T. Bauer, *West African Trade: A Study on Competition, Oligopoly and Monopoly in a Changing Economy,* Cambridge 1954.

5. C. Wrigley 'Some aspects of the political economy of Nigeria', Institute of Commonwealth Studies, University of London, 13 June 1968.

6. 'Development objectives' in A. Ayida and H.M.A. Onitiri (eds.), *Reconstruction and Development in Nigeria,* Ibadan, Oxford University Press 1971.

7. Robin Cohen, *Labour and Politics in Nigeria, 1945-71,* London, Heinemann 1974, p.144.

8. That Nigeria has an unstable state is widely recognized. See Martin Dent, 'Nigeria's third (and last?) military coup', *World Today*, September 1975, p. 355; Peter Waterman, 'Third World strikes: an invitation to discussion', *Development and Change*, vol. 7, no. 3 (1976), pp. 331-44; Terisa Turner, 'Multinational corporations and the instability of the Nigerian state', *Review of African Political Economy*, no. 5 (June 1976).

9. The backwardness of manufacturing in Nigeria may reflect the lucrative opportunities commerce has historically presented to entrepreneurs. The Third Plan (1975-80) states that despite a high rate of G.D.P. growth (12.2%) over the last decade 'the share of manufacturing and craft increased by only 2.15 per cent rising from 5.64 per cent of G.D.P. in 1962 to 7.79 per cent in 1972 [current prices]. The current 8 per cent share of manufacturing in G.D.P. compares quite unfavourably with the 15 per cent to 20 per cent share attained in many countries at a similar stage of economic development . . . . While part of the difference between the actual and the expected share of the sector in the G.D.P. can be explained by the unusual importance of the oil sector, Nigeria's manufacturing sector nevertheless is underdeveloped relative to the size and the general level of development of the whole economy'. *Plan*, Ministry of Economic Development, Lagos 1975, vol. 1, p. 147.

10. 'Comprador' is the Portuguese word for buyer. The cadre of professional intermediaries who dealt with the foreign trading houses in the coastal enclaves were dubbed 'comprador elements' by the Chinese marxists.

11. 'In order to sell and export a substantial total of this country's goods and services the exporter must pay a "commission" (for want of a better word) to the importer or his agents and intermediaries (of which there may be many). . . . Any exporter or exporter's agents unwilling to recognize this "custom" of paying a "commission" has little, if any, chance of selling his goods or services. In one African country at least, it is well known that goods will not be unloaded from the ships unless a number of financial "arrangements" are concluded with the carrier's agents and employees, and often a whole chain of other characters as well.' Letter commenting on Shell and B.P.'s secret payments to Italian political parties, *Sunday Times* (London, 25 April 1976, p. 12.

12. Gavin Williams, 'Nigeria, a political economy', in Gutkind and Waterman (eds.), op. cit.

13. Michael Tanzer, *The Energy Crisis, World Struggle for Wealth and Power*, New York and London, Monthly Review Press, 1974, p. 62.

14. 'What is missing in Nigeria today is an outward looking economic nationalism which alone will . . . generate . . . collective self-reliance and the will to develop.' A. Ayida, then Permanent Secretary in the Ministry of Economic Development at the 1969 Ibadan conference on development. Ayida and Onitiri, op. cit., p. 8.

15. The ideas included in 'development theory' are well-developed in Ayida and Onitiri, ibid. The notions of 'take off into self-sustaining growth' and maximising growth without attention to the distribution of wealth are perhaps the most prominent.

16. Federal Ministry of Finance, 'Report of the Fact-Finding Mission on Petroleum Taxation, Problems Affecting Petroleum Revenue and

Miscellaneous Matters on the Petroleum Industry', Lagos, hereafter referred to as the 'Report of the Fact-Finding Mission'. This key document was compiled in response to Federal Executive Council Conclusion 39(68)4 of 27 November, 1968 and summarizes the policy proposals which technocrats sought to have implemented. In July 1969 Members of the Mission visited Algeria, Libya and OPEC Headquarters in Vienna.

17. 'Report of the Fact-Finding Mission', pp.33-40.
18. 'The Draft Operating Agreement' (Lagos, mimeo, 18 June 1973) left virtually all day-to-day concerns in company hands.
19. ' . . . in this sector [the provision of oilfield services] there is a lot of scope for well-run private Nigerian companies which the National Oil Corporation will patronize directly or indirectly through its existing partnership arrangements.' Phillip Asiodu, Permanent Secretary of the Ministry of Mines and Power; 'Nigerians and their oil industry', Remarks at the Round Table of the Nigerian Institute of International Affairs, Lagos, Ministry of Information, 3 March 1972, pp. 11-12.
20. Oil income for 1976 amounted to $7.9 billion which is 90 per cent of foreign exchange earnings on exports and 95 per cent of federal revenues. Of total federal government income in 1976, Shell-B.P. provided 54 per cent.
21. U.S. Government, *Multi-National Corporations and United States Foreign Policy* (Hearings before the Subcommittee on Multinational Corporations of the Committee on Foreign Relations, United States Senate, Part 12), Washington, U.S. Government Printing Office 1976.
22. These effects are discussed in Terisa Turner, 'Two Refineries: A case study of technology transfer to the Nigerian refining industry', *World Development,* 1977.
23. Tanzer, op. cit., p. 29.
24. *Oil and Gas Journal* carries statistics on oil industry materials costs. A further drawback associated with delays is the loss of market opportunities.
25. On 8 December 1975 the government ' . . . urged foreign companies operating in the country to deal directly with government ministries and departments instead of through middlemen and commission agents . . . [and] said any cases of middlemen trying to extort money from foreign businessmen on behalf of public officers should be promptly reported to the military authorities.' Reuters, Lagos, 8 December 1975. In contrast, the Iraqi government requires that middlemen be registered and that foreign firms report data on commission payments to the state. Penalties include long jail terms. 'Report of the Fact-Finding Mission', pp. 42-3.
26. *Annual Reports,* 1963-64 to 1970-71, Ministry of Mines and Power, Division (later Department) of Petroleum Resources, Lagos.
27. 'The general object is to remove the distinctions in grading between very high levels where expatriates predominate and the levels immediately below them with the effect of increasing the total population of the group. It is relatively easy then to show that 60 per cent of the enlarged group is composed of Nigerians . . . ' (senior Nigerian administrator in foreign oil company, interview, November 1975, Lagos).

28. Strikes are prohibited by a Trade Disputes Decree. Robin Cohen reports that ' . . . the highest levels of strike activity since 1964 have occurred in 1971 (Adebo) and 1974-75 (Udoji) during a period when strikes were either illegal or severely restricted under a Trade Disputes Decree. The ban on industrial action has been extended annually . . . in the case of the most recent agitation strong statements by Gowon ("this is a deliberate attempt to undermine the Government's authority") and the Inspector-General of Police ("the government won't tolerate violations in the Trade Disputes Decree") were ignored by striking workers.' 'Civilian politics and the trade unions, (July 1975, mimeographed), p. 25.

29. The manpower shortage myth is based on notions of efficiency and experience which have no relation to the way in which work is organized. It may be that an oilworker's competence, dedication and sense of responsibility are functions of the extent to which the oil organization was set up and is controlled by the worker both for his or her immediate well-being, but more important, for the well-being of a larger community of which the oilworker is part.

30. In 1972 Shell-B.P. paid N2,784,000 to 400 expatriate staff and N6,108,000 to 2,700 Nigerian staff, excluding external payments and pension fund payments. The average payment to expatriates was N6,960 or more than three times the average payment to a Nigerian oilworker.

31. A relationship is non-antagonistic if the victory of one party over the other does not imply the destroying of the structure in which both exist. But ' . . . structures which contain non-antagonistic contradictions can only be changed from outside themselves, by actions emanating from the antagonistic contradictions of primary structures.' Ken Post, *Arise Ye Starvelings: Jamaican Labour Rebellion of 1938 and its Aftermath,* Millwood, N.Y., Kraus-Thomson, forthcoming.

32. Technocrats are not likely to favour the elimination of capitalism, private property or the role of the oil companies. Immanual Wallerstein has pointed out that 'The state bureaucrat, the university graduate, the technician may still aspire via a combination of individual competence and astuteness, political influence, and corruption to translate his training into wealth . . . he can only do this to a significant degree if the society legitimizes large-scale property-holding in the form of economic enterprises. It is this "option" that complete public ownership of the means of production cuts off . . . It is here that the analysis of the indigenous property-owning bourgeois and the skilled professional blurs together. For the latter almost always seeks to be the former . . .' 'Semi-peripheral countries and the contemporary world crisis', McGill University, Montreal, 1975, mimeo.

11. Oil and the Venezuelan State

Wolfgang Hein

The Capitalist State in an Oil-exporting Country

Venezuela is a rich country: with a per capita Gross Domestic Product of $2,210 in 1975[1] it falls within the top group of Third World countries; and because of its relatively high income from oil exports during the last few decades, the typical problems of under-developed countries (balance of payments deficits, lack of capital etc.) have been of only marginal importance for the country. But the majority of the Venezuelan population is poor: in 1970 20 per cent of Venezuelans controlled 65.0 per cent of income whereas the poorest 40 per cent had only 7.9 per cent.[2] In 1974 15.9 per cent of the active population were unemployed, and another 10 per cent underemployed.[3] Moreover 45 per cent of those employed in 1971 were still earning less than 500 bolivars (about $110) a month,[4] while 75 per cent of all families remained below the minimum subsistence wage of 1,500 bolivars a month.[5] The majority of the agricultural population still depends predominantly on subsistence production;[6] they, as well as a high precentage of the urban population, suffer from inadequate housing, and lack of medical and educational facilities. Infant mortality has increased in the early 1970s; the housing supply has deteriorated;[7] the number of inhabitants per hospital bed is higher, and the percentage of pupils in school between 5 and 14 years old is lower than in several other Latin American countries with a much lower *per capita* income (e.g. the Dominican Republic).[8]

The economic causes of this seemingly paradoxical situation have been analysed in many studies.[9] Basically, oil export earnings led to an availability of foreign exchange which facilitated imports and discouraged internal production. This effect was accentuated because of the exchange rates of the Venezuelan bolivar, which was determined by the high productivity of the oil sector and totally unrelated to average productivity in the rest of the Venezuelan economy. Thus imports became much cheaper and internal wages much higher than in neighbouring countries, while the destruction of traditional economic activities was greatly accelerated and the process of import-substitution delayed. In addition to all that, the availability of capital supported the use of capital-intensive equipment and the establishment of capital intensive sectors (e.g. the emphasis on basic industries).[10]

So, though traditional sectors were rapidly destroyed, the modern sector was slowly expanding and a growing percentage of the population became economically and socially marginalized.

In Venezuela oil revenues reached unprecedented heights after 1973 and government revenue more than tripled within two years.[11] But the mass of the people continues to suffer from inadequate nutrition and a lack of basic public services, with no hope of any immediate change. Such a situation is politically highly explosive and fuels class struggle. Here lies the real paradox of Venezuelan society: for, contrary to all expectations, the last 15 years have seen the *end* of both armed struggle and insurrectional attempts by the army and a permanent strengthening of a U.S.-style presidential democracy. Accion Democratica (A.D.) and COPEI, the Christian Democratic Party (which differ from each other little more than Republicans and Democrats do in the U.S.A.) are seen as the basic political alternatives.[12] The two socialist groups, M.A.S. (Movimento al Socialismo) and the alliance between M.E.P. (Movimento Electoral del Pueblo — a group which split off from A.D. at the 1968 elections) and the Venezuelan Communist Party (P.C.V.), are a significant minority (about 10 to 15 per cent of the vote). But neither has a chance of winning an election in the near future nor even of posing a radical political alternative. M.A.S., for example, did not even demand the nationalization of the oil industry in its 1973 election programme, and after the election supported the basic aspects of the Peréz government's development strategy: nationalization and the use of the bulk of oil revenue for the establishment and expansion of basic industries. M.A.S. agitation merely concentrated on criticizing administrative corruption and the huge inequality of income in the country — aspects which were condemned by the government itself.[13]

The large number of American publications claiming to explain the paradox of Venezuelan political development are hardly illuminating.[14] They use concepts developed in North American and West European political science (like political culture, conflict theory and modernization theory) which merely serve to indicate how Third World political systems are supposedly approaching the forms of bourgeois democracy that exist in the metropolitan countries (hence the stress on national integration, institutionalization of conflict resolution, etc.). The latter are usually treated as the ideal forms of political organization.[15] It is a consequence of the compartmentalization of bourgeois science that this approach hardly discusses the role of the oil sector in determining political development — this, despite the fact that the economic literature acknowledges that the oil sector has determined the dynamics of Venezuelan economic development since the 1930s and the fact that oil revenues have provided 60 per cent and more of state revenues during the last thirty years.[16]

Venezuelan Marxist analyses, on the other hand, often suffer from a somewhat muckraking character when it comes to politics. Denouncing Accion Democratica as an anti-revolutionary party is certainly important in the Venezuelan political context, but this itself does not *explain* the crucial role of A.D. in the political system.[17] An explanation of the character of this system, however, is of basic importance for discussion about the direction of further struggles to be undertaken by the Venezuelan Left. Such an explanation is also important for an analysis of the effects of the oil sector on the political development of oil-exporting countries in general.

The second problem — probably the principal one within the context of this book — has to do with a basic methodological question of Marxist political analysis. By stressing the necessity of analysing social phenomena in the totality of their relationships, Marxist analysis avoids the error of trying to make causal inferences from a simple correlation between variables. This statement can also be reversed: the fact that there are few obvious similarities between the political systems of Venezuela, Algeria, Saudi Arabia and Iran does not mean that there are no common effects of the oil sector on the development of the state in these countries. It is only an expression of the concrete articulation of the oil sector with other, different determinants of social and political development. But how is it possible, in an always limited amount of time and space, to analyse a social situation integrating the totality of relevant determinants?

Regrettably, neither Marx nor Marxists after him wrote very much about the methodological problems of analysing the historical development of capitalist societies in their totality, of how to connect theoretically the abstract analysis of capital accumulation as given in *Capital* with the concrete historical process of capital accumulation as it develops in a particular social setting and as it continuously tranforms this setting.[18] On a very general level, however, Marx, in referring to his method of abstraction, did point the way to the reverse process:

> The economists of the seventeenth century, e.g., always begin with the living whole, with population, nation, state, several states, etc.; but they always conclude by discovering through analysis a small number of determinant, abstract, general relations such as division of labour, money, value, etc. As soon as these individual moments had been more or less firmly established and abstracted, there began the economic systems, which ascended from the simple relations, such as labour, division of labour, need, exchange value, to the level of the state, exchange between nations and the world market. The latter is obviously the scientifically correct method. The concrete is concrete because it is the concentration of many determinations, hence unity of the diverse.[19]

Applying the methodological postulate implied in this statement to the analysis of class struggle and the state in Venezuela involves establishing the hierarchy of abstract determinations of Venezuelan politics. Here, of course, we have to rely on some general characterizations of the society, mostly undisputed — for example that Venezuela is a *peripheral* capitalist society. At the same time we have to rely on some general results of the Marxist critique of political economy. These are not always undisputed and therefore preliminary choices are necessary, as we are not able to solve all the theoretical problems of Marxism before we start with the analysis of concrete class struggles.[20]

Furthermore, if these abstract determinations are not helpful in explaining the historical processes being studied they have to be revised. This dialectical inter-relationship between theoretical approaches and empirical research, however, is part of the research process itself and will not usually appear in the presentation.

Five ascending steps from the abstract to the concrete will be introduced to establish the theoretical framework for the analysis of the effects of the oil sector on the development of the capitalist state in Third World oil-exporting countries:

a) Talking about the *capitalist* state implies that *the laws of motion of capital are the basic determinants of social development.*

b) *Capitalist development has a necessarily uneven character*: i.e. while the laws of motion of capital — basically the law of value, the consequence of the drive of all commodity owners to maximize their revenues — are valid wherever the capitalist mode of production is dominant, social formations in the Third World have nevertheless been fundamentally affected by their development at the periphery of the capitalist world system. *Capitalist production in peripheral societies does not develop as a self-centred process of unfolding of the social division of labour; rather it is based on the production of a few types of commodities which are only single links in the chain of the social division of labour on the world scale.* Thus the historical development of different social formations in the Third World differs considerably in relation to the character of the commodities which link a particular society to the world market.[21] Here we find the basic theoretical argument for the fundamental influence of oil on the social formations of oil-exporting countries. As we are, however, focusing on the role of the oil sector in the development of the state, we have to introduce two additional intermediate steps.

c) The capitalist state embodies the generalized, 'public' aspect of capitalist domination (in contrast to the direct domination of the bourgeoisie over the working class in the labour process). By guaranteeing the *formal* freedom and equality of all commodity owners (including owners of the commodity 'labour power') and the role of money as the general equivalent for the exchange value of commodities, the state secures the pre-conditions for the operation of the law of value and, thus, for generalized commodity production. As such, the state has to develop as an extra-economic instance, in the sense that it is not simply forced to maximize its revenue as a commodity owner on the market.[22] Due to the ever-present confrontation of the capitalist mode of production with other forms of production on the one hand, and the immanent contradictions of capital accumulation on the other, the capitalist state always has to interfere in the social process to support particular class or fractional interests in order to guarantee the accumulation process as a whole. This goal implies that the disruptive effects of the class and fractional struggles about the determination of state actions need to be minimized. To ensure this the state apparatus has to develop forms of institutionalizing class struggle.[23]

These are basic features the capitalist state has to assume in order to permit the generalization of commodity production. They are independent of the concrete forms of state and regime which superficially characterize and differentiate various states. In the Venezuelan case this means that state power cannot be directly tied to a traditional oligarchy. The struggle for power can no longer be decided by the strength of the private armies of regional caudillos, as was the case during the nineteenth century.[24]

d) There are, however, some particular problems which characterize the capitalist state in the Third World, related to *a particular contradiction of the national state in peripheral societies:* while their political form as nation state corresponds to that of metropolitan societies, they lack an economic basis congruent with the national territory. Since the centre of gravity of their accumulation process is situated outside their territory – for example, is dependent upon the demand for a single significant export product – the possibilities for effective political intervention in the accumulation process are very limited. Because of the blatant social contradictions in Third World societies (extreme inequalities in living conditions, mass poverty, sprawling cities with entirely inadequate infrastructures, etc.) and, related to all this, an often low degree of mass commitment to the political system, this structural ineffectiveness of the state tends to keep the peripheral capitalist state in a constant state of crisis. In stark contrast, metropolitan capitalist societies possess a self-centred process of accumulation. Here political conflicts tend to originate in the basic contradictions of capitalism (the increasingly *social* character of production ranged against the *private* appropriation of surplus value; the concentration and centralization of capital tending to distort the operation of the law of value; and the antagonistic interests of capital and labour generally). In contrast, *class struggle in peripheral societies is often dominated by particular contradictions originating in the specific character of their integration into the capitalist world market*. Countries which are producing, for example, agricultural raw materials on large plantations with mainly pre-capitalist relations of production are certainly dominated by different political conflicts from those producing labour-intensive manufactured goods for the world market.

e) For our analysis of Venezuelan political development, therefore, *the particular characteristics of an oil-mediated integration into the world market have to be determined*. Two attributes of the oil sector have a fundamental impact on the social and economic structure of all societies in which oil production for export has become the dominant economic activity (oil is not, of course, the dominant activity in all OPEC countries: in Ecuador, for example, oil's share of total exports in 1976 was only 48.6 per cent, while oil income accounted for only 12.9 per cent of the G.N.P. in 1975).[25] Firstly, oil is one of the few primary commodities for which there has been a continuous increase in world demand over the last fifty years, due to the rapid increase in overall world energy consumption on the one hand, and the growing role of oil among the various sources of energy on the other; the long-term increase in oil prices is a result of this. Secondly, the extraction of oil is, compared to the production of other primary products, extremely capital-intensive and highly productive. On the surface these two attributes seem to be extraordinarily desirable, as fluctuations in the world market prices of other raw materials and the tendency for their terms of trade to deteriorate are one basic cause of the chronic balance of payments problems and limited ability of most Third World countries to import the capital goods they need. The structural consequences of these characteristics, however, have already been mentioned above: though the oil revenues constitute a potentially important aspect for supporting industrial development, the insertion of the oil countries into the capitalist world market tends to transform the oil sector into an element which delays industrialization. Within a context of free world trade, oil revenues would be spent on financing imports, not for financing a process of national industrialization.

All this points to *the crucial role of the state in oil countries.* Whereas in other peripheral societies there are only limited sources of internal capital accumulation (these include the agricultural export sector, sometimes in local hands, and sometimes some manufacturing industry which may be competitive because of low wages and under-valuation of the national currency), these sources are usually too small to support accumulation in the hands of the state. The situation in the oil-exporting countries is now the opposite. As their oil sectors have been generally established originally by foreign oil companies[26] and have been developing as extreme examples of enclave economies, *their predominant link to the local society is through the state.* The state receives royalties and taxes from the oil companies, channelling these funds into the local economy and guaranteeing the repression of the oil workers (and whatever other social forces might jeopardize the capitalist labour process within the oil sector).

Without state intervention the conditions of accumulation for local capitalists are even worse in the oil-producing countries than in many peripheral societies. This is because the tendency to over-value national currencies prevents the survival, let alone the creation, of other export sectors in local hands. The fate of the Venezuelan agricultural export sector during the 1930s provides a pertinent example.[27] An over-valued currency also provides a general incentive to import. *Because of the oil revenues, however, the state – and the state alone – disposes of effective financial means to support an internal process of accumulation.*

Now this relationship between the oil sector, the state and internal capital accumulation leads to a peculiar class constellation in oil-exporting countries. The surplus value created in the oil sector provides the main source of accumulation. Even the other economic sectors do not mainly accumulate through the normal capitalist process of squeezing surplus value from their workers, but accumulate in one way or another through the transfer of resources from the oil sector itself. These transfers mitigate the principal antagonistic conflicts between capital and labour in those other economic sectors which incorporate the majority of the population.

Let us now turn to another aspect. The oil sector extracts natural resources from land. Thus the value of oil is not determined like that of manufactured goods by the socially necessary labour time required in its production under *average* conditions, but by the labour time necessary to extract it (or a product with an equivalent use value) under *marginal* conditions. Oil is predominantly used as a source of energy and is cheaper than most other sources. Since the total global demand for energy cannot be satisfied by oil or other cheaper sources of energy, the value of energy is much above the average extraction costs of oil. Thus the oil companies can realize enormous surplus profits which would, however, under conditions of fully capitalist landownership, be completely transformed into absolute and differential rent, appropriated by the landowner.[28] The oil revenues appropriated by the state in oil-exporting countries, therefore, originate in the differential rent created by the difference between the costs (i.e. socially necessary labour time) of the most expensive source of energy for which there is still a social demand, and the average costs of oil extraction in the particular country.[29] As these differences are enormous, it is possible both to pay oil workers well above the costs of the reproduction of their labour power (in order to create a reliable labour aristocracy) and to support accumulation in other sectors out of the differential rent appropriated from oil extraction.

If this analysis is right, the struggle for the appropriation of surplus profits from the oil sectors will assume a dominant role. On the one hand, there is the 'real' struggle between the oil multinationals and the internal bourgeoisies of the oil countries over the sources of accumulation. On the other hand, the struggle between these actors appears as a convenient ideological mechanism for the internal bourgeoisie (and the oil companies as well) to prevent the dominated masses from struggling for their own control of the oil revenues. As long as this ideological mechanism – a particular brand of nationalism – is effective, the internal conflicts will concentrate on the distribution of the oil rent.

The analysis that follows of Venezuelan political development shows how these features combine with particular characteristics of Venezuelan society to provide an explanation of the paradox of growing wealth and worsening poverty. Beyond that, some general propositions about the political development of oil-exporting countries are made.

Class Struggle and the Development of Bourgeois Democracy in Venezuela

The Fight for Oil Sector's Surplus Profits and Establishment of A.D. System, 1928-48

Oil was first produced in Venezuela in 1914 under the rule of Juan Vincent Gómez (1908-35). He initially granted oil concessions to Venezuelans who, in turn, sold them at a large profit to foreign oil companies. The economic and social dynamics unleashed by the development of the oil sector strengthened the Gómez dictatorship in the short run through increasing state revenues. However, these forces contained elements which in the long run put an end to the caudillism Gomez represented and led to the development of a capitalist state.

With the oil sector, an important nucleus of the Venezuelan working class developed. The number of workers increased rapidly during the 1920s until in 1929 there were 27,000 oil workers in the country.[30] As they were concentrated in a few camps around the oil fields and all lived under similarly appalling conditions (hard work, low wages, extremely primitive accommodation), their organizational potential was high. Due to their increasingly crucial role in the reproduction of Venezuelan society, their potential economic impact through strikes became significant. In June 1925 12,000 of them organized the first major strike in Venezuelan history paralysing oil production for two weeks. The strike was put down by the military, but it achieved the first wage increases in the oil industry (of six to seven bolivars a day).[31]

The development of the oil sector stimulated a rapid process of urbanization. The population of the capital, Caracas, grew from 92,212 in 1920 to 269,030 in 1941,[32] partly as a result of the management and lobbying activities of the oil companies, but more because of the rapid expansion of the state apparatus and commercial activities. This, and the professionalization of the army, led to the development of a 'new' middle class oriented towards modernization and democratization, as the only way to gain political influence at the expense of the oligarchical clique around Gómez. In the late 1920s the most active sectors of this new middle class were students of law and medicine and educated army officers.

To a very limited degree the urbanization process led to the establishment of a tiny, but slowly growing industrial bourgeoisie (based in textiles, building and building materials, food and beverages). But Gómez's politics of special privileges for himself and the ruling clique deprived aspiring entrepreneurs of funds for accumulation and denied them legal equality with the oligarchy. Thus the social transformation induced by the oil sector exerted pressures for the transformation of the state.

The development of a new export sector based on capitalist relations and the slow expansion of capitalist production for the internal market required a state able to guarantee the formal freedom and equality of commodity owners. This entailed guaranteeing the mobility of labour (and its repression), as well as legal equality for competition between individual capitalists. A state which was run as the private fief of a caudillo had to become more and more in conflict with the requirements of capital accumulation.[33]

A characteristic of pre-capitalist social relations is the absence of a built-in mechanism that forces social actors to maximize their revenues. Such a mechanism is, however, the driving force in the transition to capitalist social relations. The state has earlier in this chapter been defined as extra-economic, in so far as it is not forced to maximize its revenue as a commodity owner on the market. But the capitalist state is subject to this driving force of capitalist

231

development in so far as it is continually pressured by the bourgeoisie to maximize resources for capital accumulation.

While in most capitalist societies this maximization of resources is a central focus of internal class and fractional struggles, the situation is different in oil-exporting countries. In the absence of an independent internal source of accumulation, oil revenues become a basic means of supporting internal accumulation. The caudillist state, as the owner of oilfields, acts like latifundists who have no interest in intensifying the exploitation of their lands because they cannot consume a higher income than they already earn. In contrast, an incipient bourgeoisie will immediately start pressing the state to maximize the revenue available to support internal accumulation by asserting its power as a capitalist landowner. Economically, this means that *surplus profits are to a degree transformed into differential rent and appropriated by the state.*

Gómez did succeed, however, in replacing himself with his chosen successor, Lopez Contreras. But a period of intense political agitation followed which culminated in an unsuccessful general strike in 1935. Subsequent developments in 1936-37 typified the relationship between the bourgeoisie and the working class in Venezuela that lasted right up to the stabilization of bourgeois democracy in the 1960s.

The internal structural consequences of the oil sector outlined above were felt in full force during the Great Depression. The huge loss in export income forced other Latin American countries to devalue their currencies and introduce measures to discourage or restrict imports, stimulating internal industrial production. But the foreign exchange earnings of the Venezuelan oil sector did not decrease significantly and already exports in 1935 surpassed the value of 1930 (itself the highest before the impact of the Depression). Since Venezuelan imports decreased relative to exports, there was pressure on Venezuela to *revalue* her currency. The revaluation by 64 per cent relative to the dollar between 1929 and 1938 had two important structural consequences.[34] It led to the rapid decay of the agricultural export sector, the earnings of which had already been reduced by the fall in world prices and were further depressed by the revaluation. Moreover, it limited the growth of an internal industrial bourgeoisie while strengthening the position of the commercial bourgeoisie.

Thus, through the development of the oil sector itself, the oil companies lost one of their main allies within the country — the agricultural oligarchy — and left their other ally, the commercial bourgeoisie, in a somewhat ambiguous position. While they profited from liberal economic foreign policies, the commercial bourgeois also had an interest in the transformation of the companies' surplus profits into rent paid to the Venezuelan state, which would enlarge Venezuelan purchasing power for imported commodities. This interest, and the hope of stopping any further radicalization of the masses, motivated the commercial bourgeoisie to make rapid concessions to the demands of the democratic movement in early 1936.

The two major forces within Venezuelan society, the incipient industrial bourgeoisie and the intellectual/bureaucratic middle classes, had to rely on the working class to strengthen their political position, since both were much more dependent on the capitalist transformation of the state than was the commercial bourgeoisie. The industrial bourgeoisie sought an increase in the transfer of surplus profits from the oil companies, while the middle classes sought the opportunities that an expanded state apparatus would offer them in the way of well paid positions and political influence. Neither had any revolutionary interests beyond the fight for a capitalist state, but they could realize their potential roles only in alliance with the working class. Only this class was in a sufficiently strong position to challenge the power of the oil companies and the traditional oligarchy through the oil workers' crucial role in oil production.

There was no return to a Gómez-style personalistic dictatorship under Lopez Contreras. The movement to form labour unions which had started in February 1936 with the foundation of the *Sindicato de Obreros y Empleados Petroleros de Cabimas* was not immediately stopped. The total number of unions reached 246, with 69,139 members, in 1939. Prior to 1940 the oligarchy had not regained sufficient power to deny the registration of new labour organizations, while the bourgeoisie had no interest in dissolving the labour movement but only wanted to get it under control. This approach was reflected in the bourgeoisie's attitude to the first great strike of oil workers, which took place from 12 December 1936 to 22 January 1937. The strikers demanded a minimum wage of 10 bolivars a day, improvements in working conditions and health care and sanitary conditions, equal wages for Venezuelans and foreigners, and the recognition of the unions as the only legitimate representatives of the workers. The same conservative newspaper (*El Esfera*), which earlier had denounced the opposition to López Contreras as 'communist', now supported the oil workers' strike as a 'national battle to make the country independent from foreign regimentation'.[36] Though the results were meagre — López Contreras ended the decree and conceded only a small increase in minimum wages — the strike did show that the new bourgeoisie had a stronger interest in asserting Venezuelan property rights over the oil resources than in supporting the political struggle for democracy.

An even clearer expression of the fight for Venezuelan sovereignty over the oil sector was the petroleum law of 1938. This increased royalties, cancelled the guarantees against any further increase in royalties before the expiration of contracts, and stipulated that Venezuelan laws protecting the national economy and national industries had priority over existing contracts.[37] On the other hand, the fact that the government was never able to enforce this law against the resistance of the oil companies[38] made it clear that the bourgeoisie was in fact dependent upon the labour movement in their fight for a transformation of the oil companies' surplus profits into rent to be paid to the state. But the repression of the working class by Lopez Contreras deprived the bourgeoisie of the possibility of using the labour movement for their own ends.

The events in 1936-37 in Venezuela in some ways resembled bourgeois revolutions in metropolitan countries. The bourgeoisie in Europe needed a

temporary alliance with the masses in order to defeat the feudal aristocracy, but broke this alliance when the masses threatened to take control
of the course of events. Capital accumulation in the metropolitan centres
then led to a phase of sharpened contradictions between the bourgeoisie
and the working class. In contrast, Venezuelan development during the
1940s showed the possibility of a rather more stable alliance between these
classes in an oil-exporting, peripheral capitalist society.

This development can only be explained by reference to particular
characteristics of the working class in such a society. A principal anomaly
is the fact that the structurally most powerful sector of the working class,
the oil workers, does not confront the internal bourgeoisie in the production
process. High surplus profits in the oil sector, based on differential rent,
allow for the payment of wages well above the cost of reproduction of labour
power without jeopardizing the accumulation capacity of the oil companies.
Thus, within the framework of the Venezuelan national economy, there is
no antagonistic contradiction between the two classes. High profits also allow
a continuous flow of subsidies towards the internal manufacturing sector
and thus a mitigation of class struggle within this sector.

The comparatively simple character of the production process in traditional
manufacturing industries and its comprehension by the work force make a
workers' take-over of the production process a realistic political aim. In
comparison, the technical complexity of the oil sector is somewhat of an
obstacle. Dependence on the technological skills of foreign oil companies
is a material and psychological drawback. Until quite recently even socialist
parties in Venezuela did not demand the nationalization of the oil sector.[39]
Furthermore, the excellent opportunities for jobs and influence within an
oil-rich reformist capitalist state have an integrative effect on intellectuals. This
tends to deprive the working class of an important vanguard.

A new political party entered the Venezuelan political arena during the
early 1940s: Acción Democrático (A.D.), formed in 1941 as a successor to
those political groups which had been founded in 1936 and afterwards driven
underground. It first concentrated its efforts on unionizing the agricultural
workers,[40] but also gained a foothold in the trade union movement. In
particular it sought to create its own parallel unions, a characteristic of the
methods by which A.D. has maintained its hold over the labour unions to
this day, showing little respect for majority decisions or for the unity of the
labour movement.

A.D. took over political power through a military putsch in October 1945,
in alliance with a group of young officers[41] and a rising fraction of the bourgeoisie. The latter were interested in breaking the ties of the presidency with
the traditional oligarchy which blocked their access to state subsidies from
oil revenues.[42] The following three years, the so-called *Trienio*, were decisive
in institutionalizing a system of A.D. dominance in Venezuelan politics. This
system was based on close ties between the party and the labour movement
on the one hand, and between A.D. and the industrial bourgeoisie on the other
hand.

The *Trienio* saw a great expansion of the labour unions, stimulated and dominated by A.D., the number of registered unions and union members both increasing dramatically.

A.D. also supported the development of close links between the bourgeoisie and the state. The FEDECAMARAS, founded in 1944 as a confederation of local chambers of commerce,[43] was offered a dominant position in the Corporación Venezolana de Fomento (C.V.F.), which was a crucial instrument to channel oil revenues into the process of capital accumulation. Congress and the FEDECAMARAS were each to choose two members of the board of directors, while the chairperson was to be chosen by the President, Rómulo Betancourt. Since he chose a leading entrepreneur, the C.V.F. became more or less an instrument of the bourgeoisie.

The state's assertion of its role as a capitalist landowner against the oil companies was central to the capitalist transformation of the Venezuelan state after the A.D. gained power in 1945. The Petroleum Law passed under López Contreras in 1938 was ineffective. Medina's law in 1943 brought the first large increase in state revenues from the oil sector and a standardization of oil legislation.[44] The Petroleum Laws of 1946 and 1948 aimed to recover national control over oil resources. Revenue taxes were increased from between 8 and 9.5 per cent to between 9.5 and 26 per cent. All large oil companies with a profit of more than 26 million bolivars paid the 26 per cent rate. In 1948 the famous 'fifty-fifty' law was passed guaranteeing the Venezuelan state a share of 50 per cent in oil profits (taking tax and royalty payments together).[45] Additional measures were taken to assert the authority of the Venezuelan state over the oil sector. First, the companies had to reduce the internal price of petrol by 50 per cent. Second, in the period of rapidly increasing demand for oil after the Second World War, it proved profitable for the state to demand part of its royalties in kind and to market it directly. This brought additional incomes of 4.8 million bolivars Bs. in 1947 and 45 million in 1948. Third, further oil exploration was to be reserved for the Venezuelan state. No new concessions would be granted. Fourth, the state planned the construction of its own refineries and put pressure on the oil companies to refine a larger proportion of their crude oil within the country. In 1947 only 8.5 per cent of all Venezuelan oil was refined domestically. This was tripled to 24.9 per cent by 1955. Fifth, the economic use of natural gas became one of the main aspects of conservation policy. Finally, the need to integrate economically crucial workers led A.D. to support the demands of the oil workers for higher wages and improved working conditions. Between 1946 and 1949 the average wages of oil workers more than doubled from 23.06 bolivars a day to 49.22 bolivars, whereas the wholesale price index rose by only 26.1 per cent.[46] On the other hand, FEDEPETROL, an A.D.-sponsored confederation of oil workers founded in 1946, supported three-year collective agreements which led to a stabilization of labour relations in the oil sector. In early 1948 the Communists demanded the expiration of contracts after one year and security of jobs. They called a strike and were expelled from the union.

In a country in which the majority of the population lived in miserable conditions, where the health and educational systems reached only a small minority, and where basic infrastructural conditions for production and circulation were missing, the state could not restrict its activity to the collection and channelling of oil revenues into private funds of capital accumulation. The essential programmatic concept of A.D., was that of *sembrar el petroleo* ('sow the petrol'): use the oil revenues for the systematic development of the internal economic structure of Venezuela — an idea which was first elaborated in the 1940s.[47]

According to this concept, state economic activity was to concentrate on three areas: a) building-up modern infrastructure; b) establishing heavy industries to process Venezuelan natural resources within the country (refineries and a petro-chemical industry, but also a steel plant to process the important iron ore resources of the Guayana region); and c) supporting the substitution of manufactured and agricultural imports via local production. The first two parts of this strategy aimed at building up the economic base. It was suggested that import substitution would solve the country's social problems by creating jobs in industry and — based on an agrarian reform[48] — consolidating the agrarian sector.

The ideological role of this concept has to be stressed. It allowed the state to support the internal process of capital accumulation according to the interests of the bourgeoisie. At the same time the strategy could be presented as a policy for an integrated, truly national society, striving to overcome dependency. Until the present day A.D.'s policies have been presented in nationalist terms, though the party's nationalism never went far beyond the fight for national sovereignty over natural resources. Even during the *Trienio*, A.D. invited foreign capital to participate in the development of manufacturing in Venezuela. Since then the importance of *foreign* investment in manufacturing has continuously increased — from 170 million bolivars in 1950 to 4,853 million in 1974: multiplying more than 28 times. In contrast, the overall output of manufacturing industry has only multiplied by a factor of six.[49] More important than the quantitative extent of foreign investment are its structural aspects. Foreign investment has built up subsidiaries, partially financed by Venezuelan financial resources, which enjoy a highly protected internal market but have little connection with the rest of Venezuelan industry.

The economic contradictions of this development model cannot be dealt with at length here, but two points should be stressed. First, the high degree of world market dependency, the rather small internal market protected by a chaotic tariff system, [50] and the role of state subsidies (and thus of access to the state apparatus) in the accumulation process, all imply a high degree of distortion in the operation of the law of value. Extra-economic power determines the development of a particular firm more than competitiveness. i.e. Conditions prevail under which capitalist competition cannot stimulate the development of the forces of production nor promote a nationally inte-grated division of labour. Rather, these conditions support the rise of a few powerful groups of conglomerates with close connections to the state apparatus. These have a flexible investment policy in response to the chaotic structure of protection, credit facilities, and availability of techniques. In the last thirty years these monopolistic groups have appropriated an important part of the oil revenue without contributing to integrated social development.[51] Second, the present paradoxical social situation demonstrated the very limited success of thirty years of 'sowing the petrol'.

Nevertheless, considering the social pressure for state support for internal accumulation, the sheer quantity of oil revenues could not fail to stimulate a rapid, though disorganized process of industrialization. In addition, oil revenues gave rise to short-term real benefits (e.g. the agrarian reform) and opened up chances of social mobility for the poorest groups.

After October 1945 A.D. neglected to build a power base independent of the groups of army officers who had helped it to power. When the Army turned more and more against the government and allied itself with a broad coalition of anti-A.D. forces,[52] no broad mobilization of the working class existed to maintain government in office.[53] Venezuela relapsed into a military dictatorship, which rapidly lost its initial, rather populist image and extended repression from Acción Democrática to all political parties. Peréz Jiménez, the leading figure of the military junta, became President in 1952. He increasingly assumed the role of a traditional caudillo and even granted new oil concessions. A considerable part of the oil revenue again found its way into the bank accounts of the dictator's friends or was used for big prestige projects. When in 1957 the government stopped paying its bills on contracts given to private capital, the dictatorship became definitely unacceptable to the Venezuelan bourgeoisie.

The 1958 Revolution and Stabilization of Bourgeois Democracy 1958-63

The ten years of military dictatorship was more a period of stabilization than of erosion of mass support for Acción Democrática. A.D. was identified with the fight against the dictatorship and for democracy. Many A.D. militants were tortured and murdered, but they nevertheless succeeded in maintaining an effective underground organization throughout the period.

A rebellion of an Air Force and Army garrison close to Caracas on 1 January 1958 was suppressed within a few hours but nevertheless became the starting point for three weeks of demonstrations and riots in the capital. On 22 January, the *Junta Patriotica*, an alliance of opposition parties formed in 1957, called for a general strike, which was almost universally supported throughout the country. After some violent clashes between demonstators and police and soldiers, Pérez Jiménez gave up and was flown out of the country in the morning of 23 January. Once the military dictatorship seemed to be defeated, the bourgeoisie and the prospective bureaucratic elite turned against their left-wing allies. From now on, any further popular mobilization could only be dangerous to the stabilization of a *bourgeois* democratic state.

Nevertheless, in contrast to 1936, this sell-out of the popular forces did not result in a return to military rule. This points to the profound changes which

Venezuelan society had undergone since 1936 and the shift in the balance of class power. In 1936 manufacturing industry was almost non-existent: only 46,855 workers were employed in manufacturing, most of them in artisan-like firms with less than five employees.[54] By 1958 manufacturing industry employed 155,800 workers and employment in other sectors with predominantly capitalist relations of production had grown even more dramatically: in construction from 24,400 to 179,600, and in trade from 64,300 to 236,700.[55] Compared to these sectors, employment in the oil sector had increased less rapidly, varying closely not so much with actual output, but with new investment:[56]

1929:	27,221	1942:	16,470
1932:	8,832	1948:	55,170
1938:	22,496	1958:	44,720

Thus the relative proportion of oil workers within the Venezuelan proletariat decreased, although, structurally, the oil sector retained its overwhelming dominance: in 1936 oil exports represented 89 per cent of total exports, in 1958 91.7 per cent.[57] As a result of the greater share of the Venezuelan state in the oil companies' surplus profits the share of oil revenues in total state revenues increased from 26.1 per cent in 1932-33 to 64.5 per cent in 1956-57.[58]

In the revolutionary events of 1958 and the years that followed, the marginal groups or urban sub-proletariat which had greatly increased in numbers[59] proved to be very 'explosive' indeed. They had participated in the movement against Peréz Jiménez in the hopes of a definite improvement in their social and economic situation. They expressed a straightforward sympathy with Fidel Castro's Cuba and a hatred of American imperialism because of its support of Peréz Jiménez, though not from a clearly anti-capitalist perspective. American Vice-President Richard Nixon was received by a hostile mass of people with sticks and stones in May 1958 while a year later Fidel Castro was enthusiastically welcomed by a crowd of 300,000 people.[60] Also the provisional government's *Plan de Emergencia* created vast numbers of new jobs in public works programmes as well as making credits available for the improvement of the *barrios*.[61] This programme went along with the rapid formation of new *barrios* and a process of political self-organization of *barrio* dwellers in the form of *juntas-pro-mejoras,* to a large degree influenced by the Communist Party.

A.D. had demonstrated in the 1940s that the old guard around Rómulo Betancourt would co-operate with the bourgeoisie rather than support popular self-organization in co-operation with the Communist Party. Betancourt's first move was the exclusion of the Communist Party from the Pact of Punto Fijo, signed between A.D., COPEI (then a right-of-centre Christian Democratic party), and the U.R.D. The Pact had initially formed a 'government of national unity without partisan hegemonies in which all national political currents and independent sectors of the community will be represented' —

irrespective of the outcome of the elections.[62] The exclusion of the Communists – who would have been happy to support him[63] – was a clear signal that Betancourt had no interest in continuing the broad popular alliance. On the other hand, this Pact shows Betancourt's concern to integrate the traditional forces into a bourgeois democratic system and to leave no potential ally for the right-wing military.

The forces which had opposed the A.D. regime in the 1940s were now ready to work within such a framework. While the agricultural oligarchy had lost political importance, the commercial bourgeoisie was strengthened, but occupied a modified social position. From handling exports and imports for the traditional oligarchy, trading companies moved towards the import of commodities for a more and more generalized internal capitalist sphere of circulation. Thus the political guarantee of the pre-conditions of capitalist rationality became more important for the commercial bourgeoisie than the guarantee of personal privileges in a caudillist system. Their remaining conflicts of interest with the industrial bourgeoisie were negotiable, particularly in a situation of relatively abundant resources. The over-valuation of the bolivar favoured the import trade, but this was compensated for by extensive subsidies for the accumulation of industrial capital.

The oil companies were more interested in long-term political stability than short-term maximization of surplus profits. Thus, though they undoubtedly preferred a stable caudillist regime to a revenue-conscious bourgeois democracy,[64] they recognized the immanent contradiction between caudillism and political stability, particularly in the face of Cuban developments.

As for bureaucratic forces, they were obviously represented by Betancourt's fraction of Acción Democrática. The decisive question was whether A.D. could dominate the organized labour movement. Contradictions between Betancourt's integrationist strategy and the interests of the mobilized masses strained the unity of the labour movement, and even that of A.D. itself (during its underground existence under the dictatorship, A.D. had been led by young radicals closer to the popular movement of the Caracas sub-proletariat than to the old party bureaucracy). The December 1958 election results pointed to the main lines of class struggle for subsequent years: though Rómulo Betancourt won the presidential election with 49 per cent of the vote, he won only 13 per cent in metropolitan Caracas; in the marginal constituencies of the capital his vote was even lower.

The first big clash between the government and the popular forces came when Betancourt abandoned the *Plan de Emergencia*, and police and soldiers shot into the resulting protest demonstration killing several people.[65] Betancourt's open anti-Communist politics antagonized the left wing of even his own party. After coming under criticism from the party establishment, and after disagreements about negotiations with the oil companies, Américo Martín and Domingo Alberto Rangel decided to break with A.D. They formed a new party in April 1960, called the *Movimiento de Izquierda Revolucionaria* (M.I.R. – Movement of the Revolutionary Left), taking with them about 80 per cent of the party's youth movement and 14 out of 73 A.D. deputies.

239

For the overall political balance of power in the country, however, the challenge to A.D.'s *dominance* of the union movement was probably the most important aspect of the formation of the M.I.R.

At the moment of the split in A.D., the government had lost its majority within the trade union confederation's Executive Committee and General Council, but this soon changed. On 20 October 1960 six members of the M.I.R. were arrested on charges of subversion and advocating the overthrow of the regime. Ten days of demonstrations followed. The police and military stepped in, brutally killing six people and arresting about 500.[66]

Following a number of machinations within the unions[67] and the defeat of the guerrilla movement (see below), with which the anti-A.D. trade union forces were identified, A.D. managed to regain its dominance over the organized labour movement and thus deprived the left opposition of an ally essential to their success. Right from 1959 the Left had been under increasing attack. Wholesale suspensions of civil rights gave the government extensive powers of arrest and preventive detention. Increasingly Betancourt's government also identified with the U.S.[68] In this situation it was clear to the left that public pressure could not shift a government that had the support of the bourgeoisie and the strongest working class organization as well as the U.S. government — especially after Castro's victory in Cuba. Popular insurrection and armed struggle were the only remaining alternatives. The guerrilla build-up started in late 1961 as soon as the M.I.R. committed itself to the strategy of armed struggle. In December 1962 the Communist Party also formally adopted the policy of armed struggle.

The guerrilla campaign was a total defeat for the Venezuelan Left.[69] Its later self-criticisms concentrated on the difficulties of moving the centre of revolutionary activities to the countryside when the society was predominantly urban. Guerrilla activities increasingly became military operations with only a limited basis of peasant support, and alienated also from the Left's original support in the *barrios* of Caracas. This problem is closely related to a general weakness in the class analysis of the Venezuelan Left in the early 1960s. This weakness can be traced back to the orthodox Communist idea of the necessity of a national democratic revolution against feudal landowners and imperialism. The idea implies that the broad social base for such a revolution would embrace the urban sub-proletariat and even the national bourgeoisie. Several programmatic statements carefully stressed the support of the F.A.L.N. for the 'progressive entrepreneur'[70] overlooking the fact that the marginal population groups, particularly the urban sub-proletariat, provided the most important class basis for their fight. Imperialism had taken on a new character. It had virtually absorbed the old national bourgeoisie through the penetration of manufacturing by international capital.[71] These developments were ignored, as was the special effect of oil rent on the relationship between Venezuelan capital and the integrated working class.

In 1964, after the guerrillas' attempted election boycott failed, their unity began to crumble. Since then the armed struggle has continuously lost ground. In 1977 news that 'six Venezuelan soldiers were killed and five wounded in an ambush by guerrillas' merely indicates a rather marginal phenomenon in the Venezuelan political scene.[72]

Of crucial importance for the stabilization of the Venezuelan political system was the fact that the struggle with the Left did not paralyze the Venezuelan economy and so Betancourt was able to go ahead with most of his projects of reform. Two conditions favoured this development. The U.S. government gave its full support to Betancourt, building up the A.D. regime as 'the principal testing ground . . . to prove that Fidel, the Jacobin Left, and the Communists are wrong'.[73] This meant a certain amount of U.S. government support in overcoming the oil companies' opposition to an increase in government oil revenues and stricter state control over their activities.[74] It also meant all-out U.S. support through loans and technical aid for development projects, in the context of Kennedy's 'Alliance for Progress'.

The oil sector also cushioned the Venezuelan economy against the more serious effects of the prolonged political crisis. Investment in the oil sector had fallen by half between the late 1950s and early 1960s. In manufacturing, investment increased four-fold during the 1950s but then fell in 1963 when investment in construction nearly came to a halt.[75] Employment stagnated as a result, and unemployment rose to 14.7 per cent in 1962.[76] If the high levels of hidden unemployment and under-employment are taken into account, the effective rate of unemployment was much higher. Nevertheless, as oil production rose (from 2.6 million barrels per day in 1958 to nearly 3.5 million in 1965)[77] and the Venezuelan government's share in the oil revenues increased (from 52 to 65 per cent of company profits), total state revenues grew in spite of the economic slump.[78] Thus ordinary state revenue (i.e. excluding loans and non-recurrent income from the issue of new oil concessions) rose fairly steadily from 4.263 billion bolivars in 1957 to 7.174 billion in 1965. This enabled the A.D. government to initiate a development programme following the basic lines of the original *Sembrar el petróleo*. Without going into details of A.D.'s development policies, we can characterize them as the establishment of a firm alliance between the bureaucracy (which tends to transform itself into a 'state class') and the internal bourgeoisie with close links to international capital. This alliance is secured by supplementary policies to win and maintain the loyalty of the masses.

It has been stressed that the oil sector provides the Venezuelan state with a source of revenue of its own, making it financially independent of the internal bourgeoisie. Juan Pablo Pérez Alfonzo, Betancourt's oil minister, for the first time clearly demanded the appropriation of the whole differential rent by the state when he assessed the profits to which the oil companies were entitled in relation to the prevailing capital market.[79] By taking the initiative for the foundation of OPEC in 1959 (OPEC was established in September 1960), he aimed to increase the oil-producing countries' control over the activities of the oil companies, particularly as regards pricing policies. A large planning apparatus[80] and state-owned heavy industry complexes (a steel mill and aluminium industry in the Guayana province; petrochemical complexes in the northwest) were established. These further expanded and strengthened the

position of the bureaucracy as an independent social force. But this did not
give them control of the economic development process as a whole.

The internal bourgeoisie – the private sector which more and more
comprises the industrial *and* the commercial bourgeoisie – is attached to the
bureaucracy not through an open and formalized alliance, but basically
through their permeation of the state sector.[81] Through political pressure,
corruption etc., public resources are diverted into subsidies of private sector
enterprises:

> For example, economic groups which exert an influence on the granting
> of credits have brought about a situation where the instruments for
> evaluation, utilization, control, follow-up, and even control of repayment
> of loans, are either inefficient or lacking altogether.[82]

In addition to that, private sector organizations like the FEDECAMARAS,
the Asociación Pro-Venezuela, and A.V.I. (Asociación Venezolana Indepen-
diente) exert political pressure for particular political objectives (e.g. with
respect to tariffs and taxation). Given this peculiar form of political alliance,
conflicts between the two fractions of the dominant power bloc tend to take
on the appearance of fights against corruption, or for bureaucratic efficiency,
etc. The programme for developing import substitution in consumer goods
was completed around 1970. This strengthened the 'state bourgeoisie'
managing the heavy industry complexes and those parts of the private sector
attached to these complexes. They were henceforth in a position to push for
import substitution in intermediate goods as well, and eventually for the
production of non-traditional exports. However, accumulation in heavy
industries required a halt to the unplanned diversion of public resources to
subsidize non-competitive consumer goods industries.[83]

The ideological character of the *Sembrar el Petróleo* strategy has been
stressed above. This was now supplemented by policies to meet basic needs:
housing programmes, construction of water supply and sewerage systems,
health programmes, etc.[84] More important was the policy of agrarian
reform. Enormous sums of government money were spent on this reform
and a large number of families were affected: 171,500 received land titles
and 550,000 peasants became incorporated into the peasant union. The
policy did little to improve the agrarian structure but much to stablize
support for Accion Democratica in the countryside.[85]

The Oil Boom and Venezuela's Future Political Development

The 1963 and 1968 elections showed increasing confusion among the
marginal groups. Nevertheless, these groups accounted for a large element of
the protest vote. In 1963 only 54 per cent of the presidential vote (25 per
cent in Caracas) was cast for the candidates of A.D. and COPEI but by 1968
it had risen to 56 per cent (49% in Caracas). In contrast, the 1973 results

seemed to indicate a move towards a two-party system like that of the U.S. A.D. and COPEI together won 82.4 per cent of the presidential and 74.9 per cent of the congressional vote. The transfer of the presidency from A.D. to COPEI in 1968-69 and back again to A.D. in 1973-4 was also effected without problems.

The Left had undergone a period of self-criticism of its activities during the guerrilla phase. In December 1968 several hundred political prisoners, many of whom were guerrilla leaders and participants in the armed revolts of 1962, were freed. In March 1969 the Communist Party was legalized and in early 1970 the M.I.R. broke with the remaining guerrillas around Douglas Bravo and made its way back to a legal existence.[86] In 1970 discussions on the Soviet invasion of Czechoslovakia and the character of political alliances in contemporary Latin America led to the *Movimento al Socialismo* (M.A.S.) splitting from the Communist Party. M.A.S. is the most important group on the Left in the mid-1970s. Thus the left opposition agreed to work within the given constitutional framework after the failure of the armed struggle and the loss of their social base among the marginal population.

But to expect these developments to signify the beginning of a long-term stablization of the Venezuelan political system is to forget the basic characteristics of peripheral capitalism. Dependent integration into the capitalist world market makes a country vulnerable to sudden changes which are unrelated to its internal dynamics. The oil-price boom of 1973-74 would not have been possible without the long-term internal transformation of the state in the oil- exporting countries analysed above. But the sudden trebling of prices in one year and the related jumps in exports and government revenues were a consequence of a particular *global* constellation of forces. The Arab-Israeli War of 1973 and the subsequent Arab oil boycott, as well as short-term oil shortages in the United States, were in no way related to internal developments in Venezuela in the early 1970s.

The revenues of the Venezuelan state increased from 12.2 billion bolivars in 1972 to 42.6 billion in 1974 and remained at this level (ordinary revenue planned for 1978 is 40.8 billion bolivars).[87] In just four years, 1974-1977, total state oil revenues exceeded total government income from oil for the whole period of 1947-1973 (122.4 billion bolivars compared with 101.2 billion).[88] For people used to measuring wealth in monetary terms, such a bonanza ought to solve all the problems of underdevelopment and poverty. In fact, it has caused an enormous rise in expectations among the Venezuelan masses. In the short run there has also been an appreciable improvement in the situation of the poor. Emergency measures, such as the creation of unproductive jobs in the public sector (like the employment of operators for automatic lifts) and the decree that every employer of more than ten workers had to increase its labour force by 5 per cent,[89] increased employment. Jobs also resulted from the mere expansion of the internal market through increased revenues. A 175 million bolivar plan has been launched for funding self-help projects in the *barrios*.[90] After four years, however, two things are clear: first that the government programme to establish capital-intensive basic industries will not bring about a major structural change in the situation of the marginal population groups; and, second, that the programme itself has proved to be too ambitious.[91]

While oil exports are stagnating (as a consequence of a conscious conservation policy as well as of the pre-1979 slack in world demand for oil), imports have increased much faster than expected. After enormous balance of payments surpluses in 1974 and 1975, an actual deficit occurred in 1977. Part of the new financial resources from higher oil prices have been lost through the increases in world market prices of industrial equipment and through internal inflation of ten to twenty per cent. As a result, current government expenditures have increased faster than expected. Basic industry projects have proved to be much more expensive than originally anticipated and the traditional diversion of public resources into the private sector has been intensified. The process of planned expansion of the economy has also been hampered by the appearance of bottlenecks in different sectors: electricity shortages, the limited capacity of harbours to handle imports and the serious food crisis in May 1977. These developments have led to a decline in popular hopes for basic changes in their social conditions within the A.D./ COPEI system, and this may lead to a significant increase in protest votes in future general elections.[92]

In assessing the long-term political consequences of the oil boom, it is important to consider the structural changes in Venezuelan society. Three aspects must be stressed:

(1) The period of abundant financial resources has already passed. About 25 per cent of the 1977 budget had to be financed through loans. It was easy to negotiate these loans, but the resulting debt service may become a serious burden to the Venezuelan economy. Thus the conflict between the internal bourgeoisie, tied to the import substitution consumer goods sector, and the state bourgeoisie and their allies interested in the expansion of basic industries, can be expected to increase in intensity. So far the tension has been reduced by the availability of oil revenues.

(2) Venezuelan oil was 100 per cent nationalized by 1976, but it continues to be marketed in large part by international oil companies. Production remains technologically dependent upon these companies. However, national class conflicts can no longer be subsumed under a struggle for 'national interests'.

The material basis for a nationalist ideology has been undermined. Before nationalization, the state mediated in the conflicts between the oil companies and oilworkers on the one hand, and the oil companies and internal bourgeoisie on the other. Now, with its expanding role as an entrepreneur, the state is becoming an immediate opponent of an important part of the working class and of other fractions of the bourgeoisie.

(3) With the current stagnation of the oil sector and the further expansion of production for the internal market, the relative importance of surplus oil profit for fuelling the accumulation process in other sectors will decrease. This process of 'normalization' is being speeded up by the fact that oil is increasingly

extracted from more marginal sources with higher production costs. Thus surplus profits per unit of extracted oil are tending to decrease. Hence the internal accumulation process will become more and more dependent upon squeezing surplus value out of the workers in each particular sector and less and less subsidized by the transfer of surplus profits from the oil sector. Consequently, the direct conflict between capital and labour will increasingly be in the forefront of class struggle in Venezuela. Considering the experience of the last four years, it is very doubtful whether the intended process of developing an integrated national economy can compete with this process of 'normalization' of class struggle. A phase of reviving class struggle is much more probable than the transformation of Venezuela into a developed capitalist society guided by some kind of a social democratic perspective, as envisaged by Acción Democrática.

Conclusion

This chaper has attempted to explain the dynamics of class struggle in Venezuela by reference to a hierarchy of determinants. These have ranged from the general capitalist character of Venezuelan society down to the particularities of Venezuelan historical development. The dominance of the oil sector as the mediator of world market integration determines the general framework of class struggle. In particular, it modifies the relationship between the internal bourgeoisie and the working class. The chapter has illustrated how concrete class struggles develop within this framework.

A comparison of Venezuelan development with that of other oil countries is beyond the scope of this study. Nevertheless, a few remarks can be made on this subject. The methodology employed here suggests an explanation for the puzzling similarity of the development strategies pursued by the governments of oil countries with apparently very different class characters, such as those of Venezuela, Algeria and Iran. In all three countries, the development of basic industries (petrochemicals and steel) is seen as the engine of the development process. The development of agriculture and the whole employment problem are treated – in practice if not in ideology – with relative neglect. The explanation suggested here is that, because the state is a mediator between the oil companies and the national societies and is the owner of the oil sector, the state bureaucracy has the particular important ability to dispose of the oil revenues. As a result, the bureaucracy is relatively independent of the rest of the society. By transferring oil revenues into state-owned basic industries the bureaucracy is 'sowing the petrol' more in the sense of broadening its own economic base than of building up a base for internal accumulation. This coincides with ideological trends that stress the paramount importance of heavy industry for the process of economic development. These trends can be found within both the bourgeois and Marxist traditions.

The different class character of the political systems in Venezuela, Algeria and Iran can be explained by reference to the alliances through which the respective state bureaucracies won their dominating role, in short, by which classes came together to put the bureaucracy into a position to appropriate the surplus profits realized in the oil sector in the form of differential rent. In Venezuela this class alliance comprised the nascent bourgeoisie and the working class (the organization of which was to a large degree controlled by the bureaucracy itself); in Iran the alliance included the traditional oligarchy and excluded the working class; in Algeria, liberation from French colonialism required the broad mobilization of workers and peasants.

References

1. I.M.F., *International Financial Statistics,* July 1977.
2. Klaus Esser, *Oil and Development: Venezuela,* West Berlin 1976, p.18.
3. Ibid., p.22.
4. Michael Zink, *Venezuela: Daten zur Beschäftigungssituation und Einkommensverteilung,* Bonn, Forschungsinstitut der Friedrich Ebert Stiftung 1976, p.38.
5. Esser, op.cit., p.18.
6. Ibid., p. 13; Theodore van der Pluijm, 'An analysis of the agrarian reform process in Venezuela', *Land Reform, Land Settlement and Co-operatives,* 2 (1972), 1-21, p.3.
7. Esser, op.cit., pp.24-6.
8. Statistisches Bundesamt (Federal Republic of Germany), *Allgemeine Statistik des Auslandes: Landerkurzberichte: Haiti,* Wiesbaden 1976, p.26.
9. E.g. Weine Karlsson, *Manufacturing in Venezuela,* Stockholm, 1975; Héctor Malavé Mata, 'Formación histórica del antidesarrollo de Venezuela', in *Venezuela: Crecimiento sin desarrollo,* Mexico 1974; D.F. Maza Zavala, *Venezuela, Una Economía Dependiente,* Caracas 1964.
10. See Héctor Silva Michelena, 'Beschäftigungsprobleme in einem Öl-Land', in Armando Córdova and Héctor Silva Michelena, *Die Wirtschaftliche Struktur Lateinamerikas,* Frankfurt 1969, pp.42-62.
11. Banco Central de Venezuela, *Informe Económico 1975,* Caracas 1976, p.A-219: total government revenue in 1972 was Bs.12,547 million, in 1974 Bs.42,799 million.
12. See Domingo Alberto Rangel, *Elecciones 1973: El Gran Negocio,* Caracas 1974.
13. For the theoretical background of M.A.S. politics, see Teodoro Petkoff, *Socialismo para Venezuela,* Caracas 1970, and T. Petkoff, *Proceso a la Izquierda,* Barcelona 1976; as an example of M.A.S.'s fight against corruption see J.V. Rangel and J. Pulgar, *Quien encubre a los culpables?,* Caracas 1975.
14. North American studies of the 1960s mirrored the exemplary role attributed to Venezuela in the context of the Alliance for Progress by idealizing Acción Democrática and the political developments after 1958; see Robert J. Alexander, *The Venezuelan Democratic Revolution,*

New Brunswick, N.J. 1964. In the early 1970s the application of the theoretical concepts of North American political science became the central focus; see Daniel H. Levine, *Conflict and Political Change in Venezuela*, Princeton, N.J. 1973.

15. The joint study by C.E.N.D.E.S. (the Venezuelan Centre for Development Studies) and M.I.T., published as Frank Bonilla and José A. Silva Michelena, *The Politics of Change in Venezuela* (3 vols.), Cambridge, Mass. 1967-1971, appears to me as an unsuccessful attempt to link up North American political science with dependency theory; this publication shows both approaches side by side, but in no way integrated.

16. Ignacio Purroy, 'Staat und Industrialisierung in Venezuela', unpublished M.A. thesis, Hamburg 1976, p.A-10.

17. See Salvador de la Plaza and Jacques Duclos, *Antecedentes del Revisionismo en Venezuela*, Caracas 1973; Douglas Bravo, 'L'Impérialisme Pétrolier', *Les Temps Modernes*, 29/328 (1973), pp.832-58; Hemmy Croes, *El Movimiento Obrero Venezolano*, Caracas 1973.

18. Most Marxist discussion in this area concentrated on the concept of class analysis, which, however, is generally only related to the analysis of particular historical *situations* and, furthermore, analyzes institutions only in their relationship to classes (thus implying the danger of instrumentalist interpretations), not as part of the totality of social development.

19. Karl Marx, *Grundrisse*, Harmondsworth 1973, p.100ff.

20. It is a problem of many Marxist studies that they take as given certain assumptions although they are in fact disputed even among Marxists; my methodological approach builds to some degree on Jurgen Ritsert, *Probleme politisch-ökonomischer Theoriebildung?*, Frankfurt 1973.

21. This approach to the analysis of peripheral capitalism has been developed in Wolfgang Hein, 'Kapitalakkumulation im Weltmapstab und die Rolle des Nationalstaates in der Dritten Welt', in *Lateinamerika: Analysen und Berichte 2*, Berlin 1978, pp.53-78. Its starting point is a critique of Samir Amin's approach in 'Le modèle théorique d'accumulation et de développement dans le monde contemporain', *Tiers-Monde*, 52 (1972); see also Amin, *Unequal Development*, Hassocks, Sussex 1976.

22. This argument has been developed in German discussion of the capitalist state; see John Holloway and Sol Picciotto (eds.), *The State and Capital: a Marxist Debate*, London 1977.

23. See Joachim Hirsch, 'Bemerkungen zum Theoretischen Ansatz einer Analyse des Burgerlichen Staates' in *Gesellschaft* 8/9, Frankfurt 1976, 99-149, pp.107-9; Nicos Poulantzas, *Pouvoir politique et classes sociales*, Paris 1971, vol. 2, pp.7-8.

24. See Robert L. Gilmore, *Caudillism and Militarism in Venezuela, 1810-1910*, Athens, Ohio 1964.

25. Calculated from data in Bundesministerium für Wirtschaftliche Zusammenarbeit (West Germany), *Politik der Partner*, 2nd edn., Bonn 1977, p.143.

26. The nationalization of the oil sector does not change its basic character as an enclave, and the role of the state in linking it to the rest of the economy becomes even more obvious.

27. The fall in world market prices of primary commodities was answered

by a devaluation of the currencies of most Latin American countries; in this way, their internal revenues were stabilized. But in the case of the revalued Venezuelan currency, the proceeds from one sack of coffee fell from Bs.124.8 to Bs.41.5. See Celso Furtado, *The Economic Growth of Brazil,* Berkeley 1963, p.205, n.2; and Miguel Izard, *Series Estadisticas para la História de Venezuela,* Mérida 1970, p.200.

28. For a concentrated presentation of the Marxist theory of rent, see Robin Murray, 'Value and Theory of Rent', parts I and II, in *Capital and Class,* 3 and 4 (1977-78); for its application to oil, see M. Masserat, 'Energiekrise oder die Krise des Kapitalismus', *Probleme des Klassenkampfs,* 11/12 (1974), p.219ff and Chapter 3 in this book.

29. How much of the surplus profits realized by the oil companies is in fact transformed into differential rent, and thus appropriated by the state, is of course politically mediated.

30. Pedro Esteban Mejia Alarcon, *La industria de Petroleo en Venezuela,* Caracas 1972, p.343.

31. E. Lieuwen, *Petroleum in Venezuela,* 2nd edn., New York 1967, p.50; Luis Vallenilla, *Auge, Declinacion y Porvenir del Petroleo Venezolano,* Caracas 1973, pp.73-4.

32. Izard, op.cit., pp.54-60.

33. Caudillism should not be confused with military dictatorships in general, which, like most of the present dictatorships in Latin America, might quite perfectly guarantee the formal freedom and equality of commodity owners as economic subjects.

34. Izard,op.cit. pp.216-7.

35. Rómulo Betancourt, *Venezuela Politica y Petroleo,* Mexico 1956, p. 84.

36. Betancourt, op.cit., p.89; Vallenilla, op.cit., pp.132-3.

37. Edith Blendon, 'Venezuela and the United States, 1928-1948: The Impact of Venezuelan Nationalism', Ph.D. thesis, University of Maryland 1971, pp.105-6.

38. Betancourt, op.cit., pp.97-112.

39. The programme of M.A.S. in 1973 demands a first phase in which the state would have the right to 'supervise' the oil sector (whatever that means), only in the second phase should the sector be socialized; see *Hacia una victoria del socialismo: Bases y objectivos de la candidatura de José Vicente Rangel,* Caracas June 1973.

40. John Duncan Powell, *Political Mobilization of the Venezuelan Peasant,* Cambridge, Mass. 1971, pp.60-1.

41. The dominant reason was probably their animosity towards the older, militarily badly-trained clique of officers who had deprived the younger, well-trained, professionally-oriented officers of military promotion as well as political influence. Conspiracy against Medina started in 1942 and, in the summer of 1945, led to the formation of the Unión Patriotica Militar (U.P.M.), which in alliance with A.D., played the leading role in the putsch. See Glen L. Kolb, *Democracy and Dictatorship in Venezuela, 1945-58,* Hamden, Connecticut 1974, pp.10-13.

42. On the surface the fight against corruption was the unifying ideological element between the bourgeoisie and A.D. Essentially, this meant the fight against the immediate control of the state apparatus by the traditional oligarchy. See Betancourt, op.cit., pp.177, 187.

43. The abbreviation, FEDECAMARAS, stands for *Federación de Cámaras y Asociaciones de Comercio y Producción*; for its role as an effective organization of the Venezuelan bourgeoisie see Robert D. Bond, 'Business Associations and Interest Politics in Venezuela', Ph.D. thesis, Vanderbilt University, Nashville, Tenn. 1975.
44. Blendon, op.cit., pp.109-19.
45. For the petroleum laws of 1946 and 1948, see Betancourt, op. cit., pp.237-50.
46. Calculated from Banco Central, *La Economia Venezolana*, op. cit., pp. 141, *en los Ultimos Treinta Años* Caracas 1971, p.271. The data are for the Federal District; for this period there are no data available for Venezuela as a whole.
47. This is, besides the development of A.D., the central focus. See Betancourt, op.cit.
48. On A.D.'s Agrarian Reform law of 1948, see ibid., pp.342-62; and Powell, op.cit., pp.69-86.
49. Calculated from Banco Central, *La Economia Venezolana*, op. cit., pp. 141, 271,313 (foreign investment); and Banco Central de Venezuela, *Informe Economico, 1975* Caracas 1976, pp.A-188 and A-262.
50. This was to a large degree due to the fact that the majority of imports were excluded from special tariff protection as a consequence of the 1939 Reciprocal Trade Agreement with the U.S., which was in force until 1973. See Meír Merhav, *Posibilidades de Exportación de la Industria Venezolana,* Caracas 1973, pp.58-62.
51. See in particular the study by James Petras, *Nationalization and Capitalist Development,* State University of New York at Buffalo, Council on International Studies, Special Studies no. 76, Buffalo 1976.
52. See the case study by Levine, op.cit., pp.62-93.
53. Interestingly enough, it was the reproach that A.D. policies were anti-nationalist which brought about the seemingly strange alliance between the Communists and the traditional oligarchy which purged A.D. in 1948.
54. Tomas Enrique Carrillo Batalla, *El Desarrollo del Sector Manufacturero Industrial de la Economía Venezolana,* Caracas 1962, p.15.
55. Purroy, op.cit., p.A-4.
56. Mejía Alarcon, op.cit., p.343.
57. Franklin Tugwell, *The Politics of Oil in Venezuela,* Stanford, California 1975, pp.182-3.
58. For 1932-33, see Izard, op.cit., pp.168-9,172-3; for 1956-57 see Purroy, op.cit., p.A-10.
59. The population of Caracas increased from 200,000 in 1936 to 1.4 million in 1961, but employment did not keep pace with the accelerated pace of urbanization.
60. Richard Gott, *Rural Guerrillas in Latin America,* Harmondsworth 1973, pp.161,163-4.
61. Talton F. Ray, *The Politics of the Barrios in Venezuela,* Berkeley 1969, p.32.
62. Gott, op.cit., p.163.
63. Ibid., p.165.
64. The fact that Gulf Oil, the most important oil company operating in Angola, supported the M.P.L.A. quite rapidly after its victory in the

Civil War in 1975-76 provides an interesting illustration for the thesis
that political stability is more important to the oil companies than the
particular political orientation of the government.

65. Robert J. Alexander, *The Communist Party of Venezuela,* Hoover
Institution Studies no. 24, Stanford, California 1969, p.59.

66. Gott, op.cit., p.170.

67. See in particular Croes, op.cit., pp.193-5,205-9, and 213-25.

68. A detailed account of these events is given in Manuel Cabieses Donoso,
Venezuela Okay! Santiago de Chile 1963, pp.133-60; and in Gott, op.
cit., p.175ff.

69. For an overview of the guerrilla campaign in Venezuela and the self-
criticism by the Left, see Gott, op.cit., pp.175ff.,190ff.,211,258, and
265.

70. See ibid., p.198. The code of honour of F.A.L.N. stressed: 'No damage
will be done nor will operations be carried out against small and medium-
sized Venezuelan businessmen, manufacturers, farmers or tradesmen . . .';
p.205. The Programme of Action of the F.L.N. stated: 'Workers, farmers,
students . . . ., businessmen with progressive ideas, . . . all who desire a
Venezuela mistress of her own destiny and her own riches, belong to this
broad united front of liberation . . .'

71. It is one of the chief merits of dependency theory that it stressed this
point. See Andre G. Frank, 'Lateinamerika: Kapitalistische Unterentwick-
lung oder sozialistische Revolution' in Frank, *et. al., Kritik des burgerlichen Anti-Imperialismus,* Berlin 1969, pp.91-131 (in Spanish in
Pensamiento Critico, February 1968).

72. *Latin American Political Review,* vol. 11 no. 46 (25 November 1977),
p.328. For the development of the guerrilla since 1964, see Gott, op.cit.,
pp.210-65.

73. Alexander, *Venezuelan Democratic Revolution,* op.cit., p.315.

74. According to Tugwell, op.cit., p.52, 'the U.S. State Department cautioned
company representatives to be more politic in their behaviour.'

75. Banco Central, *La Economía Venezolana,* op.cit., p.203.

76. Ibid., p.76.

77. Tugwell, op.cit., p.183.

78. Banco Central, *La Economía Venezolana,* op.cit., p.259.

79. Tugwell, op.cit., pp.53, 60-7 (on the foundation of OPEC).

80. See Fred D. Levy, *Economic Planning in Venezuela,* New York, 1968.

81. See Esser, op.cit., particularly pp.54-9; and Petras, op.cit., pp.6-7.

82. Esser, op.cit., p.56.

83. See 'Reforma administrative y V Plan de la Nacion: Instrumentos del
sector emergente de la burguesía', *Proceso Politico,* no. 2, Caracas 1976,
pp.22-53.

84. Alexander, *Venezuelan Democratic Revolution,* op.cit., pp.271-94; for
the inefficiency of these policies cf. Esser, op.cit., pp.20-3.

85. Van der Pluijm, op.cit., for the generation of political support for A.D.;
cf. Blank, op.cit., pp.143-7. A.D. was in all elections between 1958 and
1968 strongest in the countryside.

86. Gott, op.cit., pp.255-65.

87. Banco Central, *Informe Económico, 1975,* op.cit., p.A-219; Economist
Intelligence Unit, *Quarterly Economic Review of Venezuela, Surinam,*

Netherlands Antilles, 2nd Quarter 1978, p.7.
88. Ibid., and Tugwell, op. cit., pp. 179-81.
89. Esser, op.cit., p.48.
90. David Watts, 'Caracas tries self-help to break ring of poverty', *The Times,* 12 January 1977, supplement on 'Venezuela', p.VII.
91. For critical assessments of Venezuelan development politics since 1973, see Esser, op.cit.; Petras, op.cit.; and *Latin America: Venezuela Special Report,* Supplement to Latin American Economic Report, January 1978.
92. See different issues of the *Latin American Political Review*: vol. II, no. 33 (26 August 1977), p.261; vol. 12, no. 12 (24 March 1978), p.89; vol. 12, no. 17 (5 May 1978), pp.134-5.

12. Class and Oil in Alberta
Edward Shaffer

Canada is the only industrialized capitalist country which has sufficient oil
and other forms of energy to meet its needs. Most of its conventional crude
oil, natural gas, tar sands, heavy oils, and a substantial part of its coal are in
the Province of Alberta. Alberta today is the 'Texas of Canada', providing
the country with most of its oil requirements.

Lying directly east of the Rocky Mountains, Alberta covers an area of
255,000 square miles (660,000 square kilometres). It is larger than any
country in Europe, with the exception of the Soviet Union, and larger also
than oil states like Iraq, Kuwait, Oman, Qatar and the United Arab
Emirates. Its population of 2 million is approximately the same as Libya's.
In 1977 it produced slightly more than one million barrels of conventional
crude oil per day, an amount greater than such countries as Algeria, Mexico,
Oman and Qatar. It contains the world's largest reserves of tar sands, which,
if the proper technology is developed, will be able to produce more oil than
the Middle East. Alberta is thus an important oil 'state', both in Canada and
in the world.

Because of Alberta's present importance and future potential, a study of
the political economy of oil in that province has significance far beyond its
boundaries. Furthermore, the Alberta experience is unique in that oil was
discovered and produced there *after* the province had become well-integrated
in the world capitalist economy. Therefore, the impact of oil in Alberta
could be expected to differ from that in Third World countries where large
sections of the population live outside the market economy.

The experience of Alberta, however, might serve as a guide to what could
happen in the more recently discovered oil areas — the North Sea and
Alaska — which are also already well integrated in the world capitalist economy. Its experience might be particularly useful to countries like Australia,
whose political institutions are similar to those of Canada. Both countries are
federal states in which power is divided between provincial authorities and
the central government. This division often exacerbates conflicts which may
not even exist in a unitary state.

This chapter is divided into two parts. The first analyses the impact of oil
exploitation on Alberta's industrial structure. Using labour force and

employment data, it shows how oil has fostered the growth of the non-productive, rather than productive, industries. The second part examines changes in the class structure flowing from the discovery of oil. It shows how oil is creating an indigenous bourgeoisie who are strengthening their position at the expense of the working class, farmers and petty bourgeoisie.

Industrial Structure

When oil was discovered in Alberta in 1947,[1] the Province was living mainly off agriculture. It exported wheat to world markets and cattle to domestic ones. Its economy was similar to that of its sister Prairie provinces, Saskatchewan and Manitoba.

In 1941, when the last census before the discovery of oil was taken, 49 per cent of Alberta's labour force was still engaged in agriculture. A similar portion, 48 per cent, was engaged in agriculture in the other two Prairie provinces. In contrast, only 20 per cent of the labour force was so engaged in the rest of Canada. By the time of the next census, in 1951, Alberta had already begun to show the effects of oil. Agriculture's share had fallen to one-third. While it had also fallen in the other Prairie provinces, the decline was not so pronounced: the share in these provinces was 37 per cent. This divergence in labour force patterns has continued to the present day. In 1971, the year of the most recent census, agriculture accounted for only 13 per cent of Alberta's labour force, but almost one-fifth of the force in the rest of the Prairies. (See Table 1.)

Table 1
Agricultural Labour Force as Per Cent of Total Labour Force
(1941 = 100)

Year	Alberta %	Other Prairie provinces* %	Canada (Excl. Prairies) %	Alberta	Other Prairie provinces*	Canada (Excl. Prairies)
1941**	49.0	48.0	19.8	100.0	100.0	100.0
1951	32.6	36.8	11.3	66.5	76.7	57.1
1961	21.2	26.9	6.9	43.3	56.0	34.8
1971	12.9	19.1	3.8	26.3	39.8	19.2

*Saskatchewan and Manitoba.
** excludes those on active service.

Calculated from: Statistics Canada, *1971 Census of Canada, Labour Force and Individual Income, Historical-Labour Force, For Canada and Provinces, 1911-1971*. Catalogue No. 94-702, Ottawa, November 1974, pp. 1.1-1.4.

There is little question that the growth of the oil industry in Alberta contributed to the relative decline in its agriculture *vis-à-vis* the other Prairie provinces. But this relative decline has not brought about a corresponding increase in the industrial labour force. Instead Alberta has experienced a relative increase in the non-productive labour force, i.e. in workers engaged in tertiary industries — services and distribution.[2]

The very large expenditures of the oil industry in the Province have failed to create an industrial base. The Canadian Petroleum Association, an organization representing the international oil companies operating in Canada, claims that the oil industry spent nearly (Can.) $26 billion[3] in the Province between 1947 and 1976.[4] If these expenditures, which include payments to the provincial government in the form of Crown reserve sales, lease rentals, royalties and all taxes (except income tax), were evenly divided over this thirty year period, they would have pumped into the province over $800 million a year, an amount equivalent to a *per capita* income of $400 a year based on 1977 population estimates. That such substantial expenditures had a significant impact on Alberta's economy should be self-evident.

That impact, however, has been far different from what might be inferred from orthodox theory, especially from the more optimistic versions of the staple theory of economic growth.[5] This theory, as enunciated by H.A. Innis and his followers, views the export of a staple — a staple being a raw material exported in an unprocessed form — as an engine of economic development. The production of a staple induces linkages between the staple industry and other industries in the domestic economy. The export industry presumably encourages the establishment of domestic firms supplying that industry. It also supposedly encourages the growth of local firms which use the raw materials extracted by the staple industry. Finally, the rise in incomes brought about by the transfer of labourers from those sectors in which marginal productivity is low to the export sector, and to the industries linked to the export sector, increases the demand for consumer goods, thereby encouraging the establishment of consumer goods manufacturing. Eventually these industries, all spawned by the staple industry, cut their umbilical cord to the mother industry, become independent, and grow at a much faster rate than the staple industry itself. Over time these new industries become the important ones and the relative significance of the staple industry diminishes.[6]

This process, as has already been noted, has not occurred in Alberta. The importance of goods-producing industries in general, and of manufacturing in particular, has declined. In 1951, for instance, the goods-producing industries (agriculture, mining, manufacturing and construction), which employ the bulk of productive workers, absorbed 55 per cent of the labour force; manufacturing alone employing 10 per cent.[7] By 1976 the goods-producing share fell to 36 per cent and manufacturing to 9 per cent.[8] This meant that it was the service industries (containing the bulk of non-productive workers) that absorbed a considerable portion of the transfers from agriculture and of the new entrants to the labour force.

Those linkages that have occurred have been between oil expenditures, on the one hand, and employment in financial, commercial and other services, on the other. Employment in these particular sectors expanded at a much faster rate than in the other sectors in the period between 1961 and 1976.[9]

Employment, it must be admitted, also expanded in construction. Its share rose from 9 per cent in 1961 to 10 per cent in 1976. This rise was, however, merely temporary in that in 1976 many construction workers entered the Province to work on the huge $2 billion Syncrude tar sands project, which has since been completed. Most of these workers have now left the province. Until 1976 construction's share had been declining, reaching a low point of 8 per cent in 1975.[10]

What is most interesting is the decline in manufacturing's share, which fell from approximately 13 per cent in 1961 to 11 per cent in 1976. Part of this fall could be attributed to the temporary rise in construction's share, but if we compensate for this by taking construction out of the totals, we still find that manufacturing's share has fallen. While this relative decline in manufacturing has been a feature of all advanced capitalist economies, it should not have occurred in Alberta if the staple theory had worked as the optimists had predicted. Furthermore, this decline was steeper than in the neighbouring Prairie provinces, as can be seen in Table 2.

Table 2
Manufacturing's Share of Employment in Secondary and Tertiary Industries, Alberta and Other Prairie Provinces, 1961 and 1976

	Share %		*Index* (1961 = 100)
	1961	*1976*	*1976*
Including the Construction Sector			
Alberta	12.6	11.2	88.9
Other Prairie*	14.1	13.2	93.6
Excluding the Construction Sector			
Alberta	13.9	12.5	89.9
Other Prairie*	15.0	14.0	93.3

*Saskatchewan and Manitoba.
Calculated from: Statistics Canada, *Estimates of Employees by Province & Industry, 1971-1976.* Ottawa, Ministry of Industry Trade & Commerce, May 1978, catalogue no. 72-516.

Oil, it would seem, has retarded rather than expanded industrialization in Alberta. This conclusion is reinforced by more precise estimates of the number of jobs actually created by oil activity. I have previously made estimates for the years 1961 to 1970[11] and more recently for 1961 to 1976, including some revisions of my original estimates (see Table 3). I made these estimates by contrasting developments in Alberta with those in the other Prairie provinces.[12]

Table 3
Estimates of Employment Created by Oil Industry Activity in Alberta's
Secondary and Tertiary Industries

	1961 to 1970		1961 to 1976	
Industry	*(000s)*	*(%)*	*(000s)*	*(%)*
Productive	22.0	25.7	46.3	25.5
Manufacturing	8.9	10.4	18.6	10.2
Construction	13.1	15.3	27.7	15.2
Non-Productive	63.7	74.3	135.3	74.5
Transportation, Communication				
& Other Utilities	7.9	9.2	22.9	12.6
Trade	12.6	14.7	33.3	18.3
Finance, Insurance & Real Estate	4.5	5.3	11.3	6.2
Commercial Services	9.4	11.0	25.0	13.7
Non-Commercial Services	25.0	29.2	30.9	17.0
Public Administration & Defence	4.3	5.0	11.9	6.5
Total	85.7	100.0	181.6	100.0

Table 3 indicates that oil expenditures created a considerable number of
jobs outside the oil industry, accounting for slightly more than 50 per cent of
the increase in total employment in the secondary and tertiary sectors during
both time periods. At the same time employment in the oil industry itself
did not expand as rapidly as total non-agricultural employment. In fact, oil's
share of employment fell from 3.0 per cent in 1961 to 2.8 per cent in 1970
and 2.6 per cent in 1976. Between 1961 and 1970, oil employment increased
by only 3,300 while total non-agricultural employment rose by 168,000;
between 1961 and 1976, oil employment went up by only slightly more than
8,000 while total employment rose by 359,000. In 1976 there were only
17,000 employees in Alberta's oil industry.[13]

This seemingly large multiplier effect is much greater than most students
of the Alberta economy anticipated. In a study conducted for the Canadian
Pacific Railroad in the 1950s, Caves and Holton predicted that 'the local
repercussions of the petroleum and natural gas development are likely to be
distinctly limited'.[14] Though they correctly observed that 'employment in
those manufacturing industries supplying the new primary producers in the
present case is probably negligible'[15] and that relatively small amounts of
refining and petrochemical activity would take place in Alberta because such
processing 'is market-oriented to a considerable degree',[16] they seriously
underestimated the linkages to service industries. It was precisely because of
these linkages that the impact of oil on Alberta's economy has been significant rather than 'negligible'. Caves and Holton in particular neglected the
importance of what I call 'discretionary' linkage. This is the linkage that
results from public policy rather than from the normal operations of the
market mechanism — i.e. the linkage flowing from the policies pursued with

respect to the collection and disbursement of economic rents. In Alberta the government initially used these economic rents to expand significantly the public sector.

In Table 3 the growth of the public sector is measured by changes in employment levels in non-commercial services. According to Statistics Canada these services consist of 'employment in education and related services, hospitals, welfare organizations, religious organizations and private households'.[17] Between 1961 and 1970, changes in non-commercial services accounted for almost 30 per cent of the increase in oil-induced employment (more than in any other industry). Most of the increase was in educational institutions, especially in universities and other post-secondary institutions, and hospitals. In Alberta, as in the rest of Canada, these are funded mainly by the public sector.

Between 1961 and 1976 the share of non-commercial services fell to 17 per cent. Nevertheless its share was exceeded only by trade, which accounted for 18 per cent of the increase in oil-related employment. The reasons for the very rapid expansion of non-commercial employment in the first period and its much slower expansion in the second will be discussed in the section on the class structure.

The growth of most of the other industries in the non-productive sector represents the 'automatic' linkages between the oil industry and these other industries, i.e. the linkages brought about by the market mechanism. These linkages created employment for a host of occupations serving the oil industry: lawyers, geologists, engineers, chemists, chemical engineers, economists, management and financial consultants, real estate agents, distributors of parts and equipment and many others.

The important point to remember about the jobs created by both the 'discretionary' and 'automatic' linkages to the non-productive industries is that they do not create a base for the economy to transform itself from one dependent on a staple export to one relatively independent of that export. They have, in fact, increased the dependency on the oil industry since the demand for these jobs fluctuates with the fortunes of that industry.

Only manufacturing is capable of breaking the umbilical cord tying it to the mother industry. But, as we have already noted, the oil-induced manufacturing employment growth has been relatively small. As Table 3 shows, manufacturing absorbed only 10 per cent of oil-related employment in both time periods. In the 1961-76 period only 'finance, insurance and real estate' had a smaller share of employment growth. What is also significant is that most of this growth in manufacturing occurred in what Hirschman calls 'satellite' industries. These are industries whose 'principal output is a — usually — minor input of the master industry' and whose 'minimum economic size is smaller than that of the master industry'.[18] They, like the non-productive industries, cannot develop a base of their own. Their fortunes also rise and fall with those of the oil industry.

Most of Alberta's manufacturing industries linked to the oil industry are satellite industries. These industries, which employed 44 per cent of all

257

workers in manufacturing in 1974,[19] are listed in Table 4. As can be seen from this Table the average size of establishment in most of these industries is quite small. In only two, primary metals and petroleum refineries, does the average number of employees per establishment exceed one hundred. Of these two, only primary metals has the possibility of growing independently of the oil industry. While this may happen, it has not occurred so far.

Table 4
Average Number of Employees Per Establishment in Alberta's Manufacturing Industries Linked to the Oil Industry, 1974

Industry	Employees
Primary Metals	140.2
Metal Fabricating	25.9
Machinery	39.2
Transportation Equipment	65.1
Electric Products	43.1
Non-Metallic Mineral Products	40.3
Petroleum Refining	182.4
Chemical & Chemical Products	46.3
Miscellaneous Manufacturing	7.9

Calculated from Alberta Bureau of Statistics, *Alberta Statistical Review, Annual 1976*, Table 67, pp. 69-72.

Fewer than six per cent of Alberta's manufacturing employees work in primary metals. Its share is smaller than that of such industries as meat packing, wood working, printing and transportation equipment. It also accounts for less than six per cent of the value of shipments in manufacturing.[20] Its existence is still dependent upon the well-being of the oil industry.

Manufacturing development has thus up to now reinforced, rather than weakened, the dependency on oil. Given the significant growth of oil-related jobs in both the manufacturing and non-productive sectors, the province has become more 'locked into' oil than ever before. The industrial development envisaged by the more optimistic versions of the staple theory just has not happened.

In summary, the oil industry made significant changes in the industrial structure of Alberta: it accelerated the decline in the agricultural labour force; it spurred the growth of the non-productive industries rather than manufacturing; and — within manufacturing — it encouraged the development of 'satellite' rather than independent industries. The combined effect of these structural changes has increased the dependency on oil. We now turn to examine the changes in the class structure wrought by oil.

Class Structure

When oil was discovered in Alberta, individual commodity producers – family farmers – represented the largest single group in the economy. The indigenous bourgeoisie was relatively weak, consisting mainly of ranchers, a few wealthy merchants and real estate speculators. It was essentially a petty bourgeoisie.

The economy was dominated by a few large, national monopolies based in Toronto and Montreal, namely the Canadian Pacific Railroad, the Hudson's Bay Company and the chartered banks. The dominance of these Eastern Canadian interests fostered a form of economic nationalism – or to be more precise, economic provincialism – within Alberta. This economic provincialism received support from most segments of the population and manifested itself in various reform movements, which succeeded in electing governments: that of the United Farmers of Alberta after the First World War, and then that of the Social Credit Party (Socreds), which governed the Province from 1935 to 1971. The United Farmers of Alberta had a 'leftist' programme (and could in fact be considered as one of the ancestors of the New Democratic Party, Canada's present-day social democratic party) while the Social Credit Party had a right-wing monetarist approach which supported free enterprise but demanded reforms in the banking system. But despite these differences, both governments attempted to introduce measures designed to rid the province of its dependent status.

It is not surprising, therefore, that the Social Credit government, which was in power when Imperial Oil, the Canadian subsidiary of Exxon, found oil in 1947, welcomed both the discovery and its exploitation by American-owned companies. It viewed the development of a foreign-financed oil industry as a means of ending Alberta's domination by Eastern Canada.

Fortunately for the Socreds, the institutional and political arrangements of Canada enabled them to give active encouragement to the oil companies. These arrangements gave the Province ownership of sub-surface mineral rights on land not settled before 13 October 1887. Since most of Alberta was not settled by Europeans on that date, these arrangements gave the Province ownership of mineral rights lying under 81 per cent of its territory.[21]

Despite its free enterprise philosophy, the Socred government chose to retain ownership over these rights. It did so because, among other things, it would be able to set the terms of entry in the oil industry. These terms were more favourable to the large than to the small oil companies.[22] Many of the latter, it should be pointed out, were locally owned. As a result of this policy, the major oil companies now control most of Alberta's reserves and production. In 1977, for instance, six of the major international oil companies[23] produced almost 50 per cent of Canada's crude oil and gas liquids.[24]

The entrance of the international oil companies ended the dominance by the Eastern Canadian bourgeoisie. American monopolies replaced Canadian ones as the kingpins of the economy. In addition, the leading role of the oil companies unquestionably hampered the industrialization of the province.

Nowhere in the oil extraction areas of the world have the international oil companies fostered industrialization. There are many reasons for this. First, these companies prefer to build their processing facilities in areas where a market already exists. Aside from the purely 'economic' reason that it is generally cheaper to ship crude over long distances than refined products,[25] there is probably a more basic reason. The establishment of refineries in the market areas increases the bargaining power of the oil companies *vis-à-vis* the crude producing areas. As long as these latter do not have refineries, they cannot process their crude and sell it on the world market. To make the crude marketable, they must first bring it to the refineries. By keeping the refineries outside the political jurisdiction of the crude oil areas, the oil companies can effectively cut these areas off from world markets by refusing to refine their oil. Since the international oil companies control most refineries in the capitalist world, they can keep recalcitrant areas in line through threats of boycott.[26]

The international oil companies thus have a policy of exporting oil in crude form. Oil that could be used for domestic development goes elsewhere. In this connection, Mikesell noted that:

> No important petroleum export industries exist in developing areas that are not operated by foreign firms. Mexico's nationalized petroleum industry has been successful in supplying that country's domestic requirements. However, before nationalization, Mexico's petroleum industry accounted for a substantial share of the world's exports outside the United States.[27]

The oil companies implemented this policy in the case of Alberta by exports of crude and, later, natural gas, to the more developed areas of Canada and to the United States. Though they have constructed some large refineries in the Province in recent years, they still export the bulk of their oil in the form of crude.

Another reason why the oil companies have not fostered industrialization is the existence of reciprocal relationships. These relationships, which often exist among large firms, can prevent small, independent manufacturers from selling to large firms. For instance, oil company A might agree to buy all its tools from a subsidiary of steel company B. In return, steel company B agrees to buy all its fuel from oil company A. These inter-corporate trade patterns squeeze out independent manufacturers, like local Alberta firms eager to sell to the oil industry.

Another factor is that oil companies do not look with favour at the development of an independent manufacturing base in areas where they have extensive holdings. Such a base challenges the dominant position of these companies. Furthermore, it can generate a militant industrial proletariat, which could undermine 'political stability'.

This aversion to industrialization was shared by the Socreds. Reflecting their rural and petty-bourgeois base, they feared that industrialization would raise wages to exorbitant levels, bankrupt small businessmen and undermine the quality of life. This fear of industrialization placed them in a quandary arising from the Province's ownership of sub-surface mineral rights, which not only enabled them to control entry into the oil industry but also gave them economic rents in the form of royalties, lease rentals and bonuses. A substantial portion of the economic rents was thus socialized; because of this the discovery of oil did not spawn a large class of oil millionaires, as occurred in Texas.

The Socreds' quandary stemmed from the concentration of this surplus in their hands. They had to decide how to dispose of these funds in a manner consistent with their philosophy. Once they had ruled out industrialization as a goal, they were left with few other choices. They could use the funds to reduce income inequalities and end poverty. But this was ruled out because such a redistribution would undermine the very basis of the market system — income inequality, essential for the survival and the efficient functioning of capitalism.

They finally decided to spend these funds in such a way as to minimize the redistributional effects and to satisfy the demands of their rural and petty bourgeoisie supporters. They did this by significantly expanding the health care system and educational facilities. The first measure was extremely popular and was supported by all segments of the population. The second measure benefited chiefly the wealthier farmers and middle classes, who provided the bulk of university students. Nevertheless some of the benefits extended to the poorer farmers and working class in the sense that more of their children now had the opportunity to receive a post-secondary education. It also provided the oil companies with a skilled work force which they could either hire directly or through contracting with supplier companies. While both measures did redistribute income, this effect was limited and had a minimal impact on incentives.

Ironically, the expansion of the public sector combined with the activity of the oil industry undermined the political base of the Socreds. As already noted, the decline in the agricultural labour force proceeded in Alberta at a much more rapid pace than in the other Prairie provinces. In addition, an important urban professional elite group arose, consisting of some members of the greatly expanded public sector and of the sellers of services to the oil companies. This group opposed the Socreds' rural orientation and did not share their fear of industrialization. In fact, they welcomed it because they viewed it as a means of increasing their power in Canada. Unlike the Socreds, who were mainly interested in reducing Alberta's dependent status, this new group aimed to change that status to one of domination. Their goal was to shift the locus of power in Canada away from the East.

This group came to power in 1971 with the election of a Progressive Conservative government.[28] They immediately began to reduce the rate of expansion of the public sector. While they were undoubtedly influenced by the actions of the Canadian and other capitalist governments in the West, who were responding to the growing economic crisis by cutting back public expenditure, they were mainly interested in using the oil revenues to accumulate capital for expansion of the productive sector. The rise in oil prices after 1973 and the subsequent huge flow of oil revenues into the provincial treasury gave them the opportunity to realize this goal. Most of this increased revenue has since that time been going into funds designed to spur industrialization. The thrust of this policy can be seen in Table 5, below.

Table 5
Province of Alberta: Government Income and Selected Expenditure, 1946-75

	In $ Millions				
Income	*1975*	*1971*	*1966*	*1956*	*1946*
Total	3,009.8	1,130.6	603.9	247.6	43.3
Minerals	1,372.0	235.6	250.1	128.1	3.4
Deficit	----	100.8	----	----	----
Expenditure					
Education	516.7	379.4	123.2	37.5	4.8
Health and Welfare	578.0	322.1	159.7	40.1	8.7
(Total Social					
Services	1,094.7	701.5	282.9	77.6	13.5)
Industry and					
Manpower	67.4	7.3	6.2	1.2	0.3
Surplus	772.3	----	78.5	15.9	11.6
	In Percentages				
Income					
Total	100.0	100.0	100.0	100.0	100.0
Minerals	45.6	20.8	41.4	51.7	7.9
Deficit	----	8.9	----	----	----
Expenditure					
Education	17.2	33.4	20.4	15.1	11.1
Health and Welfare	19.2	28.5	26.5	16.2	20.1
(Total Social					
Services	36.4	62.0	46.9	31.3	31.2)
Industry and					
Manpower	2.3	0.7	0.9	0.5	0.7
Surplus	25.7	----	13.0	6.4	26.8

Calculated from: Government of Alberta, *Public Accounts of the Province of Alberta.*

Table 5 shows the Alberta provincial government's income and expenditure in selected fiscal years from 1946 to 1975. As can be readily seen from the top half of the Table, there has been a great expansion in both income and expenditure. Alongside this overall expansion there has also been a growth in the relative importance of social service expenditures — education, health and welfare — between 1946, one year before the Leduc oil discovery, and 1971, the last year of the Social Credit era. As the bottom half of Table 5 shows, expenditure on education rose from 11 per cent of income in 1946 to 33 per cent in 1971, while that on health and welfare rose from 20 to 29 per cent, which together made social services spending as a whole rise from 31 per cent to 62 per cent. This rise was a continuous one and even took place in the 1966-71 period when oil revenues actually declined. In addition, the proportion of funds going to industry and manpower did not rise significantly during the Socred government era.

Since 1971 the pattern of expenditure has changed dramatically. The share going to education has fallen to 17 per cent; that going to health and welfare to 19 per cent, making that going to social services as a whole fall to 36 per cent. In contrast, the share accruing to industry and manpower has risen from 0.7 per cent in 1971 to 2.3 per cent in 1975. The counterpart to the decline in social services has been the generation of a surplus, amounting to 26 per cent of total government income. In contrast to the surplus of 1946, which was used to retire debt, this present surplus has been placed in the Alberta Heritage Savings Trust Fund (A.H.S.T.F.), which is the government's main instrument of industrialization.

Established in 1976, the A.H.S.T.F. received $1.5 billion from the Treasury initially and is to receive a specified percentage of all future revenues from non-renewable resources.[29] Early in 1978 the Fund's assets had grown to $3.7 billion and are expected to reach $4.7 billion by early 1979.[30] The bulk of these funds, at least 65 per cent, are to be invested in projects which 'will yield a reasonable return or profit to the Trust Fund and will tend to strengthen and diversify the economy of Alberta'.[31] Interestingly, the disposition of these funds will be determined by the Cabinet and does not require approval of the Legislature.[32]

This provision, giving the Cabinet sole authority over the investment of this surplus, runs counter to the very essence of bourgeois parliamentary democracy. Not surprisingly, it was opposed by some Progressive Conservatives and by many segments of the bourgeoisie throughout the Province. But it is a necessary step to foster a new, industrial bourgeoisie. Despite the changed composition of Alberta's population, the farmers and petty bourgeoisie are still strong in many areas. Even though many have switched their allegiance to the Progressive Conservatives, they have not overcome their antipathy towards industrialization. Their representatives in the Legislature might well oppose many industrialization projects. The Cabinet, anxious to create an industrial bourgeoisie, found it necessary, therefore, to impose a dictatorship of the industrial bourgeoisie over the bourgeoisie as a whole, by denying the Legislature any authority to veto their investment decisions.

By early 1978, the Fund had invested $370 million in the huge Syncrude project. This $2 billion scheme, designed to extract oil from the tar sands, is a joint venture between three governments — Alberta, Ontario and the Federal Government — and three oil companies — Exxon, Gulf and Cities Services. The Fund's investment in the project consists of $179 million in equity and $191 million in debentures of Gulf and Cities Services.[33] The Syncrude joint venture is an example of how the socialized rents are being used to foster private accumulation.[34]

Another example is the Alberta Energy Company (A.E.C.). The A.H.S.T.F.'s investment of $76 million in this Company has given it 50 per cent of its equity.[35] Under legislation establishing the Company, the Province is to retain a 50 per cent share in the Company via the A.H.S.T.F.[36] The Fund's investment can rise to much as $250 million when the Company finally issues all of its authorized 100 million shares. To date, the Company has issued only 15 million shares,[37] of which half have been purchased by private interests. The legislation provides that these private shares be offered first to residents of Alberta and then, if Albertans fail to purchase the entire offering, to 'residents and citizens of Canada'.[38] As it turned out, Albertans purchased the entire offerings. In early 1978 the Company had more than 50,000 private share-holders, 96 per cent of whom were residents of Alberta.[39] These residents, most of whom own only a few shares, constitute only 2.5 per cent of the Province's population.

The government is using the A.E.C. to funnel private, as well as public funds, into industrial development. The A.E.C. intends to use these funds to develop 'Alberta's industrial and resource potential' through policies which 'presently emphasize new, large, long-range, capital intensive projects'. The Company plans to participate in these projects on its own and 'through affiliated companies and joint ventures'.[40] Thus, the A.E.C. has invested in the power plant and pipe-line of the Syncrude project. It has participated in joint ventures in steel and natural gas marketing. Significantly, the government have sold certain oil and gas fields to it at a relatively low price. This sale was another means by which public interests were transferred to private ones.

Through both the A.E.C. and the A.H.S.T.F. the government are mobilizing capital to promote industrialization. By making the A.E.C.'s shares available to the petty bourgeoisie, they are broadening their political base and giving this class a vested interest in industrialization. By concentrating both A.E.C. and A.H.S.T.F. funds on joint ventures, they have resolved the dilemma of how to use public funds in a way consistent with private appropriation. This is the essence of state monopoly capitalism.

At present, through their joint ventures and other links, they have formed an alliance with the multinational oil companies through which they hope to strengthen the industrial bourgeoisie both within the Province and in the nation at large. The government know that the international oil companies are interested in obtaining access to the provincial surplus. The government are willing to grant them access provided the companies increase their purchases of goods and services within Alberta. Because the government have these funds at their disposal, they are able to form reciprocal arrangements with the multinationals, arrangements which will have the effect of channelling public funds into the hands of the indigenous bourgeoisie.

In addition, the Progressive Conservatives are continuing the Socred policy of using the multinationals in their conflicts with the Eastern Canadian bourgeoisie. The oil companies, for their part, are encouraging the local bourgeoisie. They would prefer to deal with a host of relatively weak provincial governments than with a strong federal one. In this way they can play one province against another, and the provinces against the national government. Through such a policy they can prevent the various governments from extracting the maximum possible economic rents.[41]

Table 6
Pre-tax Corporate Profits as Percentage of G.D.P., 1961-1976

Year	Alberta	Canada (excl. Alberta)	Saskatchewan	Manitoba
1961	11.7	9.7	11.8	8.2
1962	10.7	10.0	9.9	8.0
1963	11.7	10.4	10.1	8.7
1964	14.1	11.0	11.4	8.4
1965	12.2	11.0	11.3	8.6
1966	12.4	10.5	10.2	8.4
1967	13.3	9.8	10.9	7.5
1968	13.7	10.1	10.4	7.7
1969	13.0	9.7	8.2	7.7
1970	12.3	8.3	8.7	7.7
1971	12.9	8.6	9.1	6.6
1972	14.9	9.5	10.0	8.1
1973	17.2	11.3	10.1	9.9
1974	17.1	12.0	9.6	8.4
1975	15.8*	n.a.	n.a.	n.a.
1976	14.9*	n.a.	n.a.	n.a.

1961-1971 – Social Credit government in power.
1971-1976 – Progressive Conservative government in power.
Calculated from Statistics Canada, *Provincial Economic Accounts, 1961-1974: Experimental Data,* Ottawa n.d.
* Calculated from Alberta Bureau of Statistics, *Alberta Economic Accounts – 1976,* Edmonton 1977, p.23.

The oil companies also benefited financially from this alliance. Their rate of accumulation, which was always high, skyrocketed under the Progressive Conservatives. Table 6 above, which shows corporate profits as a percentage of Gross Domestic Product (G.D.P.), is a rough measure of the rate of capital accumulation. As can be seen in the Table, corporate profits' share in Alberta has been consistently higher than in Manitoba, or Saskatchewan, or in the rest

Oil and Class Struggle

of Canada generally. During the years of the Social Credit government (1961-71) the corporate share, while displaying a rising trend, fluctuated considerably. In 1964, for instance, it peaked at 14.1 per cent, only two years after having reached a low of 10.7 per cent.

Since the Progressive Conservatives came to power in 1971, corporate profits' share of G.D.P. shot up to over 17 per cent in 1973 and 1974, the latest year for which Canada-wide figures are available. This rise was much steeper than that in the rest of Canada and in the other two Prairie provinces. In 1976 the share in Alberta was still 14.9 per cent; though below that of the peak years of 1972 and 1973, it was nevertheless at a very high level.

The drop in the corporate profits' share in 1976, which in Alberta is essentially the oil companies' share, does not imply that the rate of accumulation had fallen over the previous two years. For the drop was offset by the rise in what Statistics Canada calls 'Interest and Miscellaneous Investment Income'. For some strange reason, Statistics Canada has slipped royalties into this category. As can be seen in Table 7, this item has risen significantly under the Progressive Conservatives.

Table 7
Interest and Miscellaneous Investment Income as Percentage of G.D.P., 1961-1976

Year	Alberta	Canada (exc. Alberta)	Saskatchewan	Manitoba
1961	5.7	3.5	5.2	3.2
1966	6.9	3.6	5.5	3.7
1971	7.6	4.6	6.9	5.0
1974	10.9	5.0	7.5	5.5
1976	13.4	n.a.	n.a.	n.a.

See Table 6 for sources and notes.

When we combine corporate profits, interest, and miscellaneous investment income, we find that accumulation has steadily increased under the Progressive Conservatives, amounting to more than one-fourth of provincial G.D.P. (See Table 8.)

Table 8
Profits, Interest, and Misc. Investment Income as Percentage of G.D.P., 1961-1976

Year	Alberta	Canada (excl. Alberta)	Saskatchewan	Manitoba
1961	17.4	13.4	17.0	11.4
1966	19.3	14.1	15.7	12.1
1971	20.5	13.2	16.0	11.6
1974	28.0	17.0	17.1	13.9
1976	28.3	n.a.	n.a.	n.a.

Calculated from Tables 6 and 7.

The corollary of this increase in accumulation has been a decline in labour's share of the Gross Domestic Product. In the later years of the Social Credit government, labour's share rose considerably. It rose at a faster rate than in the rest of Canada and in the other Prairie provinces. After the Progressive Conservatives came to power in 1971, labour's share in Alberta fell precipitously even though it continued to rise in the rest of Canada. The rise in labour's share under the Social Credit government was unquestionably the result of the expansion of the public sector, which hired many highly paid professionals. Conversely the decline in the share was the result of the Progressive Conservatives' policy of halting expansion of the public sector. These changes are shown in Table 9.

Table 9
Wages and Salaries as Percentage of G.D.P., 1961-1976

Year	Alberta	Canada (excl. Alberta)	Saskatchewan	Manitoba
1961	43.2	51.4	42.0	51.7
1962	42.6	50.5	33.5	49.5
1963	41.5	50.4	29.6	49.7
1964	41.7	50.3	33.1	48.5
1965	42.5	50.9	33.9	48.8
1966	42.3	51.5	32.1	50.0
1967	44.4	52.9	38.6	52.1
1968	44.8	52.7	39.0	52.0
1969	46.8	53.4	38.6	53.2
1970	47.5	54.4	41.1	53.4
1971	47.6	54.8	38.0	53.8
1972	46.6	54.7	41.0	54.0
1973	43.4	54.2	37.0	51.9
1974	38.3	55.0	34.9	52.7
1975	40.7	n.a.	n.a.	n.a.
1976	42.2	n.a.	n.a.	n.a.

See Table 6 for sources and notes.

Both farmers and small businessmen suffered fates similar to labour. Their shares declined under the Progressive Conservatives at a much more rapid rate than under the Social Credit administration. In 1976 their respective shares were only 3.0 and 3.8 per cent — both all-time lows.[42] It is thus readily apparent that the Progressive Conservatives' policies have brought enormous benefits to the oil industry at the expense of both the working class, and farmers and small businessmen.

This *entente cordiale* between the Progressive Conservatives and the oil industry, however, may not last forever. As socialized rents grow, the economic power relationships between oil companies and indigenous bourgeoisie are likely to change, especially if the strength of the latter rises relative to the former. If this change occurs, the local bourgeoisie may decide to pursue policies designed to reinforce its position even if these policies conflict with the interest of the oil companies.

There is some evidence that this has already occurred. Alberta Gas Trunk Lines (A.G.T.L.), a company originally formed by the Social Credit government for the purpose of distributing natural gas within the Province, became involved in a bitter fight with Imperial Oil and the other major oil companies over the location and control of a pipeline designed to carry Alaskan natural gas across Canada to the U.S. market. With the full backing of the Alberta government A.G.T.L. won this fight and is making preparations to build the $10 billion ALCAN pipeline. Though privately owned, A.G.T.L. works closely with the provincial government. The government appoints four of its directors and there are close links between the president of A.G.T.L. and the provincial premier. A.G.T.L. is therefore viewed as another vehicle by which the Progressive Conservatives are pursuing their strategy of industrialization.[43] It is still too early to say whether the pipeline dispute was a mere aberration or represents 'the wave of the future'.

That it may well represent a significant development flows from Lenin's thesis of the uneven rate of development of capitalism. This changes the power relationships among various segments of the bourgeoisie and causes conflict between them.[44] To what extent this will happen in Alberta remains to be seen.

In summary, the development of oil in Alberta has brought with it the potential for industrialization and the creation of an indigenous industrial bourgeoisie. This potential was created only because the economic rents were socialized, it did not come about as a result of the normal operation of the market mechanism.

The Progressive Conservative government are trying to realize this potential by implementing policies designed to encourage industrialization and nurture this new bourgeoisie. These policies have led them to ally themselves with the multinational oil companies against the Eastern Canadian bourgeoisie. However, as the class structure of Alberta changes and the new bourgeoisie grows more powerful, it may weaken or break its links with the oil companies and even come into conflict with them.

Whether or not this happens, one thing is certain. The industrialization that will occur will have all the evils associated with capitalist development: boom and bust, over-expansion in some sectors accompanied by under-expansion in others, urban blight, and degradation of the environment. The benefits will accrue to the new bourgeoisie while the relative position of the workers, farmers, and petty bourgeoisie will continue to decline.

The Alberta experience has shown that the socialization of economic rents can strengthen the bourgeoisie. For oil to be of any benefit to the working class, it is necessary to go beyond the socialization of economic rents to the socialization of the means of production.

References

1. There were several oil discoveries in Alberta before 1947. The two most notable ones were in the Turner Valley in 1914 and in 1936. These discoveries, however, did not have the effect of the 1947 find in Leduc, 18 miles (29 kilometres) south-west of Edmonton.

2. In this essay I am using Marx's division of the labour force into productive and non-productive labour. The former creates surplus value by *directly* changing the form of matter, i.e. by changing use-values. The latter, while often useful and necessary to society, does not *directly* change the form of matter and hence does not create surplus-value. While it is often difficult to classify a particular occupation as 'productive' or 'non-productive', I am placing workers in primary and secondary industries in the 'productive' category and those in tertiary industries in the 'non-productive' one. In a period of rapid economic development the productive labour force, especially that part engaged in secondary industries, should grow relative to the total labour force.

3. Unless otherwise stated, all figures currently here are in Canadian dollars.

4. Canadian Petroleum Association, *Statistical Handbook*, Calgary, table IV, section 3B.

5. For a discussion of the optimistic and pessimistic versions of the staple theory, see Mel Watkins, 'The Staple Theory Revisited', *Journal of Canadian Studies*, Winter 1977, pp. 83-95.

6. This summary admittedly does an injustice to many of the staple theorists. As Watkins pointed out, Innis had some reservations about the efficacy of the staple process (op.cit., pp. 83-4 and 85-6). The above is merely an amalgam of the views of the market-orientated staple theorists who believe that the free-market mechanism will both allocate resources optimally and bring about economic development. For further readings on the staple theory, see: H.A. Innis, *The Fur Trade in Canada: An Introduction to Canadian Economic History*, Toronto, University of Toronto 1930; and *The Cod Fisheries: The History of an International Economy*, Toronto, University of Toronto 1940; W.T. Easterbrook and M.H. Watkins (eds.), *Approaches to Canadian Economic History*, Toronto, McClelland & Stewart 1967, Introduction & Part 1; R. Caves, ' "Vent for Surplus" Models of Trade and Growth' in R. Caves, H. Johnson and P. Kenen (eds.), *Trade, Growth and the Balance of Payments*, Chicago, Rand McNally 1965, pp. 95-115; and 'Export-led Growth and the New Economic History' in J.N. Bhagwati *et al.* (eds.), *Trade, Balance of Payments and Growth*, Amsterdam, North-Holland 1971, pp. 403-42; and M. Roemer, *Fishing for Growth: Export-led Development in Peru, 1950-1970*, Cambridge, Harvard University Press 1970, pp. 5-23.

7. Calculated from *Census of Canada, 1951*, vol. IV, table 16.

8. Calculated from: Alberta Bureau of Statistics, *Alberta Statistical Review*,

(annual, 1976), Edmonton, table 19, p. 21. This data has to be treated with caution. The 1976 data are based on a sample survey in which the variability of some of the estimates is quite high. Furthermore, some definitions and classifications have changed since 1951. Nevertheless, the comparisons between 1951 and 1976 are indicative of trends. If, for instance, there had been a substantial rise in the relative importance of manufacturing, that trend would have shown up in the data, even though its full extent might have been either under- or over-estimated. One can argue that, because of the variability in the 1976 sample, the data could also be compatible with a slight rise in the relative importance of manufacturing. While this is correct, it is nevertheless incompatible with a *significant* rise in manufacturing, as the more optimistic versions of the staple theory suggest.

9. I have chosen this particular time period for my analysis because Statistics Canada has published a consistent set of annual employment data on 10 non-agricultural industries for these years. Unfortunately, this series does not extend back before 1961, which would have given us a better estimate of the linkages produced by the oil industry. See Statistics Canada, *Estimates of Employees by Province & Industry, 1971-1976*, Ottawa, Ministry of Industry, Trade and Commerce, May 1978, catalogue no. 72-516. Employment data differ from the labour force data used above in that the former consist only of employees while the latter include employers, the self-employed, and the unemployed.

10. The above estimates were calculated from ibid., pp. 38-40.

11. See 'The Employment Impact of Oil and Natural Gas in Alberta, 1961 to 1970', Paper presented to the Pacific Northwest Regional Economic Conference, Victoria, British Columbia, 8 May 1976, and to the Geografisch Instituut, Erasmus Universiteit, Rotterdam, Holland, 31 March 1977.

12. For details of my methodology, see ibid.

13. The above were calculated from Statistics Canada, 'The Crude Petroleum and Natural Gas Industry', (annual), catalogue no. 26-213; and *Estimates of Employees by Province & Industry 1971-1976,* op cit.

14. R. Caves & R. Holton, *The Canadian Economy: Prospect & Retrospect,* Cambridge, Mass: Harvard University Press 1959, p. 215.

15. Ibid., p. 207.

16. Ibid., p. 209.

17. Statistics Canada, *Estimates of Employees by Province and Industry, 1961-1976*, op.cit., p. 74.

18. A. Hirschman, *The Strategy of Economic Development*, New Haven, Yale University Press 1958, p. 102.

19. Calculated from Alberta Bureau of Statistics, op.cit., table 67, pp. 69-72.

20. Calculated from ibid.

21. In actuality, the federal government retained title to sub-surface mineral rights until 1930, when it relinquished them to the provinces. See E. Hanson and E. Shaffer, 'Economics of Oil and Gas', in *Canadian Perspectives in Economics*, Toronto, Collier-MacMillan, Canada, 1972.

22. For details of these terms, see ibid.

23. Exxon, Texaco, Gulf, Mobil, Standard Oil of California, and Shell.

24. Calculated from *Oilweek*, 15 May 1978, p. 45. Their exact share was 47.2 per cent of Canadian production. Since Alberta produced 86 per cent of Canadian oil, these figures can be used as a proxy for concentration in Alberta.

25. Economies in the shipment of crude can often be offset by the necessity of building more refineries in market areas. Since there are significant economies of scale in refineries, it may frequently be cheaper to build a large refinery near the crude source and ship the products to the various markets.

26. With the rise of OPEC this threat has diminished, but it has by no means been eliminated.

27. R. Mikesell, 'The Contribution of Petroleum and Mineral Resources to Economic Development' in Mikesell (ed.), *Foreign Investment in the Petroleum and Mineral Industries*, Baltimore, Johns Hopkins 1971, p. 11.

28. The main political parties in Alberta are Social Credit, Progressive Conservatives, Liberals, and the New Democratic Party. The first three are right-wing. As pointed out earlier, the Social Credit Party emphasizes monetary reform. Progressive Conservatives and Liberals are more orthodox and there is little difference between them. Nationally the Progressive Conservatives are linked to the Ontario and Western bourgeoisie, and the Liberals to the Montreal bourgeoisie. The New Democrats have a social democratic orientation.

29. This was initially set at 30 per cent, but can be changed from year to year.

30. Alberta Heritage Savings Trust Fund, *1977-78 Annual Report*, pp. 2-3.

31. *The Alberta Heritage Savings Trust Fund Act*, sec. 6(1) (c) (i) and (ii); see also sec. 6 (2) (b) and 6 (3) (c).

32. Ibid., sec. (6), (4) (a) and (b).

33. Alberta Heritage Savings Trust Fund, op. cit., p. 29.

34. For an excellent analysis of the Syncrude project, see L. Pratt, *The Tar Sands: Syncrude and the Politics of Oil*, Edmonton, Hurtig 1976.

35. Alberta Heritage Savings Trust Fund, op. cit., pp. 24-5.

36. Ibid.

37. Alberta Energy Company, *Preliminary Prospectus Dated October 30, 1974*, p. 5.

38. Ibid., p. 15.

39. Alberta Heritage Savings Trust Fund, op.cit., p. 24.

40. Alberta Energy Company, op.cit., p. 5.

41. It is perhaps no accident that the civil war in Nigeria erupted after the discovery of oil there. And perhaps it is also no accident that the Scottish nationalist movement grew significantly after the discovery of oil in the North Sea.

42. Calculated from Alberta Bureau of Statistics, *Economic Accounts — 1976*, Edmonton 1977, p. 23.

43. A.G.T.L. has also gone into petrochemicals, steel, valve manufacturing and consulting. In July 1978 it purchased a controlling interest in Husky Oil.

44. See V. Lenin, *Imperialism: The Highest Stage of Capitalism*, New York, International Publishers 1969, p. 119.

13. Iranian Oilworkers in the 1978-79 Revolution

Terisa Turner

The oil industry has the population of the globe 'locked into a worldwide kaleidoscope'; it is the most advanced example of 'the international character of the capitalist regime'. Until September 1978 Iran, the world's largest oil exporter after Saudi Arabia, produced 6 million barrels a day, amounting to about 20 per cent of OPEC production. When Iranian oilworkers struck on 27 October 1978, and halted exports, the ramifications were as international as the character of the industry. Crude prices and corporate profits rose, energy importers suffered supply cutbacks, the monetary and trading systems of the capitalist world suffered yet another jolt, and Iranian radicalism spread like a corrosive acid throughout the Middle East and beyond. The four-month strike heralded the arrival of a new stage in the worldwide centralization of capital on the one hand, and the socialization of the labour process on the other. Iranian oilworkers seized and shut down the national oil installations and only reactivated them after the fall of the Shah. Given the global net established by petroleum multinationals, international repercussions were unavoidable. In addition, Iranian oilworkers made foreign policy decisions, including the halt in oil supplies to South Africa (90% dependent on Iran) and Israel (60% dependent).

The importance of Iran, then, lies in oilworkers' successful takeover and operation of the industry, an action which inevitably alters the position of all workers by posing the challenge that they consciously exercise the social power which stems from their being organized by capital into an international class.

This chapter attempts, first, to indicate how Iranian oilworkers organized the strike as an integral element of a wider revolution; second, to review strikers' actions and demands in the oil sector; and third, to outline three lessons of the oilworkers' strike which have advanced the frontiers of struggle and constitute a new point of departure for revolutionary action worldwide. To begin with, the high points of the Iranian oilworkers' struggle in 1978 and up to April 1979 can be summarized.

Beginning in early 1978, Iranians took to the streets to demonstrate against the murder of Shariati, an Islamic revolutionary, and to demand the removal of the Shah. As the momentum grew, especially after the death of over 800 people in the Rex Cinema fire in Abadan in August 1978, workers in most public offices and industries went on strike. The bazaars closed and the schools were transformed into veritable schools of revolution. In this context the oilworkers struck, beginning in October. The Shah's military forced many back to work in November; but the oilworkers regrouped to emerge by early December with a nation-wide oil union that reinstituted the strike with complete success. By mid-December the oil cutbacks focused international attention on the Iranian Revolution, and probably finally spurred the U.S. and other Western governments to jettison the Shah. During January 1979 the strike held firm, and in February oilworkers participated in armed struggle to defeat the Shah's army and force the military to disband. Production in the oilfields was begun again in early March, but this time by an entirely Iranian workforce since foreigners had been expelled. In April production continued to increase to the new intended level of about half the pre-revolution volume.

By May 1979 (the time of writing), oilworkers had secured many of their demands and were pressing others. The wider Iranian Revolution was still in process. The Bazargan government sought to reconstitute the Shah's state apparatus while the left fought for a people's army and for popular committees in the community and workplace as the new basic foci of power. Oilworkers are supported by the Mujaheddin and Fedayeen Marxists in seeking to replace the old state. But it appeared by late April that Islamic *komitehs* had established their sway in the oil towns to the extent that the rightists had ousted the revolutionary organizations. How the oilworkers will exercise their new power and experience in the period ahead is an open question. But it is clear, as Ayatollah Khomeini declared, that the Revolution only began with the Shah's expulsion. In the current stage, the technocratic state capitalist, and local private capitalist forces are struggling to capture the state. Oilworkers have developed the consciousness and links with other workers necessary to move the Revolution ahead. They have the valuable experience of controlling the oil industry in the interests of Iranians against NIOC, the state-owned National Iranian Oil Corporation. Consequently, technocratic state capitalism is not likely to be able to unfold its inherent logic – disciplining Iranian workers while integrating into international capitalism – for long without precipitating another oilworkers' strike and broad upheaval which could displace the technocracy and propel the Revolution to a higher stage.

The Organization of the Iranian Oil Industry

The Iranian oil industry is the oldest, and in terms of workers and physical plant, the largest in the Middle East. As the map indicates, oil production is centred in the province of Khuzistan. The world's largest refinery is located at Abadan. Pipelines, refineries and petrochemical plants form a national grid from Azerbaijan in the northwest to Mashhad in the northeast. Production

fields are located along the western border towards the northern extreme of
the Persian Gulf, and most oil is loaded on tankers at Kharg Island. If we add
to this national system the thousands of road tankers and distribution outlets,
the extent to which Iran is integrated by the network of oil can be
appreciated.

Who Are the Oilworkers?

Estimates of the number of oilworkers in Iran vary widely depending on the
definition of the category. Most modest is the figure (restricted to those
directly employed by the oil companies) of 19,000 supplied by the U.S.
Department of Energy.[1] As of August 1978, some 3,000 were employed by
NIOC; 10,000 worked in the Oil Service Company of Iran (OSCO) and the
remaining 6,000 were employed by the four joint-ventures and eight foreign
oil companies that had service contracts with NIOC. OSCO is a wholly-
owned subsidiary of the major's consortium, Iranian Oil Participants, which
produced 90% of Iran's oil under a May 1973 contract with NIOC.[2] Of
OSCO's 10,000 workers, some 500 were expatriates. In contrast to this
modest total of 19,000 the media has widely quoted figures ranging from
30,000 to 78,000 oilworkers. These include Iranians engaged in support work,

especially that vast army of day labourers who are organized by labour contractors. Many work in construction on NIOC projects, and for NIOC subsidiaries such as the gas company (NIGC), the petrochemical company, the tanker company and the Ahwaz Pipe Mills.[3]

Iran's present oilworkers have their roots in the first Iranian proletariat that developed with oil exploration in 1901 and production in 1908. By 1920 some 20,000 Iranians were employed in the Khuzistan oilfields and the numbers swelled to 55,000 in 1951 plus a further 15,000 contract workers. At the bottom were unskilled labourers from the Arab tribes and Bakhtiari nomads who formed the sparse, indigenous population of Khuzistan; as well as skilled labourers from Isfahan and Tehran. In 1949 some 33,000 of the total 38,000 workers at Abadan were in this group, while in the oilfields themselves 15,000 out of 17,000 were labourers in construction, maintenance, transportation, loading and work on pipelines.[4] In the middle were technical-clerical workers who initially came from India. After the nationalist mobilization of the 1950s, Iranians filled these jobs. Finally, top-level managers and technicians were British, although over half were Iranian by 1949. The consortium began retrenchment in 1957 so that the oil labour force since then has fluctuated between 40,000 and 45,000. However, the value added per employee has skyrocketed. Between 1961 and 1966 the number of workers required to produce 100 barrels of crude declined from 8.5 to 3.5, and in 1975 output per worker was 20 times higher than in the 1950s.[5]

While the most commonly accepted definition of oilworker encompasses both those directly employed by oil companies and by contracting firms, still other sources argue for also including the populations around oil operations in the number of oilworkers. This very wide definition has advantages in that it recognizes the communities' and especially women's integral part in the strikes and broader Iranian Revolution. It also fosters an understanding of the importance of Islam and the organization of the community in the strike, and it focuses attention on the crucial links between home and point of production. The oil communities of Khuzistan developed with the industry and function to supply and service oilworkers. Thus, the oil strike meant that families and communities, with all their ethnic, ideological and job-related differences, drastically re-oriented their work-a-day lives in order to provide the solidarity essential to the effectiveness of the strike. They also made demands to secure gains of their own.

The all-inclusive definition of oilworker reflects the fact that oil companies' profits depend crucially on the work of women in producing and servicing labour power: their husbands, brothers, fathers and sons. More broadly, the community is a type of 'social factory' which produces workers for industry, and thus indirectly produces profits for companies. Of the oil industry in Venezuela, Selma James argues that 'oil production is absolutely dependent on female domestic labour, [that women are revolting against the] great discrepancy between the technology of extracting and refining oil and that of extracting and refining oil workers . . . [and that] the wife of the oilworker is as productive as he is, because she daily "directly produces, trains, develops, maintains [and] reproduces labour power itself." '6 The demands in oil-rich Khuzistan for water supplies, housing, waged jobs, health care and community improvements have demonstrated the refusal of the wider category of oil-workers to service the industry under such exploitative conditions.7 So, following James, it would be correct to say that as many as 2 million workers — domestic, industrial and service — went on strike in the oil towns in the course of the Iranian Revolution.

The Oil Towns
Today the oil province of Khuzistan has a population of some 4 millions, including two million Arab-speaking Shiites. When the oil industry was established at the beginning of the century, Khuzistan was among the least urbanized areas of Iran. Oil created eight separate towns. The largest, Abadan, site of the refinery, grew from a fishing village of a few hundred in 1900 to a city of 170,000 in the late 1940s. Virtually the whole population depended directly or indirectly on the oil company for employment.'8 There the British and Americans built 'a colonial oil society with brick houses behind walls and segregated neighborhoods for workers, middle management and top executives. One of the demands now [April 1979] is for the 10 country clubs to reopen — but on a democratic basis.'9 The oil communities include two other major cities at the head of the Gulf — Khurramshahr (Iran's main port) and Ahwaz; as well as the towns of Marun where liquefied natural gas plants are under construction; Bandar Mahshahr, Bandar Shahpur Kharg and Lavan Islands, Bushehr and Bandar Abbas. Refinery centres include Tehran (two with a total capacity of 220,000 barrels a day), Shiraz (40,000 b.p.d.), Kermanshah (20,000 b.p.d.) and two topping plants at Masjed-e-Soleman (64,000 b.p.d.) and Lavan (20,000 b.p.d.). New refineries are under construction at Tabriz (80,000 b.p.d.) and Isfahan (100,000 b.p.d.). Thousands of workers operate more than 5,500 kilometers of crude and product pipelines crisscrossing the country. In 1976 an additional 3,000 kilometers of pipeline were under construction. Oil communities operate four lubricating oil plants, export natural gas to the U.S.S.R. (328 billion standard cubic feet in 1976),10 run ten tankers with a total deadweight capacity of 1.1. million tons (British supervisors were in charge before the Revolution), distribute natural gas to over 80,000 domestic consumers, manufacture three million metric tons of petrochemical products a year in six different facilities, are building $3 billion worth of new petrochemical plants, and operate foreign subsidiaries of NIOC in six countries.11

The organization of the oil industry workers has proved effective in staging the longest general strike in Iranian history, and one with unprecedented international impact. To shut down as huge a production as six million barrels a day, six refineries, thousands of miles of pipeline, tankers, an extended apparatus of contract and service operations and simultaneously to bring the community to a standstill — to do all this safely and effectively for over four months is a tremendous achievement in co-ordination.

How was it possible, especially given that there existed no popular trade unions or parties? In part, oilworkers are disciplined and united because the very process of getting oil out of the ground, through the refineries and transported to consumers is a highly co-ordinated process. No industry except aerospace has a more sophisticated communications system or a more auto-mated production process. Thus the basis of the strikers' capacity for co-ordination is the organization imposed by the oil industry itself and by the immediate communities which the industry creates. In addition, Islamic ideology and the mosque network contributed indispensably to the capacity of oilworkers, along with the mass of Iranians, to mobilize against the state.

History of Working Class Struggle in Iran

A brief review of the history of Iranian oilworkers' struggles reveals the absence of a continuous tradition of unions or parties. Consequently, decen-tralized grassroots initiatives of workers in the 1978-79 Revolution were of the greatest importance and warrant attention. Fred Halliday identifies three periods of autonomous working class action in Iran. First, in the two decades prior to the consolidation of Reza Khan's rule in the late 1920s, working class organizations began to appear among the hundreds of thousands of Iranian migrant workers who until 1917 took jobs in the Caucasus oilfields of Southern Russia. In 1922 an Iranian Communist leader Sultan Zadeh reported that 10,000 workers were organized outside of Tehran.[12] In 1928 the Pahlavi monarchy abolished all trade unions (95% of them C.P. organised). The second period of action coincided with the Allied invasion of 1941. In that year the Communists established a Central Council of the Trade Unions (CCUTU) which by 1946 claimed 400,000 members (including 90,000 oilworkers in Khuzistan) and 186 union affiliates. With the War's end, strikes broke out in the oilfields some 500 miles south of the capital, Tehran which was itself shaken by demonstrations. 'In the refinery at Abadan and in a half-dozen distinct production centers, there were major strikes in the 1945-46 period, including a three-day general strike in July 1946 over pay and working conditions. This action, in which the workers won most of their demands, was of immense significance and demonstrated how a small but strategically placed working class can play a major role in an economy like Iran's.'[13] The regime responded by setting up a rival trade union, affiliated to the U.S.-run I.C.F.T.U., and by crushing the independent workers organizations. In 1949 the communist Tudeh Party and the CCUTU were banned.

By 1950 some 70,000 oilworkers were producing 664,000 barrels a day in an industry controlled 100 per cent by British Petroleum. Mossadeq's government came to power in 1951 and on May 1 the Iranian Majlis national-ized the oil industry and created NIOC (the National Iranian Oil Corporation). This step followed the Mossadeq government's attack on striking oilworkers. The Tudeh Party and the Communist workers movement at first opposed Mossadeq. According to one account, the Tudeh 'aimed at gaining oil con-cessions in the north for the U.S.S.R. similar to the British concessions in the south. When this program failed to gain public support, they demanded that the nationalization program be dropped in favor of outright confiscation, a policy Mossadegh's National Front was ideologically, politically, organizationally and militarily incapable of successfully implementing.'[14] Oilworkers were on strike in March-April 1951 demanding confiscation. In a major confrontation, the local Iranian governor attacked the strikers and arrested their leaders 'on the grounds that mass action against the company would provoke a British military intervention and thereby undermine the oil nationalization campaign.' By June 1951, a month after nationalization, BP had in any case effectively blocked oil exports by threatening to contest the sale of any Iranian production in the courts of importing countries. The leading issues between BP and Mossadeq's government concerned the employment of more Iranians in oil, BP's financial obligations to the state[15] and the prices charged by BP for oil products to Iranian customers. By late 1951 the unions fell into line behind Mossadeq who allowed the still-banned CCUTU to operate in a semi-legal manner. Deprived of oil revenues, the economic situation became tense. Over 200 strikes on economic matters erupted in the 1951-53 period. Huge demonstrations built up and led to the expulsion of the Shah on 16 August 1953.

The United States was vitally interested in securing access to Iranian oil and anxious to get it flowing again.[16] Within a week of the Shah's expulsion, the C.I.A. had reinstated him. The five U.S. major oil companies and five independents got 40 per cent of the new oil consortium, which left BP with only 40 per cent as C.F.P. (French) and Shell (Anglo-Dutch) got 5 and 14 per cent respectively.[17] The nationalization was retained but as an empty shell, and the foreign majors' consortium produced and sold the oil and implemented a Saudi-style 50-50 profit split. With the coup of 1953, the unions were also crushed.

In 1957 the trade unions were formally banned and a series of labour laws were introduced in 1959, 1960 and 1963, along with the Shah's system of state-run workers' organizations. These bodies sought the active cooperation of the working class in the Shah's industrialization process and fulfilled the dual function of mobilization and control. An I.L.O. study of 1971 reported a total of 397 such organizations of which 26 were in oil. These apparently were plant and factory based and designed to prevent the emergence of national workers' organizations.

The third period of autonomous working class action began in 1973 with strikes, mostly in individual plants over economic issues of wages, bonuses, and hours of work. A considerable number of economic gains were made. For instance, strikes over wages in the oil industry in August and October 1973 and in March 1975 were apparently met by concessions. Industrial action continued at a lesser pace up to 1978 when strikes again erupted in all sectors of the economy.

Iran's working class, in and out of oil, had thus acted autonomously in three periods before the 1978-79 Revolution. However, the repression in the '30s and since 1953 has denied Iranians a political tradition apart from the heritage of Islamic resistance to dictatorship. The strikes of the Mossadeq period are remembered, but the CCUTU activity may have been too brief to have had a lasting impact. Officially induced fragmentation, arrest of leaders and state acquiescence in economic demands have all been obstacles to the emergence of a working class movement in Iran. While reports on the influence of the Tudeh in the oilfields vary, it is thought that the Party's significance is small.[18] In short, oilworkers were without unions or parties. Given these negative conditions for organization, the general strike of Iranian workers, and the oil shutdown in particular, are all the more remarkable.

The 1978-79 Oil Strike: Actions and Demands

The immediate context of oilworkers' strikes was the expiration in July 1978 of the 5-year service contract between the foreign consortium, OSCO, and NIOC. The terms of the agreement had been the source of much dispute, especially over the price OSCO was expected to pay for Iranian crude under contract and over employing Iranian personnel.[19] The strikes began in the oilfields of Ahwaz in September when day labourers demanded and got pay raises.[20] On October 13 the Abadan refinery went on strike, to be followed on October 18 by the staff employees in the Ahwaz oilfields.

We are fortunate to have a first-hand account of the oilworkers' strike by a founding member of the Association of Oil Industry Staff Employees. The description of 'How We Paralyzed the Shah's Regime', included in this book as Chapter 14, takes the story up to late November. By 19 November the first 33-day strike period was ended, the Shah's military had forced oil-workers back to work, and the national oilworkers union was being organized to re-institute the strike even more effectively.

The account of how the oilworkers' strike was organized speaks for itself. But given that this is among the most sustained, powerful and advanced revolutionary mobilizations in history, it is instructive to underline certain points in the workers' account that deal with organization and demands. First, the most outstanding feature of the organization of the strike was the absence of any organization apart from that provided by the work process. The existing relationships proved highly effective and appropriate to the situation. As such they were the basis of the oilworkers' actions, not because a party or union or other externally derived organization was desired but missing, but because the oilworkers deliberately chose to rely on networks established by the industry.

Second, a high level of democracy was complemented by a rejection of leaders. For instance, delegates were elected in mid-October in Ahwaz, but 'the purpose of electing or setting up a committee was not to set apart a leadership.'[22] A *Le Monde* report of 16 November 1978 stated that in Abadan:

The workers we meet use the same words. Who has given them instructions to strike? No one in particular. Everyone agrees. There is really no organization. It's too bad. But by firing on us, the army has forced us to organize ourselves and even to arm ourselves. We listen to Khomeini and read the tracts of the Mujahidin . . . .

Another account from Ahwaz noted that:

Interviews with two young leaders of the spontaneous co-ordinating committee running the strike at the Abadan refinery suggested a devotion to utopian ideals rather than the give-and-take of labor-management struggles. Claiming no prior ties with any political opposition party, religious or communist, the leaders spoke disdainfully of a new 10 per cent pay offer which the government made Wednesday [Nov. 8] in hopes of breaking the strike.

Third, oilworkers were completely in charge of the day-to-day operations of the industry, and of the formulation of plans and strategies of production. This effective control from the bottom was exercised with a high sense of responsibility for safety and social needs, and in opposition to top technocrats in NIOC and the foreign experts from OSCO who pose everywhere as essential to the administration of the industry.

Some examples of the oilworkers' awareness that only they could stop and start the industry and their responsible execution of these tasks are in order. Oilworkers discussed whether to 'extend the strike through the entire oil industry, or whether some facilities such as hospitals, part of the telecommunications network, and some teams that do emergency repairs on the oil pipelines should be kept in operation . . . . So we said that we would designate a group of workers to make emergency repairs if there was an accident or if someone did something deliberately.' After NIOC management failed to get the oil flowing again, using 200 retired workers ('They burned out a couple of pumps and turbines') and later on 200 technicians from the navy 'who got rattled when they realized that they did not know the direction of the oil flow in the lines', the authorities 'finally realized that we were the only people who can operate the oil industry in Iran'. By the first week in November the military had occupied the oilfields and were attempting to force workers to produce at gunpoint.

A fourth feature of the Iranian oilworkers' organization of the strike was the combination of high levels of co-ordination with decentralization of decision-making and implementation. For instance, the issue of providing oil for domestic Iranian consumption, as winter approached, was resolved through co-ordinated discussions with production units, refiners and transporters. But the final decision was taken by the workers on the ground who knew the immediate situation most intimately. In December it was 'decided finally to assure the supply for domestic needs . . . . So we assigned some of the workers in Ahwaz to continue to operate one of the wells . . . . We began discussing with the [striking] refinery workers and urging them to refine the crude we were producing and pumping to their plants.' But the oil products were seized by the military. So the refinery workers 'said that they were resuming their strike, believing that we would agree with their decision. We told them that was fine, since they knew the local situation better than we did.' When Ayatollah Khomeini, then in Paris, sent the Bazargan Commission in late December to urge the oilworkers to produce and refine for local use, they refused. Cockcroft reported Dr. Yazdi's account that 'the workers, believing their production could not be adequately monitored to keep oil from the military, obeyed only in part. On January 24th, the U.S. Government announced that it was shipping diesel fuel and gasoline to Iran's military.'[23]

In December, the strike was re-instituted with total effectiveness, bringing production down from around 4 million barrels a day (as a result of forced labour at gunpoint) in late November, to nothing. Oil exports were effectively halted. Prices in the international market started to rise as earlier crude oil surpluses began to disappear. U.S. Government concern about the Iranian Revolution intensified after December 10, when the masses in Tehran's Azadi Square passed the key resolution of the period, calling for the return of the Ayatollah and rejecting the Shah. In an interview with Cockcroft in late December outside Paris, Khomeini said that from 9-10 December, 'so long as the head of any government which supports the Shah is in power we will cut off the oil. We will also cancel all contracts signed after those two days.' This is most likely the point at which imperialism began seriously to consider scuttling the Shah.

A fifth feature of the oilworkers' strike action was flexibility, itself made possible by the high level of organization. For example, after repeated attacks by the military on gatherings of oilworkers, they 'came up with a new tactic. It was to prepare our agenda and our instructions to the striking workers, get everyone together at a given place, and give them the instructions. We could do this in the half hour it took before the troops could come and drive us away.' After forced labour increased production, the strikers 'decided to go back to work along with other workers and prepare for a new strike. We did not consider ourselves defeated . . . .' The workers' flexibility reduced the regime's ability to control or halt the strike. As a participant noted, 'one group would retreat one day, and the next day would resume the struggle in a different form and propel it forward.' A report by Ibrahim in the *New York Times, 19 November* 1978, noted that: 'Despite threats by the military, thousands of workers are continuing slowdowns in the oilfields and factories, or staying away from their jobs . . . . Settlements reached with the workers in the morning come unglued in the afternoon, and new demands are made every day. Intimidating policies, such as rounding up the leaders of the revolt, seem to have little effect. . . .'[24]

Finally, these five features of strike organization were complemented by an emphasis on communication. On their first day back at work after 33 days on strike, the Ahwaz staff held an assembly which elected a 15-person Co-ordinating Committee ' to contact other organizations and individuals to solicit help' and also a 6-person Communications Committee to deal with

NIOC's Board of Directors, telegrams, media, and the development of support from all sections of the population. In fact, the strikers' organizational energies seem to have been directed mainly at communications with others, as a basis for co-ordination of action with them.

The oilworkers' demands are remarkable in their universality. They came from production, refinery and staff oilworkers, but also from striking teachers in Ahwaz. The interests of women and housewives were also recognized. They were national demands which combined economic and political concerns. The oilworkers shut down the industry on behalf of the whole population, and thereby dispelled the myths about the conservative labour aristocracy and the economism of the modern proletariat. Magdoff and Sweezy wrote in February 1979 that:

> There have been few spectacles in recent history so inspiring and heart-warming as that of 70,000 oil workers, far and away the best paid and most privileged segment of the working class, bringing to a complete halt the huge production and refining complex which is the Iranian oil industry, and doing it not for better pay or special privileges, but in support of the quintessentially *political* demand of the whole Iranian people that the Shah and all he stands for must go.[25]

In mid-November, as the oil strike got underway, the Ahwaz staff workers decided 'to define our aims . . . . We had to specify our demands. Everyone had a few demands in mind, but all of them had to be put together and presented to the company in a list.' On the October 29 list were the following demands:[26]

1. End martial law;
2. Full solidarity and co-operation with the striking teachers;
3. Unconditional release of all political prisoners;
4. Iranianization of the oil industry;
5. All communications to be in the Persian language;
6. All foreign employees to leave the country;
7. An end to discrimination against women staff employees and workers;
8. The implementation of a law recently passed by both houses of parliament dealing with the housing of oil workers and staff employees;
9. Support for the demands of the production workers, including the dissolution of SAVAK;
10. Punishment of corrupt high government officials and ministers;
11. Reduced manning schedules for offshore drilling crews.

Negotiations between strikers and Hushang Ansary, head of NIOC, opened on October 24. Ansary told the assembly that: 'he would consider the economic demands but that the others were outside his sphere. We told him that we were not going to make any distinction between our economic and non-economic demands. We told him that we had only one set of demands, from number one to twelve.'[27]

The oilworkers' strike drove a wedge between various interests within the Iranian state, and also dramatized to all the fact that real power lay with the oilworkers and not with the state. While prime minister Emami declared the strike 'an act of treason', Mr. Shariatmadari 'praised us as acting in the service of the nation'. Then the Complaints Commission declared 'that our strike was illegal, and no one had any right to declare it illegal and try to break it.' When NIOC refused to negotiate with the oilworkers, they 'called on all the people of Iran to consider this crucial political question, so that they could understand where the responsibility really lay for the continuation of the strike.'

Oilworkers, as defined broadly here, include members of the oil communities, such as teachers, judges and ayatollahs, who supported the strike and national mobilization. *Le Monde* carried the following account of the struggle in Abadan and the involvement of the broader community:

> Saturday, November 4, there is a meeting where 1,700 representatives gather from all the factories. It is held at the refinery in the presence of the military governor. The delegates lay out their demands and announce that a thousand persons will spend the night in the administrative buildings. The governor accepts this, but towards midnight he sends troops to drive them out. Result: eleven wounded of whom two die. Monday, the teachers march at Abadan and at Khorramshahr in solidarity with the oil workers, while in Tehran the government of General Azhari is formed. After Tuesday, the 7th, the army moves every night to arrest workers in their homes and to threaten others. Friday, the management of NIOC brings together the workers' delegates to announce 'If you don't start work again, you will be killed.' The army prevents the ayatollah of Abadan from giving his sermon and arrests another religious leader at the cemetery for having given the eulogy at the funeral of the demonstrators who had been killed . . . . At the Khorramshahr court house, the judges have been served with legal complaints by the victims' families; they decide to go on strike.[28]

Participants in the Abadan refinery strike indicated their sense of identity with others in the community:

> 'We were suppressed for so many years. We suffered for so long,' one leader said, 'that now we have burst. It was not the Shah who liberalized,' he added vehemently, 'but we who grasped liberalization from him. We took it.' 'I say why did my father not act and I do not want my son to ask me the same question,' his colleague said. 'We know we might be killed, but we say we are no better than the people who were killed in the Rex Cinema here in Abadan or in Saleh Square in Tehran.' he added.[29]

In Ahwaz, the strike united the whole community:

Despite threats by the military, thousands of workers are continuing slowdowns in the oilfields and factories, or staying away from their jobs . . . . [They are avoiding] direct confrontations with the soldiers, . . . call the soldiers their 'brothers' and are trying to win them over . . . . It is clear that, regardless of the diversity of their material demands, the various factions in this city of 450,000 people are unanimous in their rejection of the Shah's rule . . . .

At the Khazalah supermarket, where striking oilworkers continue to shop, a laborer named Yassin said that he is not concerned about Iran's financial losses resulting from decreased oil exports. 'We never saw any of that money anyway,' he said. 'It was all going into the pocket of Ali Baba and his forty thieves.' . . . Interviews with a dozen workers here revealed that their support for Khomeini is motivated more by his opposition to the Shah than by religious dictates. A worker for the Water and Power Authority said the Ayatollah 'has brought the eyes of the world on our problem here and made them see that the Shah is a puppet of the foreigners who are stealing our money.'

The feeling that foreigners, particularly Americans, control Iran's fate and policies is pervasive in this town, which is the capital of Khuzistan Province, the oil centre of Iran. Among the educated Iranian technicians at the oil companies in Ahwaz, the resentment of foreign experts takes on . . . a realistic dimension. One engineer for an Iranian-American metal company . . . said that most of the foreign workers in his company were not needed. 'We have technicians here who can do their jobs,' he said, 'but the government lets the foreigners run this company as they please, and I know that they don't work for the best interests of our country or our industry. Their purpose is to keep Iran dependent forever . . . .'[30]

The B.B.C. reported on its December 4 Farsi-language broadcast that the oilworkers had set up a nationwide union and initiated a general strike demanding that the Shah abdicate. On December 3, Khomeini announced that 'the strike in the oil industry in particular, which prevents looting of the nation's wealth, is an act of obedience to God.'[31] On December 15, General Azhari warned the oilworkers to return to their jobs or be dismissed. Their only response was to bring oil production to a 27-year low. Demonstrations continued to grow in size in all the major cities and the Shah in a last desperate act designated Bakhtiar as the next Prime Minister. On January 15, 1979, Ayatollah Khomeini named a provisional government and the next day the Shah left Iran. His troops continued to kill demonstrators, and oilworkers as a result threatened to stop providing even limited amounts of domestic oil. After several days of clashes between troops and demonstrators, on January 27 more than a million marched peacefully in Tehran in support of Khomeini who was welcomed four days later by some three million Iranians. By February 8 hundreds of soldiers were joining pro-Khomeini marches. The following day technicians at Homafar airforce base declared allegiance to the Ayatollah and battled elite troops. On February 10 the pro-Khomeini airforce cadets fought army troops loyal to Dr. Baktiar who resigned on the 11th.

In the armed struggle hundreds of thousands of weapons were seized by the people. The call went out for a people's army, and for community and workplace control through popular committees (or *Komitehs*). Polarization along class lines developed quickly as Khomeini and his appointee Bazargan sought to re-establish production and state authority. The conflict was . between those forces seeking to destroy and replace the old state and the Iranian bourgeoisie seeking to exercise state power. Writing about the French state in 1851, Marx observed that, 'All revolutions perfected this machine instead of smashing it. The parties that contended in turn for domination regarded the possession of this huge state edifice as the principal spoils of the victor.'[32] Khomeini's call for arms to be handed in went ignored as Iranians sought to secure their demands. On February 24 the marxist guerrilla group, the Fedayeen, asked why Khomeini's revolutionary committee did not have oilworkers on it, and protested at the secrecy of trials and summary executions. Helfgott outlined the pattern of class struggle that was emerging in February after Khomeini's return:

> Khomeini and the mullahs have no economic program precisely because the interests of their constituencies are so divergent. The wealthy merchants seek to control capitalist development, the artisans and shopkeepers reject capitalist development for fear of imminent proletarianization, and the day workers seek a form of economic well-being and social equality only possible under socialism.
>
> As the focus of the struggle moves from politics to economics, from anti-monarchical constitutionalism to class conflict, a realignment of class forces will develop. The wealthy merchants, probably Khomeini's most influential supporters, will align with the leading bourgeois fractions in the modern sector in the interests of property. It is likely that religious fervor will carry the artisans and shopkeepers with them for a brief period.
>
> The propertied classes will then attempt to isolate the day workers and industrial proletariat and re-establish a stability based on the centrality of private property.
>
> The service bourgeoisie and the students are the two elements that link the pre-capitalist sector to the modern sector and that have the potential of uniting the day workers and the industrial workers into a socialist movement . . . . The leftist intellectuals in the Khomeini movement will form an alliance with the poor to attempt to force the religious leader to the left. When this fails, they will turn to the Tudeh Party and the industrial proletariat. This merger would produce a mass-based and powerful socialist movement based in both economic sectors. However, there are numerous forces in Iran that mitigate against the success of such a socialist alliance.[33]

In late February a new set of demands were issued from the oilfields. According to an Associated Press report, 'the oil industry is in the hands of radical workers who demand a major role in deciding who gets the oil and the price to be paid for it. They expect the government to heed their demands for (1) redistribution of oil income, (2) an end to foreign control of the industry, (3) the right to reject management appointees, and (4) a substantial increase in oil prices above the level set by OPEC.' By the first week in March oil production was underway, and within 2 weeks reached 2.7 million barrels a day, near the limit the government then judged to be suitable. Mr. Nazih, the Khomeini appointee to head NIOC, announced on March 19 that, contrary to detractors' estimates,[34] it took only four rather than eight weeks to get production going again. He added that oilworkers were going to increase output to six million barrels for a single day, to demonstrate that they could do it in the absence of 800 foreign oil experts who had been expelled.

Throughout April and May, 1979, the oilworkers maintained their influence through workplace committees (*Komitehs*) which challenged the appointments of several senior NIOC officials. After meeting with oilworkers in Abadan in April the journalist, Kai Bird, wrote that 'Western importers will still face a pinstripe executive from the National Iranian Oil Company, but behind that executive will stand the worker *komiteh*, exercising its collective will over the country's oil policies.' As of April 1979, the oil industry was controlled by dozens of independent workers' *komitehs* which participated in all the decisions related to oil production, refining and export. Bird reported that:

> ... the worker *komitehs* have now been running the oilfields and refineries for more than six months — without their toprank Iranian managers and without the expertise of some 800 foreign technicians ....
>
> The presence of these *komitehs* in nearly every phase of Iranian oil operations is responsible for a new national policy based on conservation, diversification of exports, a ban on exports to South Africa and Israel, the cancellation of expensive capital investments like the gas injection projects and a determination to eliminate the multinational middlemen in the marketing of their oil.[35]

The oilfield *komitehs* are markedly to the left of Bazargan's Provisional Revolutionary Government[36] and are viewed by social democratic Iranians 'as an important counterweight in the present conservative tide'. Some oilworkers are religious, but favour a radical reorientation of Islam along the lines set out by the revolutionary intellectual, Dr. Shariati. As the elected speaker of the Abadan oil refinery central *komiteh* said in April, 'It is true that many of us feel the Revolution is moving too slowly. There are problems with some of the mullahs .... They are what we call Saffavi Shi'ia. We are followers of the reformist theology preached by the late Dr. Ali Shariati.'[37] Oilworkers share with many educated Iranians a marked preference for Ayatollah Taleghani who was imprisoned with and has close contacts with Marxists. A boilermaker in the Abadan refinery, stated that:

> We give Khomeini due respect for so stubbornly refusing to compromise with the Shah, but after all, Dr. Shariati wrote this revolution. Khomeini only led it. And now that we have an Islamic Republic, Khomeini must

rely on people like Taleghani if the revolution is to continue.[38]

The 800 miles separating the oilfields from Tehran have long kept the oil communities somewhat isolated from political developments. Bird reported in April 1979 that they were unaware that the Bazargan government had chosen to suppress ' − occasionally by force − labor unrest, peasant land grabs and ethnic minority demands for regional autonomy. The Government has repeatedly condemned attempts by worker *komitehs* in the automobile factories to shut out their managers. And, in several instances, the army has been used to expel peasants who had occupied their landlords' farms, chanting, "The land belongs to Allah, and Allah is the people!" '

In part because of this isolation, the expectations of oilworkers for radical reform are high. The *komitehs* remained in place and functioning two months after Khomeini's new government came to power, despite steps to destroy them. For instance, just prior to the March 21 meeting of OPEC, NIOC chief, Nazih, drafted a memo instructing a number of *komitehs* to disband. According to NIOC sources, Nazih was told to withdraw the memo by the Central Revolutionary Council. After all, the central *komiteh* of the Abadan refinery has been managing this, the largest plant in the world, for over six months, and the Ahwaz *komitehs* actually locked out the six most senior managers in the oil exploration and production departments. Bird quoted an Ahwaz production engineer's views on the strength of the *komitehs* and oilworkers in any struggle with NIOC or government forces:

> We support Nazih so far because he has listened to our suggestions. He has not insisted on reinstatement of these discredited managers. He has agreed to scrap the expensive and wasteful gas injection projects, which were only needed when the Shah required us to produce at maximum capacity. And he has agreed not to produce more than 3.7 million to 4 million barrels per day. We believe anything above that level damages the reservoirs − and in any case, this country cannot effectively spend oil revenues from more than 3 million barrels per day of exports. But if this government ever began to squander our national treasure, I tell you, we'd strike the fields again.[39]

Some professional oilworkers' *komitehs* have announced that they are willing to take pay cuts (from $25,000 a year). Worker *komitehs* have made public demands for the right to supervise their own jobs. In April 1979 a young Abadan welder stated that:

> We are not going to be slaves to these machines. Labor in the West is forced to obey management and produce only for consumption, always more and more consumption. It is your God. But in an Islamic Republic, the community and not consumption is the main goal.[40]

The 30-member central worker *komiteh* in the Abadan refinery has voted a change in work rules and is drafting a wage increase proposal for presentation to the government. The delegates meet every second day inside the refinery to plan and manage production and to secure their demands. There is every likelihood that further strikes will shut down the industry if the state capitalist management of NIOC fails to yield control to the workers who have so unmistakenly taken it.

Oilworkers' demands that OSCO, the foreign oil consortium, be expelled from Iran and that oil prices increase have been won. No oil is being sold to OSCO, although some of the major oil companies with an interest in the now defunct consortium are buying oil directly from NIOC. The demise of OSCO raises serious questions about the domination of most OPEC member countries' oil operations by 'service firms' which are actually the former concession-holders. The oil companies have long claimed the technology transfer function as their special preserve. Iranian oilworkers have demonstrated the dispensable nature of such service groups.[41] Several Western companies and governments have bought Iranian oil since the Revolution. In May, Shell signed a contract to buy 235,000 barrels a day to the end of 1979 at $16.57 per barrel, while Gulf contracted for over 150,000 a day at the same price. British Petroleum reached agreement on a 500,000 barrel a day arrangement at $16.55 The official Iranian crude price of $16.57 for April was higher than the OPEC price, and reflected tight world oil supplies. Production was up to 4.4 million barrels a day by early April.[42]

Three lessons from the Oilworkers' Strike

Among the many lessons of the ongoing Iranian Revolution, one of the most important is that technical knowledge and experience are built up in the very process of class struggle to throw out foreign 'experts' and their local managerial allies. In recounting their demands, an Ahwaz staff employee said that:

> In regard to the expulsion of the foreign staff employees, we said that this should be done gradually and according to a plan. Some of these employees were simply superfluous. They were drawing salaries and doing nothing. Such people could leave Iran very quickly, or else we would expel them. As for the others, there should be a plan to start replacing them.[43]

The remarkable action of Iranian oilworkers in shutting down the fields, maintaining them during the closure, and then re-starting production after four months of general strike should lay to rest for all time the 'manpower myth' which denigrates Third World technical competence and potential in order to justify imperialist control.

Second, Iranian oilworkers have demonstrated that the 'state capitalist solution' to instability in the relations between producing countries and international oil companies is really no solution at all. Multinational oil companies, prior to 1973, owned concessions in oil producing countries, but these have come under the legal control of state corporations via a process of 'participation' and phased nationalization. The strategies of multinational oil corporations were based on buying stability and time by giving way to these superficial 'nationalizations'.

The multinational corporations were responding to economic nationalism. A form of 'state capitalism' had developed through the creation of national, state-owned corporations in most Third World oil producing countries. These corporations, run by technocrats or state capitalists, united with foreign oil companies in a new kind of alliance to operate the oilfields. It appeared on the surface that national sovereignty over natural resources had been exercised. The oil corporations, in many self-congratulatory statements from 1974 to 1977, heralded a long future without upheavals in the oil business. For instance, the chairman of Shell stated in 1977 that with participation 'the oil industry now has a more comfortable role than it used to have . . . . OPEC successfully removed the oil companies as a target from that particular firing line.[44]

But the strategy of placing the OPEC states between multinational capital and the local population, especially the oilworkers, lasted no more than four years. Iranian oilworkers charged NIOC management with being corrupt puppets of foreign oil companies. This illustrates that the strategy of big oil merely placed state capitalism on the firing line, shielding multinational capital. Both state and foreign capital have been fundamentally challenged by the Iranian Revolution.

Third, Iranian oilworkers have initiated an open, national debate on what a Third World country should do with its natural resources. This debate over control was made possible by the exercise of popular control over oil production, destination, and use of revenues. Iran, by cutting off oil to South Africa, has made a significant contribution to changing the balance of forces there, as well as in Namibia and Rhodesia which get their oil through South Africa. The racist regimes are still getting oil but at much higher prices. If Iranian oilworkers, along with others, are able to enforce their policy of no oil to South Africa, not only will they contribute substantially to bringing down the apartheid regimes, but they will expand their control and mastery of the oil industry into the world market. In the current debate on the management of Iran's natural resources there is a strong emphasis on internationalism that follows unavoidably from the global character of the energy industry.

Among the issues now under public scrutiny in Iran are the underdevelopment associated with rapid oil production, inflows of huge amounts of revenue which OPEC economies are unsuited to absorb, purchase of arms and foreign property under immense international pressure, and the insistence of the capitalist West that oil money be recycled back into the industrialized economies. This fundamental and long-range planning is an approach to oil wealth that has great significance for other OPEC countries. Iranian oilworkers have made it clear that they are going to supply definite amounts of oil to specific customers, and that they want a voice in redistributing the oil money inside Iran. They are also capable of shutting down the fields and refineries, and have stated their intention to do just that, if these directions are not pursued. Thus, the questions are being posed for all societies — whether to rape finite natural resources through profligacy and corruption in order to develop Western capital, or whether to employ resources wisely in the organization of a new political economy.

References

1. Interview with Denis O'Brien, International Affairs, U.S. Department of Energy, Washington D.C., 1 March, 1979.
2. OSCO is a private company owned by Iranian Oil Participants Ltd. which in turn is owned by British Petroleum (40%), Royal Dutch Shell (14%), Compagnie Francaise des Petroles (6%), Exxon, Gulf, Mobil, Standard Oil of California and Texaco (7% each), and Iricon Agency Ltd. (consisting of 6 U.S. independents: Atlantic Richfield, Getty, Standard of Ohio, Charter, and American Independent, who share 5% ownership of IOP).
3. The gas and petrochemical subsidiaries of NIOC each have their own autonomous operation and administration.
4. Fred Halliday in *Iran: Trade Unions, Agriculture and Nutrition,* MERIP 71, 1978, p.9.
5. Ibid.
6. Selma James, 'Wageless of the world' in *All work and no pay,* edited by Edmond & Fleming, Falling Wall Press, Bristol, 1975, p. 26. The internal quote is from Marx, *Theories of Surplus Value,* part 1, Lawrence & Wishart, London, 1969, p. 127.
7. *New York Times,* 23 April 1979.
8. Halliday, op. cit., p. 9.
9. *New York Times,* 23 April 1979.
10. A huge $2.5 billion gas export pipeline is under construction, to increase U.S.S.R. supplies to 699 billion standard cubic feet per year by 1981.
11. NIOC's foreign activities in 1977 included a Madras Refinery and fertilizer plant in India, a 63,000 b.p.d. Sasolburg Refinery in South Africa (17% NIOC ownership), a 50-50 joint venture with South Korea for a refinery there with crude supplied from Iran, another similar venture for a 30,000 b.p.d. refinery for Senegal (including development of a phosphate mine, port facilities and a fertilizer plant), negotiations with Italy's ENI for a 50-50 deal concerning present and future refining and marketing activities in Western Europe (excluding Italy). NIOC also has exploration activites with BP, Socal and Norway's SAGA in the North Sea.
12. Halliday, op. cit., p. 8. Halliday quotes Schapour Ravasani, *Sowjetrepubl Gilan,* Berlin n.d. pp. 221 ff. It is not stated that these 10,000 organized workers were in the oil industry.
13. Halliday, op. cit. He cites L.P. Elwell-Sutton, *Persian Oil,* London 1975.
14. Linda Heiden letter to the editor, MERIP 75/76, March/April 1979, vol.

9, nos. 2/3, p. 39.

15. British Petroleum refused to follow the December 1950 Saudi Arabian example of Aramco (Arabian-American Oil Company) with its 50-50 profit-sharing formula.

16. Three reasons for U.S. interest in Iranian oil were: first, Iran was the largest Eastern Hemisphere producer and the reconstruction of Europe and Japan under U.S. auspices (and with energy supplied by U.S. companies under the Marshall Plan) was dependent on oil from Iran; second, because the U.S. and allied forces in the Korean War of 1950 depended on Middle East oil; and third, the U.S. was anxious about Soviet and Tudeh Party influence growing in Iran during the upheaval.

17. The eight major world oil companies shared Middle Eastern oil after the 1953 coup which reduced BP's control from about half to a quarter of overall production in the region.

18. Richard Falk, Chairman of the U.S. People's Committee in Iran, visited Iran in January 11-21, and interviewed Ayatollah Khomeini. Falk also met with representatives from the refineries and the production workers: 'The sense we got was that there are important communist, left elements within the oil workers movement, but by far the dominant force within that setting accepts the guidance of Khomeini.' MERIP 75-76, p. 10. Also see Ervand Abrahamian, 'Iran in revolution: the opposition forces', in the same issue for a concurring assessment.

19. OSCO refused to take Iranian oil that was priced above the level the majors were willing to pay. As a result, by 1978, NIOC was marketing about 25 per cent of the oil. Sales were made through state-to-state deals with India, Brazil, Taiwan, Bulgaria, Israel and South Africa. Sales were also made to smaller companies like Ashland, and in some cases bartered for missiles, tanks, and warplanes.

20. *Washington Post*, 10 November 1978.

21. This information is provided in an account of how the oil workers' strike was organized by a founder of the Association of Oil Industry Staff Employees. It appeared in December 29 edition of *Payam Daneshjoo*, was translated for January 29 edition of *Intercontinental Press/Imprecor*, and published in MERIP, *Iran in Revolution*, 75/76, p. 20.

22. *Washington Post*, 10 November 1979.

23. James Cockcroft, 'Interview with Ayatollah Khomeini', *Seven Days*, (New York), 7 February 1979, p. 21.

24. *New York Times*, 19 November 1978.

25. Harry Magdoff and Paul Sweezy, 'Iran: new crisis of American Hegemony', *Monthly Review*, February 1979, vol. 30, p. 17.

26. The first nine demands are listed in the Ahwaz staff employee account, in the appendix to this chapter. The last two are from the *Washington Post*, 10 November 1978. However, elsewhere in the Ahwaz workers' statement reference is made to twelve demands. In addition, other lists were issued subsequently.

27. That was the only meeting with Ansary who fled Iran with some $ 70 million, according to the Ahwaz staff employees' account. On November 10, 1978, Randal reported in the *Washington Post* that 'Ansary appeared

at one negotiating session two weeks ago. He is now reported out of the country — like many of the shah's once closest lieutenants — pursued by demands for his arrest on corruption charges lodged by strikers in the central oil company office in Tehran.'

28. *Le Monde,* November 16, 1978. Printed in MERIP, no. 75/6, *Revolution in Iran,* March-April 1979, p.18-19.

29. *Washington Post,* 10 November 1978. The oilworker was referring to a fire in the Rex Cinema in which some 400 people were burned to death in August, and to the September massacre of several hundred Iranians by troops in what is known as Bloody Friday.

30. *New York Times,* 19 November 1978.

31. *Quoted in *The Militant* (New York), 15 December, 1978, p.3.

32. Karl Marx, *The 18th Brumaire of Louis Bonaparte,* New York, New World Paperbacks, International Publishers, (1852), 1967, p.122.

33. Leonard Helfgott, 'Is class struggle emerging in Iran?,' *In These Times,* (New York), 7-13 February 1979, p.17-18.

34. Kai Bird wrote in *The Nation* (New York) of April 21, 1979 that '. . . the Western press has concerned itself with minor technical questions about the Iranians' capacity to produce significant oil for export without the benefit of expatriate engineers (the answer is an unequivocal yes) . . .' p.426.

35. Ibid. The discussion of oilworkers' *komitehs* is based on Bird's article.

36. Evidence of the conservative stance of Iran's new government was provided in a March 31, 1979 speech by former Minister of Economy Ali Ardalan who 'remarked that the United States dollar needed support, and that Iran was willing to recycle its petrodollars to the West. In support of this policy, Ali Ardalan cited his Government's decision to maintain Iranian investments in West Germany's Krupp industries and complete the construction of at least two West German-manufactured nuclear plants in Busher.' Ibid.

37. Ibid., p.427. The term Saffadi Shi'ism (or state Shi'ism) is a reference to the Saffavi Dynasty's 16th century subjugation of the clergy to secular power. Reformist theologians, like the late Dr. Ali Shariati, charge that many corruptions of the religion, including the wearing of the chador for women, were introduced during the Saffavi dynasty. Ibid.

38. Ibid.

39. Ibid., p.427-8.

40. Ibid.

41. The OSCO staff were expelled and no oil will be sold to the service company which, as a result, is facing collapse. *Platts Oilgram News* reported on 18 April 1979 that 'A spokeswoman at the Consortium's headquarters here [London] conceded that morale has worsened in the last couple of weeks. Employees haven't been given final notices, she said, but the feeling is they are only a matter of weeks away. There is little to do in the daily routine except "cleaning out desks," she said.' vol. 57, no. 75, p. 3.

42. *Platts Oilgram News,* 12 April 1979, vol. 57, no. 72, p.3.

43. See Chapter 14.

44. C.C. Pocock, op.cit., p.2.

14. How We Organized Strike That Paralyzed Shah's Regime

Firsthand Account by Iranian Oil Worker

The way the strike started was that the very broad movement that developed in our country made us realize that we staff employees in the oil industry were part of this nation too, and so we also had to participate in this movement. We knew from the start that, if we walked out, our strike could play a very important role in this movement.

So, on October 18, various sections began going out. In two or three days almost all the sections had joined us. Of course, five days before, we had heard that the Abadan refinery had gone on strike. But there had been no confirmation of this.

From the beginning, we felt the need to organize a committee that could give systematic direction to the strike. The purpose of electing or setting up a committee was not to set apart a leadership. In fact, a lot of people felt that, if we singled out a certain group as leaders, they would be immediately arrested and that would put us in a difficult situation. But at that time there was another development that made organizing a strike committee seem to be more called for. They told us that we could set up a staff employees association. So we decided to elect one representative for every fifty persons. However, if a section had more than 200 or 300 people, it still should not have more than three or four representatives. The representatives were not elected by secret ballot. The vote took place in front of everyone. We put up a list on the wall. People came and signed their names next to the name of their candidate. There were usually five or six candidates per office. The first duty of these representatives was to organize the professional and office workers association. So, we called this body the Organizing Committee of Oil Industry Staff Employees.

But from the very first days of the strike, we realized that there were more important questions facing us. The strike itself had to be organized. We had to define our aims. We had to clarify for our co-workers what our overall aims were. This was not clear to many of them. We had to specify our demands. Everyone had a few demands in mind, but all of them had to be put together and presented to the company in a list. Thus, the strike committee spent more of its energy organizing the strike and defining the demands of the strike than in building the association. We said, there will be enough time for that in the future. We sat down to plan the strike and work out a policy. We spent a lot of time discussing some questions. But at the end we made some good decisions.

One such question over which there was a lot of discussion was whether we should extend the strike through the entire oil industry, or whether some facilities such as hospitals, part of the telecommunications network, and some teams that do emergency repairs on the oil pipelines should be kept in operation. In particular, there is always a danger of explosions in oil pipelines, and if such accidents occur people may be killed along the route of the lines. So, we said that we would designate a group of workers to make emergency repairs if there was an accident or if someone did something deliberately. Thus, the final decision in the meeting was that this group of workers should remain on the job simply so that they would be able to take care of any such problems if they arose.

There was also a lot of discussion about maintaining production for domestic consumption. We decided finally to assure the supply for domestic needs. Domestic consumption is about 250,000 to 350,000 barrels a day. You know, oil consumption is generally less in the summer. But in the winter it gets cold in Iran. The cold weather was on its way, and so we knew that consumption was going to be high. We had to provide at least 350,000 barrels. So, we assigned some of the workers in Ahwaz to continue to operate one of the wells, namely Well No. 2. This well furnishes crude to those refineries that supply the needs of internal consumption. We came to the decision that we would let this plant continue operating, and it did maintain production. We also allowed Well No. 1, which includes the pumping system, to continue functioning and pump the crude to the refineries in Abadan and elsewhere.

But later on, we found ourselves facing another problem. We were in fact producing the amount of oil required for domestic needs, even more than the necessary 250,000 or 350,000 barrels a day. But we discovered that the RAY refinery had gone on strike. In other words, they would not refine the crude that we were producing and pumping to them. The same thing happened with the Abadan refinery. We began discussing with the refinery workers and urging them to refine the crude we were producing and pumping to their plants. We reasoned with them, explaining that the government would exploit this situation. So as not to allow the government to misrepresent our action, to set one section of the people against another, to open up a propaganda campaign against us, we thought that it was better for them to go ahead and refine the crude that we were producing to cover domestic needs. If they did that, we argued, the government would not be able to divert people's attention from the central issues involved in the strike by playing up the long lines in front of the gas stations and petroleum distributors.

The workers at the refineries accepted our arguments and decided to go ahead and produce. But the next day, they reported to us that the government was taking all the fuel being refined and using it for military purposes. They said that they were resuming their strike, believing that we would agree with their decision. We told them that was fine, since they knew the local situation better than we did. They should go ahead and do what they thought best. We reaffirmed that the essential aim was to meet the needs of domestic con-

consumption. But if, for any reason, they thought that they were not achieving this objective they should act accordingly. Their decision was to go back on strike for eleven days. They also called on all workers to boycott the plants. The reason for this was that previously some workers were showing up at the plants to stage a slowdown. The call for a boycott was to keep the workers from turning up at the plants at all.

This is why a fuel shortage developed in many cities, including Tehran, and why long lines of cars and people formed in front of the gas stations.

Three or four days later the production workers in Ahwaz sent a delegation to our staff employees association, pledging their support to our strike. They said that they would collaborate with us provided we went all the way and stuck with them to the last. They warned us not to stop at a halfway point. We agreed to this since we had already decided to keep up our strike as long as necessary to attain our objectives. We told the production workers that that was our intention, and they joined with us.

At that point, we ourselves had about sixty representatives and we had no hall large enough for them to meet in. We discussed this problem with the production workers, explaining that if they elected seventy to eighty representatives, we would then have about a hundred and forty representatives and it would be a real problem finding a place big enough to hold so many people. They said that they had already elected twenty to thirty representatives, but in view of this problem they would send only seven to ten persons to represent them, if we agreed. Although this procedure was not very democratic, we decided to go ahead with it since there was no other choice.

After the production workers joined us, news of the strike reached practically all the oil fields. Perhaps I should mention the names of some of the oil producing areas in Iran. They are as follows: Ahwaz, Aghajari, Maroon, Gachsarran, and secondarily Nafte Safeed, Babahakim, and Kazerun. The oil workers and staff employees in all these places also joined us. As a result, oil production dropped sharply. The average daily oil production in Iran is, or was, 6.5 million barrels. It dropped off abruptly to 800,000 barrels. It was at this point that oil tankers coming to Kharg Island to load had instead to drop anchor and wait up to forty hours. There was no oil. In the following days, production dropped to an even lower level — to about 500,000 barrels a day.

Both the government and Iranian Oil Company officials suddenly realized that we were serious about the demands we had been putting forward from the start. We had presented a list of twelve demands. Three of these were not economic, and had been raised separately. They were as follows: end martial law, full solidarity and co-operation with the striking teachers, and unconditional release of all political prisoners. Our economic demands included Iranianization of the oil industry, all communications to be in the Persian language, and for all foreign employees to leave the country. In regard to the expulsion of the foreign staff employees, we said that this should be done gradually and according to a plan. Some of these employees were simply superfluous. They were drawing salaries and doing nothing. Such people could leave Iran very quickly, or else we would expel them. As for the others, there should be a plan to start replacing them.

The second economic demand was for an end to discrimination against women staff employees and workers. The third demand called for implementation of a law recently passed by both houses of parliament dealing with the housing of oil workers and staff employees. Another demand was for revision of the regulations governing retirement of staff employees. Our final demand was for support to the demands of the production workers. The production workers had raised a demand not included in the list presented by the oil industry staff employees. It was for dissolution of SAVAK. The other demands raised by the production workers coincided entirely with ours.

When we presented our demands, the oil company officials realized that they had to come and discuss these demands with us. Oil production had been completely halted. It was no longer profitable for them to load the tankers. Moreover, on Kharg Island the dock workers and staff employees had already struck. Even if we were to produce oil there was no one to load the tankers and they could not get any oil out. Since Kharg is a very small island, they usually do not keep the tankers there for very long after they have been filled up. This is extremely dangerous. So, when oil is not being transported out, they keep the tankers empty to avoid the risk of explosions.

We saw that Mr. Ansari [Iranian Oil Company official] went first to the southern oil producing regions. He began an inspection tour, stopping at such secondary fields as Gachsarran and Aghajari. Apparently he thought that in these areas he would be able to convince or intimidate the workers more readily. Only later did he go to Kharg Island, and Aghajari again. In these places the workers who talked to him and his entourage told him that their demands were the same as those raised by the workers in Ahwaz. In fact, the workers had realized what he was up to. We had told them that his objective was to start with them, since they were in a minority, and to force them to go back to work. Then we in turn would be forced back ourselves. We told them that they should not go back and that they should refuse to negotiate with Ansari. So the oil workers in Abadan told Mr. Ansari that their demands were the same as those raised by the oil workers in Ahwaz. He said, then they must know what those demands were and should present them. The workers replied that since he was ready to discuss the demands, the Ahwaz workers should be brought there so that they could present the demands themselves. Ansari tried again to get the Abadan workers to present the demands, and they again refused. As a result, he left Abadan, having achieved nothing in his talks. He had no choice but to go to Ahwaz.

In Ahwaz, Ansari participated in our assembly, trying to sell the government's proposals. He said that he had come there to discuss all our demands. Making money was his specialty, he said, and if we wanted more pay or more retirement benefits, he would be willing to meet such demands. He also made a number of other promises. He said that since there were a lot of us there, close to 7,000 persons, he could not possibly talk to all of us. He asked us to elect a number of representatives so that he could meet with them, in the hope that some sort of agreement could be worked out. In that same meeting, we once again laid out all of our twelve demands. He said that he would consider the economic demands but that the others were outside his sphere. We said that we only expected him to convey these demands to the government, since he was the highest official in the oil company. He said that he would be happy to do that. At this point we decided to hold another general assembly.

The meeting was scheduled for 5.30 the next afternoon. Mr. Ansari did not arrive until an hour after the meeting had actually begun, even though it had started an hour late for some other reason. He came at about 7.30, and asked us to present our demands. In order to speed things up, we had elected some-one to speak for us. Our representative began reading the list of demands, and the first was for an end to military rule. At this point Mr. Ansari broke in, asking him not to read the non-economic demands. He said that they had nothing to do with him. We reminded him that he promised us that he would take all the demands to the government. Ansari said that he could not do that and asked us to read just the economic demands.

When we realized that he had not been honest with us, we told him that we were not going to make any distinction between our economic and non-economic demands. We told him that we had only one set of demands, from number one to twelve. Up till now we had considered demands one through three as non-economic, and from four to twelve, economic; but now we had just one set of demands, from one to twelve.

Ansari insisted that we should not present our non-economic demands, but we would not accept this. At this point, he pulled a trick on us. Someone came to the meeting telling him that he had an important telephone call. Ansari left the assembly, ostensibly to answer the call, but he never returned. All in all, our meeting with him lasted about three minutes. Later on he sent a message complaining that the air in the meeting was really impossible and suggested that three, four, or five of us meet with him in another location. We replied that not only were we not going to accept this proposal but that we insisted that any meeting had to be held in the same room with the same number of people and had to begin that very day. That is, it had to start that day, and it might last three, four, or five days. He did not accept our offer and went off to Tehran.

It seems that it was the Shah's birthday, and Ansari wanted to take part in the royal ceremonies. Later on, his stooges began spreading it around that we had insulted him; supposedly we had put our feet on the table. We had not spoken to him with due respect, we had not stood up in reverence before him, and so on. They also said that we had some kind of complexes. The purpose of these stories was to sow division between our representatives and the ranks. But fortunately these divisive tactics did not work. We reported the proceed-ings of the meeting as they occurred to our fellow workers. A great majority of them agreed with us, but some did not, thinking that Ansari may have had a point. At any rate, we found it necessary to act to neutralize these tactics. At the same time, our co-workers were pressing us, wanting to know what we were going to do next. They wanted to know who we wanted to talk to since we had refused to talk with Ansari. We replied that we did want to talk to him. He was the one who was not willing to talk.

So, in order to outdo Ansari in using this tactic, we sent a telegram to the Association of Iranian Jurists with copies to the newspapers *Kayhan* and *Ettela'at* , as well as the Complaints Commission of the lower house of parliament. Another copy was sent to the Association of Iranian Lawyers. In this telegram we described the context in which the oil strike was taking place and pointed to the harm it was doing to the economy of the country. We also said in the telegram that the responsibility for the continuation of the strike rests on Mr. Ansari's shoulders, since he was not willing to negotiate with us. At the end, we called on all the people of Iran to consider this crucial political question, so that they could understand where the responsibility really lay for the continuation of the strike

When Mr. Ansari found out that we had sent a copy of the telegram to the Complaints Commission, he got in touch with Mr. Pezashkpour, the head of this body. Ansari said that the workers had lied, and that he was willing to meet with us at any time, in any place in Iran, and with any number of workers' representatives. Mr. Pezashkpour, in turn, telephoned us, and relayed what Mr. Ansari had told him. We told Mr. Pezashkpour that we had not slandered Mr. Ansari. And in order to prove to Mr. Pezashkpour that Ansari had lied, we declared our willingness to meet with him at any time and in any place in Iran. Pezashkpour invited us to send about fifteen representatives to the Complaints Commission and meet with him, which we agreed to do. Since Iran Air was also on strike, we used the oil company's plane to travel to Tehran, and availed ourselves of their hotel. We used all their facilities.

When we arrived at Mr. Pezashkpour's office, he handed us a message from Mr. Shariatmadari [a religious leader] supporting our strike. This was in spite of the fact that Mr. Sharif Emami, the prime minister at the time, had called our strike an act of treason because it had dealt irreparable damage to the country's economy. In his message, Mr. Shariatmadari not only did not call us traitors but praised us as acting in the service of the nation.

In his capacity as head of the Complaints Commission, Mr. Pezashkpour declared that our strike was legal, and no one had any right to declare it illegal and try to break it. He also pointed out that the three non-economic demands we had raised were really national demands, since the entire nation supported them. So, Mr. Pezashkpour met with the fifteen representatives we had sent, but Mr. Ansari never showed up. On that very day, he left Iran, taking with him 480 million tumans [nearly $70 million]. In his place, Mr. Ansari had sent two lawyers, Mr. Najmabadi and Najand. We started the meeting, and the first question we asked was: Where is this Mr. Ansari who was willing to meet with us at any time and in any place? The answer was that he was ill. Later on they said he had a heart ailment and had to go to the United States or France for treatment.

At any rate, we had exposed Ansari pretty well by that time. We had already told the entire nation that he would not meet with us to negotiate. Once again we sent a statement to the press pointing out that he had not showed up for this meeting. So the entire nation approved of what we had done.

In the meeting, Mr. Najmabadi tried to give us a lecture on the history of the Iranian Oil Company. We told him there was no need for that because we knew that history better than anyone. What he really wanted to do was confuse things and stall. Mr. Najmabadi also refused to listen to our non-economic demands, saying they did not concern him. As for our economic demands, he said they had been attended to, and no more raises would be granted.

So, they started using methods of intimidation to force us back to work. In the meantime, they came up with another tactic for breaking the strike. They brought in 200 retired workers and employees, paid them enormous sums of money, and tried to get them to operate the wells. But these people were unable to get the installations functioning. They were not fully familiar with the new equipment that had been introduced since their retirement. They burned out a couple of pumps and turbines.

After this tactic failed, they brought in 200 technicians from the navy. These are trained technicians who are usually sent abroad for education. They got one of the pumping stations operating for a while but got rattled when they realized that they did not know the direction of the oil flow in the lines. That, of course, is a very alarming situation, since a fire can result from doing the wrong thing. Finally, our people went in to help them shut down the equipment and get out of the area.

The authorities finally realized that we were the only people who can operate the oil industry in Iran. And that is why they went with troops to the homes of workers in Aghajari and Gachsarran to pull workers out of their houses and take them to the plants, where they forced them to work. But the workers in Aghajari had seen this coming and had left the area for the weekend, so that they were not forced to go back to work.

The authorities did succeed in forcing some of the workers from Gachsarran back to work with the help of armed soldiers. And so, oil production picked up a little, gradually reaching 500,000, 800,000, 900,000 and even one and a half million barrels a day. When the workers returned to Aghajari after the weekend to see their families, they were picked up by the troops and forced to go to work. This forced labor operation finally raised oil production to four million barrels a day.

At this point, we realized that our strike had suffered a setback. It was no longer effective. The government could have continued this sort of thing, forcing the workers back until oil production was restored to the 6.5 million barrel level. So, we decided to go back to work. But at this point, a couple of things happened that threw a monkey wrench into the government's strike-breaking operation. In those days, during the premiership of Mr. Sharif Emami, when radio and TV censorship was partially lifted, they would broadcast the list of all the governmental or non-governmental organizations that had come out in support of our strike. Sometimes this would go on a whole hour. This showed the support that existed for our strike, but we needed more substantial backing.

Of course, Ayatollah Khomeini had issued a statement supporting our strike and pledging financial help. We were not overly worried about money at that time since everyone could have endured the financial hardship for a few months. And we did not think that it would last longer than two or three months. Since the entire nation had joined the movement, we thought that sooner or later the government was going to have to retreat and grant our demands. But this did not happen.

The government did all it could to isolate our strike and keep it from getting help from other sectors of the population. Students and teachers at various universities across the country had tried to open up their schools and stage demonstrations. This would have helped take the military pressure off the oil strike. But the government kept the schools from being opened.

Here I should mention some things about the military pressure brought to bear on us and about the military occupation of the oil fields. When we first began the strike, we used to gather in the halls and rooms in the main office building. The troops surrounded the building, occupied it, and forced us to disperse. Later we gathered in the parking lots of the main office building. But special troops and Ranger units occupied these areas and forced us to disperse. We moved our assembly site to an area in front of the company hospital. We were able to gather there for a couple of days, but we were again driven away. Finally, we came up with a new tactic. It was to prepare our agenda and our instructions to the striking workers, get everyone together at a given place, and give them the instructions. We could do this in the half hour it took before the troops could come and drive us away.

Despite all our tactics, many of our mates had been forced back to work and production had gone up considerably. At this point, we decided to go back to work along with other workers and prepare for a new strike. We did not consider ourselves defeated, since it was obvious that there was a continuing movement of the entire Iranian people.

What was happening was that one group would retreat one day, and the next day would resume the struggle in a different form and propel it forward. This is why we decided to go back to work and prepare everyone to strike again. This gave us a chance to draw a balance sheet of our strengths and weaknesses and to get ready for the next battle. At the same time, we decided to build up the structure of the Association of Oil Industry Staff Employees.

Our first strike lasted thirty-three days. The first day we went back to work, we held an assembly. The agenda dealt with setting up the association. We elected a committee of fifteen persons. Their primary task was to contact other organizations and individuals to solicit help and coordinate our work. We called this body the Co-ordinating Committee. It was also given the task of drawing up a constitution for the association. A preliminary draft was prepared and distributed among the employees. I think by this time, the constitution must have been approved by a general assembly of the membership.

I should mention another point. When our strike began, it was virtually ignored by all the major press including *Kayhan* and *Ettela'at*, and even the BBC. We decided to boycott the daily papers since they would send their reporters to meetings but never give us any coverage. When we complained to the papers about the lack of coverage of our actions, they said that their reporters were having difficulty getting the straight facts at our meetings. They said that they would be glad to report our actions, if we would elect a person or a number of persons to keep touch with them, and inform them of our strike demands.

So, we decided there was a need for a committee to keep in touch with the press. We set up a Communications Committee, including six persons. One of these was in charge of communications between the strike representatives and the Board of Directors of the Oil Company. Another was in charge of receiving and sending telegrams. Another was responsible for contacting the media. The work of this committee helped to get us a lot of support from all sections of the population.

Index